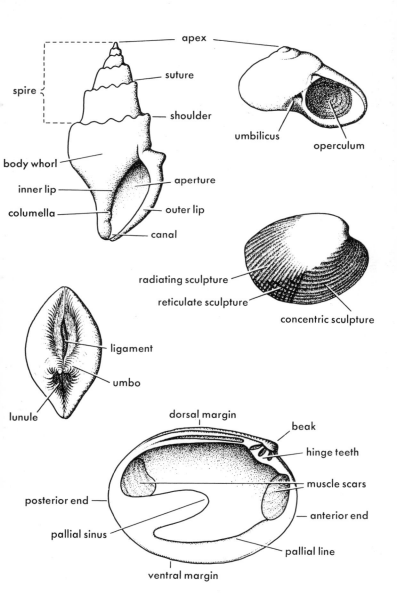

TERMINOLOGY OF UNIVALVE AND BIVALVE SHELLS

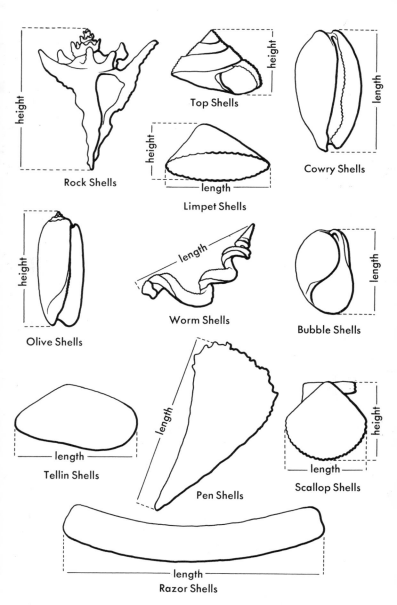

Rock Shells

Top Shells

Cowry Shells

Limpet Shells

Olive Shells

Worm Shells

Bubble Shells

Tellin Shells

Pen Shells

Scallop Shells

Razor Shells

SHELL MEASUREMENTS

THE PETERSON FIELD GUIDE SERIES®

Edited by Roger Tory Peterson

THE PETERSON FIELD GUIDE SERIES®

A Field Guide to
Shells

Atlantic and Gulf Coasts
and the West Indies

R. TUCKER ABBOTT
and
PERCY A. MORRIS

Photographs by
R. TUCKER ABBOTT

Fourth Edition

*Sponsored by the National Audubon Society,
the National Wildlife Federation,
and the Roger Tory Peterson Institute*

HOUGHTON MIFFLIN COMPANY

BOSTON • NEW YORK

1995

For information about permission to reproduce selections from this
book, write to Permissions, Houghton Mifflin Company,
215 Park Avenue South, New York, NY 10003

PETERSON FIELD GUIDES and PETERSON FIELD GUIDE SERIES
are registered trademarks of Houghton Mifflin Company.

Library of Congress Cataloging-in-Publication Data

Abbott, R. Tucker (Robert Tucker), 1919–
A field guide to shells of the Atlantic and gulf coasts and
the West Indies / R. Tucker Abbott, Percy A. Morris ;
photographs by R. Tucker Abbott.—4th ed.
p. cm.   (The Peterson field guide series ; 3)
Sponsored by the National Audubon Society, the National
Wildlife Federation, and the Roger Tory Peterson Institute.
Includes bibliographical references and index.
ISBN 0-395-69780-8.   ISBN 0-395-69779-4 (pbk.)
1. Shells—Atlantic Coast (U.S.)—Identification.   2. Shells—
Mexico, Gulf of—Identification.   3. Shells—West Indies—
Identification.
I. Morris, Percy A., 1899– .   II. Title.   III. Series
QL416.A22 1994
594'.0471'097—dc20   94-14421
CIP

Printed in the United States of America

MP 10 9 8 7 6 5 4 3 2 1

EDITOR'S NOTE

When I was a boy more than half a century ago many lads
my age collected birds' eggs, and in so doing launched their
interest in natural history. Eggs were a popular outlet for
that craving of all boys to collect. Finding nests was a kind
of treasure hunt: the eggs were the gems and could be
hoarded. With some youngsters the hobby became a mild
form of kleptomania; others, more thoughtful, took only a
set or two of each species and eventually became deeply in-
terested in the birds themselves. Many ranking ornitholo-
gists can trace their involvement to this juvenile hobby. A
few deplore the fact that egging is no longer allowed, but in
the interests of conservation this was inevitable. With the
advent of the binocular, the "list" has become the egg sub-
stitute.

Although butterflies are easily collectible, and so are minerals (more so than plants), none of nature's varied produc-
tions lend themselves more to the gratification of the collecting instinct than shells. Because of their calcareous
texture and delicate colors, shells have some of the same
tactile and visual appeal of jewels, jade, and fine porcelain.
That is the attraction to the esthete. Others, aware that the
shell is but the garment of a once-living animal, take the
naturalist's point of view and concern themselves with classification and distribution. All too few inquire into the life
of the living mollusk, its ecology and its habits.

Recognition, however, always comes first. That is why
the Field Guide Series was launched — as a shortcut to rec-
ognizing and naming the multitude of living things that pop-
ulate America. The first volume to appear, *A Field Guide to
the Birds*, met with instant approval; then followed *A Field
Guide to Western Birds*; the third was Percy Morris's admi-
rable *Field Guide to the Shells* (1947), now presented in its
fourth edition.

Whether your interest in the seashore is that of a bird
watcher (no seascape is ever devoid of birds), that of a surf

fisher casting for channel bass, or merely that of a beach-comber, you cannot overlook the shells. From the rocky headlands of Maine to the long sandy beaches of the Texas coast stretch thousands of miles of good collecting grounds. Rock, sand, and mud offer radically different environments. Some specimens are found at the line of high tide, where the sea has cast them up. Others occur commonly in tide pools. Still others can only be obtained in deep water. And here we add a cautionary conservation note: some mollusks are so rare that we do not encourage the collecting of the living animal except for scientific purposes. Commercialization of such rarities could eliminate low-level populations. Among the mollusks there are endangered species as vulnerable as certain birds or mammals.

Like many other books in the Field Guide Series, this guide has evolved considerably from its earlier beginnings. The second edition (1951) added 112 species of mollusks not covered in the original book. Six new plates of photographs were added and seven of the earlier plates were rebuilt with new photographs. The use of common or popular names was extended and much of the text was rewritten.

In the third edition, the area covered had been enlarged to include the West Indies and the number of plates increased from 45 to 76 (68 in black and white, 8 in color). Common names were adopted for all shells and these are given priority in the species headings.

Percy Morris died shortly after preparing the manuscript of the third edition, and it fell to Dr. William J. Clench, former Curator of Mollusks at the Museum of Comparative Zoology, Harvard University, to act as technical editor, checking the nomenclature and also the many details that would have fallen to Mr. Morris had he lived to see his book through to publication. To Dr. Clench we are much in debt for his scholarly assistance.

We are very pleased that this fourth edition has been assembled by Dr. R. Tucker Abbott, director of the Bailey-Matthews Shell Museum. He was trained by and was long associated with Dr. Clench at Harvard University. This edition includes 74 new color plates. Many of the inaccessible deep sea species have been omitted; emphasis has been put on the living animals of the mollusks.

Take this book with you whenever you go to the shore. Do not leave it home on your library shelf; it is a Field Guide, meant to be used.

Roger Tory Peterson

ACKNOWLEDGMENTS

It has been a great pleasure and honor to have revised this well-known and useful guide. During my college days I was well acquainted with its original author, Percy A. Morris, who at that time was president of the Connecticut Shell Club and in charge of the scientific mollusk collections at the Peabody Museum of Natural History at Yale University. Percy Morris had a way of popularizing shell studies that led me further into the field.

All previous editions had a minor assist from me, despite my beginner's knowledge, but perhaps more influential was the major input that my Harvard professor, William J. Clench, gave to the third edition. He, his assistant Ruth Turner, and a host of other malacologists and private shell collectors all contributed to the successful enlargement of this indispensable identification guide.

I am grateful to many who have helped me assemble this fourth edition. For an opportunity to consult literature and photograph museum specimens I wish to thank Dr. Kenneth J. Boss at the Museum of Comparative Zoology; Dr. Fred Thompson and Kurt Auffenberg at the Florida Museum of Natural History; and Dr. M.G. Jerry Harasewych at the Smithsonian Institution. The colored photographs of living mollusks are the field work of Bob Lipe of St. Petersburg Beach; Frank Frumar of St. Louis, Missouri; Steven F. Barry of Panama City, Florida; and from the Shell Vision Bank of the Bailey-Matthews Shell Museum on Sanibel Island. The shells illustrated in a number of the color plates are from the excellent private collection of Edith and Harry Chippeaux of Ft. Myers, Florida.

All American naturalists, young and old, owe a great debt of gratitude to Roger Tory Peterson for launching his Field Guide series so many decades ago. The publishing house of Houghton Mifflin Company in Boston and its present-day editors have kept alive this great educational tradition. You need only read Dr. Peterson's Editor's Note to sense his enthusiasm for collecting natural history specimens and for the thrill of learning the names of the creatures that inhabit our fragile world.

R. Tucker Abbott
Bailey-Matthews Shell Museum
Sanibel Island, Florida

CONTENTS

ILLUSTRATIONS

Line illustrations

INTRODUCTION

Shell collecting today is no longer a hobby or occupation of amassing a collection of as many species or specimens as one can acquire. The "trophy" spirit has been changed by the realities of today's increase in human activities in the ocean and along our shores. Pollution and habitat destruction are causing us to think about how we can study living mollusks in their natural habitats and how best we can protect populations in the wild.

Yet, shelling has a lure to those who love to collect, wish to set things in orderly arrangements, identify species, and study the intricate life histories of this miraculously variable and interesting molluscan phylum. Fortunately, shell collecting by amateur conchologists and scientific malacologists, if done with intelligent restraint, is no threat to living populations. Nearly all marine mollusks exist by the millions, and only a small fraction of their natural territories are within reach of the average collector.

Modern research in oceanographic ecology, increased educational efforts by such organizations as the National Audubon Society and the National Wildlife Federation, and major aquaculture projects around the world are all helping to protect what live populations still flourish. If you must collect live specimens, follow the dictum of many shell clubs: "Don't be a pig. Leave some for the person who may follow you." Your careful and selective shell collecting will keep alive the learning experiences and appreciative aspects of natural history.

There are three major activities involved in shell collecting:

1. The field work, which includes the observation of the living mollusks in their natural habitats, and the hunting down and collecting or photographing of specimens.
2. The creation and maintenance of a properly organized

study collection. This involves cleaning, preserving, sorting, identifying and cataloging your finds.

3. Literature research about your collection. This can be followed by exhibiting in shell shows or teaching others about conchology and environmental awareness.

Collecting your shells: There is an old adage that "shells are where you find them," and this is true because each of the thousands of marine species have their own environmental conditions in which they flourish. Because of the vagaries of ecological conditions, the presence or relative abundance of a species may vary from month to month.

Beachcombing seems a logical and easy way to begin, but in reality the harsh action of waves, shifting sands, and exposure to bright sunlight are unpleasant conditions for living mollusks. Beaches are generally the graveyards for shells uprooted from offshore habitats and cast up along the windrows at the upper tide level. The worn and bleached dead shells are at least a clue to what might be found on sand flats at extreme low tide or in nearby shallow waters. In some areas, particularly after a windy storm, the beaches may be laden with live, stranded specimens.

For collecting, one should wear old clothes and sturdy shoes. Be aware of the dangers of excessive sunburn and extreme current and tidal variations. Never collect barefooted, because many shells, buried in the sand, have razor-sharp edges, to say nothing about broken glass. You will need a bag or sack for carrying specimens, a jar or two of seawater to protect fragile specimens until you can care for them later, and a few small vials for minute forms. A stout bar of some sort for probing and overturning stones is useful; a shovel or trowel is a necessity. A pair of tweezers for handling tiny mollusks is helpful.

One scarcely needs to be told where to find shells. The beginner usually starts by walking along the shore and keeping a sharp eye for specimens that have been washed in by the tides. While many excellent shells may be obtained in this way, a large majority will be wave-worn, eroded, broken, or otherwise imperfect. Bivalve shells will usually be represented by single valves, and the lips of univalves will show broken edges, worn sculpture, or damaged spires.

The novice collector soon learns that to build up a really fine collection he or she must look for living specimens. But it's important to limit collecting to only a few well-chosen specimens and to take care that the habitat is not unduly disturbed. When examining the underside of a rock, carefully roll it over into its original position in order not to disturb young or obscure egg cases.

Each species has its own preferred marine territory. A vast assemblage of different forms live on rocky shores, clinging to or hiding under the rocks while the tide is out. Others prefer sandy flats, where they burrow into the sand during the ebb tide. Many like nothing better than a muddy bottom, and the blacker and stickier the better. Some will live only in the purest seawater, tolerating no mixture with freshwater at all, whereas others seem to like it better where the water is brackish.

A large and interesting part of our molluscan fauna lives in what is known as the *littoral zone,* that portion of the beach between high and low tides that is exposed to the sun usually twice each day. Others live out beyond the low-water level, and many species are found in deep water, even up to several miles in depth. Temperature controls the distribution of most varieties, and we shall find a different group in Maine from those at Cape Hatteras. Yet some of the shells that may be collected close to shore in northern waters are to be found living in deeper water farther south.

On rocky coasts the receding tides leave pockets of water in all depressed areas, and in these tide pools one can find various kinds of molluscan life carrying on in a business-as-usual manner. It will reward the collector to scan these miniature aquariums carefully. The pilings and undersides of wharves are rich collecting grounds too, as the logs are generally covered with a heavy growth of marine algae that conceals many of the smaller mollusks.

The best time to collect is at low tide, when it's possible to get out to the low-water limits. Any stone, plank, or section of driftwood should be turned over; a host of marine creatures, including mollusks, take refuge under such objects to await the return of the next tide. A good practice is to roll the stone or log back the way it was after you are through searching. On sand and mud flats the presence of bivalves can usually be detected by small holes that reveal the location of the clam's siphons. As you trudge along the sand flat the mollusk quickly draws in its siphons, commonly ejecting a thin squirt of water as it does so. The snails generally burrow just beneath the surface and produce small telltale mounds. By energetic digging in likely places while the tide is out, one should come up with a good representative collection of the species inhabiting that particular beach, all of them "taken alive" specimens, far superior to the old and empty shells picked up along the shoreline.

Nevertheless, the collecting of dead shells is not to be neglected altogether, since many fine examples may be so obtained. This is particularly true of the minute forms. On nearly every exposed beach you will find a long wavy line of flotsam and jetsam — known as sea wrack, beach litter, or beach drift — which marks the high-tide limit. It will pay you to examine this debris carefully. Here you will find large pieces of seaweeds that have been torn from their moorings and washed up on the shore. Concealed in the folds and among the roots you may find scores of tiny mollusks that live out in deeper waters. If you gather freshly washed-up material, such as on a day following a violent storm, most of the mollusks will be live ones. Sections of sponges should be pulled apart and examined, and pieces of driftwood broken up to reveal piddocks and shipworms. Dead crustaceans and sea urchins are worth looking over for parasitic mollusks. The fine material in the beach litter should be run through a sieve to eliminate most of the sand grains, and the remaining shelly particles searched for tiny bivalves and gastropods. Most collectors take home small bags of this material, commonly called "grunge," to work on in evenings or on rainy days.

Try collecting at night with a strong flashlight. Most of our snails are nocturnal, and certain species that have to be searched for under stones and in crevices during the daylight hours will be found crawling over the rocks and the sandbars after dark. For safety reasons, night collecting should be done with a companion or two.

One of the most exciting as well as rewarding types of collecting is dredging. We cannot all afford the boats, winches, and heavy gear to do this on a large scale, much as we would like to, but it does not cost very much to rig up a small iron frame, attach a netting or fine wire bag, and drag it along the bottom from a rowboat in 15 to 20 feet of water. Low tide is the best time. Try all sorts of bottoms — sandy, muddy, gravelly, and so on. After dragging your scoop for several minutes, pull it to the surface, jiggle it a bit to wash out most of the mud and silt, then haul it over the side of the boat and empty it into a basin or tub of water. Separating your catch in this way is easier, and small fragile shells are less likely to be injured than if you dumped the contents out onto the deck.

· · ·

Preparing your shells: While the collecting of shells is sheer pleasure, the necessary cleaning and preparing comes under the label of work; but it is work that has to be done if we are to gather living material. First, get rid of the animal in the shell, unless you plan to do anatomical studies. Soft parts of mollusks are best preserved in 70 percent grain alcohol. Avoid the use of formaldehyde, as it tends to etch away the calcitic shell. To extract the soft parts, it is common practice to place the shells in a pan of water and boil them 5 to 10 minutes. Small live gastropods may be placed in a half-open plastic bag and cooked in a microwave oven at high temperature for a minute or two. Cooked bivalves present no problem: the valves gape open and the soft parts can be removed with no difficulty, though the muscle scars generally require a slight scraping. Valves with an external ligament will remain attached in pairs. After the interior has been thoroughly cleaned, the two valves can be closed and the whole shell wrapped with strong thread until the ligament has dried. In each tray of specimens you will want a pair of valves that are separated to show the interiors. Freezing bivalves overnight and then thawing them is also an effective way to remove the soft parts.

With univalves, the animal will have to be drawn out of its shell by a hook or bent wire. After being boiled, the soft parts generally slip out without too much trouble, but sometimes the small end will break off and stay in the upper whorls. Soaking in plain water for several days often will rot and soften this part so that it can be flushed out. If this fails, the usual practice is to put the shell in a 70 percent solution of alcohol for a few hours to harden the animal matter. Then the shell can be dried in a shady place, and after this there should be no offensive odor. Very tiny snails are generally kept in the 70 percent alcohol solution for several days and then dried.

Many snails have an *operculum* attached to the body in such a manner that when the "foot" is withdrawn it serves as a door, effectively blocking the aperture (see left endpaper). Opercula may be horny, leathery, or calcareous. This structure must be cut away from the flesh and its reverse side scraped clean. When the shell is prepared and ready for the cabinet, the operculum is glued to a tuft of cotton and then inserted in the aperture and positioned as it would be in life. When cleaning your gastropods, take special care to see that each operculum is kept with its own shell.

Some of the larger bivalves, particularly of the genera

Spondylus and *Chama,* usually have their shells more or less coated with worm tubes, barnacles, calcareous algae, and other foreign growths. They can be cleaned only by careful and painstaking work with small chisels, needles, and scrapers. Some collectors paint the unwanted encrustations with a weak solution of muriatic acid, but although the acid will dissolve all limy deposits, it will also attack the shell itself, so its use is not recommended. Soaking dirty shells in a weak solution of Clorox often helps.

The *periostracum* (a noncalcareous covering that protects the outside of many shells) can be removed by soaking the shell in a solution of Clorox. Most collectors, however, prefer their specimens in a natural state, even though some — such as the cone shells *(Conus)*—do not reveal their beauty until the periostracum has been removed. It is ideal to have two or three examples of each species in a tray, one denuded of its periostracum and the others as they were in life.

After your shells are cleaned, washed, dried, and are ready for their trays or the cabinet, they may be lightly rubbed with a small amount of mineral oil applied with a tuft of cotton. This will impart a slight luster to the surface, make them fresh-looking, and aid somewhat in preserving the delicate coloring. Some workers use olive oil, but that may in time become rancid and it also may attract insects. Never coat your shells with lacquer, varnish, or shellac.

Arranging your shells: A collection's value is proportional to its labeling. The precise locality and date are far more important than having the shell correctly named. Any competent malacologist can put the right name on your shell at any time, but you and *only you* can provide the exact location and date. Adopt some form of label that provides space for a number (which will be entered in your catalog and written in waterproof ink on each specimen), the name, date, and locality. This last should be as exact and detailed as possible. "West Indies" and "southern Florida" do not mean very much, but "$1/2$ mile south of Mayaguez, Puerto Rico" and "Cape Romano, s. Florida" tie the specimen down accurately. The collector's name should be included, and most collectors can be depended upon not to neglect that. Under the entry number in your catalog you may include notes on the tide conditions, the weather, whether or not the mollusk was a living specimen or an empty shell and, if the former, what type of bottom it was living on, its relative abundance at that time and place, and anything else that may seem per-

YALE PEABODY MUSEUM
Division of Invertebrate Zoology

YPM No. *26971*

Nassarius obsoletus (Say)

Mud flats, 1 mile W. /*6602*/
of New Haven, Conn.

Coll. *H. M. Woolsey* Date *7-21-1954*

tinent. Above is a sample of a label used by the writer.

The number in the small box is an accession number applying to all shells from a certain collection. For example, if we spend an hour or a day or a week at some particular locality all the shells gathered on that trip can have the same accession number; or if we purchase a complete collection from some source we may give an accession number to the whole lot. Then, although each species will eventually have its catalog number, the number in the box instantly associates each shell with a certain group. In the accessions catalog you will have detailed information about the trip or the purchase.

Names of shells: The beginner is apt to be confused and at first annoyed by some of the "jawbreaking" names that have been given to shells. This is true in any branch of natural history but is perhaps more apparent in the molluscan field, since many of our species are rarely seen by the average person and only a few kinds have become well enough known to have acquired common or popular names. Perhaps this is a good thing, because English names are very likely to be too local in character. Thus the same shell may be called one thing in one place and be known by a completely different name a few miles down the coast, and in three widely separated localities the same name may be applied to three totally different shells.

Scientists have agreed upon Latin as best for the naming of animals and plants for very good reasons. It is a dead language and therefore not subject to change. Serious scholars all over the world, regardless of their individual nationalities, are familiar with it, so it is about as close as one can get to an international tongue. The name "Crown Conch" means something to a resident of Florida but it means nothing to a French or a Japanese person, or to most Californians. Use the snail's scientific name of *Melongena corona*, however, and every shell enthusiast, whatever his country, knows what shell we are talking about.

In this book common names are given for all the shells. However, the serious collector is strongly urged to learn their scientific names. These names are not difficult after we become familiar with them. We use the words alligator, boa constrictor, and gorilla commonly enough without stopping to realize that they are perfectly good scientific names. In botanical reference we all speak or write of our iris, forsythia, geranium, crocus, delphinium, and scores of others with the greatest of ease, just because we are familiar with them. Who dares say that chrysanthemum or rhododendron is easier to say or spell than *Murex, Tellina,* or *Littorina?*

It has been found convenient to give each animal two names: first, a general, or generic, name (always capitalized) to indicate the group *(Genus)* to which it belongs; second, a special, or specific, name (not capitalized) to apply to that animal alone as the species name. In older works the specific name was capitalized if a proper name, but that practice has been discontinued for many years.

Take the well-known Junonia, that vividly spotted shell hopefully looked for by nearly all collectors on Florida beaches. This was named *junonia* by Lamarck in 1804; Lamarck placed it in the genus *Voluta.* Since the name of the person who first describes a species, known as the *author,* follows the scientific name, as well as the year in which it was published, our snail became listed officially as *Voluta junonia* Lamarck, 1804. This serves as a very useful bibliographic tool in tracking down any reference. If later research proves that a species belongs in a genus different from the one to which the author has allocated it, it is removed to the proper genus but the species name is retained and parentheses are placed around the author's name to indicate that a change has been made from the original allocation. In this case the gastropod was put in the genus *Scaphella,* so our name now reads *Scaphella junonia* (Lamarck, 1804). The parentheses are a technicality of importance chiefly to specialists; many books for nonspecialists do not use them, although the International Rules of Zoological Nomenclature insist that they are a valid part of the name.

Your fellow collectors: One of the many joys connected with "shelling" is meeting others with the same interests. One cannot search the sandflats or pry under driftlogs and stones for any length of time without running into someone similarly occupied; many lasting friendships have been initiated on the beach. Shell people like to get together, and shell clubs have been organized in many places throughout the country. In fact, their growth during the past decade has been little short of phenomenal. Most are affiliated with the Conchologists of America. Anyone seriously collecting shells should consider joining this society. The only requirement is an interest in mollusks. The membership of this nonprofit organization is mainly made up of amateur conchologists. They issue an attractive quarterly shell magazine. The membership director is Mrs. Bobbie Houchin, 2644 Kings Highway, Louisville, KY 40205. Professional malacologists and college students, as well as some serious amateurs, may join the American Malacological Union, which issues a technical journal on mollusks, by writing Mrs. Connie Boone, 3706 Rice Boulevared, Houston, TX 77005. Any inquiry about these associations will receive prompt attention.

Some of the eastern shell clubs are listed in Appendix D. If you are within commuting distance of any, by all means get in touch with the secretary and plan to attend one of the meetings. Here you will find kindred souls, perhaps enrich your own collection by exchanges, enjoy the good fellowship of local field trips, and obtain help in the identification of puzzling material. Many of these shell clubs issue a publication for the benefit of club members, possibly a bimonthly newsletter or monthly bulletin that varies from being a mimeographed list of members with program notes and local items to including short articles about collecting and classification or presenting discussions on a particular group or genus.

The Phylum Mollusca: The Animal Kingdom evolved some 700 to 900 million years ago from primitive forms of single-celled Protista. The kingdom may be roughly divided into the vertebrates (Chordata) and the invertebrates (those without backbones), although animals are now divided into Phyla to show a more realistic relationship to each other.

The two main stocks of animals are the arthropod-annelid worm-mollusk line and the chordate line, which includes the backboned vertebrates (fish, reptiles, birds, and mammals).

Most mollusks, with the exception of several thousand specialized kinds, produce a calcareous shell. Seashore visitors should realize that other shelled creatures may belong to other phyla, such as the barnacles and crabs which are crustacean Arthropoda, and the sand-dollars and sea-urchins which belong to the phylum Echinodermata.

The Mollusca are a very diverse group of animals, ranging from the very simple, wormlike Aplacophora to the advanced and complicated Cephalopoda, or squid, octopus and nautilus. All have in common a fleshy mantle capable of producing an external shell, and in most cases a set of many teeth within the mouth, called the radula. Unlike the arthropods, they do not have truly segmented bodies or long jointed leg appendages.

This group is one of the major branches of the animal kingdom, including as it does the clams, oysters, scallops, the snails, whelks and slugs, as well as the chitons, squids, octopuses, and some others. About 100,000 living forms are known throughout the world, besides many thousands of fossil species, for the group is represented in the most ancient fossil-bearing rocks of the Lower Cambrian 500 million years ago. The mollusks are now divided into the 7 major living classes that follow:

1. The *Monoplacophora*, or gastroverms, are a limpetlike primitive group with some paired organs. They were known only as ancient fossils and were believed to have become extinct about 250 million years ago until 1957, when living specimens were first dredged from abyssal depths off Guatemala. Today there are about a dozen known species of these limpet-shaped shells. The first one found was named *Neopilina galatheae* Lemche, 1957. None are included in this popular guide.

2. The *Aplacophora*, or solenogasters, are wormlike inhabitants of deep water. Most of the known 250 species are less than 2 inches in length. The shell is reduced to small spicules scattered over the outer surface. They glide along with the aid of a very narrow foot. They feed on detritus, and the radula is very reduced.

3. The *Polyplacophora*, chitons or coat-of-mail shells (once called the Amphineura) are primitive mollusks of very

Monoplacophora: Gastroverms

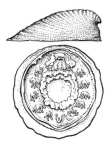

Amphineura: Chitons

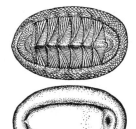

Gastropoda: Univalves
Snails, periwinkles, whelks, conchs

Bivalvia (Pelecypoda): Bivalves
Clams, oysters, mussels, scallops, cockles

Cephalopoda: Squids,
Octopuses, Nautiluses

Scaphopoda:
Tusk Shells

THE SIX CLASSES OF MOLLUSKS

sluggish habits, mostly preferring shallow water close to shore. The typical chiton (the common name) is an elongate, depressed mollusk, without tentacles or cephalic eyes, bearing a shelly armor of 8 saddle-shaped plates, or valves, arranged in an overlapping series along the back. The foot is broad and flat and serves as a creeping sole or sucking pad, by which the creature clings to the rocks. The ancestral mollusk, from which all existing forms have been evolved, is believed to have been very similar to the present-day chiton.

4. The *Gastropoda*, or univalves, are numerically the largest division of the Mollusca. Examples occur in marine and fresh waters, and also as terrestrial air-breathing animals. There is but a single valve, usually spiral or caplike, and a few are shell-less. There is a distinct head, often with eyes, and the mollusk is provided with a toothed radula, or lingual ribbon, which it uses to shred its food. Gastropods may be either herbivorous or carnivorous.

5. The *Scaphopoda*, or tusk shells, are elongate mollusks enclosed in a tapering conical shell open at both ends and slightly curved. From the larger end project the foot and several slender filaments. Through the narrow end, usually protruding up from the sandy bottom, fresh seawater is inhaled and exhaled. Scaphopods live in clean sand, from shallow water to considerable depths.

6. The *Bivalvia (Pelecypoda* or *Lamellibranchiata)* are entirely aquatic and predominantly marine, with a pair of valves joined by a hinge and held together by strong muscles within. The animal has no head and feeds upon microscopic plant and animal matter drawn into the mantle cavity through the siphon. There is commonly a muscular foot for burrowing, although some live permanently attached to rocks or coral.

7. The *Cephalopoda* are highly specialized mollusks, keen of vision and swift in action. The head is armed with a sharp parrotlike beak and is surrounded by long flexible tentacles studded with sucking disks. Besides the well-known devilfishes (octopuses), this class includes the delicate Paper Argonaut and the beautiful Pearly Nautilus of the western Pacific. *Spirula*, a delicate, white, chambered shell frequently washed up on our southern beaches, belongs to this class, and the spectacular *ammonites* and *nautiloids* found as fossils in rocks of Jurassic and Cretaceous periods were cephalopods too.

ABOUT THIS BOOK

In this fourth edition of the Atlantic Coast shell guide, the focus is on the shallow-water species found from Labrador to Texas. We have excluded the many deep-sea species, particularly those described by Dr. A. E. Verrill at Yale, that were featured in the third edition. We felt that the average shore collector would have little opportunity to do deep-water dredging. Accounts and illustrations of these rare deep-sea species may be found in *American Seashells* by Abbott or in the scientific journal, *Johnsonia,* formerly edited at Harvard by Clench and Boss. Because of their particular interest to many advanced collectors, we included colored photographs and accounts of the pleurotomarid slit-shells and the only East Coast deep-sea abalone, *Haliotis.*

Similarly, we have eliminated several common species found only in the West Indies, but have retained those Caribbean species that regularly live in the Lower Florida Keys. The West Indian fauna consists of about 3,000 species, many deep-water, and many are adequately described and illustrated in shell books, such as *Caribbean Seashells* by Abbott and Warmke.

The book has been largely rewritten and illustrated in color, with the addition of helpful drawings of minute species. Most desired by advanced shell collectors is the addition of the author and date along with the scientific name. This feature is important in the field of malacology because it serves as a useful tool in tracking down original descriptions and in distiquishing homonyms (similar names given to different species).

More than 20 years have passed since the last edition was edited by the late William J. Clench, with the assistance of Dr. Ruth D. Turner. It is no surprise that the 40,000-or-so scientific papers and mongraphs published in that time have shown advances in our knowledge of malacology. New species have been described, some old ones now found to be a mixture of two species, and many found to have been synonyms. Some species and genera have been relocated into other families, as for instance in the move of the Woodlouse genus, *Morum*, from the Cassidae (helmet shell family) to the Harpidae (harp family).

It is hoped that this revised edition will prove useful to the growing army of enthusiasts embracing shell collecting as a hobby. The present author, as well as the originator of this guide, the late Percy Morris, has tried to include all of the common mollusks that the collector is likely to discover on trips to the seashore, and it is hoped that the selection herein presented will prove adequate for building a foundation of knowledge about one of the most interesting animal groups in nature. For more advanced identification work, the reader is referred to the technical works listed in the bibliography.

Classification: Unlike books on birds, minerals, or flowers, shell books rarely agree on the arrangement of families, or in other words the classification of mollusks. This is because of the enormous number of known species and the imperfect state of our knowledge. The accepted plan begins with the most primitive forms and works up to the most advanced or complex forms. This is determined largely by the mollusk's anatomy. The early conchologists were concerned chiefly with the characters of the shell rather than with the soft parts. Modern workers have arrived at a fairly satisfactory listing, certainly better, bringing together those forms most closely related, and the classification is constantly being improved as more anatomical work is done. For example, most writers used to begin their gastropod sections with *Patella* and *Acmaea*, the true limpets, followed by the keyhole limpets, *Fissurella*, *Diodora*, and so on. It is now recognized that the keyhole limpets are more primitive than the true limpets, so in modern listings they precede them. As more intensive research is done it can occasionally be demonstrated that whole genera should be taken out of one family and placed in another. We can hope that someday the classification will be stabilized, but there may never be complete agreement between equally competent malacologists.

The arrangement in this book is taken from the review work of Kay C. Vaught, *A Classification of the Living Mollusca*, edited by Abbott and Boss, 1989, American Malacologists, Inc. This outline of the Phylum Mollusca lists in taxonomic order over 6,500 supraspecific names (orders, families, genera, and subgenera). While in many cases we have listed species in alphabetical order under the genus, in some cases we have grouped similar-looking species near each other in order to facilitate comparisons.

Nomenclature: The nomenclature of any branch of natural science is never static but always subject to change. Although name changes are often annoying to the amateur collector, they are necessary if we are to abide by the rules and eventually arrive at something resembling stability. The International Commission on Zoological Nomenclature is a body set up to formulate rules and pass judgment on such matters; and perhaps the most important rule is the law of priority that states that the first published name is to be the valid one, even if it is misspelled or misleading. A common clam from our East Coast carries the name of *Lucina pensylvanica*, with one *n*, and a helmet shell coming only from the Caribbean, but originally thought to be from the island of Madagascar, was named *Cassis madagascariensis*.

Let us consider the reasons for name changes in a well-known eastern freshwater shell. An abundant ram's horn snail of ponds and streams was named *Planorbis bicarinatus* by Thomas Say in 1816. In 1834 Timothy Conrad described the same snail as *Planorbis antrosum*. Of course Say's name had priority, and *antrosum* became a synonym. Later it was discovered that Lamarck had used the name *bicarinatus* for a Paris Basin planorbid, before Say's publication, so *bicarinatus* became unavailable for our American shell since it was a homonym, and the next in line, Conrad's *antrosum*, became official. In 1840 William Swainson created the subgenus *Helisoma* for the planorbids of the New World, and in 1928 F. C. Baker elevated it to full generic rank, so our snail became *Helisoma antrosum* (Conrad, 1834). It was eventually discovered that the same mollusk had been described in a German publication by Karl Menke in 1830. Menke named it *Planorbis anceps*, based upon the illustration in a work by Martin Lister, and since his is the earliest naming our common pond snail it is now correctly known as *Helisoma anceps* (Menke, 1830).

The nomenclature in this Field Guide is believed to be as up-to-date as possible at the time of publication, but in the years ahead, possibly in the months ahead, there undoubtedly will be additional name changes. In many listings you will find species, subspecies, and forms (formerly called varieties). A form is simply a color variety or ecologically induced morphological variation occurring within a population. It has no taxonomic validity. A subspecies, on the other hand, differs slightly but constantly from the typical species; more important, it occupies a different geographic range, so that, except where the two forms meet and perhaps overlap a bit, there can be no intergrades. However, this law is not absolute, for we have what is termed a sympatric subspecies. This is a form slightly but demonstrably different from the typical, which though occupying the same geographic range is confined to a particular ecologic niche and ordinarily does not come in contact with the typical species.

Measurements: The *length of a bivalve* shell is the distance, in a straight line, from the anterior to the posterior end. The *height* is a straight line from the dorsal margin to the ventral margin (see right endpaper). It should be noted that with some shells, such as *Lima,* the height may be greater than the length. The *anterior* end of a bivalve is usually (but not always) the shorter; that is, it is closer to the beaks than the *posterior* end, and the beaks generally incline forward. In some cases, especially with orbicular shells, one has to see the interior to be sure. The foot protrudes from the anterior end and the siphons from the posterior. The pallial sinus, when present, opens toward the posterior end. Oysters, irregular in form but commonly elongate, are usually measured in length from the beaks to the opposite end.

Bivalves have *right* and *left* valves. When a clam is held with the dorsal margin up, and the anterior end away from the observer, the right valve is on the right and the left valve on the left. With sessile bivalves such as oysters and jewel boxes, one usually refers to the valves as upper and lower. The same is true of some of the scallops, particularly where one valve is deeply cupped (lower) and its mate is more or less flat (upper).

With *gastropods* it is always a question whether to give the distance between the apex and the opposite end as height or length. Since most of our snails customarily carry their shells in a horizontal or semihorizontal position, it is probably more correct anatomically to regard this measurement as length; but because virtually all illustrations of gastropods show them with the apex uppermost, that dimension will be given in this book as height. As with the bivalves, there will be some exceptions. With the *limpets* the height is the distance of the apex, or summit, above the place of the snail's attachment, and the length is a straight line from the anterior to the posterior end. *Cowries*, which crawl about on the apertural area and thus have an upper and lower surface, are measured from end to end as length, and length is also used for the maximum distance from apex to aperture in the elongate worm shells (see right endpaper).

Measurements in this book refer to average, mature shells. The collector will find many young examples that are smaller than the stated dimension and may obtain occasional specimens that exceed them. For the interest of some collectors, there is an official list of the known largest specimens of many species published in *World Size Records* by American Malacologists, Inc., Melbourne, Florida. The maximum known size, owner, and place and date of collection are recorded now by Barbara Haviland and R. T. Abbott.

Range and habitat: The ranges cited are based on records compiled over many years by collectors and many research museums. Ranges may be extended from time to time as new material is collected and evaluated. Long- or short-term changes in oceanic weather may influence ranges. For the purposes of this book the term *shallow water* ranges from the tidal area to a depth of about 30 feet; *moderately shallow water* from 30 to about 80 feet; *moderately deep water* from 80 to about 200 feet; and *deep water* anything beyond 200 feet.

A FIELD GUIDE TO SHELLS
OF THE ATLANTIC AND GULF COASTS
AND THE WEST INDIES

CLASS BIVALVIA (Pelcypoda): BIVALVES

SUBCLASS PROTOBRANCHIA

ORDER SOLEMYOIDA

■ **AWNING CLAMS: Family Solemyidae**

In this family the valves are equal and considerably elongated. There is a tough and glossy periostracum (noncalcareous covering) extending well beyond the margins of the shell. These are rather uncommon bivalves, but the family is nearly worldwide in distribution and is represented on our East Coast from Canada to the West Indies by five species. They live in a U-shaped burrow open at both ends.

● **Genus *Solemya* Lamarck, 1818**

BOREAL AWNING CLAM *Solemya borealis* Totten, 1834   **Pl. 19**
Range: Nova Scotia to Connecticut.
Habitat: Shallow water; burrows in sand and mud.
Description: Fragile, attains a length of 3 in. Oblong; beaks scarcely elevated. Weak radiating ribs, nearly concealed by strong, shiny periostracum that overhangs margin of shell as a ragged fringe. Color tan to greenish brown; interior lead-colored.
Remarks: Like its more common relative, the Atlantic Awning Clam (below), it is a good swimmer, progressing by extending and rapidly withdrawing its foot, forcing water from the shell by spurts and traveling by a series of sudden dashes.

WEST INDIAN AWNING CLAM
Solemya occidentalis Deshayes, 1857
Range: Florida to the West Indies.
Habitat: Moderately shallow water.
Description: Length about ¼ in. An oval shell, rounded and

gaping at both ends. Beaks inconspicuous, hinge toothless. Surface smooth, covered by shiny brown periostracum.

ATLANTIC AWNING CLAM *Solemya velum* Say, 1822   **Pl. 18**
Range: Nova Scotia to Florida.
Habitat: Shallow water; burrows in sand and mud.
Description: Fragile, 1 to 1½ in. long. Shape oblong, ends rounded. Surface smooth, with about 15 slightly impressed double lines, most conspicuous on posterior margin. Greenish brown periostracum firm and elastic, shiny; projects far beyond the shell itself, where it is slit at each of the radiating lines and gives edges a ragged, fringed appearance. Interior bluish white.
Remarks: Also known by such popular names as Swimming Clam and Veiled Clam, this bivalve is easily recognized by the tough covering that overhangs the edge of the shell like a veil. Specimens of *Solemya* are exceedingly fragile when dry and should not be kept loose in trays. Attach them by a drop of adhesive to a card cut to fit the tray, or place them on soft cotton.

ORDER NUCULOIDA

■ NUT SHELLS: Family Nuculidae

Three-cornered or oval, small shells, with no pit for the ligament between the umbones (beaks). There is a series of tiny but distinct taxodont teeth on each side of the beak cavity. The inside is polished, often pearly, and the inner margins are crenulate. Distributed in nearly all seas but commonest in cool waters. Eleven species, mainly deep-water, are found in eastern North America.

● Genus *Nucula* Lamarck, 1799

CANCELLATE NUT SHELL
Nucula atacellana Schenck, 1939
Range: Cape Cod to Virginia.
Habitat: Moderately deep water.
Description: Slightly under ¼ in. long. Shell oval, yellowish brown, inside only somewhat pearly. Surface cancelled by minute radiating and concentric lines.

Remarks: Formerly listed as *N. cancellata* Jeffreys and *N. reticulata* Jeffreys, both names being previously used.

DELPHINULA NUT SHELL   **Pl. 18**
Nucula delphinodonta Mighels & Adams, 1842
    Range: Labrador to Maryland.
    Habitat: Moderately shallow water in mud.
    Description: Length less than $1/4$ in. Obliquely triangular, beaks near posterior end. Posterior end short, anterior sloping to rounded point. Hinge with 3 teeth behind and 7 before beaks. Surface smooth, color greenish olive; interior moderately pearly.
    Remarks: This tiny bivalve is usually recovered from the stomachs of cod fishes.

ATLANTIC NUT CLAM *Nucula proxima* Say, 1822   **Pl. 18**
    Range: Nova Scotia to Texas; Bermuda.
    Habitat: Sheltered bays and harbors; muds.
    Description: Slightly more than $1/4$ in. long and white, with a thin olive-green periostracum (commonly missing in beach specimens). Shell triangular, beaks somewhat elevated. Surface marked with scarcely perceptible striae (fine lines). Interior pearly and highly polished; margins crenulate. Teeth of hinge sturdy, the posterior series very distinct and regular.
    Remarks: Our most abundant nut shell close to shore. Common in the stomachs of marine fishes; it is also eaten by various bottom-feeding ducks.

SMOOTH NUT CLAM *Nucula tenuis* Montagu, 1808   **Pl. 18**
    Range: Circumboreal; Labrador to Maryland.
    Habitat: Moderately deep water.
    Description: Thin and fragile, length $1/4$ in. Outline more oval than triangular. Hinge teeth usually number 4 or 5 before and about 8 behind the beaks. Color pale yellowish green; interior silvery white but not pearly.
    Remarks: *N. expansa* Reeve, 1855, is a synonym.

NUT CLAMS AND YOLDIAS: ORDER NUCULANOIDEA

■ Family Nuculanidae

These were formerly classed with the Nuculidae. The shell is more or less oblong, usually rounded in front and prolonged into an angle behind. Margins are not crenulate. There are 2 lines of hinge teeth, separated by an oblique pit for the ligament. Distributed in nearly all seas, but chiefly in cool waters.

● **Genus *Nuculana* Link, 1807**

POINTED NUT CLAM *Nuculana acuta* (Conrad, 1831)   **Pl. 18**
Range: Massachusetts to Texas and the West Indies.
Habitat: Sandy mud just offshore.
Description: Length ½ in. Anterior end broadly rounded, posterior prolonged to an acute tip. Shell sculptured with distinct concentric grooves. Hinge composed of a number of V-shaped teeth, interrupted by a central pit for the ligament. Color white, with a very thin brownish or greenish periostracum; interior white, highly polished.
Remarks: A moderately uncommon shell in the north, it occurs rather frequently in the south, where living examples can often be obtained by sifting the bottom material just offshore.

CARPENTER'S NUT CLAM   **Pl. 18**
Nuculana carpenteri (Dall, 1881)
Range: N. Carolina to the West Indies.
Habitat: Moderately deep water.
Description: A narrow, elongate shell slightly less than ½ in. long. Anterior end broadly rounded, posterior drawn out to a small square tip. Dorsal line concave, the beaks closer to front end. Hinge teeth delicate and few. Surface quite shiny, with faint concentric lines. Color greenish gray.
Remarks: A graceful small bivalve; not common and considered a prize in most collections.

CONCENTRIC NUT CLAM
Nuculana concentrica (Say, 1824)
Range: Florida to Texas; also Pleistocene.
Habitat: Moderately deep water.
Description: Slightly under ½ in. long, the shell thin and not inflated. Posterior end double the length of anterior and narrowed to a nearly acute tip. Surface with a series of concentric regular, equidistant, rounded striations. Hinge teeth angulated toward beaks. Color pale yellowish brown; interior white.

MINUTE NUT CLAM *Nuculana minuta* (Fabricius, 1776)
Range: Labrador to Maine; also Pacific Coast from Arctic Ocean to California.

Habitat: Moderately deep water.

Description: A small brown species only about ¼ in. long; interior white. Anterior end broadly rounded; posterior slightly prolonged, narrowed at the tip, where it is abruptly truncate. Very fine concentric lines present on the valves.

MÜLLER'S NUT CLAM *Nuculana pernula* (Müller, 1771)

Range: Circumpolar; Greenland to Massachusetts.

Habitat: Moderately deep water.

Description: Length about ¾ in. Rather thin, with a prolonged but only slightly narrowed posterior end. Hinge teeth sharp. Sculpture consists of rather weak concentric lines. Color olive-green; interior white. Also found in Alaska.

SULCATE NUT CLAM
Nuculana tenuisulcata (Couthouy, 1838)

Range: Gulf of St. Lawrence to Rhode Island.

Habitat: Shallow water; muds.

Description: Averaging about ½ in. long, this shell is quite thin, the valves scarcely inflated at all. Posterior end double the length of anterior and narrowed to a truncate tip. Surface with strong, concentric, closely spaced grooves. Color pale yellowish brown; interior white.

Remarks: Commonest of *Nuculana* on the New England coast. Specimens are not often found on the beach, but individuals may sometimes be obtained by dragging in the soft mud well out beyond the low-tide limits. Commonly found in the stomachs of cod fishes.

■ YOLDIA CLAMS: Family Yoldiidae

● Genus *Yoldia* Möller, 1842

ARCTIC YOLDIA *Yoldia arctica* (Gray, 1824)

Range: Greenland to Gulf of St. Lawrence.

Habitat: Moderately deep water.

Description: A rather squarish or oblong shell, well inflated, attaining length of nearly 1 in. Beaks quite prominent, located closer to anterior end, which is regularly rounded. Posterior truncate, basal margin sloping upward to form a blunt point. From 12 to 14 teeth in each series. Color lead-gray, with thin greenish periostracum; interior white.

Remarks: Fossil shells (Pleistocene) are to be found in New Brunswick and Maine.

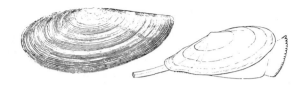

Figure 1. File Yoldia *Yoldia limatula*

FILE YOLDIA *Yoldia limatula* (Say, 1831)   **Fig. 1 & Pl. 19**
  Range: Gulf of St. Lawrence to New Jersey; West Coast from Alaska to San Diego.
  Habitat: Moderately shallow water; muds.
  Description: A handsome, shiny, light green clam 2 to $2\frac{1}{2}$ in. long. Shell oval, elongate, and thin; beaks nearly central but low. Anterior and basal margins regularly rounded, posterior end drawn out to a pointed and partially recurved tip. Teeth along hinge prominent, about 20 on each side. Interior bluish white.
  Remarks: This streamlined bivalve may be recognized by its length (more than twice as great as its height) and by the peculiarly upturned, snoutlike posterior tip. It is an active mollusk, living in mud but capable of swimming and leaping to an astonishing height.

COMB YOLDIA *Yoldia myalis* (Couthouy, 1838)   **Pl. 18**
  Range: Labrador to Massachusetts; Alaska.
  Habitat: Moderately shallow water; muds.
  Description: Smooth, elongate-oval, averages slightly less than 1 in. Beaks low, situated close to middle of shell. Both ends slightly rounded, posterior one somewhat narrower. About 12 teeth in each series. Color yellowish olive, and there is a thin periostracum that in fresh specimens is often arranged in alternate dark and light zones. Interior glossy yellowish white.

SHORT YOLDIA *Yoldia sapotilla* (Gould, 1841)   **Pl. 18**
  Range: Labrador to North Carolina.
  Habitat: Moderately shallow water; muds.
  Description: Length 1 in. Oval, somewhat elongate, thin and fragile, green. Anterior end regularly rounded, posterior end

narrowed. Interior white, with about 50 teeth on each side of beak cavity.

Remarks: Found commonly in stomachs of fishes taken off New England coast; single valves are often found among the beach litter that marks the high-tide limits.

BROAD YOLDIA *Yoldia thraciaeformis* Storer, 1838   **Pl. 19**
Range: Arctic Ocean to N. Carolina; West Coast from Arctic Ocean to Oregon.
Habitat: Moderately shallow water; muds.
Description: Length averages about 2 in. A strong, firm, squarish shell, broadest behind and gaping at both ends. An oblique fold extends from the beaks to posterior third of basal margin, giving exterior a wavy appearance. Hinge with a spoon-shaped cavity for the ligament, about 12 robust teeth on each side. Color yellowish brown; interior pure white, not shiny.
Remarks: The general shape strongly suggests the blade of an ax. With its squarish outline, wavy surface, and salient rows of V-shaped teeth along the hinge line, this species is not likely to be confused with any other shell. Placed in the subgenus *Megayoldia*.

ORDER ARCOIDEA

■ ARK SHELLS: Family Arcidae

In this group the shell is solid, strongly ribbed or cancellate, the hinge line bearing numerous teeth arranged in a line on both valves. Usually a heavy, commonly bristly periostracum (noncalcareous covering). There is no siphon. Some prefer to attach themselves by a silky byssus (threadlike anchor). Worldwide, from shallow water to considerable depths (1800 ft.). Extensively eaten in the Orient.

● Genus *Arca* Linnaeus, 1758

MOSSY ARK *Arca imbricata* Bruguière, 1789   **Pl. 19**
Range: N. Carolina to West Indies and Brazil; Bermuda.
Habitat: Attached to rocks in shallow water.
Description: Some 2 in. long, boxlike and elongate. The Mossy Ark is well named. Its shell is purplish white inside and outside, but the mollusk is almost completely covered

with a dark brown, mossy periostracum. Beaks prominent and widely separated, with a broad area between them often scored with a geometric pattern. Anterior end rounded, the longer posterior end sharply carinated (keeled). Valves gape at ventral margin. Surface of shell irregularly cross-ribbed by growth lines. Margins smooth, not scalloped or crenulate.
Remarks: Formerly listed as *A. umbonata* Lamarck.

TURKEY WING *Arca zebra* (Swainson, 1833)   **Pl. 19**
Range: N. Carolina to the West Indies; Bermuda.
Habitat: Attached to rocks in shallow water.
Description: From 2 to 4 in. long, the shell is sturdy, oblong, and gaping at both ends. Beaks slightly incurved and rather widely spaced, a broad and flat area between them. Hinge line perfectly straight, with about 50 small teeth. A colorful clam, fresh specimens yellowish white, irregularly streaked with reddish brown; interior pale lavender. It is eaten in pies in Bermuda.
Remarks: Formerly listed as *A. occidentalis* Philippi, 1847.

● **Genus *Barbatia* Gray, 1842**

RED-BROWN ARK *Barbatia cancellaria* (Lamarck, 1819)   **Pl. 19**
Range: Florida to the West Indies.
Habitat: Moderately shallow water.
Description: Another shaggy shell, from 1 to 2 in. long and purplish brown. Differs from the Mossy Ark, *Arca imbricata* (above), by being rounded at both ends and in lacking flattened area between beaks. Valves decorated with numerous fine, closely set radiating lines, each faintly beaded throughout its length. Hinge typically comblike, the teeth small and few. A heavy, hairy periostracum.
Remarks: Formerly listed as *Arca barbata* Linnaeus, but that name belongs to a Mediterranean species.

WHITE BEARDED ARK *Barbatia candida* (Helbling, 1771)   **Pl. 19**
Range: N. Carolina to Texas; West Indies.
Habitat: Attached to stones in shallow water.
Description: Length 2 to 3 in. Shell compressed, rounded at anterior end and bluntly pointed at posterior. Surface sculptured with fine ribs and concentric growth lines, imparting a somewhat beaded appearance. Notch at ventral margin for byssus. Hinge teeth quite small. Color white, with soft and shaggy yellowish brown periostracum.

WHITE MINIATURE ARK   Pl. 18
Barbatia domingensis (Lamarck, 1819)
Range: Cape Hatteras to the West Indies; Bermuda.
Habitat: Shallow water; under coral and stones.
Description: About 1 in. long. Strong and rugged, moderately inflated. Posterior end abruptly pointed, with a distinct ridge running from the posterior point to neighborhood of the beaks. Surface with strong radiating ribs that cut across stronger concentric beads and produce a distinctive network pattern. Hinge line short, teeth medium. Margins of shell crenulate. Color yellowish white; periostracum yellowish brown.

DOC BALES' ARK *Barbatia tenera* (C. B. Adams, 1845)   Pl. 19
Range: South Florida to the West Indies.
Habitat: Moderately shallow water.
Description: About $1\frac{1}{2}$ in. long. Beaks swollen, front end the shorter. Shell thin and considerably inflated. Sculpture of fine radiating lines. Color white, with a thin brownish periostracum. *Arca balesi* Pilsbry and McLean, 1939, is a synonym.

● **Genus *Arcopsis* Koenen, 1885**

ADAMS' MINIATURE ARK *Arcopsis adamsi* (Dall, 1886)   Pl. 18
Range: Cape Hatteras to Brazil.
Habitat: Shallow water; under stones.
Description: Nearly $\frac{1}{2}$ in. long, shape oblong. Both ends rounded, anterior end broadly and posterior more abruptly. Shell relatively thick, decorated with numerous very fine beaded lines. Beaks well elevated. Hinge line bears teeth that are moderately large but few. Inner margins smooth. Color yellowish white.

● **Genus *Anadara* Gray, 1847**

INCONGRUOUS ARK   Pl. 19
Anadara brasiliana (Lamarck, 1819)
Range: N. Carolina to Brazil.
Habitat: Moderately shallow water; gravelly bottoms.
Description: Length $1\frac{1}{2}$ to 2 in., height nearly the same. Inequivalve, one valve slightly overhanging the other. Considerably inflated. Beaks high and not well separated, so that in

many cases there are specimens with the beaks showing signs of wear (frequently flattened). About 25 broad ribs with narrow grooves between them, the ribs crossed by equidistant lines, less conspicuous toward posterior end. Row of comblike teeth is graduated, the smaller teeth at center. Color white. See Chemnitz's Ark for similarity.

Remarks: It has been pointed out that when looking directly at the basal ventral margin, with the beaks directed away from the viewer, the margin presents a gentle curve instead of a straight line as in most bivalves. This species used to be known as *Arca incongrua* Say, 1822.

CHEMNITZ'S ARK *Anadara chemnitzi* (Philippi, 1851)   **Pl. 19**
Range: Texas to the West Indies and Brazil.
Habitat: Moderately shallow water; gravelly bottoms.
Description: About ½ in. long, this species appears at first sight quite like the Incongruous Ark. It is slightly inequivalve, short and high, and well inflated. There are some 25 rounded or flattened ribs, crossed by distinct grooves. Beaks more widely spaced and considerably higher than in Incongruous Ark, and ventral line lacks characteristic curve of that species. Color white.
Remarks: This is chiefly a West Indian shell, uncommon in Florida.

CUT-RIBBED ARK *Anadara floridana* (Conrad, 1869)   **Pl. 19**
Range: N. Carolina to Texas; West Indies.
Habitat: Moderately shallow water.
Description: From 3 to 5 in. long, a sturdy white shell with a brownish periostracum. Beaks low, slightly incurved, hinge line straight. About 35 radiating ribs that widen as they approach the margin, each rib bearing a deep central groove for most of the length.
Remarks: Formerly listed as *Arca secticostata* Reeve. *Anadara lienosa* (Say) is a fossil shell from Florida (Pleistocene).

EARED ARK *Anadara notabilis* (Röding, 1798)   **Pl. 19**
Range: Bermuda; Florida to Brazil.
Habitat: Shallow water; grassy and muddy bottoms.
Description: Thick, heavy, sturdy, rather oblong, attains length of 3½ in. Beaks well elevated. Anterior end short and rounded, posterior longer and squarish. Hinge teeth numerous and small. About 25 strong radiating ribs crossed by threadlike lines. Color white, with a silky brown periostracum.

Remarks: Known as the Eared Ark from the thin dorsal edge of the posterior tip. Formerly listed as *Arca auriculata* Lamarck, but that species comes from the Red Sea. It was also called *Arca deshayesi* Hanley, 1843, but Röding's name has priority.

BLOOD ARK *Anadara ovalis* (Bruguière, 1789)   **Pl. 19**
Range: Massachusetts to the West Indies and Brazil.
Habitat: Shallow water; sandy bottoms.
Description: About 2 in. long, shell thick and solid, with prominent beaks terminating in points nearly in contact, so that viewed from the end the shell is heart-shaped. About 35 radiating ribs. Color white, but lower half of shell covered with a thick and bristly greenish brown periostracum.
Remarks: This clam derives its popular name from being one of the very few mollusks that has red blood. It used to be listed as *Arca pexata* Say, *A. campechiensis* Gmelin, 1791, and *A. americana* Wood, 1825.

TRANSVERSE ARK *Anadara transversa* (Say, 1822)   **Pl. 19**
Range: Massachusetts to Texas; West Indies.
Habitat: Shallow water; sandy bottoms.
Description: Length about 1 in. Shell transversely oblong, the beaks incurved and set closer to anterior end. Valves slightly unequal, so margin of one commonly passes a little beyond that of its mate. About 12 radiating ribs. Color white, the hairy periostracum dark brown.
Remarks: This small white ark is very common in shallow waters, particularly in the South.

■ **Family Noetiidae**

● **Genus *Noetia* Gray, 1857**

PONDEROUS ARK *Noetia ponderosa* (Say, 1822)   **Pl. 19**
Range: Virginia to Texas.
Habitat: Shallow water; sandy bottoms.
Description: Length 2½ in. Shell somewhat oblique, quite thick and sturdy. Beaks prominent, inclined to turn backward. Some 30 strong ribs covered near the margins by deeply chiseled lines. The comblike teeth are larger at the ends, smaller at the center. Color white. In life the shell is covered with a heavy, velvety periostracum that is nearly black.

Remarks: Single valves are now and then washed up on the beaches at Cape Cod, Nantucket, and Long Island, but these are believed to be fossil shells, and the species is not thought to be living north of Virginia at present. It is common in the Gulf of Mexico.

■ LIMOPSIS: Family Limopsidae

These are chiefly small oval clams with a soft, furry periostracum. The beaks are nearly central, and the toothed hinge line is slightly curved. They are inhabitants of deep waters as a rule.

● Genus *Limopsis* Sassi, 1827

SULCATE LIMOPSIS   Fig. 2 & Pl. 19
Limopsis sulcata Verrill & Bush, 1898
  Range: Massachusetts to the West Indies.
  Habitat: Deep water from 10 to 349 fathoms.
  Description: Length about ¹/₂ in., shape obliquely oval. Posterior margin prolonged and obtusely rounded, dorsal margin short and straight. Beaks small but prominent. About 18 strong teeth, the posterior series curving downward. Surface sculptured with rather strong concentric grooves marked by faint vertical lines. Margins crenulate. Color grayish, with brownish, furry periostracum.

Figure 2. Sulcate Limopsis *Limopsis sulcata*

■ BITTERSWEET SHELLS: Family Glycymerididae

These are rather solid, roundish, and well-inflated shells with strong hinges bearing curved rows of teeth. Living chiefly in warmer waters, they are popularly known as bittersweet clams.

● Genus *Glycymeris* da Costa, 1778

AMERICAN BITTERSWEET   Pl. 19
Glycymeris americana (Defrance, 1829)
   Range: Virginia to Texas to Brazil.
   Habitat: Moderately shallow water.
   Description: About $1/2$ in. long in the northern section of its range. It grows to nearly 5 in. in the southern section. Shell circular, rather compressed, the beaks centrally located. There is a curving row of hinge teeth, becoming feeble or absent beneath the beaks. Surface bears numerous, fine striations; margins crenulate. Color grayish tan, sometimes weakly mottled with yellowish brown.
   Remarks: A relatively rare species.

DECUSSATE BITTERSWEET   Pl. 19
Glycymeris decussata (Linneaus, 1758)
   Range: South Florida; West Indies, and south to Brazil.
   Habitat: Moderately shallow water.
   Description: About $1/4$ in. long. Outline orbicular, moderately inflated. Shell solid. Numerous radiating lines. Cream-colored, variously blotched with chestnut brown. See the Atlantic Bittersweet (below) for similarity.
   Remarks: Formerly listed as *G. pennaceus* (Lamarck).

COMB BITTERSWEET   Pl. 19
Glycymeris pectinata (Gmelin, 1791)
   Range: N. Carolina to the West Indies.
   Habitat: Shallow water on a sand and gravel bottom.
   Description: Generally less than 1 in. long. Shell rather compressed, with about 20 well-rounded radiating ribs crossed by minute growth lines. About 10 teeth on each side of beak cavity. Color white to yellowish white, with spotted bands of yellowish brown.
   Remarks: This is a pretty shell when obtained fresh and in good condition. Specimens rolled about in the surf and left drying on the beach lose much of their delicate color.

ATLANTIC BITTERSWEET   Pl. 19
Glycymeris undata (Linnaeus, 1758)
Range: N. Carolina to the West Indies to Brazil.
Habitat: Moderately shallow water.
Description: About 1³/₄ in. long. Shell solid, moderately inflated. Surface appears smooth but there are numerous fine radiating lines. Color pale cream to white, variously blotched with brown.
Remarks: Easily confused with the Decussate Bittersweet (above), but its radiating lines are finer and the beaks point toward each other; in *G. decussata* the beaks are inclined to point backward. It used to be known as *G. lineata* Reeve.

ORDER MYTILOIDEA

■ MUSSELS: Family Mytilidae

Shells with equal valves, the hinge line very long and the umbones (beaks) sharp. Some members burrow in soft mud, clay, or wood, but the majority are fastened by a byssus (threadlike anchor). Most mussels are edible, though seldom eaten in this country. In Europe the mussel is farmed much the same as the oyster is here, and it forms an important item of European seafood. Worldwide, and best represented in cool seas.

● Genus *Mytilus* Linnaeus, 1758

BLUE MUSSEL   Fig. 3 & Pls. 5, 20
Mytilus edulis Linnaeus, 1758
Range: Greenland to S. Carolina; Alaska to California; Europe.
Habitat: Intertidal; usually attached to submerged hard surfaces.
Description: Length about 3 in. Shell roughly an elongate triangle, the beaks forming the apex. Anterior margin generally straight, posterior margin broadly rounded. Surface bears many fine concentric lines and is covered with a shining periostracum. Color bluish to bluish black; interior white, the margins violet. Young specimens are usually brighter-colored, and may be greenish or even banded or rayed.
Remarks: Acres of blue mussels are exposed at low tide all along the Atlantic Coast to the Carolinas. We find them attached to stones and pebbles where the water is clear, on

pilings of wharves, and in rocky places generally. They are attached by a series of strong byssal threads but are capable of moving about to some extent. This clam is a tasty morsel, much relished by those who have tried it; for some reason — probably because of the abundance of other larger bivalves — it has never become very popular here, although it is eaten extensively in Europe.

● **Genus *Modiolus* Lamarck, 1799**

TULIP MUSSEL *Modiolus americanus* (Leach, 1815)   **Pl. 20**
Range: N. Carolina to the West Indies.
Habitat: Moderately shallow water.
Description: From 2 to 4 in. long, the anterior end is short and narrow, posterior end broadly rounded. Beaks swollen anterior, not terminal. Shell rather thin in substance and moderately inflated. Surface smooth, periostracum glossy. Color yellowish brown; interior purplish.
Remarks: Formerly listed as *M. tulipa* Lamarck. Compare with the False Tulip Mussel.

NORTHERN HORSE MUSSEL   **Pl. 20**
Modiolus modiolus (Linnaeus, 1758)
Range: Arctic Ocean to north Florida; Arctic to California.
Habitat: Moderately deep water.
Description: Length of adults 4 to 6 in. Shell heavy and coarse, oblong-oval, the beaks placed slightly to one side. Anterior end short and narrow, posterior broadly rounded. Surface marked by lines of growth, and sometimes a few radiating lines. Color bluish black, with a thick and leathery periostracum.
Remarks: This large mussel is generally considered unfit for food. The empty valves, noticeable because of their size, are thrown up on nearly every northern beach exposed to the open sea. Bleached shells often turn pale lavender or reddish.

FALSE TULIP MUSSEL   **Pl. 20**
Modiolus modiolus squamosus Beauperthuy, 1967
Range: North Carolina to Texas; West Indies.
Habitat: Shallow water; attached to rocks and wharf pilings.
Description: Length 1 to 2 in. Exterior brownish, with an oblique whitish ray. Interior purplish to white. Umbones small, not swollen, always white.
Remarks: Common in cooler water. Do not confuse with the Tulip Mussel which is fatter and has rosy, swollen umbones.

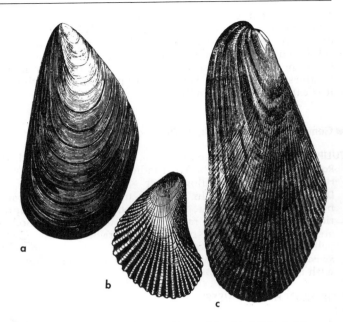

Figure 3. a) Blue Mussel *Mytilus edulis* **b)** Ribbed Mussel
Geukensia demissa **c)** Hooked Mussel *Ischadium recurvum*.

● **Genus *Geukensia* Poel, 1959**

RIBBED MUSSEL   Fig. 3 & Pl. 20
Geukensia demissa (Dillwyn, 1817)
　Range: Nova Scotia to Florida.
　Habitat: Intertidal in marshes.
　Description: Length 2 to 4 in. Shell moderately thin, oblong-
oval, and much elongated. Surface ornamented with numerous radiating, somewhat undulating ribs that occasionally
branch. Color yellowish green to bluish green. Interior silvery white, often iridescent.
　Remarks: This common mussel found on muddy flats and in
brackish waters seems to thrive best in partially polluted situations. Formerly listed as *M. plicatulas* Lamarck. Florida
specimens are sometimes listed as a subspecies, *G. demissa
granosissima* (Sowerby, 1914). It has twice as many ribs as
the northern form.

● **Genus _Brachidontes_ Swainson, 1840**

YELLOW MUSSEL   **Pl. 18**
Brachidontes modiolus (Linneaus, 1767)
  Range: South Florida to the West Indies.
  Habitat: Moderately shallow water.
  Description: About 1¹/₄ in. long and fan-shaped on one side; this gives the outline a peculiarly lopsided appearance. Surface ornamented with numerous fine wavy riblets. Color yellowish brown; interior purplish, often with a metallic sheen.

SCORCHED MUSSEL   **Pl. 18**
Brachidontes exustus (Linneaus, 1758)
  Range: Cape Hatteras to West Indies to Brazil.
  Habitat: Moderately shallow water.
  Description: About 1 in. long, this species is not as elongate as Yellow Mussel. Shell thin, fan-shaped on one side. Surface ribbed, strongest near margins. Color bluish gray, with a yellowish brown periostracum.
  Remarks: Commonly washed ashore in clusters attached to other shells and seaweeds. _B. citrinus_ (Röding, 1798) is a synonym.

● **Genus _Ischadium_ Jukes-Brown, 1905**

HOOKED MUSSEL   **Fig. 3 & Pl. 18**
Ischadium recurvum (Rafinesque, 1820)
  Range: Cape Cod to the West Indies.
  Habitat: Shallow water.
  Description: Length 1 to 2 in., triangular shell moderately solid, slightly inflated, strongly and obliquely curved. Surface decorated with a pattern of fine, elevated lines that often divide as they approach posterior end. Color bluish black; interior polished, purplish with a whitish margin.
  Remarks: Formerly listed as _Mytilus hamatus_ Say. Living specimens have been taken in Long Island Sound and at Cape Cod, but it is believed that these were imported with young oysters from more southern waters, and that this mussel is unable to live through our northern winters.

● **Genus _Gregariella_ Monterosato, 1884**

ARTIST'S MUSSEL   **Pl. 21**
Gregariella coralliophaga (Gmelin, 1791)
  Range: N. Carolina to the West Indies.
  Habitat: Bores into rocks and other shells.

Description: A small mussel, about ³/₄ in. long. Outline some-what cylindrical, the tips drawn out to a point and often frayed. Color reddish brown; interior highly iridescent.

Remarks: This diminutive mussel sometimes bores into other shells or stone but more often it attaches itself to some support and becomes encased in a small mound of cemented sand grains. *Mytilus opifex* Say, 1825, is synonym of this variable species.

● **Genus *Amygdalum* Mühlfeld, 1811**

PAPER MUSSEL *Amydalum papyrium* (Conrad, 1846)   **Pl. 18**
  Range: Texas and Maryland to Florida and Mexico.
  Habitat: Moderately shallow water.
  Description: Length to 1¹/₂ in. An elongate shell, very thin and fragile. Front end short, posterior long and widening to a rounded tip. Hinge weak. Surface glossy, with delicate pale green periostracum.
  Remarks: Commonly attaches to the marine tassel grass, *Ruppia*, in shallow water.

● **Genus *Musculus* Röding, 1798**

DISCORD MUSSEL *Musculus discors* (Linneaus, 1767)
  Range: Labrador to Long Island Sound; Arctic seas to Puget Sound.
  Habitat: Moderately deep water.
  Description: A rather plump little mussel about 1 in. long, oblong-oval, and slightly produced at the posterior end. Weak radiating lines are discernible on both ends of the shell, and there is a slightly excavated channel across the middle of each valve. Color brownish black; interior bluish white and somewhat iridescent.

LATERAL MUSSEL   **Fig. 4 & Pl. 23**
Musculus lateralis (Say, 1822)
  Range: N. Carolina to the West Indies and Brazil.
  Habitat: Moderately shallow water.
  Description: Length nearly ¹/₂ in. An oblong shell, moderately inflated, with radiating lines at both ends; the center shows only concentric growth lines. Color pale brown; interior slightly iridescent.
  Remarks: This small, abundant species is placed in the sub-genus *Ryenella* Fleming, 1959.

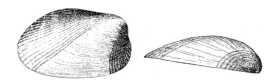

Figure 4. Lateral Mussel *Musculus lateralis*

LITTLE BLACK MUSSEL *Musculus niger* (Gray, 1824)
Range: Arctic Ocean to N. Carolina; Arctic seas to Puget Sound.
Habitat: Moderately shallow water.
Description: Shell thin and oval, 1 to 2 in. long. Beaks close to front end. Rather prominent radiating lines at both ends, a relatively smooth area at center of each valve. Color deep brownish black, with a rusty brown periostracum; interior pearly.
Remarks: This mussel is rather more active than most of the others and easily moves from place to place, using its foot as a prehensile organ and spinning a new byssus when a satisfactory situation has been found.

● **Genus** *Crenella* **Brown, 1827**

LITTLE BEAN MUSSEL *Crenella faba* (Müller, 1776)
Range: Greenland to Nova Scotia.
Habitat: Moderately shallow water.
Description: Length $\frac{1}{4}$ to $\frac{1}{2}$ in. Oval, with a small portion of the hinge line straight. Anterior acutely rounded, posterior broadly rounded. Sculpture consists of numerous distinct radiating lines that make the margins crenulate. Color yellowish brown; interior lead-colored but polished.

GLANDULAR BEAN MUSSEL
Crenella glandula (Totten, 1834)
Range: Labrador to N. Carolina.
Habitat: Moderately shallow water.
Description: Slightly more than $\frac{1}{2}$ in. long. Shape oval, beaks close to anterior end. Surface bears fine but distinct radiating lines crossed by even finer concentric lines. Color yellowish brown; interior bluish white.

● **Genus *Botula* Mörch, 1853**

CINNAMON MUSSEL *Botula fusca* (Gmelin, 1791)   **Pl. 20**
   Range: N. Carolina to the West Indies; Bermuda.
   Habitat: Shallow water; bores into rocks and wood.
   Description: An oddly shaped shell, about ³/₄ in. long. Beaks situated at one end, which they sometimes overhang, producing a hooked effect. Shell rather cylindrical and somewhat curved. Surface smooth but coarsely wrinkled by growth lines. Dark chestnut brown, with a shiny periostracum.
   Remarks: *B. cinnamomea* Lamarck, 1819, is a synonym.

● **Genus *Lioberus* Dall, 1898**

SAY'S CHESTNUT MUSSEL   **Pl. 20**
Lioberus castaneus (Say, 1822)
   Range: Florida to the West Indies to Brazil.
   Habitat: Shallow water.
   Description: About ³/₄ in. long, beaks close to front end. Shell slightly cylindrical. Color light brown; usually the posterior half is shiny and the posterior part is covered by a grayish, feltlike periostracum; interior lavender.
   Remarks: These mussels may be found living in clusters, attached to stones and dead shells.

● **Genus *Lithophaga* Röding, 1798**

GIANT DATE MUSSEL   **Pl. 20**
Lithophaga antillarum (Orbigny, 1842)
   Range: South Florida to the West Indies to Brazil.
   Habitat: Moderately shallow water; bores into limestone.
   Description: Length 2 to 4 in. Shell thin, elongate, cylindrical; wedge-shaped when viewed from above. Beaks low and insignificant, hinge line without teeth. Surface with numerous concentric furrows, most pronounced on posterior end. When young this species suspends itself from rocks by a byssus; when adult it forms a cavity in limestone and other moderately soft rocks which corresponds to the shape of its valves. Color brown, the thin periostracum also brown.

SCISSOR DATE MUSSEL   **Pl. 20**
Lithophaga aristata (Dillwyn, 1817)
   Range: N. Carolina to Texas and the West Indies.
   Habitat: Moderately shallow water; bores into soft rocks.

Description: A small rock borer about 1 in. long. Pale brown and cylindrical. This species is instantly recognized by the extension of the extremities of the valves, which cross each other at the posterior end of the shell.

MAHOGANY DATE MUSSEL   Pl. 20
Lithophaga bisulcata (Orbigny, 1842)
Range: N. Carolina to the West Indies; Bermuda.
Habitat: Moderately shallow water; bores into soft rocks.
Description: About 1 in. long. A smooth and somewhat polished shell bearing a pair of radiating furrows from beaks to posterior end of shell. Anterior end bluntly rounded, posterior abruptly tapering. Color pale brown, but surface generally covered by a calcareous encrustation.

BLACK DATE MUSSEL *Lithophaga nigra* (Orbigny, 1842)   Pl. 20
Range: South Florida to the West Indies.
Habitat: Moderately shallow water; bores into coral.
Description: Length 1 to 2 in. Color dark brown or black. Cylindrical, surface with strong concentric growth lines, crossed by prominent vertical striations. Heavy, glossy periostracum.
Remarks: Fleshy parts of the animal are luminous in the dark.

ORDER PTERIOIDA

■ PURSE SHELLS: Family Isognomonidae

These are greatly compressed shells, characterized by a hinge with vertical parallel grooves. The interior is pearly. Inhabitants of warm seas around the world.

● Genus *Isognomon* Lightfoot, 1786

FLAT TREE OYSTER *Isognomon alatus* (Gmelin, 1791)   Pl. 21
Range: South Florida to Brazil; Bermuda.
Habitat: Mangrove roots and submerged brush near shore.
Description: Length about 3 in. Shell greatly compressed, the right valve flat and the left slightly inflated. Hinge line short, perpendicular grooves on inside. Surface may be smooth or scaly; color brown, black, or purplish; juvenile

examples often rayed. Inside with pearly layer that does not extend all the way to the margins.

Remarks: This genus may be found in old books under the names *Perna* Bruguière or *Pedalion* Dillwyn. This is a common species.

LISTER'S TREE OYSTER   Pl. 21
Isognomon radiatus (Anton, 1839)

Range: South Florida to Brazil; Bermuda.

Habitat: Shallow water; attached to rocks.

Description: Length to 3 in. Elongate, irregular in outline. Valves compressed, hinge with vertical grooves. Surface wrinkled, color greenish brown, commonly with paler rays; interior pearly.

Remarks: Formerly listed as *I. listeri* (Hanley, 1843).

■PEARL OYSTERS: Family Pteriidae

In this group the shells are very inequivalve, the right valve with an opening under its wing for the passage of a byssus (threadlike anchor). This family contains the valuable pearl oysters, *Pinctada*. Found generally on rocks, sea fans, and other firm objects.

●Genus *Pteria* Scopoli, 1777

ATLANTIC WINGED OYSTER   Pl. 21
Pteria colymbus (Röding, 1798)

Range: N. Carolina to Brazil; Bermuda.

Habitat: Shallow water; attached to sea fans.

Description: Moderately solid, $1^1/_2$ to 3 in. long. Hinge line straight, posterior margin broadly rounded, the wing strongly notched. Surface wrinkled; young specimens usually covered with prickly spines. Color brownish purple, with radiating lines of paler brown; interior pearly.

Remarks: Formerly known as *Avicula atlantica* Lamarck, 1819, this is a member of the pearl oyster group. The valuable shells of this group, however, are found in Ceylon, Australia, and the Persian Gulf, although some pearl fishing is done off Baja California, Panama, and Isla Margarita in Venezuela. This species commonly washes ashore in western Florida.

● Genus *Pinctada* Röding, 1798

ATLANTIC PEARL OYSTER   Pl. 21
Pinctada imbricata Röding, 1798
   Range: South Florida to the West Indies; Bermuda.
   Habitat: Shallow water; attached to rocks.
   Description: About 2 in. long; larger in the southern part of its
   range. Valves flattish and nearly equal in size. Hinge line
   straight; byssal notch under right wing. Surface sculptured
   with scaly projections arranged concentrically, although
   these may be lacking in some specimens. Color variable,
   generally some shade of brown or green; interior very pearly.
   Remarks: Formerly called *P. radiata* (Leach, 1814). May produce a pearl of gem quality.

■ **PEN SHELLS: Family Pinnidae**

   Large wedge-shaped bivalves, thin and fragile, and gaping at
   the posterior end. They are attached by a large and powerful
   byssus and live partially buried in mud or sand. Clothing
   articles, such as gloves and stockings, have been woven from
   the byssus of a Mediterranean species. There are large edible
   muscles in both valves. Occurring in warm seas, some grow
   to a length of more than 2 feet, and occasional specimens
   contain black pearls. A small commensal crab is sometimes
   found inside the mantle cavity.

● Genus *Pinna* Linnaeus, 1758

AMBER PEN SHELL *Pinna carnea* Gmelin, 1791   Pl. 21
   Range: South Florida to the West Indies; Bermuda.
   Habitat: Shallow water; attached to pebbles in coarse sand.
   Description: Thin, fragile, and wedge-shaped, more than 1 ft.
   long when fully grown, but most specimens are less than
   that. Posterior end rounded and gaping; shell tapers to a
   point at the other end, where the beaks are situated, so that
   one might almost say there is no front end. Valves decorated
   by a number of undulating, radiating folds with smaller lines
   in between. Color pale yellowish orange.
   Remarks: In the genus *Pinna*, on the inside there is a narrow

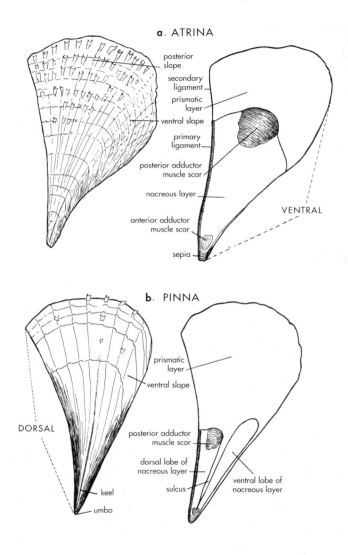

a. ATRINA

posterior slope
secondary ligament
prismatic layer
ventral slope
primary ligament
posterior adductor muscle scar
nacreous layer
anterior adductor muscle scar
sepia

VENTRAL

b. PINNA

prismatic layer
ventral slope
posterior adductor muscle scar
dorsal lobe of nacreous layer
sulcus
ventral lobe of nacreous layer

DORSAL

keel
umbo

Figure 5. a) Pen Shell *Atrina* **b)** Pen Shell *Pinna*

groove down the center separating the iridescent portion into two lobes. In the genus *Atrina* (below) this groove is absent and the iridescent part is undivided.

● **Genus *Atrina* Gray, 1842**

HALF-NAKED PEN SHELL
Atrina seminuda (Lamarck, 1819)
Range: N. Carolina to Texas and to Argentina.
Habitat: Offshore in shallow water, buried in sandy bottoms.
Description: 5 to 9 in. in length. Very similar to the Stiff Pen Shell, but on the inner surface the small, round muscle scar is well surrounded by the nacreous area. Its living mantle edge is pale yellow.

STIFF PEN SHELL *Atrina rigida* (Lightfoot, 1786)   **Pl. 21**
Range: N. Carolina to the West Indies.
Habitat: Shallow water; gravelly mud.
Description: Large but delicate, growing to a length of 1 ft. Shell wedge-shaped in outline — dorsal margin straight, ventral rounded, and posterior gaping. Valves decorated with about 15 rounded and slightly elevated ribs, which fade near beaks. Highly elevated tubular spines adorn the ribs, particularly near margins. There is a strong silky byssus. Color of shell purplish black.
Remarks: The Half-naked Pen Shell, *A. seminuda* (Lamarck) occupies about the same range and cannot be distinguished from the Stiff Pen Shell externally, although it is usually a more tan-purple; differences are in the soft parts and muscle scars.

SAW-TOOTHED PEN SHELL   **Pl. 21**
Atrina serrata (Sowerby, 1825)
Range: N. Carolina to Texas and the West Indies.
Habitat: Shallow water; sandy mud.
Description: A yellowish brown shell from 8 to 12 in. long. Shaped like Stiff Pen Shell but more delicately sculptured. With about 30 rows of smaller but much more numerous scales.
Remarks: Commonly washed ashore with *rigida*.

■ SCALLOPS: Family Pectinidae

The valves are commonly unequal, the lower strongly convex, the upper flat or even concave. Surface usually ribbed and margins scalloped. Juvenile specimens may be attached by a byssus, but adults generally are free-swimming. The bivalve progresses through the water by a series of jerks and darts produced by rapidly opening and closing its valves, forcing a jet of water out from between the wings so that the mollusk travels with the hinge backward. This locomotion is powered by a single large muscle — the only part of the scallop we eat. A row of tiny eyes fringes the mantle, each eye complete with cornea, lens, and optic nerve. Scallops are found in all seas, from shallow water to great depths. Shells of this family have always had a certain artistic appeal. The Crusaders employed the shell as a badge of honor, using a Mediterranean species (*Pecten jacobaeus* Linnaeus, 1758), and at present, a scallop shell is the well-known trademark of a large oil company. All of the scallops used to be placed in the genus *Pecten;* the great diversity within the group, however, has led to the erection of many genera and subgenera.

● **Genus *Euvola* Dall, 1897**

RAVENEL'S SCALLOP *Euvola raveneli* (Dall, 1898)   **Pl. 22**
  Range: N. Carolina to the West Indies.
  Habitat: Moderately shallow water.
  Description: About 2 in. long, a pinkish to purplish and occasionally golden-yellow scallop. Upper valve is quite flat and deeply colored with irregular dark markings. Very convex lower valve decorated with about 25 strong, grooved ribs with wide spaces between them. Hinge line straight, the wings unequal; basal margin forms an almost perfect semicircle.
  Remarks: A rather uncommon species, sometimes confused with the Zigzag Scallop, but it is a smaller shell, more lightly colored, and the ribs on the flat valve are rounded and fewer.

ZIGZAG SCALLOP *Euvola ziczac* (Linnaeus, 1758)   **Pl. 22**
  Range: Bermuda; N. Carolina to the West Indies.
  Habitat: Moderately shallow water.
  Description: Length 2 to 4 in. This species has a flat upper

valve, often with a central concavity, and a lower valve that is deep, cup-shaped, and overlaps the upper. Lower valve has low radiating ribs, so low that the surface seems rather smooth, and the color of this valve is a mottled brown, verging on reddish. The flat, heavily blotched upper valve bears crowded ribs and is ornamented with zigzag lines of black.
Remarks: Sometimes mistaken for Ravenel's Scallop (see above). Fished for food in Bermuda.

PAPER SCALLOP *Euvola papyracea* (Gabb, 1873)   **Pl. 22**
Range: Gulf of Mexico to the West Indies and to Brazil.
Habitat: Moderately deep water.
Description: A rather flattish, smooth and glossy shell, some 2 in. long, each valve only slightly arched. Exterior polished and without ribs of any kind, but there are distinct radiating ribs on the inside. Upper valve reddish brown, lower one pure white, sometimes with a yellow border. Inside, this valve nearly always has a rim of bright yellow.
Remarks: A larger species, *C. laurenti* (Gmelin, 1791) from the West Indies is used for food.

● **Genus** *Chlamys* **Röding, 1798**

ICELAND SCALLOP *Chlamys islandica* (Müller, 1776)   **Pl. 22**
Range: Greenland to Massachusetts.
Habitat: Moderately deep water.
Description: Length to 4 in. Shell oval, upper valve slightly more convex than the lower. Surface with about 50 narrow, crowded, radiating ribs bearing numerous small, erect scales; ribs frequently grouped, forming a number of unequal ridges. Wings very unequal, the posterior one shorter. Pale orange to reddish brown, lower valve paler tone. Interior glossy white, muscle scar large and shallow.
Remarks: A popular edible species in the Maritime provinces of Canada.

● **Genus** *Caribachlamys* **Waller, 1993**

LITTLE KNOBBY SCALLOP   **Pl. 22**
Caribachlamys imbricata (Gmelin, 1791)
Range: South Florida to the West Indies; Bermuda.
Habitat: Moderately shallow water.
Description: Length about 1½ in., the height somewhat more.

Unusually flat, the valves scarcely arched at all. Ribs stout, 9 or 10, each with a series of regularly spaced hollow knobs. Wings unequal in size. Color mainly white, sometimes variegated with pinkish; interior yellowish, the margins and hinge area purplish.

ORNATE SCALLOP   Pl. 22
Caribachlamys ornata (Lamarck, 1819)
   Range: South Florida to the West Indies and to Brazil.
   Habitat: Shallow water under rocks.
   Description: About 1 in. long. Approximately 20 strong ribs, a few of which are usually unspotted, so they stand out as plain white lines. Ribs studded with short but sharp spines, especially near margins. Wings very unequal, one scarcely discernible. Color white, spotted with red and purple.

SENTIS SCALLOP *Caribachlamys sentis* (Reeve, 1853)   Pl. 22
   Range: South Florida to the West Indies and to Brazil.
   Habitat: Shallow water under rocks.
   Description: A small species 1 to 1½ in. long. Wings very unequal. Surface with numerous crowded ribs, each with tiny scales. Often bright scarlet, but may be brown, purple, or even white. Both valves generally colored alike with about 5 riblets.

● **Genus** *Placopecten* **Verrill, 1897**

ATLANTIC DEEP-SEA SCALLOP   Pl. 22
Placopecten magellanicus (Gmelin, 1791)
   Range: Labrador to N. Carolina.
   Habitat: Moderately deep water.
   Description: Commonly from 6 to 8 in. long. This scallop's shell is large, orbicular, somewhat higher than long, and moderately thick and solid. Lower valve nearly flat, upper slightly convex. Surface sculptured with a multitude of narrow radiating lines and grooves, wings about equal in size. Upper valve reddish or pinkish brown, sometimes rayed with white, lower valve pinkish white; interior glossy white, with very prominent muscle scar.
   Remarks: The convex valves were commonly used as dishes by the Indians, and today visitors to our northern shores nearly always take home a shell or two to be used as ashtrays. This species has been listed as *Pecten tenuicostatus* Mighels and Adams, 1841, and *P. grandis* Solander, 1789, an invalid name.

● Genus *Bractechlamys* Iredale, 1939

ANTILLEAN SCALLOP   Pls. 23, 24
Bractechlamys antillarum (Récluz, 1853)
   Range: South Florida to the West Indies; Bermuda.
   Habitat: Shallow water, uncommon.
   Description: Small, rather flattish, not quite 1 in. long. Valves
   thin, about equal in shape and convexity. About 15 low ribs,
   with relatively wide spaces in between. Color buffy yellow,
   pale orange, or light brown, sometimes mottled with white.

● Genus *Nodipecten* Dall, 1898

LION'S PAW   Pls. 3, 22
Nodipecten nodosus (Linnaeus, 1758)
   Range: Cape Hatteras to West Indies and to Brazil; Bermuda.
   Habitat: Moderately deep water.
   Description: Shell very robust and heavy, 4 to 6 in. long.
   Valves equal in size and shape and slightly arched. Surface
   with numerous closely spaced radiating ribs, and about 10
   broad folds, the crests of which are marked at regular intervals with blunt raised knobs. Interior has channels corresponding to the outside folds. Color reddish brown to bright
   orange; glossy interior generally some shade of pink or
   salmon.
   Remarks: A handsome shell eagerly sought by collectors and
   seldom found on shore. Single valves can be picked up at
   Sanibel Island after a storm, but most of the fine specimens
   seen are brought in by shrimp fishermen.

● Genus *Argopecten* Monterosato, 1889

CALICO SCALLOP   Pls. 4, 22
Argopecten gibbus (Linneaus, 1758)
   Range: Maryland to Brazil; Bermuda.
   Habitat: Shallow water.
   Description: Length 1 to 2 in., most specimens about $1\frac{1}{2}$ in.
   Shell inflated, with about 20 rounded radiating ribs marked
   by numerous growth lines that give the shell a somewhat
   rough surface when not wave-worn. Wings about equal.
   Color patterns of this little clam are numerous; various
   combinations of mottled white, rose, brown, purple, and
   orange-yellow, the colors most striking on the upper valve.
   Remarks: This is now a popular seafood in Florida. See Nucleus Scallop (below) for similarity.

BAY SCALLOP   Pls. 3, 22
Argopecten irradians (Lamarck, 1819)
   Range: Nova Scotia to Florida and Texas.
   Habitat: Shallow water.
   Description: Shell roughly round, well inflated, length 2 to 3
   in. Wings nearly equal-sized, covered with small radiating
   ridges. Valves about equally convex. This species is divided
   into 3 subspecies, each illustrated on Plate 22. (1) Bay Scallop, *A. i. irradians* (Lamarck, 1819), is found from Nova
   Scotia to Long Island; it has 17 or 18 rounded radiating ribs;
   color grayish brown, more or less mottled, and the valves are
   nearly the same color. (2) Southern Scallop, *A. i. concentricus* (Say, 1822), is found from New Jersey to Florida; it has 20
   to 21 ribs that are somewhat squarish in cross section;
   slightly more inflated than the typical form and commonly
   more brightly colored, being orange-brown to bluish gray,
   occasionally with concentric bands; lower valve usually uncolored. (3) Gulf Scallop, *A. i. amplicostatus* (Dall, 1898), occurs in Gulf of Mexico along the Texas coast; it is the stout-
   est of the three subspecies, with only 12 to 17 ribs; color
   mottled gray and black, the lower valve usually pure white.
   Remarks: This is the common scallop of our East Coast; tons
   are dredged annually for the markets. It prefers to live
   among eelgrass. The unfortunate disappearance of eelgrass
   in many localities has led to a corresponding scarcity of scallops. Fishermen obtain them by dragging a rakelike dredge
   through this grass.

NUCLEUS SCALLOP *Argopecten nucleus* (Born, 1778)   Pl. 22
   Range: South Florida to the West Indies.
   Habitat: Shallow water.
   Description: About 1 in. long, well inflated. Very similar to
   Calico Scallop (above) but slightly more globose and with a
   few more ribs. Colors the same, except that the Nucleus
   Scallop does not show the bright shades of red or orange.
   Remarks: This scallop is sometimes listed as a subspecies, *A.
   gibbus nucleus* Born.

● **Genus *Aequipecten* P. Fischer, 1886**

THISTLE SCALLOP   Pl. 23
Aequipecten acanthodes (Dall, 1925)
   Range: South Florida; Bermuda and Caribbean.
   Habitat: Shallow protected waters among turtlegrass.

Description: About 1 inch, slightly broader than long, rather flat, minutely spined. Bright colors vary from orange, rusty red, and deep purple to yellow. Differing from the much fatter Rough Scallop in having the short ear square, rather than U-shaped at the edge.

Remarks: This species swarms in protected canals in the Florida Keys in the springtime.

ROUGH SCALLOP   Pl. 22

Aequipecten muscosus (Wood, 1828)

Range: N. Carolina to the West Indies.

Habitat: Shallow water.

Description: About 2 in. long, the shell is sturdy, with wings of unequal size. Surface with about 20 strong ribs, each composed of a bundle of smaller ribs. Lower portions studded with erect sharp scales, giving the surface a rough, spiny appearance. Pinkish red to deep reddish brown; some individuals are bright lemon yellow.

Remarks: Formerly listed as *Pecten exasperatus* Sowerby. The yellow examples are eagerly sought by collectors (Pl. 22).

● Genus *Cryptopecten* Hayami, 1984

SPATHATE SCALLOP   Pl. 24

Cryptopecten phrygium (Dall, 1886)

Range: Cape Cod to the West Indies.

Habitat: Deep water.

Description: Length 1 in. Shell fan-shaped, rather flattish. Both valves sculptured with about 18 ribs; interspaces nearly equal. Each rib has a sharp median keel, made up of tiny scales. Wings unequal. Color greenish gray, with irregular bands of dull pink.

■ FILE SHELLS: Family Limidae

These shells are obliquely oval and usually winged on one side. The ends gape and the hinge is toothless, with a triangular pit for the ligament. Color is generally white. Members of this family are most often called file shells. They are as competent in swimming as the scallops, but they dart about with the hinge foremost instead of backward, often trailing a long sheaf of filaments. Some of them build nests of broken shells and coral, held together by byssal threads, which act as an anchor. There are many fossil forms.

● **Genus *Lima* Bruguière, 1797**

SPINY FILE SHELL *Lima lima* (Linnaeus, 1758)   **Pl. 26**
Range: South Florida to the West Indies; Bermuda.
Habitat: Shallow water.
Description: About ½ in. long, sometimes slightly longer, with a white, moderately thick shell. Its rasplike surface does remind one of a file. Shell obliquely oval, ends only slightly gaping. Surface bears about 20 broad ribs, each with many closely set erect scales.
Remarks: This file shell occurs in one of its forms almost everywhere around the world in warm seas. *L. tetrica* Gould, 1851, is found in the Gulf of California and *L. squamosa* Lamarck, 1819, is from the Mediterranean Sea.

ANTILLEAN FILE SHELL *Lima pellucida* C. B. Adams, 1846
Range: N. Carolina to the West Indies.
Habitat: Shallow water.
Description: Length 1 to 1½ in. Shell thin but sturdy, oblique, considerably inflated, and gaping at both ends, so that the valves are in contact only at the hinge and basal margin. Surface sculptured with fine lines, often with tiny lines in between. Color pure white.
Remarks: Formerly listed as *L. inflata* Lamarck, which is a South American shell. It lives in crevices and under stones, attached by a byssus, and frequently constructs a crude nest of byssal threads, plastered with bits of seaweed and pebbles; but the mollusk can cast all this aside and go zigzagging off with speed and dispatch when the occasion demands action.

ROUGH FILE CLAM *Lima scabra scabra* (Born, 1778)   **Pl. 26**
Range: Off South Carolina to Brazil.
Habitat: Shallow water.
Description: About 2 in. long, but attains height of nearly 4 in. A moderately thick and robust shell, oval and not as oblique as most of this group. Valves rather compressed, gaping somewhat near hinge, and decorated with closely set ridges covered with small pointed scales. White in color, it usually bears a thin, yellowish brown periostracum.
Remarks: The species formerly known as *L. tenera* Sowerby, 1843, is now regarded as only a form of *L. scabra.* It has the same shape, generally is slightly smaller, and the surface bears many very fine radiating lines notched by small, sharp scales, so the shell has a satiny luster. This form has the same range as *L. scabra* (see Pl. 4).

● Genus *Limatula* Wood, 1839

SMALL-EARED FILE SHELL
Limatula subauriculata (Montagu, 1808)
Range: Greenland to the West Indies; Alaska to Mexico.
Habitat: Moderately deep water.
Description: Length $1/2$ in. Elongate-oval, hinge at top. Sculptured with very fine radiating lines. Two ribs along middle of shell are slightly stronger and more conspicuous, and these can usually be seen on the inside of the shell. Color white.

■ SPINY OYSTERS: Family Spondylidae

These bivalves are attached to some object, commonly coral, by their right valves. The surface is ribbed or spiny and the hinge consists of interlocking teeth in each valve. Many species are highly colored. They are confined to warm seas.

● Genus *Spondylus* Linnaeus, 1758

ATLANTIC THORNY OYSTER   Pl. 25
Spondylus americanus Hermann, 1781
Range: Off N. Carolina to Brazil.
Habitat: Moderately deep water; on coral.
Description: Heavy and strong-shelled, from 3 to 5 in. long. Color varies from white to brown and purplish, and sometimes bright yellow or red. Shell attached by its right valve, which has a broad triangular hinge area; crowded conditions often produce irregularly shaped individuals. Surface with many radiating ribs and numerous scattered spines, some short and needlelike and some long, broad, and blunt. Interlocking teeth are present in each valve, so a pair can be opened only partway without being fractured.
Remarks: Also known as the Spiny Oyster and Chrysanthemum Shell, the latter because of the frilled, varihued appearance. Shells are sometimes found partially imbedded in chunks of coral washed ashore, and upper valves, badly worn, are not uncommon on Florida beaches. The display specimens, however, are generally obtained by divers working with hammer and chisel on old wrecks and coral growths.

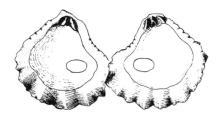

Figure 6. Kitten's Paw *Plicatula gibbosa*

■ KITTEN PAWS: Family Plicatulidae

Small, trigonal, thick-shelled bivalves with broad radiating ribs or folds. Hinge with two heavy, interlocking teeth. They live attached to rocks and coral (by either valve) in warm seas.

● Genus *Plicatula* Lamarck, 1801

KITTEN'S PAW   **Fig. 6 & Pl. 25**
Plicatula gibbosa Lamarck, 1801
Range: N. Carolina to the West Indies.
Habitat: Intertidal and shallow water.
Description: About 1 in. long, although most individuals found on beach are smaller. Shell solid and fan-shaped, with 6 or 7 broad folds radiating from beaks. Right valve is larger of the two. Color white, often with gray or reddish lines.
Remarks: Very common in the drift along shore, but the delicate pencil-like coloring fades rapidly when the shell is exposed to the sun's rays, and most specimens picked up will be a lusterless white. Synonyms include *imbricata* Reeve and *spondyloidea* Meuschen.

■ OYSTERS: Family Ostreidae

Shell irregular, with unequal valves, and is often large and heavy. The lower valve usually adheres to some solid object; the upper valve generally is smaller. Distribution is worldwide in temperate seas as well as warm seas. Probably the most valuable of the food mollusks belong to this family.

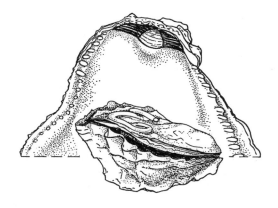

Figure 7. Crested Oyster *Ostreola equestris*

● **Genus *Ostreola* Monterosato, 1884**

CRESTED OYSTER   Fig. 7 & Pl. 25
Ostreola equestris (Say, 1834)
    Range: Virginia to Brazil.
    Habitat: Moderately shallow water.
    Description: About 2 in. long. Shell roughly oval, with raised and fluted margins. Color yellowish gray; interior dull gray with a greenish tinge. Muscle scar uncolored.
    Remarks: This species seems to prefer saltier waters than the commercial common Oyster, *Crassostrea virginica* (below).

● **Genus *Dendostrea* Swainson, 1835**

'COON OYSTER *Dendostrea frons* (Linnaeus, 1758)   Pl. 25
    Range: N. Carolina to the West Indies.
    Habitat: Mangrove roots and submerged brush.
    Description: Length 1½ to 2 in. Shell moderately thin and curved, and there is a broad longitudinal midrib with coarse folds from it to the margins. The attached valve bears several processes that clutch the stems of sea plants or tree roots. Color rosy brown to deep brown; interior white, usually with violet margins.
    Remarks: 'Coon Oysters are found growing together in huge

masses sometimes larger than a bushel basket. They derive their name from the fact that raccoons delight in feeding upon them.

● Genus *Cryptostrea* Harry, 1985

SPONGE OYSTER   Fig. 8 & Pl. 25
Cryptostrea permollis (Sowerby, 1891)
  Range: N. Carolina to the West Indies.
  Habitat: Moderately shallow water; in sponges.
  Description: A small, rather soft-shelled oyster, in the majority of cases living imbedded in masses of the "bread sponge." Slightly over 1 in. long, it is a golden-brown shell outside and bluish white inside. Shell compressed, variable in outline, with a narrow hinge. Lower valve flat, upper slightly convex. Surface wrinkled by irregular wavy ridges, and covered by a periostracum that is thick but soft.

● Genus *Parahyotissa* H. Harry, 1985

McGINTY'S OYSTER   Pl. 25
Parahyotissa mcgintyi H. Harry, 1985
  Range: Southeast Florida and the West Indies.
  Habitat: Below low tide on rocks and shipwrecks.
  Description: Three in., generally circular in outline, and sometimes with a sawtooth margin. Under a hand lens, the shell appears to be filled with numerous bubbles. Colors variable.

Figure 8. Sponge Oyster *Cryptostrea permollis*

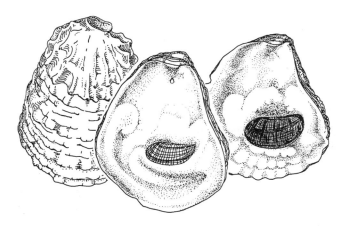

Figure 9. Common Atlantic Oyster *Crassostrea virginica*

● **Genus *Crassostrea* Sacco, 1897**

COMMON ATLANTIC OYSTER   **Fig. 9 & Pl. 25**
Crassostrea virginica (Gmelin, 1791)
   Range: Gulf of St. Lawrence to Florida.
   Habitat: Moderately shallow water.
   Description: From 6 to 10 in. long and lead gray. The rough and heavy shell is generally narrow, elongate, gradually widening and moderately curved, but it varies in surface and shape according to the position in which it has lain during growth. Upper valve smaller and flatter than lower and moves forward as the shell advances in age; growth of the ligament leaves a lengthening groove along beak of the adhering valve. Interior dull white, the muscle scar nearly central and deep violet.
   Remarks: This well-known shellfish is our most important commercial bivalve. The tiny young (called spat) are free-swimming for a short period before they settle upon some hard object and become sessile for life. Those individuals that chance to settle in the mud perish, so to minimize the annual loss oystermen spread tons of broken shells (called clutch) over the beds each year. The oyster's chief enemies are the starfish and various snails, especially the Oyster

Drill *(Urosalpinx cinerea)*. The starfish wraps its 5 arms or rays around the unlucky oyster and exerts a steady pull that may last for hours, until the bivalve's muscles are exhausted and it is forced to gape a little; then the starfish is rewarded with a good meal. The Oyster Drill bores a neat round hole through the shell by means of its filelike tongue (radula) and feeds upon the succulent parts within. Contrary to popular belief, valuable pearls are not likely to be found in the valves of the Common Oyster. The shell lining is not pearly but is smooth and dull, so that any pearl formed is porcelaneous and without luster or iridescence.

■ JINGLE SHELLS: Family Anomiidae

These are thin, translucent clams, usually pearly inside. They are attached to some solid object by a stalklike byssus (threadlike anchor) that passes through an opening in the lower valve; the byssus becomes calcified and the bivalve is permanently attached. The cuplike upper valve is the one that is washed ashore after the animal dies, and the perforated lower valve is not so often found. Native to warm and temperate seas.

● Genus *Anomia* Linnaeus, 1758

PRICKLY JINGLE SHELL
Anomia squamula Linnaeus, 1758
 Range: Maine to N. Carolina; northern Europe.
 Habitat: Moderately shallow water.
 Description: About ³/₄ in. long and yellowish gray. Shell rounded, upper valve convex, lower thin and flat. Surface of upper valve covered with minute prickly scales, commonly arranged in radiating rows; lower valve with perforation near beaks for passage of byssus. Interior purplish white. Formerly called *A. aculeata* Gmelin, 1791.

JINGLE SHELL *Anomia simplex* Orbigny, 1842   **Pl. 25**
 Range: Nova Scotia to the West Indies.
 Habitat: Shallow water.
 Description: About 1 to 2 in. long and varies in color, which ranges from sulphur yellow to coppery red, and many specimens silvery gray or black. Shell circular and variously distorted according to object on which it is attached. Margins sometimes undulating or jagged. Surface minutely scaly and

of a waxy luster. Upper valve convex; lower smaller, flat, with subcircular hole for passage of a fleshy byssus, by which the mollusk adheres.

Remarks: These are greatly admired by children at the seashore, and perhaps are the most abundant and familiar shells on many beaches. It used to be a popular custom to string these shells on cords and hang them in an open window or doorway at a shore cottage, where each passing breeze produced a pleasing tinkle. The raw flesh of this bivalve is extremely acrid to the taste.

● **Genus** *Pododesmus* **Philippi, 1837**

FALSE JINGLE SHELL *Pododesmus rudis* (Broderip, 1834)   **Pl. 25**
Range: Florida to the West Indies.
Habitat: Moderately shallow water.
Description: Length 1 to 2 in., sometimes longer. A moderately solid shell, the upper valve decorated with very coarse and irregular radiating ribs. Lower valve has a much larger hole than does that of the true jingle shells. Pale yellowish white; interior greenish.
Remarks: Formerly listed as *P. decipiens* Philippi, 1837.

ORDER VENEROIDA

■ ARCTIC HARD-SHELLED CLAMS: Family Arcticidae

Shells large and thick, almost circular, the periostracum thick and wrinkled. There is no lunule (depressed area in front of beaks). Native to cold seas.

● **Genus** *Arctica* **Schumacher, 1817**

OCEAN QUAHOG *Arctica islandica* (Linneaus, 1767)   **Pl. 27**
Range: Arctic Ocean to Cape Hatteras.
Habitat: Moderately deep water.
Description: A large and robust bivalve, 4 in. long when fully grown. Shell thick and heavy, roughly circular. Beaks elevated and turned forward, nearly in contact. Periostracum black or deep brown, coarse, shiny, and roughened with crowded and loose wrinkles. Interior white.
Remarks: Also known as the Black Clam. Large colonies are dredged south of Cape Cod and taken to the Cape to be

cleaned, diced, and quick-frozen for shipment to hotels and restaurants.

■ MARSH CLAMS: Family Corbiculidae

These are mollusks of brackish or semifresh waters. The shell is somewhat oval, and there is a rough periostracum, often eroded in places. They inhabit warm and temperate seas.

● Genus *Polymesoda* Rafinesque, 1820

CAROLINA MARSH CLAM   **Pl. 27**
Polymesoda caroliniana (Bosc, 1801)
  Range: Virginia to Texas.
  Habitat: Brackish water.
  Description: Oval, considerably swollen, length 1½ in. Valves more or less corroded in neighborhood of beaks, as a rule, owing to the mollusk's preference for living in brackish waters where acids are apt to be present. Shining greenish periostracum.
  Remarks: At first glance this species appears to be like a typical river clam. It is generally abundant in tidal marshes and river-fed lagoons. It was eaten extensively by the Calusa Indians of southeast North America.

MARITIME MARSH CLAM   **Pl. 27**
Polymesoda maritima (Orbigny, 1842)
  Range: Florida to Texas.
  Habitat: Brackish water.
  Description: About 1 in. long, shell thin but sturdy. Outline oval, beaks moderately inflated. Anterior end rounded, posterior prolonged. Hinge structure weak. Thin periostracum. Color purplish white, darker at margins. Interior may be white with purple margin or it may be solid purple.
  Remarks: Generally abundant in mangrove swamps. Formerly known as *Pseudocyrena floridana* (Conrad, 1846).

■ ASTARTES: Family Astartidae

Small brownish bivalves, usually sculptured with concentric furrows. The ligament is external, lunule distinct. Soft parts

commonly brightly colored. There are many species, distributed chiefly in cool seas. This is a confusing group. The
species making up the genus *Astarte* all are much alike but
at the same time show some variation; many of them have
been named and renamed, with the result that a shell could
be listed under several different names in early conchological literature. Take for example the species *borealis:* this
bivalve was named by Schumacher in 1817; it was named
semisulcata by Leach in 1819, *veneriformis* by Wood in
1828, *withami* by Smith in 1839, *richardsonii* by Reeve in
1855, *lactea* by Broderip in 1874, *producta* by Sowerby in
1874, *placenta* by Mörch in 1883, and *rhomboidalis* by
Leche in 1883. Its correct name is *A. borealis* Schumacher.

● **Genus *Astarte* Sowerby, 1816**

NORTHERN ASTARTE   **Pl. 26**
Astarte borealis Schumacher, 1817
   Range: Circumpolar; Greenland to Massachusetts.
   Habitat: Moderately shallow water.
   Description: Shell solid and oval, about 1¼ to 2¾ in. long.
   Beaks rather low, centrally located. Surface bears distinct
   concentric furrows on upperpart of each valve, but they fade
   toward the margins. Color deep brown; interior white.
   Remarks: Differs from the Lentil Astarte in being more ellip-
   tical in side view and in having the beaks near the middle.

ELLIPTICAL ASTARTE *Astarte elliptica* (Brown, 1827)   **Pl. 26**
   Range: Greenland to Massachusetts.
   Habitat: Offshore in sand; common.
   Description: One in., broadly ovate in outline; beaks ⅓ back
   from the front end. Has microscopic, meshlike surface on
   the red-brown periostracum. Margin of valves smooth.

CHESTNUT ASTARTE *Astarte castanea* Say, 1822   **Pl. 26**
   Range: Nova Scotia to off New Jersey.
   Habitat: Moderately shallow water.
   Description: Shell small but solid, rather compressed, about 1
   in. long. Somewhat kidney-shaped, beaks nearly central and
   considerably elevated. Surface bears numerous concentric
   wrinkles but it lacks the deeper furrows so characteristic of
   most of this group, or has them only weakly defined. Shell
   covered with a thick chestnut brown periostracum, often
   eroded near the beaks. Interior shiny white.

Remarks: In life the foot of the animal is bright vermilion, and when seen protruding from the partly open valves in shallow water it presents an extremely colorful sight.

LENTIL ASTARTE   **Pl. 26**
Astarte subaequilatera Sowerby, 1854
   Range: Labrador to Florida.
   Habitat: Water 80 to 180 ft. deep.
   Description: Slightly more than 1 in. long. Anterior slope a bit concave, posterior end broadly rounded. Some 15 squarish concentric ridges, more or less obsolete toward posterior end. Margin finely crenulate within. Periostracum yellowish brown.
   Remarks: Formerly listed as *A. lens* Stimpson.

WAVED ASTARTE *Astarte undata* Gould, 1841   **Pl. 26**
   Range: Labrador to Maryland.
   Habitat: Moderately shallow water.
   Description: Length 1¼ in. Shell robust and roughly triangular. Posterior slope rather straight. Beaks elevated and pointed. Surface decorated with about 15 strongly developed concentric ridges and furrows, widest and strongest at center of shell and vanishing at each end. A thick and glossy reddish brown periostracum; interior of shell polished white.

■ CRASSATELLAS: Family Crassatellidae

Shells thick and solid, equivalve, and often rostrate (beaked) posteriorly. Strong hinge structure. Occur in shallow to moderately deep water.

● Genus *Eucrassatella* Iredale, 1924

GIBBS' CLAM *Eucrassatella speciosa* (A. Adams, 1852)   **Pl. 27**
   Range: N. Carolina to the West Indies.
   Habitat: Moderately shallow water.
   Description: Strong and robust, length 2 in. Anterior end rounded, posterior partially truncate and bearing a weak ridge. Beaks near center, not high. Surface sculptured with closely spaced concentric ridges. Inside, the hinge is very strong and the muscle scars deep. Color yellowish brown, with a thin periostracum; interior generally pinkish.
   Remarks: Formerly listed as *Crassatella gibbesii* Tuomey &

Holmes, 1856, but the genus *Crassatella* is now restricted to fossil species.

● Genus *Crassinella* Guppy, 1874

LUNATE CRASSINELLA   Fig. 10
Crassinella lunulata (Conrad, 1834)
   Range: Massachusetts to Texas and to Brazil.
   Habitat: Shallow water.
   Description: A small but rugged shell up to ¹/₂ in. long. Shape triangular, beaks forming the apex. Anterior and posterior slopes pronounced, basal margin rounded. Hinge thick and sturdy. Surface has 15 to 17 undulating concentric waves and very minute radiating lines (striae). Color yellowish green; interior often brownish or pinkish.
   Remarks: Formerly listed as *Gouldia mactracea* Linsley, 1845.

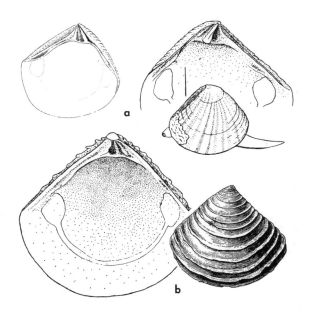

Figure 10. a) Lunate Crassinella *Crassinella lunulata*
b) Martinique Crassinella *Crassinella martinicensis*

MARTINIQUE CRASSINELLA   **Fig. 10**
Crassinella martinicensis (Orbigny, 1842)
   Range: Gulf of Mexico and the West Indies.
   Habitat: Offshore in sand.
   Description: Small $1/16$ in., triangular, somewhat inflated. Color white to brown, 8 to 15 sharp concentric ribs over all of the outside.

■ CARDITAS: Family Carditidae

Small, generally solid shells, equivalve, and usually strongly ribbed. There is an erect, robust tooth under the umbones (beaks). These bivalves are found in warm, temperate, and cold seas.

● Genus *Glans* Mühlfeld, 1811

DOMINGO CARDITA   **Pl. 24**
Glans dominguensis Orbigny, 1845
   Range: Southeast U.S. and the West Indies; offshore.
   Habitat: Shallow water.
   Description: An oval shell about $1/4$ in. long. Beaks set closer to front end, and valves moderately inflated. Sculpture consists of strong radiating ribs, some of which are weakly beaded, so surface has a rough appearance. Color pinkish white.

● Genus *Carditamera* Conrad, 1838

BROAD-RIBBED CARDITA   **Pl. 27**
Carditamera floridana Conrad, 1838
   Range: Florida to Mexico.
   Habitat: Shallow water.
   Description: About 1 in. long, sometimes a little more. Shell heavy and solid, bluntly oval. About 20 robust, scaly, radiating ribs. Yellowish white, blotched with purple and brown. Old individuals may be unspotted. Interior porcelaneous and white.
   Remarks: Many thousands of shells are used annually in the manufacture of shell novelties. The clam lays jellylike blobs with eggs within.

WEST INDIAN CARDITA   Pl. 27
Carditamera gracilis (Shuttleworth, 1856)
Range: West Indies.
Habitat: Shallow water.
Description: Length to 1¹/₂ in. An elongate shell, sturdy and strong. Anterior end rounded and short; posterior long and broadly rounded. Surface with strong, flattened radiating ribs, scaly on posterior. Color grayish brown; interior white, heavily stained with purplish brown.

● **Genus *Cyclocardia* Conrad, 1867**

NORTHERN CARDITA   Fig. 11 & Pl. 27
Cyclocardia borealis (Conrad, 1831)
Range: Arctic Ocean to Cape Hatteras.
Habitat: Moderately shallow water.
Description: Length about 1 in. Shell thick and solid, beaks elevated and incurved. About 20 radiating ribs, wider than the spaces between them. Grayish white, with thick and shaggy brownish periostracum; interior glossy white.

● **Genus *Pteromeris* Conrad, 1867**

FLAT CARDITA *Pteromeris perplana* (Conrad, 1841)
Range: N. Carolina to Florida.
Habitat: Moderately shallow water.
Description: Length about ¹/₄ in. Shaped much like Northern Cardita, but smaller and less inflated. Color pinkish brown, often more or less mottled, interior white. No periostracum.

Figure 11. Northern Cardita *Cyclocardia borealis*

● Genus *Pleuromeris* Conrad, 1867

THREE-TOOTHED CARDITA   Pl. 24
Pleuromeris tridentata (Say, 1826)
  Range: N. Carolina to Florida.
  Habitat: Moderately shallow water.
  Description: Length ¼ in. Trigonal in shape, considerably inflated. Beaks at apex of triangle and point forward. Hinge sturdy, dominated by 3 teeth. About 15 strongly beaded ribs. Grayish brown; interior white.

■ DIPLODONS: Family Ungulinidae

Mostly small, thin-shelled bivalves, orbicular and well inflated. Hinge with 2 cardinals, one of which is split. They generally are white and live in the sands from shallow water to moderate depths. Formerly called the family *Diplodontidae*.

● Genus *Diplodonta* Bronn, 1831

ATLANTIC DIPLODON *Diplodonta punctata* (Say, 1822)   Pl. 24
  Range: N. Carolina to the West Indies; Bermuda.
  Habitat: Moderately shallow water.
  Description: Length about ½ in. Very inflated, its shape almost globular. Surface appears smooth, but under a lens you can see fine concentric lines. Color pure white.
  Remarks: Formerly in the genus *Taras* Risso 1826.

PIMPLED DIPLODON   Pl. 24
Diplodonta semiaspera (Philippi, 1836)
  Range: South Florida to the West Indies.
  Habitat: Shallow water, common in sand.
  Description: Length about ½ in. A nearly orbicular shell, beaks about central. Well inflated. Sculpture is distinctly pustulate; color is chalky white.

VERRILL'S DIPLODON *Diplodonta verrilli* (Dall, 1900)   Pl. 27
  Range: Massachusetts to N. Carolina.
  Habitat: Moderately deep water.
  Description: A thin-shelled clam, highly inflated, with full beaks swollen at the umbones. Length ¼ in. Outline nearly round, surface quite smooth. Color pure white.
  Remarks: Formerly in the genus *Taras* Risso 1826.

Figure 12. Atlantic Cleft Clam *Thyasira trisinuata*

■CLEFT CLAMS: Family Thyasiridae

These are small bivalves with a furrow, or cleft, on the posterior portion of each valve. Usually white, the shell fragile. Chiefly from cool seas.

●Genus *Thyasira* Lamarck, 1818

ATLANTIC CLEFT CLAM   Fig. 12
Thyasira trisinuata (Orbigny, 1842)
   Range: Nova Scotia to the West Indies.
   Habitat: Moderately deep water.
   Description: An oblong shell ¹/₂ in. long. Shell quite delicate, hinge weak. Posterior slope bears a weak cleft. Surface smooth, grayish white.

■LUCINES: Family Lucinidae

Shells generally round, compressed, and equivalve, with small but definite beaks. Members of this family are distributed mostly in tropical and subtropical seas and are usually white. In many species the foot makes a passageway in the sandy mud up to the water. The siphons are very short.

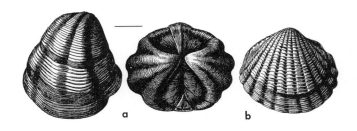

Figure 13. a) Decorated Lucine *Lucina amiantus*
b) Four-ribbed Lucine *Lucina leucocyma*

● **Genus *Lucina* Bruguière, 1797**

PENNSYLVANIA LUCINE   **Pl. 28**
Lucina pensylvanica (Linnaeus, 1758)
    Range: N. Carolina to the West Indies.
    Habitat: Shallow water.
    Description: Length to 2 in. Nearly circular and moderately
well inflated. A deep fold extends from the beak to posterior
margin, giving impression of one shell cupped in another.
Surface marked with widely separated concentric ridges.
Color white, with pale yellow or brownish periostracum.
    Remarks: In the original description of this species in 1758,
the name Pennsylvania was misspelled; so according to the
rules of scientific nomenclature the specific name of this
clam must be spelled with only one *n*.

DECORATED LUCINE *Lucina amiantus* (Dall, 1901)   **Fig. 13**
    Range: N. Carolina to the West Indies; Brazil.
    Habitat: Moderately deep water.
    Description: Length about 1/2 in. Nearly round, moderately in-
flated. Very ornate; about 12 broad radiating ribs with narrow furrows between them, and these are cut by concentric
ridges that are bladelike in character. A row of tiny nodes
decorate the posterior slope. Pure white.

FOUR-RIBBED LUCINE *Lucina leucocyma* Dall, 1886   **Fig. 13**
    Range: N. Carolina to the West Indies.
    Habitat: Moderately deep water.
    Description: Small but sturdy, length slightly more than 1/4 in.
Shape somewhat triangular, with prominent beaks at apex.

Shell with 5 broad folds, producing a lobed effect at the margins. Sculpture of fine concentric lines. Color white. Interior margins finely crenulate.

Remarks: This species is the type of the subgenus *Pleurolucina* Dall, 1901.

● **Genus *Lucinoma* Dall, 1901**

ATLANTIC LUCINE   Pl. 27
Lucinoma atlantis R. A. McLean, 1936
   Range: Maryland.
   Habitat: Deep water in mud.
   Description: Two in., almost circular, compressed, white, with a dark brown periostracum. Beaks small. Sculpture of fine, but distinct, rather widely spaced, raised concentric ridges. No anterior lateral tooth present.
   Remarks: The illustrated specimen is the holotype at the Museum of Comparative Zoology at Harvard.

NORTHERN LUCINE   Fig. 14 & Pl. 27
Lucinoma filosus (Stimpson, 1851)
   Range: Newfoundland to Florida and Texas.
   Habitat: Moderately deep water.
   Description: Length 2 in. Shape nearly circular, hinge line nearly straight. Valves slightly swollen, beaks small but prominent. Sculpture of sharp concentric ridges, rather widely spaced. Color white to tan.
   Remarks: Unlike most of this group, it is a cold-water lover and is found at increasingly greater depths as it passes southward. Southern specimens are usually not as large. Formerly in the genus *Phacoides* Gray 1847.

Figure 14. Northern Lucine *Lucinoma filosus*

● **Genus *Pseudomiltha* P. Fischer, 1885**

FLORIDA LUCINE   Pl. 28
Pseudomiltha floridana (Conrad, 1833)
  Range: West Florida to Texas.
  Habitat: Shallow water.
  Description: Length about 1½ in. Valves thick and solid, circular in outline and considerably compressed. Beaks small but prominent, inclined to turn forward. Fold from beak to posterior margin less conspicuous than for many of this group. Surface with fine concentric lines. White, with thin yellowish periostracum.

● **Genus *Parvilucina* Dall, 1901**

MANY-LINED LUCINE   Fig. 15
Parvilucina multilineata (Tuomey & Holmes, 1857)
  Range: N. Carolina to Florida; Brazil.
  Habitat: Shallow water.
  Description: Length ¼ in. Beaks nearly central, shell nearly circular and well inflated. Surface with numerous fine, crowded, radiating lines. Color white.

● **Genus *Phacoides* Blainville, 1825**

SPINOSE LUCINE *Phacoides muricata* (Spengler, 1798)   Pl. 24
  Range: South Florida to the West Indies; Brazil.
  Habitat: Moderately shallow water.
  Description: A very pretty shell, circular and about 1 in. long. Valves well compressed, decorated with sharp concentric and radiating lines that cover the surface with a fine network of sharp ridges. Color pure white. See Woven Lucine for similarity.
  Remarks: Formerly in the genus *Lucina* Bruguière.

Figure 15. Many-lined Lucine *Parvilucina multilineata*

WOVEN LUCINE *Phacoides nassula* (Conrad, 1846)   **Pl. 24**
  Range: N. Carolina to Florida and n. Gulf Coast.
  Habitat: Shallow water.
  Description: Less than $^{1}/_{2}$ in. long. Closely resembles Fancy Lucine but is smaller and slightly more inflated. Sculpture of fine but distinct radiating lines. Where the lines meet there is a sharp point; consequently the surface is almost filelike. Color white.

THICK LUCINE *Phacoides pectinatus* (Gmelin, 1791)   **Pl. 27**
  Range: N. Carolina to the West Indies.
  Habitat: Shallow water.
  Description: Length about 2 in. Heavy and solid, roughly circular and slightly inflated. The characteristic fold is conspicuous on the posterior end. Surface with many fine concentric ridges, rather widely spaced. Color pale yellowish white.
  Remarks: Formerly in the genus *Lucina*.

● **Genus** *Anodontia* **Link, 1807**

BUTTERCUP LUCINE *Anodontia alba* Link, 1807   **Pl. 28**
  Range: N. Carolina to the West Indies.
  Habitat: Shallow water.
  Description: About 2 in. long, dull white, the interior bright yellow to orange. Shell strong, considerably inflated, with rounded margins; beaks low but prominent. Though surface appears smooth there are numerous very faint growth lines. Ligament bright red in living specimens.
  Remarks: Formerly listed as *Loripinus* or *Lucina chrysostoma* Philippi, 1847. The Chalky Buttercup resembles the Buttercup Lucine, but its interior is uncolored.

CHALKY BUTTERCUP   **Pl. 28**
Anodontia philippiana (Reeve, 1850)
  Range: N. Carolina to the West Indies; Bermuda.
  Habitat: Moderately shallow water.
  Description: Length of 2 to 4 in. Shell strong and quite globose, with well-rounded and centrally placed beaks. Surface with fine concentric lines. Dull chalky white; interior uncolored.
  Remarks: Formerly listed as *Loripinus schrammi* Crosse. Similar to the Buttercup, but that species has brightly colored interior.

● **Genus *Codakia* Scopoli, 1777**

COSTATE LUCINE *Codakia costata* (Orbigny, 1842)   **Pl. 28**
 Range: N. Carolina to the West Indies.
 Habitat: Moderately shallow water.
 Description: About $^1/_2$ in. long, sometimes slightly longer. Valves more inflated than in Great White or Little White Lucines, and the lunule (depressed area in front of beaks) is proportionally smaller. Radiating ribs commonly arranged in pairs and crossed by fine concentric lines. Color white, sometimes tinged with yellow.

TIGER LUCINE   **Pl. 28**
Codakia orbicularis (Linnaeus, 1758)
 Range: Florida to the West Indies.
 Habitat: Moderately shallow water.
 Description: A handsome and showy shell about 3 in. long. Orbicular, solid, and slightly inflated. Lunule small, heart-shaped. Beaks sharp and prominent, hinge teeth large and sturdy. Surface marked with many narrow radiating ribs crossed by elevated growth lines which give the shell a crossribbed appearance. Color white; sometimes with a border of pink or lavender on the inside.
 Remarks: Popularly known as the Tiger Lucine, after its former listing of *Lucina tigrina* (Linnaeus) from the Indo-Pacific.

DWARF TIGER   **Pl. 28**
Codakia orbiculata (Montagu, 1808)
 Range: N. Carolina to the West Indies.
 Habitat: Moderately shallow water.
 Description: Length 1 in. Very much like a small edition of the Tiger Lucine, but the lunule is elongate instead of heart-shaped. Shell sturdy, circular, and surface bears distinct radiating ribs crossed by numerous fine concentric lines. Pure white inside and outside.

● **Genus *Divaricella* von Martens, 1880**

DENTATE LUCINE *Divaricella dentata* (Wood, 1815)   **Pl. 28**
 Range: West Indies.
 Habitat: Moderately shallow water.
 Description: Very like Cross-hatched Lucine, but generally slightly larger, sometimes $1^1/_2$ in. long, and having the inner margin smooth instead of crenulate.

CROSS-HATCHED LUCINE Pl. 28
Divaricella quadrisulcata (Orbigny, 1842)
Range: Massachusetts to the West Indies.
Habitat: Moderately shallow water.
Description: An odd shell, ivory-white and about 1 in. long. Shell moderately solid, circular, and rather plump. Surface sculptured quite unlike any similar shell, with prominent grooves bent obliquely downward at both ends. Inner margins of valves minutely crenulate.
Remarks: See Dentate Lucine for differentiation.

■ MARSH CLAMS: Family Cyrenoididae

● Genus *Cyrenoida* Joannis, 1835

FLORIDA MARSH CLAM Pl. 27
Cyrenoida floridana (Dall, 1896)
Range: Georgia to southern Florida
Habitat: Brackish to fresh water. Common.
Description: Thin, delicate, rounded, white with a pale, silky, yellowish periostracum. Surface smooth. Ligament short. Hinge with 2 cardinals. No lateral teeth.

■ JEWEL BOXES: Family Chamidae

Thick, heavy, and irregular shells with unequal valves. They are attached to some solid object, the fixed valve being the larger and more convex. Native to tropical and subtropical seas.

● Genus *Chama* Linnaeus, 1758

CORRUGATED JEWEL BOX Pl. 28
Chama congregata Conrad, 1833
Range: N. Carolina to the West Indies; Bermuda.
Habitat: Shallow water.
Description: Usually less than 1¹/₂ in. long. Surface marked with wavy corrugations. Upper valve is the one not attached. Often spiny. Color white, more or less mottled or streaked with purple. Interior generally reddish.

LEAFY JEWEL BOX *Chama macerophylla* Gmelin, 1791 Pl. 28
Range: N. Carolina to the West Indies.

Habitat: Moderately deep water.

Description: A thick and ponderous oysterlike bivalve 1 to 3 in. long. Shell irregularly rounded in outline, the adhering valve the larger of the two and also deeper-cupped. Surface sculptured with many distinct scalelike foliations. Pallial line extends from the outer edges of the muscle scars. Inner margin finely crenulate. Color varies from pink and rose to yellow.

Remarks: These mollusks are usually firmly attached, so a hammer and chisel are necessary parts of the collector's equipment. See Smooth-edged and Left-handed Jewel Boxes (below) for similarities.

CHERRY JEWEL BOX *Chama sarda* Reeve, 1847   **Pl. 28**

Range: South Florida to the West Indies.

Habitat: Shallow water.

Description: About 1 in. long. Robust for its size. Surface with many wavy, tubular scales arranged like shingles and often frondlike in character. Lower valve white; upper sometimes with reddish rays.

SMOOTH-EDGED JEWEL BOX

Chama sinuosa Broderip, 1835

Range: South Florida to the West Indies.

Habitat: Moderately deep water.

Description: Length 2 to 2$\frac{1}{2}$ in. Almost identical with Leafy Jewel Box (above), but differing in a few ways: inner margins not crenulate; pallial line runs only to anterior and posterior muscle scars instead of past them as in the Leafy Jewel Box. Color white; interior often greenish.

● **Genus *Pseudochama* Odhner, 1917**

LEFT-HANDED JEWEL BOX   **Pl. 28**

Pseudochama radians (Lamarck, 1819)

Range: South Florida to the West Indies.

Habitat: Moderately deep water.

Description: Length 1 to 3 in. Almost the same as Leafy Jewel Box (above), except that the adhering valve turns the other way. Members of the genus *Chama* are attached by their left valves, but in this genus it is the right valve that is anchored to a solid object. Color whitish or grayish; interior often brownish.

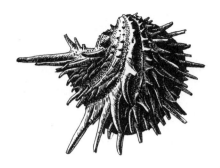

Figure 16. Caribbean Spiny Jewel Box *Arcinella arcinella*

● **Genus *Arcinella* Schumacher, 1817**

CARIBBEAN SPINY JEWEL BOX   Fig. 16 & Pl. 29
Arcinella arcinella (Linneaus, 1767)
   Range: West Indies to S. America.
   Habitat: Moderately deep water.
   Description: About 1 in. long. Very much like the next species but usually smaller and with about 20 rows of spines. Strong attachment scar on right valve. Color yellowish white, often marked with rosy purple, especially on inside.
   Remarks: This name was for many years applied to the common Spiny Jewel Box of Florida, which is correctly named *A. cornuta* (Conrad). The genus *Echinochama* Fischer, 1817, is a synonym.

SPINY JEWEL BOX *Arcinella cornuta* (Conrad, 1866)   Pl. 29
   Range: N. Carolina to Florida and Texas.
   Habitat: Shallow water.
   Description: Length about $1^{1}/_2$ in. Shell robust and solid, beaks curved forward. Each valve has 7 or 8 strong ribs, spread fanwise, each with erect tubular spines throughout the length. Surface between ribs covered with beadlike pustules. Color white; interior often shows splashes of red.
   Remarks: It is attached to some solid object in its youth and later in life it becomes free, but the attachment scar (in form of a smooth area) is always present and visible in front

of the umbo on the right valve. Formerly listed as *E. arcinella* (Linnaeus), but that name is now reserved for a closely related species from the Caribbean region (see above).

■ COCKLES: Family Cardiidae

Shells equivalve and heart-shaped, frequently gaping at one end. Margins of the shell are serrate or scalloped. Native to all seas, this family contains the cockles, or heart clams. In Europe these bivalves are regularly eaten, and cockle-gathering is a recognized seaside activity, but they are not used as food to any extent in this country. For many years all of the shells belonging to this family were assigned to the genus *Cardium* Linnaeus, 1758, and those found on our Atlantic Coast are listed in old books as *Cardium muricatum, C. islandicum,* etc. It is now recognized, however, that the genus Cardium should be restricted to those forms living in the eastern Atlantic, so our species have had their subgeneric names elevated to full generic rank.

● Genus *Trachycardium* Mörch, 1853

FLORIDA PRICKLY COCKLE   **Pl. 29**
Trachycardium egmontianum (Shuttleworth, 1856)
  Range: N. Carolina to Florida.
  Habitat: Shallow water.
  Description: From 2 to 2½ in. long, valves well inflated and rather thin and oval. Moderately prominent beaks nearly central. Surface sculptured with deeply chiseled radiating ribs, the ends of which are studded with sharp recurring scales, most pronounced on anterior and posterior slopes. Yellowish to creamy white; interior salmon to salmon-purple, the anterior part whitish.
  Remarks: Very popular with seaside visitors. The graceful lines and delicate colors make it suitable for all sorts of articles, such as pincushions, ashtrays, shell flowers, etc. It used to be listed as *T. isocardia* (Linnaeus), but that name belongs rightfully to a slightly larger West Indian species (next).

WEST INDIAN PRICKLY COCKLE   **Pl. 29**
Trachycardium isocardia (Linnaeus, 1758)
  Range: West Indies.

Habitat: Shallow water.
Description: Length to 3 in. An elongate-oval shell, beaks well elevated. Sculpture of 30 or more radiating ribs that are set with sharp scales, almost becoming spines on posterior slope. Color creamy yellow, with irregular blotches of brown; interior coppery salmon.

MAGNUM COCKLE   Pl. 29
Trachycardium magnum (Linnaeus, 1758)
Range: Lower Florida Keys to Brazil.
Habitat: Moderately common in shallow water.
Description: Elongate, with 32 to 35 mostly smooth ribs. End ribs scaly; middle one smooth and squarish. Light cream with patches of reddish brown. Interior white, flushed with orange-buff at the center.

YELLOW COCKLE   Pl. 29
Trachycardium muricatum (Linnaeus, 1758)
Range: N. Carolina to the West Indies; Brazil.
Habitat: Moderately shallow water.
Description: Length 2 in. Yellowish white, sometimes lightly speckled with brownish red, especially on the umbones. Interior yellow. Shell roundish and inflated, valves equal in size, and heart-shaped when viewed endwise. From 20 to 40 pronounced ribs, about a dozen of the central ribs almost or quite smooth over the umbonal region, the others crossed by erect, sharp scales. Margins of valves serrate and interlocking.

● **Genus** *Dinocardium* **Dall, 1900**

GIANT HEART COCKLE   Pls. 5, 29
Dinocardiurn robustum robustum (Lightfoot, 1786)
Range: Virginia to north Floria to Texas.
Habitat: Moderately shallow water.
Description: Our largest member of this group, the length averaging between 3 and 5 in. Shell large and considerably inflated, with the posterior area flattened, dark, and polished. Beaks strongly rounded. About 35 robust flat ribs, regularly arranged. Margins of valves serrate. Color yellowish brown, irregularly spotted with chestnut and purplish marks; posterior slope brownish purple. Interior salmon-pink.
Remarks: A form living on the western coast of Florida is generally larger, more triangular in outline, and brighter in

color. This subspecies has been named Vanhyning's Heart Cockle, *D. r. vanhyningi* Clench & Smith, 1944 (see Pl. 29).

● **Genus *Americardia* Stewart, 1930**

ATLANTIC STRAWBERRY COCKLE   **Pl. 29**
Americardia media (Linneaus, 1758)
    Range: Cape Hatteras to the West Indies.
    Habitat: Moderately shallow water.
    Description: Length 1 in., sometimes a bit more; creamy white, more or less checkered with buff and purple. Shell solid, somewhat triangular; anterior margin regularly rounded and posterior margin partially truncate, forming a distinct slope on that end. Sculpture of strong, rounded radiating ribs.

● **Genus *Clinocardium* Keen, 1936**

ICELAND COCKLE   **Pl. 29**
Clinocardium ciliatum (Fabricius, 1780)
    Range: Greenland to Massachusetts.
    Habitat: Moderately deep water.
    Description: Shell large and well inflated, about $2^1/_2$ in. long. Front end a little shorter and narrower than posterior. Surface bears about 38 sharp-edged radiating ribs, the furrows between them rounded and slightly wrinkled by lines of growth. Margins scalloped. Dull white; periostracum stiff and fringelike, brown. Interior straw-colored.

● **Genus *Laevicardium* Swainson, 1840**

EGG COCKLE   **Pl. 29**
Laevicardium laevigatum (Linnaeus, 1758)
    Range: N. Carolina to the West Indies.
    Habitat: Moderately shallow water.
    Description: Length about $1^1/_2$ in. Shell thin and inflated, beaks rather small. Anterior end curved slightly more than posterior. Surface smooth and polished, but there are slight traces of ribs. Interior margin crenulate. Color ivory-white, usually with concentric bands of brownish orange. Thin brownish periostracum.
    Remarks: Occasional specimens are found that when quite fresh are very brilliantly colored, but most beach specimens are plain white. The leaping ability of this clam is well es-

tablished. One collector reports that a captive specimen made a successful getaway by using its powerful foot to leap from the boat. Formerly listed as *L. serratum* (Linnaeus, 1758).

MORTON'S EGG COCKLE   Pl. 24
Laevicardium mortoni (Conrad, 1830)
   Range: Nova Scotia to Brazil.
   Habitat: Shallow water.
   Description: Height seldom exceeds 1 in., usually somewhat smaller; length 3/4 in. Shell thin, inflated, obliquely oval. Surface weakly pebbled. Inner margins crenulate. Color yellowish white, generally a little streaked with orange. Interior generally tinged with yellow, somewhat blotched with purple on the posterior side.

RAVENEL'S EGG COCKLE   Pl. 24
Laevicardium pictum (Ravenel, 1861)
   Range: Florida to the West Indies.
   Habitat: Moderately shallow water.
   Description: Length about 3/4 in. A roundish shell, well inflated. Front end regularly rounded, posterior slightly sloping. Surface smooth, color creamy white, with zigzag bars of yellow-brown. Interior yellow, the pattern often showing through.

DALL'S EGG COCKLE
Laevicardium sybariticum (Dall, 1886)
   Range: Florida to the West Indies.
   Habitat: Shallow water.
   Description: Length 3/4 in. Shell inflated. General shape squarish with slight posterior slope. Surface shiny, color whitish with brown scrawls; umbones pinkish. Interior pale yellow, variously marked with lilac.

● **Genus *Papyridea* Swainson, 1840**

SPINY PAPER COCKLE   Pl. 29
Papyridea soleniformis (Bruguière, 1789)
   Range: N. Carolina to the West Indies.
   Habitat: Shallow water.
   Description: Length about 1 1/2 in. Shell thin, compressed, somewhat elongate, gaping at posterior end. Beaks low. Many fine radiating ribs, smooth in center of shell but provided with short spines toward extremities and sometimes

overhanging the margins. White or pink, heavily mottled with rosy brown — inside as well as outside; rarely orange.
Remarks: Formerly listed as *P. hiatus* (Meuschen, 1787) and *P. spinosum* (Meuschen, 1787), both invalid names.

● **Genus *Serripes* Gould, 1841**

GREENLAND COCKLE   **Pl. 29**
Serripes groenlandicus (Bruguière, 1789)
    Range: Greenland to Cape Cod; Alaska to Washington.
    Habitat: Moderately deep water.
    Description: A fairly large clam, length averaging between 3 and 4 in. Shell thin in substance but moderately inflated. Outline somewhat triangular, with beaks centrally located and slightly incurved. Anterior end regularly rounded. Posterior partially truncate and widely gaping. Surface bears numerous concentric lines, and several radiating ridges (most pronounced on the two ends). Color drab gray; juvenile specimens sometimes show a few zigzag darker lines.

■ **HARD-SHELLED CLAMS: Family Veneridae**

This is one of the largest bivalve families and it probably has the greatest distribution, both in range and in depth. Named for the goddess Venus, the shells of this group are noted for their graceful lines and beauty of color and sculpture. The shells are equivalve, commonly oblong-oval in outline, and porcelaneous in texture. The mollusks burrow just beneath the surface of sand or mud and are never fixed in one place. They are native to all seas, and since ancient times many of them have been used by man for both food and ornament.

● **Genus *Periglypta* Jukes-Brown, 1914**

PRINCESS VENUS *Periglypta listeri* (Gray, 1838)   **Pl. 30**
    Range: South Florida to the West Indies.
    Habitat: Shallow water.
    Description: Shell thick and solid, broadly oval, 2 to 4 in. long. Sculpture of impressed lines, crossed by concentric ridges that are both heavy and sharp. On posterior end these

ridges often expand into flaring, bladelike structures. Color grayish white.

Remarks: Formerly in the genus *Antigona* Schumacher, 1817. Moderately common in sand.

● **Genus *Ventricolaria* Keen, 1954**

RIGID VENUS *Ventricolaria rigida* (Dillwyn, 1817)   **Pl. 30**
Range: South Florida to the West Indies to Brazil.
Habitat: Shallow water.
Description: Length 2^1/$_2$ in. Front end short and abruptly rounded, with definite lunule. Posterior regularly rounded, slightly squarish at tip. Sculpture of strong concentric ribs, with smaller concentric lines in between. Color yellowish gray with brown mottlings.

QUEEN VENUS *Ventricolaria rugatina* (Heilprin, 1887)
Range: N. Carolina to the West Indies.
Habitat: Moderately shallow water.
Description: Thick-shelled, nearly round, and about 1^1/$_2$ in. long. Posterior end regularly rounded, anterior sharply rounded. Surface decorated with rather strong concentric ribs, each with a pair of smaller riblets between it and the next rib. Color yellowish white, somewhat mottled or marked with pale brown.

● **Genus *Mercenaria* Schumacher, 1817**

SOUTHERN QUAHOG   **Pl. 30**
Merceneria campechiensis (Gmelin, 1791)
Range: Off New Jersey to Florida, Texas, Cuba, and Yucatan, Mexico.
Habitat: Sandy bottom from intertidal flats to water 120 feet in depth.
Description: Similar to the Northern Quahog, but much more obese, heavier, and lacks the smooth central area on the outside. The lunule is usually as wide as long.
Remarks: The common Hard-shell Clam may sometimes hybridize with the Northern Quahog and may be considered a subspecies. The subspecies *texana* (Dall, 1902), living in inner sheltered bays of the northern shores of the Gulf of Mexico, has a glossy central area on the outside of the shell, but has large irregular, coalescing, flat-topped concentric ribs (see Pl. 30).

NORTHERN QUAHOG   Pl. 30
Mercenaria mercenaria (Linnaeus, 1758)
Range: Gulf of St. Lawrence to Florida.
Habitat: Shallow water.
Description: Length 5 or 6 in. when fully grown. Shell thick and solid, rather well inflated; beaks elevated and placed forward. Surface bears numerous closely spaced concentric lines, most conspicuous near the ends; central portion of the valves smooth. Around umbonal region the lines are rather widely spaced. Color dull grayish; interior white, often with a dark violet border.
Remarks: This bivalve has many other popular names, among them Round Clam, Hard-shelled Clam, Cherrystone Clam, and Little-necked Clam. It will be found in many lists under its old name, *Venus mercenaria.* This is the chief commercial clam of the East Coast, ranking second only to the oyster in shellfish value. When young or half grown it is the delicious cherrystone, said to have a flavor surpassing that of any other bivalve. When older it is less tender and is used extensively for bakes and chowders. That it was a favorite food of the coastal Indians is attested to by the many shell heaps of ancient vintage found scattered from Maine to Florida and by the name Quahog, by which this clam is known in New England. The noted purple wampum was made from the colored edge of this shell; this fact may explain the bivalve's name of *mercenaria.* It is not uncommon to find pearls under the mantle of this bivalve, sometimes of fair size but of no commercial value.
M. mercenaria notata (Say), which is smaller, lacks the purple border as a rule and bears a weak pattern of brownish zigzag marks on the outer surface. It is commercially maricultured on the east coast of Florida (see Pl. 30).

● **Genus *Chione* Mühlfeld, 1811**

CROSS-BARRED VENUS   Pl. 30
Chione cancellata (Linnaeus, 1767)
Range: N. Carolina to the West Indies.
Habitat: Shallow water.
Description: About 1 1/4 in. long, cloudy yellowish white, decorated with zigzag or triangular patches of purplish brown, sometimes in the form of radiating bands. Shell small, thick, and solid, the beaks elevated and situated forward. Surface sculptured with a series of well-elevated rounded ribs,

crossed by concentric ridges of the same size, forming a network of raised lines. Inner margins crenulate. Interior usually purple.

LADY-IN-WAITING VENUS   Pl. 24
Chione intapurpurea (Conrad, 1849)
Range: N. Carolina to the West Indies.
Habitat: Moderately shallow water.
Description: About 1½ in. long. Shell strong and solid, ventral
margins strongly convex. Beaks prominent but low. Many
crowded concentric ridges, generally wrinkled over posterior half. Inner surface smooth, margins crenulate. Color
white to cream; interior with a violet splotch on posterior
portion.

CLENCH'S VENUS *Chione clenchi* Pulley, 1952   Pl. 30
Range: Texas coast.
Habitat: Moderately shallow water.
Description: About 1 in. long. Anterior end short and abruptly
rounded, the posterior longer and more sharply pointed than
for most of this genus. Sculptured with broad and distinct
concentric ribs, the grooves between them quite small.
Color gray, spotted and streaked with pale purplish brown;
interior white.
Remarks: Named by Dr. Tom Pulley of Texas after his
teacher, Professor William J. Clench.

BEADED VENUS *Chione granulata* (Gmelin, 1791)   Pl. 30
Range: South Florida to the West Indies.
Habitat: Shallow water.
Description: Length 1 in. Roundish in outline, posterior end
slightly pointed. Sculptured with close radiating ribs that are
somewhat scaly. Color gray, with darker mottling; interior
generally purplish toward posterior end.

IMPERIAL VENUS *Chione latilirata* (Conrad, 1841)   Pl. 30
Range: N. Carolina to Texas; West Indies.
Habitat: Moderately deep water.
Description: Attains a length of nearly 2 in. but averages a
little more than 1 in. Shell very solid and sturdy, well inflated, irregularly triangular, and highly polished. Surface
bears a series of large and broadly rounded concentric ribs,
with deep furrows between them, the ribs not pinched out at
ends. Color grayish white, irregularly marked with lilac and
brown.

Remarks: Its broad rounded ribs, plus the high gloss, render this bivalve easy to identify, but wave-worn specimens found on the beach are apt to have lost their polish.

KING CHIONE *Chione paphia* (Linnaeus, 1767)   **Pl. 30**
Range: South Florida to the West Indies.
Habitat: Moderately deep water.
Description: May be confused with Imperial Venus (above), but it is not as heavy in build. Grows to about the same size and has about 12 rounded concentric ribs that are not as broad, and they tend to pinch out at each end. Grayish, rather heavily marked with lilac and brown; shell has a high polish.

WHITE PYGMY VENUS   **Pl. 24**
Chione pygmaea (Lamarck, 1818)
Range: South Florida to the West Indies.
Habitat: Shallow water.
Description: Small, somewhat elongate, length about $1/2$ in. Surface with delicate radiating and concentric lines; rather scaly. Color white, the teeth purple only on posterior half of hinge.

GRAY PYGMY VENUS *Chione grus* (Holmes, 1858)   **Pl. 23**
Range: N. Carolina to Florida and to Texas.
Habitat: Shallow water to 30 ft., in sand.
Description: About $1/3$ in., oblong, with 30 to 40 fine radial riblets which are crossed by very fine, concentric threads. Dorsal margin of right valve fimbriated and overlapping the left valve. Lunule narrow, heart-shaped, brown. Escutcheon very narrow and sunken. Exterior dull gray, sometimes pinkish or purplish. Purple streak on inside at both ends of the hinge.
Remarks: This common bivalve resembles the White Pygmy Venus but lacks the zebra stripes on the escutcheon and has minute fibriations on the exterior of the valves.

● **Genus *Anomalocardia* Schumacher, 1817**

WEST INDIAN POINTED VENUS   **Pl. 30**
Anomalocardia brasiliana (Gmelin, 1791)
Range: West Indies to Brazil.
Habitat: Shallow water.
Description: Length $1^{1}/_{4}$ in. This bivalve is sometimes con-

fused with the next one, but it is a larger shell, heavier in build, and considerably less elongate. Color variable, generally some shade of yellowish gray with tan and purple speckling.

Remarks: It does not occur in the U.S.

POINTED VENUS   **Pl. 30**
Anomalocardia auberiana (Orbigny, 1842)
  Range: South Florida to Texas.
  Habitat: Shallow water.
  Description: Length about 3/4 in. Shell small, thin, wedge-shaped, decidedly pointed at posterior end. Beaks slightly elevated. Surface of shell glossy, decorated with rounded concentric lines. Color varies from grayish white to greenish or brownish, often with darker mottlings. Interior pale lavender, margins crenulate.
  Remarks: Formerly called *cuneimeris* Conrad. See West Indian Pointed Venus for similarity.

● **Genus *Circomphalus* Mörch, 1853**

EMPRESS VENUS   **Pl. 30**
Circomphalus strigillinus (Dall, 1902)
  Range: South Carolina to Brazil.
  Habitat: Offshore in sandy bottoms in 100 to 600 ft.
  Description: About 1 1/2 in. long; externally resembling a small Quahog, but not as elongate and with more distinct, concentric riblets. Internally, the pallial sinus is very small, if not absent. Margin of shell thick. Left valve has buttonlike anterior lateral tooth. Color outside is whitish.

● **Genus *Callista* Poli, 1791**

GLORY-OF-THE-SEAS VENUS   **Pl. 31**
Callista eucymata (Dall, 1890)
  Range: North Carolina to Texas and to Brazil.
  Habitat: Offshore in sand, from 130 to 670 ft.; rare.
  Description: About 1 to 1 1/2 in.; fairly thin-shelled, oval, with about 50 slightly flattened, concentric ribs which have a short dorsal and long ventral slope and separated by a narrow, sharp groove. Color glossy white to pale brown, with clouds and zigzag markings of reddish brown. No escutcheon. Margins smooth and rounded.

● Genus *Tivela* Link, 1807

TRIGONAL TIVELA *Tivela mactroides* (Born, 1778)   **Pl. 31**
   Range: West Indies to Brazil.
   Habitat: Sandy mud in shallow water.
   Description: About 1 to 1½ in., solid, inflated, trigonal in shape. Variously rayed and clouded with soft brown. Surface smooth; beaks central. Three cardinal teeth in each valve. Large anterior lateral tooth in the left valve.
   Remarks: This species is not found in the waters of Florida nor the Gulf of Mexico.

● Genus *Cyclinella* Dall, 1902

ATLANTIC CYCLINELLA *Cyclinella tenuis* (Récluz, 1852)   **Pl. 30**
   Range: N. Carolina to the West Indies.
   Habitat: Moderately shallow water.
   Description: Length 1½ in. A rather thin shell, nearly orbicular. Valves moderately inflated, beaks small and inclined forward. Surface smooth but not polished. Color white.

● Genus *Transennella* Dall, 1883

CONRAD'S TRANSENNELLA   **Fig. 17**
Transennella conradina Dall, 1883
   Range: South Florida to the West Indies.
   Habitat: Moderately shallow water.
   Description: About ½ in. long. Front end rounded, posterior sloping to a rounded point. Surface shiny, color yellowish gray, often with zigzag scrawls of brown.
   Remarks: A characteristic of this genus is the shell's inner ventral margin: it presents a corded appearance, with numerous microscopic threads twisted along the edge.

          a   b

Figure 17. a) Conrad's Transennella *Transenella conradina* **b)** Cuban Transennella *Transennella cubaniana*

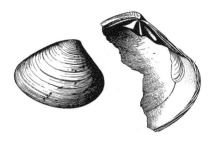

Figure 18. Stimpson's Transennella *Transennella stimpsoni*

CUBAN TRANSENNELLA   Fig. 17
Transennella cubaniana (Orbigny, 1842)
   Range: South Florida to the West Indies.
   Habitat: Moderately shallow water.
   Description: Length ¹/₂ in. Somewhat triangular, anterior end slightly shorter than posterior. Basal margin rounded. Surface with very faint concentric lines. Color white, flecked with brown; umbonal region rosy.
   Remarks: See Remarks under Conrad's Transennella.

STIMPSON'S TRANSENNELLA   Fig. 18
Transennella stimpsoni Dall, 1902
   Range: N. Carolina to Florida and Bahamas.
   Habitat: Moderately shallow water.
   Description: About ¹/₂ in. long, the shape more triangular than with *T. conradina* (above), its posterior end less elongate. Surface smooth and polished, color creamy white with radiating brown bands sometimes discernible. Interior commonly purplish.
   Remarks: See Remarks under Conrad's Transennella (above).

WAXY GOULD CLAM   Pl. 23
Gouldia cerina (C.B. Adams, 1845)
   Range: N. Carolina to Florida; Bermuda; West Indies.
   Habitat: Shallow water to 600 ft., in sand.
   Description: About ¹/₃ in., solid, trigonal in shape with beaks in the center and very small; lunule long, bounded by a minute impressed line; no escutcheon present. Sculpture reticulate in which the fine concentric ribs predominate. The

radial riblets are stronger at the anterior end. Color white, with faint brownish flecks; interior flushed with light purple or shell pink.

Remarks: This very small bivalve is quite common in warm, shallow waters. A minor variety from Bermuda was named *bermudensis* E.A. Smith, 1886.

● **Genus *Pitar* Roemer, 1857**

WHITE VENUS *Pitar albidus* (Gmelin, 1791)   **Pl. 31**
   Range: West Indies.
   Habitat: Moderately shallow water.
   Description: About 1½ in. long. Rather plump, posterior somewhat longer than anterior. Beaks not prominent. Color pure white, rarely with faint traces of radiating bands.

PURPLE VENUS *Pitar circinatus* (Born, 1778)   **Pl. 31**
   Range: West Indies.
   Habitat: Shallow water.
   Description: Length 1½ in. Very much like Elegant Venus (below) but without spines. Surface with rather strong concentric lines. Color white, with radiating rays of purplish over the upper parts of shell.

CORDATE VENUS *Pitar cordatus* (Schwengel, 1951)
   Range: Off lower Florida Keys and Gulf of Mexico.
   Habitat: Moderately shallow water.
   Description: Length 1½ in. Rather plump, beaks full. Anterior end short and rounded, posterior longer, the tip quite pointed. Ornamentation of concentric lines that are sharp and distinct. Color grayish white.

ELEGANT VENUS *Pitar dione* (Linnaeus, 1758)   **Pl. 31**
   Range: Eastern Mexico and the West Indies.
   Habitat: Moderately shallow water.
   Description: Length about 1½ in. Shell plump, with rather high beaks. Anterior end broadly rounded, posterior gently sloping. Surface bears many deeply cut concentric grooves, and a rather distinct ridge runs in an easy curve from beaks to posterior margin; this ridge has 1 or 2 rows of long spines. Color of whole shell, including spines, delicate lavender; interior white. See Purple Venus (above) for differences.
   Remarks: Considered by many to be the handsomest bivalve shell in w. Atlantic, it very nearly misses our shores. For-

merly listed as *Venus dione,* this is the species used by Linnaeus in his original description of the genus *Venus* in 1758. It is a strikingly beautiful shell, not as fragile as it appears, and is generally considered a prize in any collection.

LIGHTNING VENUS *Pitar fulminatus* (Menke, 1828)   **Pl. 31**
   Range: N. Carolina to Brazil; Bermuda.
   Habitat: Moderately shallow water.
   Description: Length about $1^1/_2$ in. Roundly oval and plump, with small beaks, the posterior end only slightly longer than the anterior. Sculpture of very fine concentric lines. Color white, with brown or orange spots commonly arranged in a radial pattern. Interior polished white, the margins smooth.

FALSE QUAHOG *Pitar morrhuanus* (Linsley, 1848)   **Pl. 31**
   Range: Prince Edward Island to N. Carolina.
   Habitat: Shallow water.
   Description: Length to 2 in. Shell roundish oval, rather thin, the valves quite convex. Anterior end about half the length of posterior. Margins regularly rounded behind and at base. Heart-shaped lunule (depressed area) in front of moderately elevated beaks. Surface smooth, color rusty gray; interior white.
   Remarks: This shell appears something like a small, wave-worn Quahog, but it is not as solid, has a smaller tooth structure, and lacks the purple border of the Quahog. Also called the Morrhua Venus.

● **Genus *Agriopoma* Dall, 1902**

TEXAS VENUS *Agriopoma texasiana* (Dall, 1892)   **Pl. 31**
   Range: Florida to Texas.
   Habitat: Moderately deep water.
   Description: Length $1^1/_2$ to 3 in. Beaks a little closer to anterior end, both ends sloping to rounded tips. Valves inflated and rather thin in substance. Surface smooth, color yellowish white.

● **Genus *Macrocallista* Meek, 1876**

CALICO CLAM   **Pl. 31**
Macrocallista maculata (Linnaeus, 1758)
   Range: N. Carolina to Brazil; Bermuda.

Habitat: Shallow water.
Description: Length 2 to 3 in., shell roundish oval. Anterior end rounded, posterior sloping. Surface porcelaneous, color yellowish buff, with squarish spots of violet-brown distributed over whole shell, but with 1 to 2 radiating bands generally present. Interior white and polished, the pattern sometimes showing through. Margins smooth.
Remarks: Sometimes called the Checkerboard, this is a handsome edible bivalve, very popular with collectors. It is most plentiful on Florida's west coast.

SUNRAY VENUS   **Pl. 31**
Macrocallista nimbosa (Lightfoot, 1786)
Range: N. Carolina to Florida and west to Texas.
Habitat: Shallow water.
Description: Large and showy, reaches a length of 6 in. Shell smooth, thick, porcelaneous, and elongate-oval, with depressed beaks. Anterior end short and rounded, posterior rounded and elongate. Surface glossy, but with very faint concentric and radiating striations. Inside polished with smooth margins. Color pinkish gray, with radiating lilac bands; in fresh specimens interior is salmon-pink.
Remarks: Half-grown 2- or 3-in. examples are generally more brightly colored than larger shells. The valves, although relatively thick, are quite brittle and break easily. It is sometimes commercially fished in northwest Florida.

● **Genus** *Dosinia* **Scopoli, 1777**

WEST INDIAN DOSINIA   **Pl. 31**
Dosinia concentrica (Born, 1778)
Range: West Indies to Brazil.
Habitat: Moderately shallow water.
Description: Length 3 in. An orbicular, somewhat compressed shell with sharp beaks almost centrally situated. Sculpture of closely spaced concentric lines, about 9 to a centimeter. Surface shiny, color yellowish white.
Remarks: Very similar to Elegant Dosinia (below) of Florida shores.

DISK DOSINIA *Dosinia discus* (Reeve, 1850)   **Fig. 19 & Pl. 31**
Range: Virginia to Florida.
Habitat: Shallow water.
Description: A trim and neat shell, about 3 in. long, resem-

bling Elegant Dosinia. Circular and considerably compressed, with small but prominent beaks. Surface decorated with numerous and crowded concentric lines. Hinge thick and strong. Color glossy white, with thin yellowish periostracum.

Remarks: The periostracum peels away easily, revealing the shiny white shell.

ELEGANT DOSINIA   Fig. 19 & Pl. 31
Dosinia elegans Conrad, 1846

Range: North Carolina to Texas.

Habitat: Shallow water.

Description: Very similar to Dosinia, also pure white and up to 3 in. long. Surface bears numerous uniformly spaced concentric lines, but not so crowded as in D. discus.

Remarks: *D. elegans* has from 8 to 10 lines to a centimeter and *D. discus* has 20.

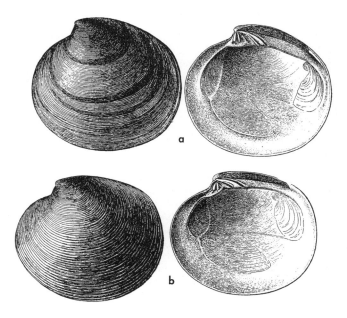

Figure 19. a) Disk Dosinia *Dosinia discus* **b)** Elegant Dosinia *Dosinia elegans*

Figure 20. a) Amethyst Clam *Gemma gemma* **b)** *Gemma purpurea*

Figure 21. Brown Gem Clam *Parastarte triquetra*

● **Genus *Gemma* Deshayes, 1853**

AMETHYST CLAM *Gemma gemma* (Totten, 1834)   **Fig. 20**
Range: Nova Scotia to Florida and Texas.
Habitat: Shallow water
Description: A diminutive shell only 1/5 in. long. Broadly triangular, with beaks about central. Surface shining, with minute, crowded, concentric lines. Inner margins crenulate. Color varies from grayish to lavender, shading to purplish on umbones (beaks).
Remarks: Several names have been applied to this shell, some of which may qualify as subspecific names. *G. gemma* is likely to be lavender over most of the shell; *G. manhattensis* Prime, 1862, is a form found in w. Long Island Sound that lacks the purplish color, being mostly gray; *G. purpurea* Lea, 1842, is whitish shading to purplish near the posterior end; *G. fretensis* Rehder, 1939, is believed to be a synonym of *G. purpurea*.
    Sometimes called the Gem Shell. Early settlers in Massachusetts sent boxes of them back to England as curiosities. There was a time when it was believed that they were the young of the Quahog.

● Genus *Parastarte* Conrad, 1862

BROWN GEM CLAM   **Fig. 21**
Parastarte triquetra (Conrad, 1846)
   Range: Florida to the West Indies.
   Habitat: Shallow water.
   Description: Length generally less than $1/4$ in. A solid little shell, higher than long, its shape triangular. Beaks elevated, prominent, situated at apex. Margins crenulate. Surface smooth, with minute concentric lines. Color white with a tinge of purple; sometimes brownish.

● Genus *Liocyma* Dall, 1870

WAVY CLAM *Liocyma fluctuosa* (Gould, 1841)   **Pl. 24**
   Range: Greenland to Maine; Alaska to British Columbia.
   Habitat: Moderately deep water.
   Description: About $1/2$ in. long. Valves thin, slightly inflated. Beaks nearly central. Sculpture of concentric ridges that fade near the margins. Anterior end shortest and broadest, both ends broadly rounded. Color white beneath a thin yellowish periostracum.

■ **ROCK DWELLERS: Family Petricolidae**

   Shells elongate, gaping behind, with a weak hinge. They are burrowing mollusks, excavating cavities in clay, coral, and limestone. The cavity is gradually enlarged until the clam attains adult size. Distributed in warm, temperate, and even cooler seas around the world.

● Genus *Petricola* Lamarck, 1801

BORING PETRICOLA   **Pls. 23, 30**
Petricola lapicida (Gmelin, 1791)
   Range: Bermuda; south Florida; West Indies.
   Habitat: Bores into coral rock.
   Description: About $3/4$ in. long. An oval, well-inflated shell, anterior end short, posterior long and broadly rounded. Surface with weak concentric lines and short radiating lines that often fork, producing a crosshatched pattern. Color dull chalky white.

FALSE ANGEL WING   **Pl. 30**
Petricola pholadiformis Lamarck, 1818
  Range: Prince Edward Island to Gulf of Mexico.
  Habitat: Intertidal; mudbanks.
  Description: Length 2 in. Shell thin, much elongated, and
  somewhat cylindrical. Anterior end very short and acutely
  rounded, posterior narrowed, elongate, and slightly gaping.
  Beaks elevated, with well-defined lunule in front. Surface
  marked by growth lines and strong radiating ribs. At poste-
  rior end ribs are crowded and faint, but at anterior they are
  large and widely spaced. Color chalky white.
  Remarks: Burrowing into peat, mud, or stiff clay, this bivalve
  bears a striking resemblance to the large and showy Angel
  Wing, *Cyrtopleura costata* (Linnaeus).

● **Genus** *Rupellaria* **Fleuriau, 1802**

ATLANTIC RUPELLARIA *Rupellaria typica* (Jonas, 1844)
  Range: N. Carolina to the West Indies.
  Habitat: Shallow water; bores into coral.
  Description: About $1^{1}/_{2}$ in. long. A plump and rough shell,
  rather elongate. Anterior end well rounded, posterior longer
  and gaping. Surface bears radiating lines, fine and close near
  ends of shell, with undulating lines of growth in between.
  Color grayish white; interior brownish.

■ **CORAL CLAMS: Family Trapeziidae**

  Elongated bivalves, with the beaks almost at the front end.
  The hinge has 3 cardinal teeth. Distributed in warm seas.

● **Genus** *Coralliophaga* **Blainville, 1824**

CORAL-BORING CLAM   **Pl. 27**
Coralliophaga coralliophaga (Gmelin, 1791)
  Range: North Carolina to Texas; West Indies; Bermuda.
  Habitat: In burrows, rocks, and coral.
  Description: A thin-shelled bivalve about 1 to $1^{1}/_{2}$ in. long.
  Shell cylindrical, rounded at both ends, slightly gaping pos-
  teriorly. Valves bear faint radiating lines but surface appears
  fairly smooth. Color yellowish tan; interior white.
  Remarks: Often found in burrows of other mollusks, some-
  times in company with the rightful owner.

■ SURF CLAMS: Family Mactridae

Shells with equal valves, usually gaping slightly at the ends. The hinge has a large spoon-shaped cavity for an inner cartilaginous ligament. Native to all seas, they live at moderate depths, commonly in the surf.

● Genus *Macronella* Marks, 1951

CARIBBEAN WINGED SURF CLAM   **Fig. 22**
Mactronella alata (Spengler, 1802)
  Range: West Indies.
  Habitat: Shallow water.
  Description: Length 4 in. An oval shell, rather thin and brittle. Beaks prominent. A moderate posterior slope bordered by a distinct ridge extending from beaks to the tip, where it frequently becomes finlike. Interior with spoonlike cavity at hinge. Color white, with thin yellowish periostracum.

Figure 22. Caribbean Winged Surf Clam *Mactronella alata*

Figure 23. Fragile Surf Clam *Mactra fragilis*

● **Genus** *Mactra* **Linnaeus, 1767**

FRAGILE SURF CLAM   **Fig. 23 & Pl. 32**
Mactra fragilis Gmelin, 1791
   Range: N. Carolina to Texas; West Indies.
   Habitat: Shallow water.
   Description: Length averages 2 in. Shell thin and moderately delicate, rather oval in outline. Sculptured with very close concentric lines. Beaks about central. Anterior end rounded, posterior with distinct radiating ridge. Color white, with thin yellowish periostracum.

● **Genus** *Spisula* **Gray, 1837**

STIMPSON'S SURF CLAM   **Pl. 32**
Spisula polynyma (Stimpson, 1860)
   Range: Greenland to Rhode Island; also n. Pacific south to Puget Sound and Japan.
   Habitat: Moderately shallow water.
   Description: Closely resembles the Surf Clam. It does not grow quite as large, seldom exceeding 4 in., and it has a less regularly rounded ventral margin. Other points of difference are: lateral teeth (short and plain in this species and long and provided with tiny saw-toothed striations in *S. solidissima*) and the pallial sinus (much larger in *S. solidissima*). Color yellowish white.

SURF CLAM *Spisula solidissima* (Dillwyn, 1817)   **Pl. 32**
   Range: Nova Scotia to S. Carolina.
   Habitat: Moderately shallow water.
   Description: A large and heavy species that resembles Stimpson's Surf Clam and attains a length of 7 in. Shell thick and ponderous in old individuals, roughly triangular. Beaks large and central, with a broad, somewhat flattened area behind them. Hinge very strong, with a large spoon-shaped cavity within, just under beaks. Surface smooth or slightly wrinkled by growth lines. Color yellowish white, with thin olive-brown periostracum.
   Remarks: Also known as the Hen Clam, it is the largest bivalve found on the north Atlantic Coast. Although not as popular as the Quahog, this species is regularly eaten and is considered excellent for clambakes. It is the main ingredi-

ent in canned clam soup. In the south its place is taken by a smaller subspecies, Southern Surf Clam, *S. s. similis* (Say, 1822), shown on Plate 32.

● **Genus *Mulinia* Gray, 1837**

LITTLE SURF CLAM *Mulinia lateralis* (Say, 1822)   **Pl. 24**
    Range: Maine to Florida and Texas.
    Habitat: Shallow water.
    Description: Length $1/2$ to $3/4$ in. Shell triangular, smooth, and polished, with beaks nearly central and inclined forward. Areas before and behind beaks are broad, flattened, roughly heart-shaped, and bordered by slightly elevated ridges. Yellowish white, with thin periostracum.
    Remarks: An important food item for many of our marine fishes, as well as for our seagoing ducks. It is sometimes known as the Duck Clam.

● **Genus *Anatina* (Spengler, 1817)**

SMOOTH DUCK CLAM
Labiosa anatina (Spengler, 1802)
    Range: N. Carolina to Florida and Texas.
    Habitat: Moderately shallow water.
    Description: Up to 3 in. long. Shell thin and swollen, with high beaks. Anterior end broadly rounded, posterior gaping and decorated with a cordlike ridge radiating from the beaks. Color white. There is a thin yellowish periostracum.
    Remarks: Formerly known as *Labiosa lineata* (Say, 1822).

CHANNELED DUCK CLAM   **Pl. 32**
Raeta plicatella (Lamarck, 1818)
    Range: N. Carolina to Texas; West Indies.
    Habitat: Moderately shallow water.
    Description: About 3 in. long. Shell oval-orbicular, gaping, very thin and fragile. Posterior slope narrowed, beaks high, swollen, and directed backward. Sculpture of evenly spaced, rounded, concentric grooves. Inside, on hinge line, is a spoonlike cavity. Color pure white.
    Remarks: Commonly washed ashore as single valves, but one is seldom rewarded by finding a complete specimen. It used to be listed in the genera *Labiosa* Moller, 1832; its specific name was *canaliculata* Say.

● **Genus *Rangia* Desmoulins, 1832**

COMMON RANGIA   Fig. 24 & Pl. 36
Rangia cuneata (Sowerby, 1831)
   Range: Maryland to Texas; Mexico.
   Habitat: Brackish water.
   Description: Length about $1^3/4$ in. A thick and solid shell, somewhat triangular. Beaks high and full, set close to the rounded anterior end. Posterior sloping and bluntly pointed. Color grayish white, with tough gray-brown periostracum; interior white and polished.
   Remarks: Used as a prepared food and the shells as a roadbed material.

BROWN RANGIA   Fig. 24 & Pl. 32
Rangia flexuosa (Conrad, 1839)
   Range: Louisiana to Texas and Vera Cruz, Mexico.
   Habitat: Brackish water to fresh water in marsh areas; uncommon.
   Description: Similar to the Common Rangia, but more pointed, with no distinct pallial sinus; short lateral teeth, and light brown inside valves. Heavy, 1 to $1^1/2$ in.

Figure 24. a) Common Rangia *Rangia cuneata*
b) Brown Rangia *Rangia flexuosa*

■WEDGE CLAMS: Family Mesodesmatidae

Oval or wedge-shaped shells with very short posterior ends. Hinge with a spoon-shaped cavity in each valve. Lateral teeth with a furrow.

● Genus *Mesodesma* Deshayes, 1830

ARCTIC WEDGE CLAM   Pl. 32
Mesodesma arctatum (Conrad, 1830)
   Range: Gulf of St. Lawrence to New Jersey.
   Habitat: Moderately shallow water.
   Description: Length $1^{1}/_2$ to 2 in. Outline wedge-shaped, the very short posterior end forming base of the wedge. Anterior end narrowed and regularly rounded. Shell thick and strong, spoon-shaped cavity at hinge. Color brown, with yellowish periostracum that often reflects a metallic luster. Interior white, muscle impressions strongly delineated.

TURTON'S WEDGE CLAM   Pl. 32
Mesodesma deauratum (Turton, 1822)
   Range: Gulf of St. Lawrence, Canada.
   Habitat: Shallow water in sand.
   Description: About $1^{1}/_2$ in., differing from arctatum in having a less truncate posterior end, and does not plunge sharply to the ventral margin.

● Genus *Ervilia* Turton, 1822

SHINING ERVILIA *Ervilia nitens* (Montagu, 1806)   Pl. 24
   Range: South Florida to the West Indies.
   Habitat: Moderately shallow water.
   Description: Not quite $^{1}/_2$ in. long. A plumpish small shell, rather triangular in outline. Beaks close to center. Surface smooth, although there are weak concentric lines. Color white, more or less tinted with pinkish.

■TELLINS: Family Tellinidae

The shells of this family are generally equivalve and rather compressed, the anterior end rounded and the posterior more or less pointed. The animals are noted for the length of their siphons. Several hundred species have been described, including many fossil forms. Within this group we find some of the most colorful, highly polished, and graceful of the bivalves. Native to all seas.

● **Genus *Tellina* Linnaeus, 1758**

NORTHERN DWARF TELLIN   Fig. 25 & Pl. 34
Tellina agilis Stimpson, 1857
   Range: Gulf of St. Lawrence to N. Carolina.
   Habitat: Shallow water.
   Description: About ½ in. long, moderately elongated and well compressed. Posterior end sloping and unusually short, with a marked ridge running from beaks to that tip. Color white, sometimes yellowish or pink.
   Remarks: Formerly listed as *T. tenera* Say, 1822.

BOSS'S DWARF TELLIN *Tellina probina* Boss, 1964   Pl. 34
   Range: North Carolina to the West Indies.
   Habitat: Moderately shallow water in sand.
   Description: About 1 in.; shaped like the Northern Dwarf Tellin but more truncate at the back end. Exterior oily white with weakly cut, irregularly spaced, concentric grooves.

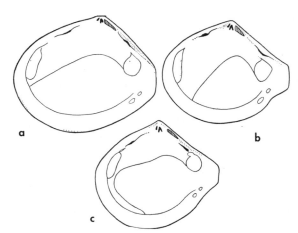

Figure 25. a) Northern Dwarf Tellin *Tellina agilis*
b) Say's Tellin *Tellina texana* **c)** Dall's Dwarf Tellin *Tellina sybaritica*

ALTERNATE TELLIN *Tellina alternata* Say, 1822   **Pl. 33**
Range: N. Carolina to Gulf of Mexico.
Habitat: Shallow water.
Description: Length 2 to 3 in. Shell compressed, oblong, narrowed and angulated at posterior end. Anterior gracefully rounded. Surface decorated with numerous parallel, impressed, concentric lines, every other line vestigial on posterior area, which is marked by an angular ridge extending from the beaks to posterior margin. Commonly white, but may be pink or yellow.

TAYLOR'S TELLIN   **Pl. 33**
Tellina alternata subsp. *tayloriana* Sowerby, 1867
Range: Texas to Tampico, Mexico.
Habitat: Shallow water in sand.
Description: Similar to the more northern subspecies, but pink throughout, with a broad, fairly strong anterior radial rib inside, with somewhat fatter valves and with stronger concentric scupture on the left valve.

ANGULAR TELLIN *Tellina angulosa* Gmelin, 1791   **Pl. 33**
Range: South Florida to the West Indies.
Habitat: Shallow water.
Description: About $1^1/_2$ in. Anterior end rounded, posterior pointed, valves compressed. Sculpture of fine concentric lines, sharp and crowded. Color delicate pink.

CANDÉ'S TELLIN *Tellina candeana* Orbigny, 1842   **Pl. 34**
Range: Bermuda; Florida; West Indies.
Habitat: Moderately shallow water.
Description: Length $^3/_8$ in. Posterior short and sloping, anterior acutely rounded. Surface polished, but under a lens one can see oblique lines on the posterior slope. Color white.

CRYSTAL TELLIN   **Fig. 26 & Pl. 34**
Tellina cristallina Spengler, 1798
Range: S. Carolina to the West Indies.
Habitat: Moderately deep water.
Description: About 1 in. long. Anterior end rounded, posterior with straight slope down to a slightly upturned tip that is square. Valves thin and well inflated. Surface shiny, with well-spaced concentric lines. Color transparent white.

GEORGIA TELLIN *Tellina nitens* C. B. Adams, 1845
Range: South Florida to the West Indies; Brazil.
Habitat: Moderately shallow water.

Description: Length $2^{1}/_{2}$ in. Anterior end longer of the two, but the prominent beaks are almost centrally located. Surface with sharp and crowded concentric lines. Color deep pink.

Remarks: Formerly called *georgiana* Dall, 1900.

IRIS TELLIN *Tellina iris* Say, 1822   **Pl. 34**
   Range: N. Carolina to Florida to Texas.
   Habitat: Shallow water.
   Description: Length $^{1}/_{2}$ in. Valves compressed. Anterior rounded, posterior rather sharply pointed. Low beaks nearly central. Surface glossy, color white, the valves thin and more or less translucent.

SMOOTH TELLIN *Tellina laevigata* Linnaeus, 1758   **Pl. 33**
   Range: Florida to the West Indies; Bermuda.
   Habitat: Shallow water.
   Description: About 2 in. long. Outline roundish, anterior end regularly rounded, the slightly shorter posterior end bluntly pointed, with a distinct angle running from the beaks to that tip. Valves moderately inflated. Surface smooth, often glossy. Color white with pale orange rays.

ROSE PETAL TELLIN *Tellina lineata* Turton, 1819   **Pl. 35**
   Range: N. Carolina to the West Indies.
   Habitat: Shallow water.
   Description: About 1 in. long and rosy pink, the umbonal area usually darker in hue. Interior same color as outside. Shell smooth and delicate, nearly as high as long. Anterior end rounded, posterior slightly pointed.
   Remarks: A common species, these dainty rose and pink valves — looking like so many rose petals — are washed ashore with every tide. Gathered extensively for the making of shell flowers and other novelties.

SPECKLED TELLIN *Tellina listeri* Röding, 1798   **Pl. 33**
   Range: N. Carolina to Brazil; Bermuda.
   Habitat: Shallow water.
   Description: Length 1 to 2 in. Shell rather long and thin, not polished. Anterior end rounded, posterior end rostrate (beaked). Beaks nearly central and low. Surface sculptured with strong, equidistant, concentric lines. Color creamy white, with crowded streaks of brownish purple. Interior polished white.
   Remarks: This species has long been listed as *T. interrupta* Wood, 1815.

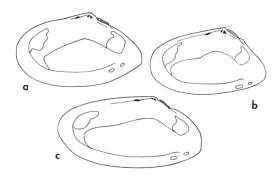

Figure 26. a) Lintea Tellin *Tellina aequistriata* **b)** Crystal Tellin *Tellina cristallina* **c)** Martinique Tellin *Tellina martinicensis*

GREAT TELLIN *Tellina magna* Spengler, 1798   **Pl. 33**
  Range: N. Carolina to the West Indies.
  Habitat: Moderately shallow water.
  Description: Our largest tellin, it attains a length of $4^1/_2$ in. Both ends slope to a rounded ventral margin, with posterior end more pointed. Valves rather thick, hinge strong. Surface marked by growth lines. Color white on left valve, yellowish or orange on the right. Interior frequently pinkish.

MARTINIQUE TELLIN
Tellina martinicensis Orbigny, 1842
  Range: Florida to the West Indies and to Brazil.
  Habitat: Moderately shallow water.
  Description: Nearly 12 in. long. A moderately inflated shell, posterior end pointed and anterior rounded. Beaks central. Surface shiny, color white.

MERA TELLIN *Tellina mera* Say, 1834   **Pl. 34**
  Range: Bermuda; Bahamas; s. Florida south through Lesser Antilles and Curaçao.
  Habitat: Shallow water.
  Description: Nearly 1 in. long. Beaks prominent, somewhat

closer to posterior end, which is bluntly pointed. Anterior broadly rounded. Surface smooth and shiny, color white.

SUNRISE TELLIN *Tellina radiata* Linnaeus, 1758   Pl. 33
Range: South Florida to the West Indies.
Habitat: Shallow water.
Description: An elongate shell, length to 3 in. Thin but sturdy, with low beaks placed about midway of the shell. Both ends broadly rounded, posterior a little less so than anterior. Surface smooth and very highly polished. Color yellowish white, with bands of pinkish rose radiating from the beaks, and commonly visible on interior.
Remarks: The broad rosy rays, coupled with the bivalve's high gloss and graceful form, make this a prime favorite with collectors. There is a form of this species that lacks the colorful rays; a form consistent in color, generally white or pale yellow. It has been listed as *T. r. unimaculata* Lamarck, 1818 (see Pl. 33).

SAY'S TELLIN *Tellina texana* Dall, 1900   Fig. 25 & Pl. 34
Range: N. Carolina to Gulf of Mexico; Bahamas.
Habitat: Shallow water.
Description: Length $1/2$ in. Rather well inflated; front end rounded, the posterior slopes gradually to a rounded tip. Beaks small, set rather closer to front end. Color glossy white.
Remarks: Frequently washed ashore. As with many of the tellins, one often finds examples with both valves attached and spread out on the sand like so many mounted butterflies. Formerly known as *sayi* Dall, 1900.

CONSOBRINE TELLIN *Tellina consobrina* Orbigny, 1842   Pl. 34
Range: Southeast Florida and West Indies; Bermuda.
Habitat: Shallow water.
Description: Length $1/2$ in., elongate, fragile, rather fat with the left valve fatter and with a posterior twist to the right. Umbones posterior to the middle. Sculpture of weak concentric lines crossed by very obscure "scissulations" (about 3 to 5 per mm.) White with pink rays or all white.

DWARF CUNEATE TELLIN *Tellina gouldii* Hanley, 1846   Pl. 34
Range: Southeast Florida and West Indies; Bermuda.
Habitat: Sand and weeds, offshore to deep water.
Description: Length $1/2$ in., milk white, glossy, solid, with very weak concentric threads that are generally evident only on the very blunt, somewhat truncated posterior end.

CANDY STICK TELLIN *Tellina similis* Sowerby, 1806 **Pl. 34**
Range: South Florida to the West Indies; Bermuda.
Habitat: Shallow water.
Description: Moderately elongate, length about 1 in. Shell thin and compressed, beaks rather prominent and situated $1/3$ closer to posterior end. Anterior end gracefully rounded, posterior end dropping off rather abruptly to rounded tip. Glossy white, often with short radiating rays of pinkish.

DALL'S DWARF TELLIN **Fig. 25 & Pl. 34**
Tellina sybaritica Dall, 1881
Range: N. Carolina to the West Indies; Bermuda.
Habitat: Moderately shallow water.
Description: Less than $1/2$ in. long. Very elongate, with beaks about central. Posterior end sloping, a bit less than anterior. Surface shiny, color generally pinkish but may be deeper red.
Remarks: Probably the smallest member of its genus on our shores.

TAMPA TELLIN *Tellina tampaensis* Conrad, 1866 **Pl. 34**
Range: Florida to Texas; West Indies.
Habitat: Shallow water.
Description: About $3/4$ in. long. Beaks high and full, anterior end short and regularly rounded, posterior somewhat longer and abruptly pointed. Valves only slightly inflated. Color shiny white. Interior often showing a pinkish tone.

DEKAY'S DWARF TELLIN **Pl. 34**
Tellina versicolor DeKay, 1843
Range: Cape Cod to Florida and Texas; West Indies to Trinidad.
Habitat: Shallow water.
Description: About $1/2$ in. long. Beaks fairly prominent, anterior end broadly rounded, posterior end short, sloping, bluntly pointed. Surface polished and iridescent. Color may be white, pink, reddish, or weakly rayed with rosy pink.

CRENULATE TELLIN **Pl. 35**
Tellina squamifera (Deshayes, 1855)
Range: N. Carolina to Florida and to Texas.
Habitat: Moderately shallow water.
Description: Length about 1 in. This is a rather thin shell, the front end broadly rounded and the posterior sloping to a somewhat truncate tip. Sculpture of fine but sharp concentric lines. Noticeable thornlike crenulations on the dorsal margins. Color white, occasionally yellowish or orange.

LINTEA TELLIN *Tellina aequistriata* Say, 1824   **Pls. 34, 37**
  Range: Cape Hatteras to Gulf of Mexico; West Indies.
  Habitat: Moderately deep water.
  Description: Not quite 1 in. long. Shell thin and rather delicate, beaks small and pointed. Anterior end rounded, posterior sharply sloping, with a slightly truncate tip. Surface
  sculptured with finely chiseled concentric lines, upturned
  on posterior slope to form a filelike edge. Color white; interior polished. Formerly *Quadrans lintea* (Conrad, 1837).

● **Genus *Arcopagia* Brown, 1827**

FAUST TELLIN *Arcopagia fausta* (Pulteney, 1799)   **Pl. 33**
  Range: N. Carolina to the West Indies.
  Habitat: Moderately shallow water.
  Description: A large and moderately heavy shell, as long as 4
  in. Both ends slope to a rounded ventral margin, the posterior end more pointed. Valves rather thick, hinge strong. Surface marked by coarse growth lines. Color whitish; interior
  often showing tinges of yellow.

Figure 27. Balthic Macoma *Macoma balthica*

Figure 28. Short Macoma *Macoma brevifrons*

Figure 29. Chalky Macoma *Macoma calcarea*

● **Genus *Macoma* Leach, 1819**

BALTHIC MACOMA   Fig. 27 & Pl. 33
Macoma balthica (Linneaus, 1758)
  Range: Arctic to Georgia.
  Habitat: Shallow water.
  Description: Length to 1½ in. Shell moderately thin, with
rounded outline, posterior end somewhat constricted. Beaks
rather prominent and nearly central. Surface bears many
very fine concentric lines of growth. Color pinkish white
with a dull finish and there is a thin olive-brown periostracum, usually lacking on the parts of the early shell.
  Remarks: This bivalve is abundant in muddy bays and coves
and commonly travels partway up many creeks and rivers.
It occurs on our West Coast and in Europe.

SHORT MACOMA *Macoma brevifrons* (Say, 1834)   Fig. 28
  Range: South Carolina to Brazil.
  Habitat: Moderately shallow water.
  Description: About 1 in. long. A small dull white shell, the
only sculpture being indistinct lines of growth. Commonly a
yellowish tint over the umbones, and interior may be buffy
yellow. Anterior end long and broadly rounded, posterior end
sloping rather sharply to a bluntly pointed tip. Thin brownish periostracum.

SHINY MACOMA *Macoma cerina* C. B. Adams, 1845   Pl. 35
  Range: Florida and the West Indies.
  Habitat: Offshore in sand.
  Description: About ⅓ in. oval, with one end narrower. Surface
smooth. Color all-white with a light flush of yellow. Um-
bones somewhat raised.

CHALKY MACOMA   Fig. 29 & Pl. 33
Macoma calcarea (Gmelin, 1791)
  Range: Greenland to Long Island.

Habitat: Moderately shallow water.
Description: Length 2 in. Elongate-oval in shape, posterior end narrowed and slightly twisted. Dull chalky white, inside and outside, with dull grayish periostracum generally present only toward base of shell.

EXTENDED MACOMA *Macoma extenuata* Dall, 1900   **Pl. 35**
Range: Cedar Key, Florida.
Habitat: Offshore, northeast Gulf of Mexico.
Description: Length 1 in., elongate, rounded at the front end; posterior narrow, pointed and with a weak, raised ridge. Color white.

TAGELUS-LIKE MACOMA   **Pl. 33**
Macoma tageliformis Dall, 1900
Range: Louisiana to Texas, and to Brazil.
Habitat: Offshore in muddy sand.
Description: Two in., oblong, left valve fatter than the right; ligamental area long and depressed. Posterior end gently rounded. Pallial sinus reaches halfway to anterior muscle scar.

CONSTRICTED MACOMA   **Pl. 33**
Macoma constricta (Bruguière, 1792)
Range: Florida to the West Indies; Texas.
Habitat: Shallow water.
Description: About $2^1/2$ in. long. Shell moderately inflated, with broadly rounded margins. Posterior end partially truncate and notched below, with a feeble fold extending from beaks to ventral margin. Color white, with a thin yellowish periostracum.

NARROWED MACOMA *Macoma tenta* (Say, 1834)   **Pl. 35**
Range: Prince Edward Island to Florida and Gulf of Mexico; West Indies.
Habitat: Shallow water.
Description: A small, thin, delicate bivalve, the length slightly less than $1/2$ in. as a rule, but it may be as much as $3/4$ in. Anterior end long and broadly rounded, posterior short and abruptly sloping. Surface bears tiny, sharp lines of growth. Color pinkish white, though surface is iridescent and reflects a rainbow of hues.

FALSE MERA MACOMA   Pl. 35
Macoma pseudomera Dall & Simpson, 1901
   Range: South Florida; Bermuda and the West Indies.
   Habitat: Offshore in sand in moderately deep water.
   Description: About $3/4$ in., ovoid with the umbones near the center. With very fine concentric lines. Color dull white.

MITCHELL'S MACOMA
Macoma mitchelli Dall, 1895
   Range: South Carolina to Texas.
   Habitat: Shallow water in fine sand.
   Description: About $1/2$ in. in length, elongate; posterior end narrowed and pointed. Exterior white and with fine concentric lines.

● **Genus *Strigilla* Turton, 1822**

ROSY STRIGILLA *Strigilla carnaria* Linnaeus, 1758   Pl. 35
   Range: Florida to the West Indies.
   Habitat: Shallow water.
   Description: Length slightly under 1 in. Shell moderately solid, rather circular in outline, and fairly well inflated. Surface appears smooth but there is a sculpture of extremely fine radial lines that become oblique and wavy over posterior area. Pale rose color, deepest over umbones (beaks); interior rosy pink.
   Remarks: The rosy color makes this common species an attractive shell for decorative purposes.

WHITE STRIGILLA *Strigilla mirabilis* (Philippi, 1841)   Pl. 35
   Range: N. Carolina to Texas; West Indies; Bermuda.
   Habitat: Shallow water.
   Description: Nearly $1/2$ in. long, oval, and well inflated. Beaks situated slightly closer to front end. Surface bears the same peculiar sculpture as in Rosy Strigilla. Color white.

PEA STRIGILLA *Strigilla pisiformis* (Linneaus, 1758)   Pl. 37
   Range: South Florida to the West Indies; Bahamas.
   Habitat: Shallow water.
   Description: Length $1/3$ in. Moderately inflated, this is an oval, slightly oblique shell, with much the same sculpture as others of its genus. Color pink, darker over the umbonal region. On inside the color is darkest centrally, often white at the margins.

● Genus *Tellidora* H. & A. Adams, 1856

CRESTED TELLIN *Tellidora cristata* (Récluz, 1842)   **Pl. 35**
   Range: N. Carolina to Florida; Texas.
   Habitat: Shallow water.
   Description: Length about 1 in. Shell compressed, left valve
   flatter than right, outline somewhat triangular. Beaks central and prominent. Ventral margin broadly rounded. Surface bears faint concentric ridges that form teeth on the lateral margins, giving the shell a saw-toothed appearance.
   Color pure white.

● Genus *Psammotreta* Dall, 1900

ATLANTIC GROOVED MACOMA   **Pl. 33**
Psammotreta intastriata (Say, 1827)
   Range: Florida to the West Indies; Bermuda.
   Habitat: Shallow water.
   Description: A large but thin shell about 3 in. long. Posterior
   end long and broadly rounded, anterior sloping and pro-
   foundly folded, so the shell has an oddly twisted appearance
   at its front end. Valves well inflated. Color pure white,
   sometimes with a tinge of yellow.
   Remarks: Formerly in the genus *Apolymetis* Salisbury, 1929.

■ **BEAN CLAMS: Family Donacidae**

   Generally small, wedge-shaped clams, the posterior end
   elongated and acutely rounded and the anterior sharply sloping and short. Distributed in all seas that are warm, where
   they live in the sand close to shore.

● Genus *Donax* Linnaeus, 1758

CARIBBEAN COQUINA   **Pl. 37**
Donax denticulata Linnaeus, 1758
   Range: West Indies.
   Habitat: Shallow water.
   Description: A sturdy shell, slightly more than 1 in. long.
   Elongate-oval, with fine radiating lines on surface. Inner
   margins crenulate. Color may be brown, violet, or yellowish,
   often with darker rays.

FOSSOR COQUINA *Donax fossor* Say, 1822
Range: Long Island to New Jersey.
Habitat: Shallow water.
Description: About $1/2$ in. long. Shell rather thick and solid, inner margins crenulate. Shaped much like the Coquina (below), of which it may turn out to be a variety. Surface decorated with fine radiating lines. Color white or bluish white, sometimes with faint rays.

POOR LITTLE COQUINA   **Pl. 37**
Donax fossor subsp. *parvula* Philippi, 1849
Range: North Carolina to northeast Florida.
Habitat: Migrates from lower beach to subtidal sand flats in summer.
Description: Similar to *variabilis,* but smaller (adults 7 mm), less colorful, without rays, and with a shorter, broader ligament holding the valves together.
Remarks: This is the southern subspecies of the northern Fossor Coquina.

ROEMER'S COQUINA *Donax roemeri* (Philippi, 1849)
Range: Texas.
Habitat: Shallow water.
Description: This is a slightly smaller form than the Fossor Coquina, and it occurs on the Texas coast. It is not as elongate, and the posterior end is blunter. The ventral margin sags down. Color tends to be more yellowish.

STRIATE COQUINA *Donax striatus* Linnaeus, 1767   **Pl. 37**
Range: West Indies.
Habitat: Shallow water.
Description: Length 1 in. Anterior end long and bluntly rounded, posterior sloping, abruptly rounded. Basal margin slightly concave. Surface smooth, a few radiating lines on posterior slope. Color bluish white.

COQUINA *Donax variabilis* Say, 1822   **Pls. 4 , 37**
Range: Virginia to Florida and west to Texas.
Habitat: Shallow water.
Description: About $3/4$ in. long. Shell wedge-shaped, posterior end prolonged and acutely rounded, anterior short and obliquely truncated. Surface bears numerous fine radiating lines, inner margins crenulate. Displays a bewildering variety of colors, ranging from pure white to yellowish, rose, lavender, pale blue, and deep purple. It is usually decorated with radiating reddish brown bands and sometimes with

concentric colored lines. Now and then a shell has both, producing a plaid pattern. Inner surface smooth, and also shows varied coloration, often deep purple.

Remarks: Known by several other popular names, among them Butterfly Shell, Wedge Shell, and Pompano. It burrows in loose sand at the midwater line, where in favorable situations individuals may be gathered by the handful with scarcely any sand mixed in; despite their diminutive size they are often so gathered and made into a delicious broth. Dead shells usually remain in pairs, connected at the hinge and spread out like so many butterflies. The color patterns are almost countless; out of 50 shells it is sometimes difficult to find 2 exactly alike. Suites of this little bivalve are often used in biology classes to demonstrate an extreme in color variation within a single species.

● **Genus** *Iphigenia* **Schumacher, 1817**

GREAT FALSE COQUINA   **Pl. 36**
Iphigenia brasiliana (Lamarck, 1818)
  Range: South Florida to the West Indies; Brazil.
  Habitat: Shallow water.
  Description: Length to 3 in. A fairly large and sturdy clam, broadly triangular. Beaks prominent and almost central. Anterior end sharply rounded, posterior with angled slope. Margins not crenulate. Color buffy white, but in life there is a rather substantial tan periostracum. Interior shiny white, often pinkish on teeth.
  Remarks: *I. brasiliensis* is a misspelling of this fairly common species.

■ **GARI SHELLS: Family Psammobiidae**

Shells somewhat like the tellins, with which they were once grouped. The animals have very long siphons. Distributed chiefly in warm seas. Formerly the family name was Sanguinolariidae.

● **Genus** *Sanguinolaria* **Lamarck, 1799**

ATLANTIC SANGUIN   **Pl. 36**
Sanguinolaria sanguinolenta (Gmelin, 1791)
  Range: South Florida; Gulf states; West Indies.
  Habitat: Moderately shallow water.

Description: About 1¹/₂ in. long. Shape oval, with a flattish top. Both ends and basal margin regularly rounded. Beaks very low. Surface fairly smooth. Color rosy pink over the beak area, fading to whitish toward the margins.

Remarks: Erroneously called *cruenta* (Solander), an elongate purplish, Caribbean species.

● **Genus *Asaphis* Modeer, 1793**

GAUDY ASAPHIS *Asaphis deflorata* (Linnaeus, 1758)   **Pl. 36**

Range: South Florida to the West Indies; Bermuda.

Habitat: Shallow water in coarse sand.

Description: Length averages 2 in. but sometimes is longer. Shell thin but strong, rather well inflated. Surface bears numerous radiating lines, most pronounced on posterior slope. Lines at both ends crossed by wavy growth lines. Color variable, ranging from white to yellow, orange, and purple, with majority of specimens tending toward latter. Interior may be yellow, orange, or purple.

● **Genus *Tagelus* Gray, 1847**

PURPLISH TAGELUS   **Fig. 30 & Pl. 36**

Tagelus divisus (Spengler, 1794)

Range: Cape Cod to Gulf states; West Indies; Bermuda.

Habitat: Shallow water.

Description: Length 1¹/₂ in. Shell thin and fragile, elongate with parallel margins, both ends rounded. Beaks nearly central. Surface smooth, generally shiny, with a thin yellowish brown periostracum. Color of shell purplish gray, faintly rayed with purple. Interior often deep purple.

STOUT TAGELUS   **Fig. 30 & Pl. 36**

Tagelus plebeius (Lightfoot, 1786)

Range: Massachusetts to Gulf states and to Brazil.

Habitat: Shallow water.

Description: Length 3 to 4 in. Shell elongate, stout, gaping, and abruptly rounded at both ends. Beaks blunt and slightly elevated; situated just off middle of shell. Surface coarsely wrinkled concentrically. Color white or yellowish, with a thin yellowish brown periostracum. Most of the shells that have been empty for any length of time are a dull chalky white.

Remarks: Formerly listed as *T. gibbus* (Spengler, 1794).

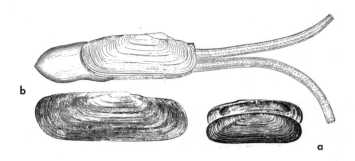

Figure 30. a) Purplish Tagelus *Tagelus divisus* **b)** Stout Tagelus *Tagelus plebeius*

● **Genus** *Heterodonax* **Morch, 1853**

SMALL FALSE COQUINA   Pl. 36
Heterodonax bimaculata (Linnaeus, 1758)
  Range: Florida to the West Indies; Bermuda.
  Habitat: Shallow water in clear sand.
  Description: About ³/₄ in. long. Triangular-oval in shape, rather solid. Posterior end short and squarish, anterior more rounded. Common shade is bluish white, and most valves bear 2 red or purple spots, and in addition there may be rays of purplish. Interior commonly spotted with brown or purple.

● **Genus** *Solecurtus* **Blainville, 1825**

CORRUGATED RAZOR CLAM   Pl. 36
Solecurtus cuminginus Dunker, 1861
  Range: N. Carolina to Texas and to Brazil.
  Habitat: Moderately deep water.
  Description: About 1¹/₂ in. long. Shape much like Stout Tagelus, *Tagelus plebeius*, with beaks closer to front and with both ends rounded. An odd sculpture, consisting of a number of prominent concentric rings, on which is superimposed a series of distinct lines that are oblique on the front portion of the valves and sharply vertical on the rear. White, with yellowish gray periostracum.

ST. MARTHA'S RAZOR CLAM
Solecurtus sanctaemarthae (Orbigny, 1842)
Range: South Florida to Brazil; Bermuda.
Habitat: Shallow water.
Description: Length to about 1 in. An oblong shell, squarish and gaping at both ends. Beaks low, set closer to front end. Surface similar to that of Corrugated Razor Clam. Color white, with thin yellowish periostracum.

■ FALSE MUSSELS: Family Dreissenidae

Small bivalves, these superficially resemble the mussels. There is a shelflike platform under the beaks for the attachment of the anterior muscle. Found in shallow waters, under brackish conditions. One freshwater species, the Zebra Mussel, *Dreissena polymorpha* (Müller, 1776) was introduced to eastern and central United States in 1986 and has become a nuisance by clogging water pipes (see Pls. 21 and 26).

● Genus *Mytilopsis* Conrad, 1857

FALSE ZEBRA MUSSEL   Pls. 21, 26
Mytilopsis leucophaeata (Conrad, 1831)
Range: New York to Texas.
Habitat: Brackish waters. Abundant attached to logs and pilings.
Description: An elongate, partially curved shell about 1 in. long. Valves considerably inflated and bluntly keeled. Beaks terminal, the beak cavity containing a small plate, or platform, where the muscle is attached. Color grayish brown; interior dull white, not polished.
Remarks: A nuisance to boats. *M. leucophaeta* is a misspelling.

■ SEMELES: Family Semelidae

Shells roundish oval and very slightly inflated, with more or less obscure folds on the posterior ends. The brown elongate, chitinous resilium is embedded obliquely within the shelly hinge. There is a deep pallial sinus. Chiefly confined to warm seas.

● **Genus** *Semele* **Schumacher, 1817**

CANCELLATE SEMELE   **Pl. 35**
Semele bellastriata (Conrad, 1837)
   Range: N. Carolina to Brazil; Bermuda.
   Habitat: Moderately shallow water.
   Description: Length to 1 in. Round-oval, with anterior end
   somewhat shorter and more sharply rounded. Surface has
   both radiating and concentric lines, so that with some specimens it appears slightly beaded. Color may be solid purplish
   gray, but often yellowish with streaks of brown. Interior polished and frequently brightly colored with yellow or lavender.

WHITE ATLANTIC SEMELE   **Pl. 36**
Semele proficua (Pulteney, 1799)
   Range: N. Carolina to Brazil; Bermuda.
   Habitat: Shallow water.
   Description: Length to 1½ in. Shell rather thin and compressed, rounded oval. Beaks small and turned forward, with
   small lunule in front. Sculpture of extremely fine but sharp
   concentric lines. Color creamy white, occasionally variegated with pinkish rays. Very thin periostracum. Interior
   yellowish and polished, occasionally lightly speckled with
   purplish or pink.

PURPLE SEMELE *Semele purpurascens* (Gmelin, 1791)   **Pl. 35**
   Range: N. Carolina to the West Indies.
   Habitat: Shallow water.
   Description: An oval shell with both ends rounded, about 2 in.
   long. Posterior end twice the length of anterior. Surface
   bears fine concentric lines, but appears quite smooth. Color
   pale yellow, rather blotched with purple or brown or orange.
   Some individuals may be uniformly deep yellow.

● **Genus** *Cumingia* **Sowerby, 1833**

SOUTHERN CUMINGIA
Cumingia coarctata Sowerby, 1833
   Range: South Florida to Brazil; Bermuda.
   Habitat: Shallow water.
   Description: Length ⅜ in. A roughly oval shell, beaks moder-
   ately elevated. Interior with spoonlike pit beneath beaks.

Surface bears concentric lines, with minute radiating lines in between. Color white.

Remarks: *C. antillarum* Orbigny, 1842, is a synonym.

COMMON CUMINGIA   Pl. 35
Cumingia tellinoides (Conrad, 1831)
Range: Nova Scotia to Florida.
Habitat: Shallow water.
Description: About ³/₄ in. long. Shell oval-triangular, quite thin, the anterior end broadly rounded, posterior considerably pointed and gaping. Surface covered by numerous sharp, elevated, concentric lines. Color white.

● **Genus *Abra* Lamarck, 1818**

COMMON ATLANTIC ABRA *Abra aequalis* (Say, 1822)   Pl. 35
Range: N. Carolina to Texas; West Indies to Brazil.
Habitat: Moderately deep water.
Description: A small, ¹/₃ in. rather plump shell. Shell rounded and slightly oblique, decorated with minute concentric wrinkles near the margins, the rest of surface relatively smooth. Color brownish white, often tinged with buff.
Remarks: An abundant, very simple-looking bivalve.

DALL'S LITTLE ABRA *Abra lioica* (Dall, 1881)   Fig. 31
Range: Cape Cod to south Florida; West Indies.
Habitat: Offshore in clear sand, down to 1,200 feet.
Description: Very small, ¹/₄ in., all white except for a small tan beak. Similar to the Common Atlantic Abra, but the beaks are nearer the front end; the shell is thinner and more elongate. Front margin of the right valve is not grooved.

Figure 31. Dall's Little Abra *Abra lioica*

■ RAZOR CLAMS: Family Solenidae

Members of this family are the true razor clams, and they are so called wherever they occur. The shells have equal valves, are usually greatly elongated, and gape at both ends as a rule. They are distributed in the sandy bottoms of coastal waters in nearly all seas, and all are edible.

● Genus *Solen* Linnaeus, 1758

WEST INDIAN RAZOR CLAM
Solen obliquus Spengler, 1794
Range: West Indies to Brazil.
Habitat: Shallow water.
Description: Length 5 to 6 in. Remarkably elongate, margins parallel. Low beaks at extremely short anterior end. Both ends squarish. Growth lines the only sculpture. Color whitish, with brown periostracum.

LITTLE GREEN RAZOR CLAM *Solen viridis* Say, 1821   Pl. 38
Range: Rhode Island to n. Florida and n. Gulf of Mexico.
Habitat: Intertidal.
Description: Length 2 to 3 in. Shell thin, elongate, somewhat compressed. Hinge line nearly straight. Gaping at both ends. Surface smooth and rather glossy, with very faint concentric wrinkles. Shiny green periostracum.
Remarks: Specimens may be distinguished from young examples of the Common Razor Clam, *Ensis directus* (below), by their straighter shells and slightness of curve.

● Genus *Ensis* Schumacher, 1817

COMMON RAZOR CLAM *Ensis directus* Conrad, 1843   Pl. 38
Range: Labrador to Florida; Europe.
Habitat: Intertidal.
Description: Most specimens 5 to 7 in. long, but the species may reach 10 in. Shell thin, greatly elongated, gaping, and noticeably curved. Sides parallel, ends squarish. Surface has glossy greenish periostracum and a long triangular space marked by concentric lines of growth. Shell itself whitish.
Remarks: Burrows vertically in sandbars, and the speed with which it can sink down out of sight in wet sand is astonishing. Also a successful if somewhat erratic swimmer. The long foot is extended and folded back against the shell, then suddenly straightened out as if it were a steel spring, and the clam is propelled like an arrow for 3 or 4 feet. Razor

clams are tender if not too large and have an excellent flavor. See Remarks under Little Green Razor Clam, *Solen viridis* (above).

DWARF RAZOR CLAM   Pl. 38
Ensis megistus Pilsbry and McGinty, 1943
   Range: Florida to Texas.
   Habitat: Intertidal.
   Description: Proportionally narrower and more fragile than Common Razor Clam, seldom exceeding 4 in. Many regard this as a subspecies of the Common Razor Clam, *E. directus.*
   Remarks: *E. minor* Dall, 1900 (not Chenu, 1843) is a synonym.

● **Genus *Siliqua* Mühlfeld, 1811**

ATLANTIC RAZOR CLAM *Siliqua costata* Say, 1822   Pl. 36
   Range: Gulf of St. Lawrence to N. Carolina.
   Habitat: Shallow water.
   Description: About 2 in. long. Oval-elliptical, thin and rather fragile, moderately elongate. Broadly rounded at each end. Beaks very low, situated closer to front. Interior strengthened by a prominent vertical rib that extends from the beaks, bending slightly backward, and, expanding, loses itself about halfway across the valve. Color pinkish white, with thin yellowish green periostracum.

SCALE RAZOR CLAM *Siliqua squama* Blainville, 1824   Pl. 36
   Range: Newfoundland to Cape Cod, Massachusetts.
   Habitat: Offshore, in sand; uncommon.
   Description: Three in. in length. Similar to the Atlantic Razor Clam, but larger, thicker-shelled, white internally, and its internal supporting ridge, or rib, slants posteriorly instead of anteriorly as in *costata.*

ORDER MYOIDA

■ ROCK BORERS: Family Hiatellidae

Shells usually elongate, valves unequal. Some very large. Members of this family commonly bore into sponge, coral, and limestone, but some burrow deeply in mud. The surface is generally irregular and rough and lacking in colors. Distributed from the Arctic to the tropics.

● **Genus** *Hiatella* **Daudin, 1801**

ARCTIC ROCK BORER *Hiatella arctica* (Linnaeus, 1767) **Pl. 36**
Range: Arctic Ocean to West Indies; Pacific coast.
Habitat: Moderately shallow water.
Description: A rough and unattractive bivalve about $1\frac{1}{2}$ in.
long and dingy white. Shell oblong-oval, coarse and irregular
in shape. Beaks rather prominent; from them run 2 faint
ridges to the rear margin. Both ends rounded, the posterior
nearly 3 times as long as the anterior. Surface coarsely
marked with lines of growth and irregularly undulated.
Remarks: It occasionally does some damage by excavating its
burrows in the cement work of breakwaters or embank-
ments. Each individual, after boring its home, attaches itself
to the walls by a byssal cord and remains fixed for life.
Young specimens are often found attached to rocks and pebbles close to shore. This shell is quite common as a fossil in
Pleistocene rocks throughout the Northeast.

● **Genus** *Cyrtodaria* **Reuss, 1801**

PROPELLER CLAM *Cyrtodaria siliqua* (Spengler, 1793) **Pl. 36**
Range: Labrador to Rhode Island.
Habitat: Moderately deep water.
Description: A thick and heavy shell about 3 in. long. Elongate-oval, beaks closer to front end. Valves widely gaping
and slightly twisted like a propeller. Surface bears concentric grooves. A thick and horny, glossy black periostracum
frequently projects beyond the valves. Beaks very low, usually eroded.
Remarks: The animal is very large, and the valves never completely cover the fleshy parts. Periostracum easily flakes off
dry shells.

Figure 32. Arctic Rough Clam *Panomya arctica*

● Genus *Panomya* Gray, 1857

ARCTIC ROUGH CLAM   Fig. 32 & Pl. 38
Panomya arctica (Lamarck, 1818)
Range: Circumpolar; Arctic Ocean to Georges Bank (off Cape Cod).
Habitat: Intertidal; gravelly muds.
Description: Rough and sturdy, rather squarish in outline, attains a length of about 3 in. Posterior end squarely cut off, gapes widely; front end slopes to a rounded point and then to the ventral margin, which is straight. Color chalky white, with a dark, almost black periostracum that peels easily from the shell, so even living examples are rarely completely covered.
Remarks: The shell usually fails to encase the animal completely.

● Genus *Panopea* Ménard, 1807

ATLANTIC GEODUCK   Pl. 38
Panopea bitruncata (Conrad, 1872)
Range: N. Carolina to Florida.
Habitat: Moderately shallow water.
Description: Length 5 to 6 in. Well inflated, with prominent beaks, regularly rounded before and rather sharply truncated behind, where it gapes widely. Surface marked with growth lines, color dull grayish white.
Remarks: A rare shell, once believed to be extinct, but a few live specimens have been collected in recent years. It might be considered the Atlantic cousin of the well-known North Pacific Gweduc, or "Gooey-duck." Formerly the genus *Panope*.

■ **SOFT-SHELLED CLAMS: Family Myidae**

Valves usually unequal and gaping. Left valve contains a spoonlike structure called a chondrophore, to which the resilium (internal cartilage in hinge) is attached. Distributed in all seas. Formerly Myacidae.

● **Genus *Mya* Linnaeus, 1758**

SOFT-SHELLED CLAM *Mya arenaria* Linnaeus, 1758   **Pl. 38**
   Range: Labrador to N. Carolina.
   Habitat: Intertidal; gravelly muds.
   Description: Length 3 to 6 in. Shell gapes at both ends. Anterior rounded, posterior somewhat pointed. Surface roughened and wrinkled by lines of growth. An erect spoonlike tooth (chondrophore) is located under beak in left valve. Dull gray or chalky white, with thin grayish periostracum.
   Remarks: Known by other popular names such as Longnecked Clam, Long Clam, and Steamer Clam, this species lives in the muds and gravels between tides, where it is exposed to air twice each day. It lives buried with only the tips of its siphons at the surface; as one walks over its territory the mollusk's position is revealed by a vertical spurt of water, ejected as the alarmed clam suddenly withdraws its siphons. Although generally regarded as inferior to the Quahog, this is a very important food mollusk, and it enjoys a steady popularity in the markets. Persistent clamming has made specimens as large as 6 in. rare and difficult to find.

TRUNCATE SOFT-SHELLED CLAM   **Pl. 38**
Mya truncata Linnaeus, 1758
   Range: Greenland to Massachusetts; Arctic seas to Washington.
   Habitat: Intertidal.
   Description: Length 2 to 3 in. Shell rather thick and solid, oblong. Anterior end rounded, posterior end abruptly truncated and widely gaping, the edges slightly flaring. Beaks moderately prominent, chondrophore in left valve. Surface roughly wrinkled. Color dingy white, with a tough yellowish brown periostracum.
   Remarks: A cold-water species, seldom found south of Maine. It is known on our West Coast as far south as Puget Sound, and also in Japan and Norway. It occurs commonly as a Pleistocene fossil throughout the northern New England shoreline.

● **Genus *Paramya* Conrad, 1860**

OVATE PARAMYA *Paramya subovata* Conrad, 1860
   Range: N. Carolina to Florida.
   Habitat: Moderately shallow water.
   Description: About $1/2$ in. long. Anterior end rounded, posterior

enlarged and bluntly rounded, rendering the shell rather square in outline. Beaks moderately prominent. Color dull white or yellowish white.

■ CORBULA CLAMS: Family Corbulidae

Shells small but solid, valves very unequal, one valve generally overlapping the other. Slightly gaping at the anterior end. An upright, conical tooth is present in each valve. White, and usually concentrically ribbed. Distributed in nearly all temperate seas.

● Genus *Varicorbula* Grant and Gale, 1931

OVAL CORBULA   Fig. 33
Varicorbula operculata (Philippi, 1848)
Range: N. Carolina and Gulf of Mexico; West Indies.
Habitat: Shallow water.
Description: Thin-shelled and glossy, length about ³/₈ in. Beaks high and curved inward. Valves so inflated the shell is almost globular; one valve slightly larger than the other. Color white, more or less tinged with pink, and with a yellowish periostracum.
Remarks: Formerly listed as *Corbula disparilis* Orbigny.

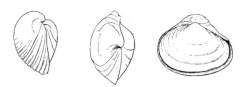

Figure 33. Oval Corbula *Varicorbula operculata*

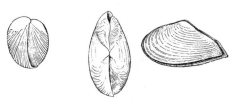

Figure 34. Contracted Corbula *Corbula contracta*

● Genus *Corbula* Bruguière, 1792

CONTRACTED CORBULA   Fig. 34 & Pl. 23
Corbula contracta Say, 1822
    Range: Massachusetts to the West Indies.
    Habitat: Shallow water.
    Description: About ¹/₂ in. long. Shell solid and inflated, anterior end rounded, posterior somewhat pointed. An angular ridge runs from beaks to rear ventral margin, giving that portion of the shell a distinct slope. Right valve overlaps left at rear. Surface sculptured with concentric ribs. Dull white, with thin brownish periostracum.
    Remarks: Also known as the Common Basket Clam.

SNUB-NOSED CORBULA   Fig. 35
Corbula chittyana C. B. Adams, 1852
    Range: North Carolina to the West Indies.
    Habitat: Uncommon in sand in shallow water.
    Description: About ¹/₄ in., oblong, fat and strongly rostrate at the posterior end. Right valve much larger than the left. Margins of valves with a thick border of dark brown periostracum. Concentric sculpture of distinct ridges. Color yellowish to brownish white.
    Remarks: Formerly misidentified as *Corbula nasuta* Sowerby, 1833, which, however, is an Eastern Pacific tropical species.

Figure 35. Snub-nosed Corbula *Corbula chittyana*

Figure 36. Dietz's Corbula *Corbula dietziana*

DIETZ'S CORBULA

Fig. 36 & Pl. 23

Corbula dietziana C. B. Adams, 1852

Range: North Carolina to Brazil.

Habitat: Offshore in moderately deep water.

Description: About $\frac{1}{3}$ to $\frac{1}{2}$ in. in length, like the Contracted Corbula, but larger, thicker-shelled and pink inside. Ventral margins are blushed or rayed with carmine-rose. Microscopic threads numerous between the few coarse, concentric ridges.

SWIFT'S CORBULA

Fig. 37

Corbula swiftiana C. B. Adams, 1852

Range: Massachusetts to Texas and the West Indies.

Habitat: In sand in moderately shallow water.

Description: About $\frac{1}{4}$ in., oblong, moderately fat. Right valve overlaps the left valve. Posterior slope in the right valve bounded by 2 radial ridges. Left valve with only one ridge. Color dull white with a thin yellowish periostracum.

BARRATT'S CORBULA

Corbula barrattiana C. B. Adams, 1852

Range: North Carolina to Brazil.

Habitat: Shallow to deep water in sand.

Description: Usually $\frac{1}{4}$ in., moderately compressed; rostrate at the posterior end, with weak concentric ridges in the beak area. Color variable: white, pink, mauve, yellow, or orange-red.

Figure 37. Swift's Corbula *Corbula swiftiana*

■GAPING CLAMS: Family Gastrochaenidae

Burrowing or boring mollusks living in coral, limestone, or dead shells of other mollusks. The valves are equal and gape considerably. Chiefly dwellers in warm seas.

● **Genus *Gastrochaena* Spengler, 1783**

ATLANTIC ROCELLARIA
Gastrochaena hians (Gmelin, 1791)
>**Range:** N. Carolina to the West Indies.
>**Habitat:** Soft coral rocks.
>**Description:** Length to about 1 in. Beaks close to front end, which slopes sharply to ventral margin. Posterior gapes widely and is somewhat twisted. Sculpture of very fine concentric lines. Color yellowish gray.
>**Remarks:** Sometimes excavates burrows in other shells, especially large examples of *Spondylus*. Formerly in the genus *Rocellaria* Blainville, 1828.

● **Genus *Spengleria* Turton, 1861**

ATLANTIC SPENGLER CLAM   **Pl. 38**
Spengleria rostrata (Spengler, 1783)
>**Range:** Florida to the West Indies.
>**Habitat:** Bores into coral and limestone.
>**Description:** A small yellowish white shell about 1 in. long. Valves sturdy, elongate, squarish, slightly twisted, and widely gaping. Anterior end rounded, posterior end squarely truncate. There is an elevated, transversely ribbed, radiating area extending from beaks to posterior margin.

■ PIDDOCKS: Family Pholadidae

These are boring clams, capable of penetrating wood, coral, and moderately hard rocks, although some live in clay and mud and a few in wood. The shells are white, thin, and brittle, generally elongate, and narrowed toward the posterior end. They gape at both ends. The front end bears a sharp abrading sculpture, and they have accessory shelly plates on the dorsal surface. Distributed in all seas.

● Genus *Pholas* Linnaeus, 1758

CAMPECHE ANGEL WING   **Pl. 38**
Pholas campechiensis Gmelin, 1791
> **Range:** N. Carolina to Gulf of Mexico; West Indies to Brazil.
> **Habitat:** Shallow water.
> **Description:** About 4 in. long. Shell greatly elongated, thin, and brittle, gaping at both ends. Rayed all over with rather distinct ribs, those on anterior end sharp and rasplike. Hinge plate reflected over the umbones (beaks) and supported by several vertical shelly plates. There are 2 accessory plates on dorsal surface. Apophyses (shelly braces) long and narrow. Color white.
> **Remarks:** This graceful shell closely resembles the Angel Wing, *Cyrtopleura costata* (below), but it is smaller and slimmer, with a sculpture that is not as coarse.

● Genus *Cyrtopleura* Tryon, 1862

ANGEL WING *Cyrtopleura costata* (Linnaeus, 1758)   **Pl. 38**
> **Range:** Cape Cod to Gulf of Mexico; West Indies to Brazil.
> **Habitat:** Shallow water.
> **Description:** Length 5 to 7 in. Shell quite thin and brittle. Rounded at front, narrowed and prolonged at rear. Sculptured with strong imbricate radiating ribs. Coarse lines of growth rise over the ribs in an undulating manner. Ribs at front end (boring end) sharp and scaly. Shelly brace (called the apophysis) under each beak projects into shell's interior and is for the attachment of the foot muscles. Valves gape widely, touching only at a point near the top. Color pure white, occasionally with pinkish margins. Thin grayish periostracum during life. See *Pholas campechiensis* (above) for similarity, and also the False Angel Wing, *Petricola pholadiformis*.
> **Remarks:** Formerly listed as *Barnea costata* Linnaeus. A single glance at the snowy white, graceful shell is enough to convince one that the name Angel Wing is a good one. It has long been a great favorite with collectors. A staple article of food in parts of the West Indies, it is not uncommon in Florida but is rare north of Virginia. "Pink Angel Wings" owe their coloration to the presence of blooms of the "red tide" algae.

● Genus *Barnea* Risso, 1826

FALLEN ANGEL WING *Barnea truncata* (Say 1822) **Pl. 38**
Range: Massachusetts to Texas and Brazil.
Habitat: Intertidal; mud and peat banks.
Description: About 2 in. long, sometimes slightly more. Valves thin and fragile, somewhat elongated, posterior end broadly truncate at tip. Surface transversely and longitudinally wrinkled, and studded on front end with small erect scales. Valves gape widely, and there is a small elongate accessory shelly plate situated between the valves just in front of the beaks. Color white, with thin grayish periostracum.
Remarks: The shell is so fragile that it is difficult to dig a specimen free without crushing it. The best way to obtain perfect specimens is to dig out a large block of mud and put it in the nearest tide pool, where it may disintegrate slowly; thus the earth is washed from the clam instead of the clam's being pried out of the earth.

● Genus *Zirfaea* Gray, 1842

GREAT PIDDOCK *Zirfaea crispata* (Linnaeus, 1758) **Pls. 5, 38**
Range: Labrador to New Jersey.
Habitat: Bores into clay and soft rocks.
Description: Length 2 to 3 in. Shell sturdy, rather oblong, rounded posteriorly and somewhat pointed at front. Widely gaping at both ends. Surface bears numerous coarse, wrinklelike ridges that become lamellar on anterior half of shell. Valves divided into nearly equal portions by a broad channel running from beaks to the middle of ventral margin. In live shells, a membranous expansion covers upperpart of shell. Strong apophysis (shelly brace) in each beak cavity. Color pure white. Accessory plate transverse, posterior to umbones.

● Genus *Martesia* Blainville, 1824

WOOD PIDDOCK *Martesia cuneiformis* (Say, 1822) **Pl. 38**
Range: N. Carolina to the Gulf of Mexico; south to Brazil.
Habitat: Bores into wood.
Description: Length ½ to ¾ in. Shell pear-shaped and rather

chubby. Anterior gapes widely in young but pedal gape (opening for foot) closed by a callum in adult. Valves divided into sections by a narrow sulcus (groove) from beaks to ventral margin. Anterior sculptured with closely packed concentric ridges; posterior with smooth, rounded, concentric ridges. Long and thin apophyses. There is a triangular accessory plate over the beaks that shows a deep crease down its center. Color grayish.

STRIATE WOOD PIDDOCK   Pl. 38
Martesia striata (Linneaus, 1758)
Range: N. Carolina to Florida; West Indies to Brazil.
Habitat: Bores into wood.
Description: Length about 2 in. Shell wedge-shaped, anterior gapes widely in young but is closed by a callum in the adult. Anterior slope sculptured with filelike ridges, posterior margin rounded. Surface transversely wrinkled and striated with elevated, minutely crenulated lines. Umbonal-ventral groove prominent. Apophyses long and thin. Accessory plate circular, cushionlike in adult. Color grayish white.
Remarks: Wood piddocks may be collected by searching in old waterlogged wood. The boring is done by the abrading surface of the valves; the clam generally works against the grain of the wood.

● **Genus *Xylophaga* Turton, 1822**

ATLANTIC WOOD BORER   Fig. 38
Xylophaga atlantica Richards, 1942
Range: Quebec to Virginia.
Habitat: Waterlogged wood.
Description: Less than $1/4$ in. long, color white. Shell gapes widely. Valves reinforced by sturdy central ribs. Apophyses lacking. Siphons short, combined, the excurrent slightly shorter than the incurrent. Dorsal accessory plate is of 2 triangular parts.
Remarks: This bivalve has all the appearances of belonging to the next group, Teredinidae, the shipworms, but lack of pallets (a pair of calcareous structures) and presence of small accessory plates on dorsal surface place it among the Pholadidae. Until fairly recently this borer was listed as *X. dorsalis* Turton, which is a European species.

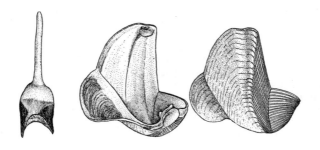

Figure 38. Atlantic Wood Borer *Xylophaga atlantica*

■ SHIPWORMS: Family Teredinidae

Shipworms, or pileworms, are wood borers. The front part of a shipworm is covered by a tiny bivalve shell, but the posterior part is enclosed in a long shelly tube. The shell is white, very much inflated, and gaping, and is decorated with closely set lines. A pair of calcareous structures called pallets at the extreme rear end is used to close the tube; the individual characters of these pallets are determining factors in identifying the different genera and species. It is next to impossible to tell some of them apart with any degree of certainty by their shells alone.

● Genus *Teredo* Linnaeus, 1758

COMMON SHIPWORM *Teredo navalis* Linnaeus, 1758   **Fig. 39**
Range: Whole Atlantic Coast; Europe.
Habitat: Bores into wood.
Description: A small, globular, bivalve shell about ¼ in. long so far as the vestigial shell is concerned, but most of the animal lives in a shelly tube that may be several inches long. Anterior part of valves provided with sharp scaly ribs for boring; posterior smooth and widely gaping. Interior with stout umbonal-ventral rib. Color white. Pallet simple, white.
Remarks: This worm lives in wood and is a great destroyer of ship and wharf timbers. It usually bores with the grain of the wood, and never intersects its neighbor's tunnel. Infested timbers are so honeycombed by the elongated galleries that they eventually disintegrate and crumble away. Painting or

soaking the wood with creosote appears to discourage the mollusk to some extent. Although this tiny clam costs the shipping industry vast sums of money yearly, its record is not entirely bad, for it performs a valuable service as a scavenger, ridding our seas of wooden derelicts and other hazards to navigation.

● Genus *Teredora* Bartsch, 1921

MALLEATED SHIPWORM   **Fig. 40**
Teredora malleola (Turton, 1822)
　Range: Bermuda; West Indies.
　Habitat: Burrows usually in floating wood.
　Description: Length ³/₈ in. Vestigial shell globular, widely gaping. Valves 3-lobed, with median furrow. Color white. Pallets with thumbnail-like depression.
　Remarks: This species has been named *Teredo thompsoni* Trvon.

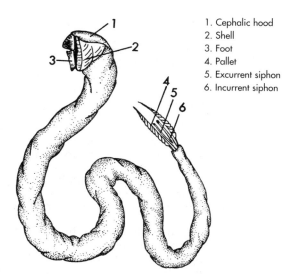

1. Cephalic hood
2. Shell
3. Foot
4. Pallet
5. Excurrent siphon
6. Incurrent siphon

Figure 39. Common Shipworm *Teredo navalis*

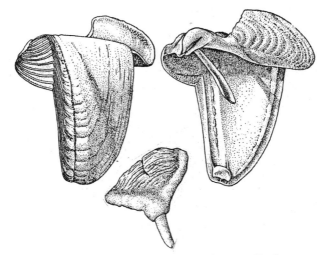

Figure 40. Malleated Shipworm *Teredora malleola*

● Genus *Bankia* Gray, 1842

There are other species of shipworms that can be found in drifting timbers along the Atlantic Coast, all having the same habit of burrowing with the grain of the wood; their specific identification is generally a task for the specialists. Since these small mollusks live in drifting timbers, their exact range is somewhat unpredictable. Their specific identification is generally a task for specialists. Consult Ruth Turner, 1966, "A Survey and Illustrated Catalog of the Teredinidae," Museum Comp. Zool., Harvard University.

GOULD'S SHIPWORM *Bankia gouldi* Bartsch, 1908   **Fig. 41**
Range: New Jersey to Brazil.
Habitat: Found commonly in submerged wood structures in shallow water.
Description: Shell ¹/₄ in., pallets about ¹/₂ in. in length. Cones deep-cupped, with smooth, drawn-out edges.
Remarks: This is the most widespread and abundant species in this genus on the Atlantic coast, hence the most destructive. There are other species of shipworms that can be found in drifting timbers along the Atlantic coast, all having the same habit of burrowing with the grain of the wood.

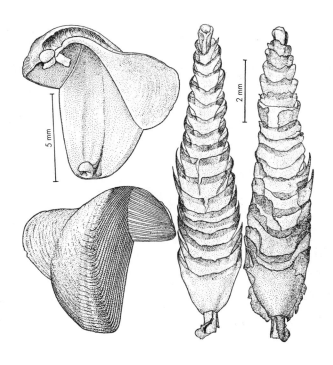

Figure 41. Gould's Shipworm *Bankia gouldi*

SUBCLASS ANOMALODESMATA

■ PAPER SHELLS: Family Lyonsiidae

Shells small and fragile, valves unequal. The hinge bears a narrow ledge to which the ligament is attached. Interior pearly. These mollusks are represented in both the Atlantic and Pacific oceans, living in shallow water on sandy bottoms as a rule.

● **Genus** *Lyonsia* **Turton, 1822**

SAND LYONSIA *Lyonsia arenosa* (Moller, 1842)   **Pl. 23**
   Range: Greenland to Maine.
   Habitat: Shallow water.
   Description: A blocky shell about ¹/₂ in. long. Full beaks ¹/₃
   closer to front end, with rear dorsal margin in straight line to
   the tip. Color silvery white, shell thin and translucent,
   quite pearly within.

PEARLY LYONSIA *Lyonsia beana* (Orbigny, 1842)   **Pl. 37**
   Range: N. Carolina to the West Indies.
   Habitat: Shallow water; often attaches to sponges.
   Description: About 1 in. long. Very unequal valves and rather
   unpredictable in shape. Posterior prolonged and gaping; one
   valve usually quite concave, the other more flat. Color shiny
   white to brownish, often polished.

FLORIDA LYONSIA *Lyonsia floridana* (Conrad, 1849)
   Range: West Florida to Texas.
   Habitat: Shallow water.
   Description: A trim but fragile bivalve about ³/₄ in. long. Shell
   very inequivalve, thin and translucent, and somewhat
   pearly. Surface bears widely spaced radiating lines and a
   paper-thin grayish periostracum.
   Remarks: Some authorities regard this as a subspecies of the
   Glassy Lyonsia, *L. hyalina.*

GLASSY LYONSIA *Lyonsia hyalina* Conrad. 1831   **Pls. 23, 37**
   Range: Nova Scotia to S. Carolina.
   Habitat: Shallow water.
   Description: Length about ³/₄ in. Shell thin and fragile, translucent and pearly. Anterior end rounded, posterior elongated,
   narrowed, and slightly truncate. Beaks prominent.
   Remarks: The surface is covered with radiating wrinkles, minutely fringed, that entangle grains of sand, with which the
   margins of the shell are often coated.

■ **PANDORAS: Family Pandoridae**

   Shells small, very thin and flat, with inconspicuous beaks;
   valves unequal. The exterior is white, the interior very
   pearly. These clams are distributed in all seas and generally
   prefer a sandy or gravelly bottom.

● Genus *Pandora* Bruguière, 1797

INORNATE PANDORA   **Pl. 32**
Pandora inornata Verrill and Bush, 1898
    Range: Nova Scotia to Massachusetts.
    Habitat: Offshore
    Description: Length $3/4$ in., similar to *gouldiana*, but more elongate, thicker shelled. Left anterior cardinal tooth is curved and thickened at the end.

GLACIAL PANDORA *Pandora glacialis* Leach, 1819   **Pl. 32**
    Range: Arctic seas to Gulf of Maine; Alaska to California.
    Habitat: Shallow to deep water.
    Description: Length $3/4$ in., quite fragile, compressed. Left valve convex and centrally inflated. Sharply concave ventrally. With weak radial scratches.

SAND PANDORA *Pandora arenosa* Conrad, 1834   **Pl. 37**
    Range: N. Carolina to Florida.
    Habitat: Shallow water.
    Description: About $1/2$ in. long. Very thin and flat; anterior rounded and posterior with square tip. Weak posterior ridge. One valve perfectly flat, the other slightly inflated. Color white; interior pearly.
    Remarks: Sometimes listed as *P. carolinensis* Bush, but Bush described it in 1885, whereas Conrad's name goes back to 1834.

GOULD'S PANDORA *Pandora gouldiana* Dall, 1886   **Pl. 32**
    Range: Gulf of St. Lawrence to New Jersey.
    Habitat: Shallow water.
    Description: About 1 in. long. Shell irregularly wedge-shaped, rounded before, with a recurved truncate tip behind. The valves are asymmetrical, the right one flat and the left slightly convex. Exceedingly thin and flat. White or grayish white; interior pearly.
    Remarks: This is the largest and most common of the Pandoras and is not infrequently found in intertidal flats in the Northeast.

THREE-LINED PANDORA *Pandora trilineata* Say, 1822   **Pl. 32**
    Range: N. Carolina to Florida; Texas.
    Habitat: Shallow water; common.
    Description: Length about 1 in. More than twice as long as high, with a marked concave area between beaks and up-turned posterior tip. With 3 distinct lines along dorsal concavity. Color white; interior very pearly.

■ THRACIAS: Family Thraciidae

This group contains some rather large bivalves, and some that are quite small. Valves unequal and more or less gaping at each end. Beaks prominent, one commonly perforated.

● Genus *Thracia* Blainville, 1824

CONRAD'S THRACIA *Thracia conradi* Couthouy, 1838   **Pl. 32**
Range: Nova Scotia to Long Island.
Habitat: Moderately deep water.
Description: Shell oval and inflated, length up to 4 in. Beaks about central and slightly turned backward; beak of right valve perforated to receive point of left beak. Right valve larger and more convex than left and projects somewhat beyond it. Hinge toothless. Anterior end rounded, posterior bluntly pointed. Surface coarsely wrinkled by growth lines. Color dingy white, with thin brownish periostracum; interior chalky white.

■ SPOON CLAMS: Family Periplomatidae

The shells are white, small, and usually fragile. Slightly gaping, they are called spoon shells from a low, spoon-shaped tooth (chondrophore) in each valve. A small triangular prominence lying next to this structure is generally lost when the animal is removed from its shell.

● Genus *Periploma* Schumacher, 1817

FRAGILE SPOON CLAM   **Pl. 32**
Periploma fragile (Totten, 1835)
Range: Labrador to New Jersey.
Habitat: Moderately shallow water.
Description: Length about $1/2$ in. Right valve rather more concave than and projecting a little beyond the left. Somewhat oval; anterior gradually rounded, posterior narrowed and slightly truncate. An elevated angular ridge extends from beaks to posterior margin. Surface minutely wrinkled, color pearly white.

ANGULAR SPOON CLAM   Pls. 32, 37
Periploma anguliferum (Philippi, 1847)
Range: Georgia to the Florida Keys and to Texas.
Habitat: Shallow water in sand.
Description: About 1 in., oblong, white, smoothish. One end short. Hinge with a single, large, spoon-shaped tooth, or chondrophore.

UNEQUAL SPOON CLAM
Periploma margaritaceum (Lamarck, 1801)
Range: S. Carolina to Texas.
Habitat: Moderately deep water.
Description: Length about $\frac{1}{2}$ in. Front end short and abruptly rounded, posterior long and broadly rounded. Surface smooth and valves moderately inflated. Chondrophore relatively large and points backward. Color white.

LEA'S SPOON CLAM   Pl. 32
Periploma leanum (Conrad, 1831)
Range: Gulf of St. Lawrence to N. Carolina.
Habitat: Moderately shallow water.
Description: About $1\frac{1}{2}$ in. long. Left valve almost flat, right convex and somewhat truncate at posterior tip; a faint ridge proceeds from the beaks to this tip. Spoon-shaped tooth (chondrophore) nearly horizontal. Pearly white, with thin yellowish periostracum.

PAPER SPOON CLAM
Periploma papyratium (Say, 1822)
Range: Labrador to Rhode Island.
Habitat: Moderately deep water.
Description: About 1 in. long. A delicate shell with a short and angled anterior end and a long and rounded posterior end. Valves moderately inflated. Spoonlike chondrophore points downward. White, with a thin yellowish periostracum.

■ POROMYA CLAMS: Family Poromyidae

Shells small, with valves unequal. Thin, and somewhat pearly within. Surface commonly granulated. Widely distributed, chiefly in deep water.

● Genus *Poromya* Forbes, 1844

GRANULATE POROMYA
Poromya granulata (Nyst & Westendorp, 1839)
Range: Maine to the West Indies.
Habitat: Deep water.
Description: Less than $1/2$ in. long. Shell oval, moderately inflated, beaks full and centrally situated. Both ends rounded. Surface bears tiny granules but appears smooth. Color yellowish brown.

■ DIPPER SHELLS: Family Cuspidariidae

Small pear-shaped bivalves, mostly confined to deep water. They are called dipper shells from their elongated handlelike posterior end (rostrum).

● Genus *Cuspidaria* Nardo, 1848

NORTHERN DIPPER SHELL   Fig. 42
Cuspidaria glacialis (G. O. Sars, 1878)
Range: Nova Scotia to Maryland.
Habitat: Moderately deep water.
Description: About 1 in. long. Beaks high, anterior regularly rounded, posterior narrowed to form a definite "handle," but since it is not as long or as pronounced as in some of this group the shell appears to be rather squat. Color cream to white and with grayish white periostracum.
Remarks: Probably the commonest dipper shell along our coast, but not likely to be found close to shore.

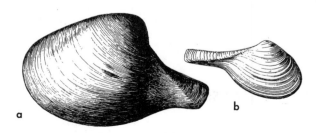

Figure 42. a) Northern Dipper Shell *Cuspidaria glacialis*
b) Rostrate Dipper Shell *Cuspidaria rostrata*

Figure 43. Costellate Dipper Shell *Cardiomya costellata*

ROSTRATE DIPPER SHELL   Fig. 42 & Pl. 37
Cuspidaria rostrata (Spengler, 1793)
 Range: Arctic Ocean to the West Indies; also Europe.
 Habitat: Deep water.
 Description: Nearly 1 in. long. Valves well inflated, anterior end sharply rounded, posterior end abruptly narrowed and drawn out to form a relatively long rostrum ("handle"). Surface bears delicate lines of growth which form strong wrinkles on rostrum. Color yellowish white; interior shiny white.

● Genus *Cardiomya* A. Adams, 1864

COSTELLATE DIPPER SHELL   Fig. 43 & Pl. 23
Cardiomya costellata (Deshayes, 1837)
 Range: Off N. Carolina to the West Indies.
 Habitat: Deep water.
 Description: Length ¼ in. A small shell, beaks nearly central. Front end regularly rounded, posterior end produced into a narrow rostrum. A series of strong radiating ribs decorate the front half of shell, which is scalloped at the margin. Surface shiny, color bluish white.

■ VERTICORDS: Family Verticordiidae

These are mostly small mollusks, very pearly inside. The valves are equal or nearly so, well inflated, and quite solid in substance. Chiefly dwellers in deep water.

● **Genus** *Verticordia* **Sowerby, 1844**

ORNATE VERTICORD   **Fig. 44**
Verticordia ornata (Orbigny, 1842)
Range: Massachusetts to the West Indies.
Habitat: Deep water.
Description: Length ¼ in. Beaks hooked forward, front end short and acutely rounded. Front half of shell sculptured with strong radiating folds that make that margin crenulate; longer posterior portion smooth. Valves considerably compressed. Color dull yellowish gray; interior very pearly.

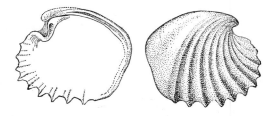

Figure 44. Ornate Verticord *Verticordia ornata*

2

CLASS GASTROPODA: UNIVALVES

Mollusks usually producing a single, calcareous shell, either coiled or cup-shaped. Rarely, as in the nudibranch seaslugs, without a shell. The head, bearing two ocular tentacles, is fused to a flattish, muscular ventral foot. A ribbon of radular teeth is present in the majority of forms. The various organs, such as the gills, anus and kidney exit-tubes, face forward instead of backward, because of torsion or twisting that always takes place in the early embryonic stage. There are about 60,000 species living in marine waters, 2,500 freshwater dwellers and about 24,000 kinds of air-breathing, terrestrial snails.

SUBCLASS PROSOBRANCHIA

■ SLIT-SHELLS: Family Pleurotomariidae

Although not likely to be personally collected by the average shell collector, a few of the primitive deep-water species are included because they sometimes come into specimen trade circles from those who dredge or scuba-dive in deep water. Four of the dozen known species are found in east American waters. These handsome, colorful shells are characterized by a narrow, open slit in the last part of the body whorl, through which water passes between two internal gills. The opercular trap door, attached to the upper part of the posterior end of the foot, is circular, thin, brown, chitinous, and has many whorls.

● **Genus *Perotrochus* P. Fischer, 1885**

LOVELY SLIT-SHELL   **Pl. 39**
Perotrochus amabilis (F. M. Bayer, 1963)
   Range: Gulf of Mexico and off Key West, Florida.
   Habitat: Deep water on submarine walls.
   Description: Adults from 3 to 3¹/₂ in., brightly colored with ax-
ial flames of reddish brown, some of which extend over the
base of the shell which has about 26 weak threads. Umbili-
cus slightly indented. Slit ¹/₄ whorl long. Rare.

QUOY'S SLIT-SHELL   **Fig. 45**
Perotrochus quoyanus (Fischer & Bernardi, 1857)
   Range: Gulf of Mexico; West Indies; Bermuda
   Habitat: Deep water, from 70 to 330 feet.
   Description: Shell pyramidal in shape; about 2 inches in length
and width. Umbilicus sealed over. Sculpture of finely
beaded, small spiral threads. The peripheral slit on the last
whorl is rather short and wide. Color orange-yellow; base
white.

Figure 45. Quoy's Slit-shell *Perotrochus quoyanus*

MAURER'S SLIT-SHELL   Pl. 39
Perotrochus maureri (Harasewych & Askew, 1993)
   Range: Off the Carolinas to northeast Florida.
   Habitat: Upper continental shelf at down to about 1,300 feet.;
   hard bottom.
   Description: Length about 2 inches, thin-shelled, without an
   umbilicus. Slit narrow, running back from the apertural edge
   about $1/8$ of the last whorl. Spire slightly concave. About 19
   fine, spiral cords on the base of the shell (whereas *P. amabilis* has 24 to 31). Color ivory with crowded, axial flames
   of brick red. Aperture iridescent. Operuclum multispiral,
   half the size of the aperture, corneous and thin.
   Remarks: Named after Richard S. Maurer, who financed the
   hall of shells at the Fernbank Museum of Natural History in
   Atlanta, Georgia. This rare species resembles *P. amabilis* but
   is smaller, has a lower spire and has fewer spiral cords on the
   base. Some workers consider this a northern subspecies of *P.
   amabilis* of the Gulf of Mexico.

CHARLESTON SLIT-SHELL   Pl. 39
Perotrochus charlestonensis (Askew, 1988)
   Range: Off the coast of South Carolina.
   Habitat: Rubble rock bottom to a depth of about 650 feet.
   Description: Shell $3^{1}/_{2}$ in., broadly turbiniform, very thin-
   shelled, fragile; spire angle 89 degrees. Slit short. Color
   creamy white with diffuse brownish orange axial streaks and
   blotches. Spiral threads very fine and numerous, with 40 on
   the base of the shell. Operculum, multispiral, translucent,
   brownish yellow.

●**Genus *Entemnotrochus* P. Fischer, 1885**

ADANSON'S SLIT-SHELL   Pl. 39
Entemnotrochus adansonianus (Crosse & Fischer, 1861)
   Range: Off Key West and the West Indies; Florida.
   Habitat: Deep water (300 to 1,000 feet).
   Description: Up to 7 in. Umbilicus round, very deep. Slit on
   periphery of whorl narrow and very long ($1/2$ of a whorl).
   Color cream to salmon with irregular, small patches of red.
   Remarks: This is the largest Atlantic Slit-shell and the first
   to be discovered. It lives on firm bottoms at 300 to 600 feet
   of water and has been obtained by scuba divers as well as
   submersible vehicles. A smaller, but very similar, subspecies

was described from Bermuda, *E. adansonianus bermudensis* Okutani and Goto, 1983.

■ ABALONES: Family Haliotidae

Shells spiral, depressed, spire small. Body whorl constitutes most of the shell. There is a row of round or oval holes along the left margin, those near the edge open. Interior pearly and often multicolored. Animals live attached to rocks like limpets. All are edible. Common in Pacific and Indian oceans, also European waters; only 1 species, exceedingly rare, known to live on our Atlantic Coast.

●Genus *Haliotis* Linnaeus, 1758

POURTALÈS ABALONE *Haliotis pourtalesii* Dall, 1881   **Pl. 40**
Range: Off Florida Keys to Texas and to Brazil.
Habitat: Deep water.
Description: Length about 1 in. About 3 whorls, spire low. Margin shows 5 open holes. Sculpture consists of rather strong wavy ridges that follow the curvature of the volutions. Color yellowish brown, with patches of orange on last (body) whorl; interior pearly white.
Remarks: A single specimen, less than 1 in. long, was dredged (alive) by Count Louis François de Pourtalès in 1869. It was taken in 1,200 ft. off s. Florida. This shell, along with much other dredged material, was sent to Dr. William Stimpson in Chicago, who was at that time engaged in a monumental work on East Coast mollusks; the whole collection, including Stimpson's notes and manuscript, was destroyed in the great Chicago fire of 1871. The unique abalone was described by William H. Dall about ten years later, working entirely from memory. Forty-two years later a second specimen was collected off Sand Key, Florida. Several imperfect shells or fragments have been taken since, including one nearly perfect example from off Key Largo in 1944. This would certainly rate as one of our rarest marine shells, and for a complete discussion of its interesting history the reader is referred to *Johnsonia*, Vol. 2, No. 21 (1946), from which this brief account has been condensed.

■ KEYHOLE LIMPETS: Family Fissurellidae

Shells conical, oval at base. The apex is perforated, or there is a slit, or notch, in the margin of the shell. Surface usually strongly ribbed. The slit ("keyhole") distinguishes these snails from the true limpets. When very young, they have a spiral shell with a marginal slit. Shelly material is added slowly until the margin below the slit is united, and then the spiral is absorbed as the hole enlarges. Distributed in warm and temperate seas as a rule.

● Genus *Fissurella* Bruguière, 1789

POINTED KEYHOLE LIMPET   Pl. 40
Fissurella angusta (Gmelin, 1791)
  Range: Florida Keys to British Guiana.
  Habitat: Intertidal.
  Description: About ³/₄ in. long. Rather flattish, somewhat pointed in front. Sculpture of about 10 rather nodulous ribs. Color whitish, with reddish brown blotches; interior greenish, pale brown around orifice.

BARBADOS KEYHOLE LIMPET   Pl. 40
Fissurella barbadensis (Gmelin, 1791)
  Range: South Florida to Brazil; Bermuda.
  Habitat: Intertidal on shore rocks.
  Description: Length about 1 in. Solid, conical, highly elevated, with round or oval orifice at top. Surface rough, with a heavy assortment of radiating ribs that project at the margins and give the shell a scalloped edge. Variable in color, generally some shade of gray, green, or pink, with brown blotches; interior usually has alternating rings of dull green and white.

WOBBLY KEYHOLE LIMPET   Pl. 40
Fissurella fascicularis Lamarck, 1822
  Range: Southeast Florida to the West Indies.
  Habitat: Intertidal in shore rock pools.
  Description: Length ³/₄ in. Rather flat. Base oval, front and back ends raised noticeably. Apex opening somewhat long and narrow, with a small notch on each side at center which forms a cross. Sculpture of numerous radiating ribs. Color

superficially a faded magenta, with a few reddish rays near the perforation; interior white, pinkish around orifice.

Remarks: When placed on a level surface, the shell rests only upon the middle of each side, like rockers.

KNOBBY KEYHOLE LIMPET   Pl. 40
Fissurella nodosa (Born, 1778)

Range: Southeast Florida to the West Indies.

Habitat: Intertidal on shore rocks.

Description: About 1 in. long. Moderately elevated, with elongated opening at summit. Sculptured with 20 or so radiating ribs that bear nodules concentrically arranged. Base broadly oval, margins deeply scalloped. Color may be white, brown, gray, or pinkish; interior white.

ROSY KEYHOLE LIMPET   Pl. 40
Fissurella rosea (Gmelin, 1791)

Range: Southeast Florida to the West Indies.

Habitat: Intertidal.

Description: Length about 1 in. Shell conical but rather flat, the summit bearing a small, usually round opening. Marginal outline egg-shaped, the front end narrower. Sculpture of close, unequal radiating lines. Color variable, commonly delicate pink with paler rays, but some individuals are deep pink or purple; interior greenish at margins, white at center, often with pinkish around orifice.

●Genus *Diodora* Gray, 1821

CAYENNE KEYHOLE LIMPET   Pl. 40
Diodora cayenensis (Lamarck, 1822)

Range: Maryland and south; Gulf of Mexico; West Indies and south to Brazil.

Habitat: Intertidal.

Description: Length 1 to $1^{1}/_{2}$ in. Shell moderately solid and highly elevated, with elongated hole at summit. Surface sculptured with numerous sharp and distinct radiating lines (every 4th one larger) and wrinkled by growth lines. Margins finely crenulate. Usually white but may be buff, pink, or dark gray; interior white or bluish gray.

Remarks: Formerly listed as *D. alternata* (Say, 1822). In the genus *Diodora* the orifice is bordered on the inside by a deep notch toward the front.

DYSON'S KEYHOLE LIMPET   Pl. 40
Diodora dysoni (Reeve, 1850)
Range: Florida to Brazil; Bermuda.
Habitat: Shallow water in reefs under rocks.
Description: Length about ¹/₂ in. Base oval, the ends somewhat pointed. Not highly elevated; perforation small, triangular as a rule and not far from middle of shell. Small knob behind orifice. Surface with strong radiating ribs, usually 3 small ones between each larger rib. Color white, with broad bands of black.

LISTER'S KEYHOLE LIMPET   Pl. 40
Diodora listeri (Orbigny 1842)
Range: Bermuda; Florida to the West Indies; Brazil.
Habitat: Intertidal; common.
Description: Length about 1¹/₂ in. Shell solid, oval, highly elevated. Apex slightly in front of middle of shell, with slitlike opening. Surface has alternating large and small ribs crossed by strong cordlike lines. Margins scalloped. Color white or buff, sometimes with darker rays; interior white.

MINUTE KEYHOLE LIMPET   Pl. 40
Diodora minuta (Lamarck, 1822)
Range: South Florida to Brazil.
Habitat: Intertidal; uncommon.
Description: Length about ¹/₂ in. Shell well arched, elongated, apex closer to front end. Sides slightly raised, so shell rests on its ends. Surface ornamented with beaded ridges that radiate from the summit. Color white, blotched or rayed with brown or black; interior white, with black ring around orifice.
Remarks: *Diodora variegata* Sowerby, 1862, is a synonym.

GREEN KEYHOLE LIMPET   Pl. 40
Diodora viridula (Lamarck, 1822)
Range: South Florida; Caribbean islands to Trinidad.
Habitat: Intertidal on rocks.
Description: Length about 1 in. Moderately arched, orifice elongated, situated closer to front end. Strong radiating ribs that are white, with smaller greenish ribs between. Interior white. Black stain around perforation, inside and outside.

●Genus *Lucapina* Sowerby, 1835

SOWERBY'S FLESHY LIMPET   **Pl. 40**
Lucapina sowerbii (Sowerby, 1835)
   Range: South Florida; West Indies south to Brazil.
   Habitat: Intertidal.
   Description: Length 3/4 in. An elongated shell with rounded
   ends and straight sides. Apex only slightly raised, shell moderately elevated. Perforation large and rounded, set close to
   anterior end. Surface bears alternating large and small ribs
   that are crossed by numerous concentric lines. Color white
   to buff, blotched with brown; interior white, no ring around
   orifice.
   Remarks: Formerly listed as *L. adspersa* (Philippi, 1845).

CANCELLATE FLESHY LIMPET   **Pls. 7, 40**
Lucapina suffusa (Reeve, 1850)
   Range: Florida to the West Indies.
   Habitat: Intertidal.
   Description: Length about 1 in. Shell conical, somewhat depressed, oval. Summit with round orifice, slightly ahead of
   middle of shell. Surface ornamented by strong radiating
   ribs, alternating in size and cancelled by regular, concentric ridges. Color buffy or white; interior white, with bluish
   ring around orifice.
   Remarks: Formerly listed as *L. cancellata* (Sowerby, 1862).

●Genus *Lucapinella* Pilsbry, 1890

FILE FLESHY LIMPET   **Pl. 40**
Lucapinella limatula (Reeve, 1850)
   Range: N. Carolina to Brazil.
   Habitat: Moderately deep water.
   Description: Length 1/2 to 3/4 in. Shell oval, only moderately elevated; orifice near center and large, often somewhat triangular. Sculpture of alternating larger and smaller radiating
   ribs, made scaly by concentric wrinkles. Color brownish,
   with spotted whitish rays; interior white.

●Genus *Emarginula* Lamarck, 1801

PYGMY EMARGINULA   **Pl. 40**
Emarginula pumila (A. Adams, 1851)
   Range: Southeast Florida to Brazil; Bermuda.
   Habitat: Shallow water.
   Description: Length about ¹/₂ in. Base oval, shell well arched,
   apex pointing backward. A very small slit at anterior margin.
   Sculpture of 11 to 13 radiating ribs and rather strong concen-
   tric lines. Color yellowish to whitish, darker between ribs;
   interior with greenish rays.
   Remarks: A similar species, *E. dentigera* Heilprin, 1889, from
   Bermuda and the Lower Florida Keys is smaller (7 mm.),
   whitish to greenish, high-spired, with 18 to 26 radial riblets.
   It is a fairly common littoral species.

●Genus *Hemitoma* Swainson, 1840

EMARGINATE LIMPET   **Pl. 40**
Hemitoma emarginata (Blainville, 1825)
   Range: Florida Keys to the West Indies.
   Habitat: Moderately deep water.
   Description: Length ³/₄ to 1 in. A highly elevated, caplike shell,
   the apex strongly curved backward. Small slit at anterior
   margin when young. Sculpture of concentric threads and radiating lines. Base oval, front end truncated and provided
   with a sharp notch. Color whitish; interior pale green.

EIGHT-RIBBED LIMPET   **Pl. 40**
Hemitoma octoradiata (Gmelin, 1791)
   Range: Florida Keys to the West Indies.
   Habitat: Shallow water.
   Description: Length 1 in. Shell solid, flattened to moderately
   arched. Apex closer to anterior, and only slightly curved
   backward. Ornamentation of 8 nodular ribs, with smaller
   lines between. Very small notch at front end. Color grayish
   white; interior grayish green, commonly with a darker zone
   near the rim.

●Genus *Puncturella* Lowe, 1827

LINNÉ'S PUNCTURELLA   **Pl. 41**
Puncturella noachina (Linnaeus, 1771)
   Range: Circumpolar; Arctic Ocean to Massachusetts.

Habitat: Shallow to deep water.
Description: About $^1/_2$ in. long. Steeply conical, with oval base, laterally compressed. Sharply pointed apex; just in front of tip is a narrow slit. Sculpture of rather sharp radiating ribs. Color dull white.
Remarks: Sometimes listed as *P. princeps* (Mighels & Adams).

■ LIMPETS: Family Acmaeidae

Shells conical, oval, open at base. There is no opening at the summit. Not spiral at any stage of growth. Mollusks of the shore region, adhering to rocks and grasses. Most Atlantic species were formerly put in the genus *Acmaea*.

● Genus *Lottia* Gray, 1833

SOUTHERN LIMPET *Lottia antillarum* (Sowerby, 1831)   **Pl. 41**
   Range: South Florida to the West Indies.
   Habitat: Intertidal.
   Description: About $^3/_4$ in. long. Rather flat, base oval, apex closer to front end. Gray or buff, with narrow black lines radiating from apex which sometimes combine to form broad rays; interior polished, bluish gray, with broadly checked border.
   Remarks: Formerly listed as *A. candeana* (Orbigny, 1845).

BLACK-RIBBED LIMPET   **Pl. 41**
Lottia leucopleura (Gmelin, 1791)
   Range: South Florida to the West Indies.
   Habitat: Intertidal; commonly on large snail shells.
   Description: Length $^1/_2$ to $^3/_4$ in. Roundish, well elevated at summit. Shell marked with radiating black lines on white background. Apex generally eroded. Interior white with a checkered rim, and the callus presents an arrow-shaped design in dark brown.
   Remarks: Synonyms are *jamaicensis* and *albicosta* C. B. Adams, 1845.

SPOTTED LIMPET *Lottia pustulata* (Helbling, 1779)   **Pl. 41**
   Range: South Florida to the West Indies; Bermuda.
   Habitat: Intertidal.
   Description: About $^3/_4$ in. long. A heavy, oval, thick shell with

parallel sides; only moderately arched. Apex nearly central. Surface decorated with coarse radiating ribs (few) and sometimes by weak concentric lines. Color yellowish white, usually with reddish specks; interior polished white, callus yellowish.

Remarks: The small form living on turtle grass leaves is very thin, light rose in color (or opaque white with two side brown rays), with a tiny sharp apex, and is occasionally flecked with red. Called the form *pulcherrima* Petit, 1846.

ATLANTIC PLATE LIMPET   Pl. 41
Lottia testudinalis (Müller, 1776)

Range: Arctic Ocean to New York.

Habitat: Shallow water; on rocks.

Description: Averages about 1 in. long, but some specimens may be close to 2 in. Shell conical, oblong-oval, moderately arched. Surface relatively smooth, color bluish white, checkered with dark brown marks radiating from the summit. Interior dark glossy brown, with a checkered gray and brown border; central area and border separated by a paler band.

Remarks: The largest specimens are found in the vicinity of Eastport, Maine. The Eelgrass Limpet, *A. t. alveus* (Conrad, 1831), is a form that lives on the narrow leaves of eelgrass instead of on rocks. It is smaller — seldom more than $1/2$ in. long — well arched, and has parallel sides; often is boldly checkered with yellowish or whitish dots, which are sometimes plainer on inside of shell than on outside. This form may be found from Maine to Connecticut.

■ BLIND LIMPETS: Family Lepetidae

Shells small, oval, somewhat depressed. Apex nearly central. Distributed chiefly in cold seas and moderately deep water.

●Genus *Lepeta* Gray, 1842

NORTHERN BLIND LIMPET   Pl. 41
Lepeta caeca (Müller, 1776)

Range: Greenland to Massachusetts; Alaska to Washington.

Habitat: Moderately deep water.

Description: About $1/4$ in. long. Oval, conical, but not highly arched. Numerous minute radiating lines, crossed by equally fine concentric lines. The resulting sculpture, when viewed under a lens, is a distinct network. Color white or grayish white, inside and outside.

■ PEARLY TOP SHELLS: Family Trochidae

Herbivorous snails, widely distributed in warm and cold seas, living among seaweeds in shallow water, and upon wave-washed rocks. The shells are composed largely of iridescent nacre, although the pearly luster may be concealed by pigmentation of various colors on the outer surface. They vary in shape but are commonly pyramidal. The operculum is thin and horny.

●Genus *Margarites* Gray, 1847

NORTHERN ROSY MARGARITE Fig. 46 & Pl. 43
Margarites costalis (Gould, 1841)
  Range: Greenland to Massachusetts; Alaska.
  Habitat: Moderately shallow water.
  Description: About ⅓ in. high. Shell thin and of depressed conical shape, with from 5 to 7 whorls, made angular by prominent revolving ridges. Umbilicus broad and deep. Aperture circular, with sharp outer lip. Color ashy white, sometimes tinged with green.
  Remarks: Formerly known as *cinereus* (Couthouy, 1838), not Born, 1778.

Figure 46. Northern Rosy Margarite *Margarites costalis*

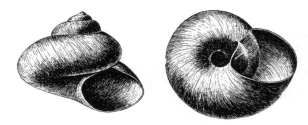

Figure 47. Greenland Margarite *Margarites groenlandicus*

Figure 48. Smooth Margarite *Margarites helicinus*

GREENLAND MARGARITE
Fig. 47 & Pl. 43

Margarites groenlandicus (Gmelin, 1791)
Range: Greenland to Massachusetts.
Habitat: Moderately shallow water.
Description: Height $^1/_3$ in., diameter about $^1/_2$ in. With 4 or 5 whorls, somewhat flattened above and undulated near sutures by short folds or wrinkles. Shell thin but strong, sculptured by numerous revolving lines. Umbilicus broad and funnel-shaped, operculum thin and horny. Color dull reddish brown; aperture pearly.

SMOOTH MARGARITE
Fig. 48 & Pl. 43

Margarites helicinus (Phipps, 1774)
Range: Greenland to Massachusetts.
Habitat: Moderately shallow water.
Description: Diameter about $^1/_2$ in. With 4 whorls; body whorl relatively large. Sutures well impressed. Surface smooth and shining, color pale yellowish or horn colored, often with iridescent sheen.

Remarks: This little snail lives on eelgrass and other marine vegetation, well below the low-water level. After storms they may be found clinging to plants that have been torn from their moorings and cast up on the beach.

●Genus *Solariella* Wood, 1842

CHANNELED TOP SHELL
Solariella lacunella (Dall, 1881)
  Range: Virginia to Florida.
  Habitat: Moderately deep water.
  Description: Height about ¼ in. Some 5 whorls, with fine revolving lines, those on the shoulders beaded. Sutures rather deeply channeled. Aperture circular, umbilicus small. Color white or pale pearly gray.

OBSCURE TOP SHELL   Fig. 49
Solariella obscura (Couthouy, 1838)
  Range: Labrador to Virginia.
  Habitat: Moderately deep water.
  Description: Height ¼ in., diameter about the same. Whorls (5) slightly angular because of single beaded line at shoulders. Umbilicus open but small, aperture circular. Color gray, often with pinkish tint.

LITTLE RIDGED TOP SHELL   Fig. 50
Solariella varicosa (Mighels & Adams, 1842)
  Range: Labrador to Maine.
  Habitat: Moderately deep water.
  Description: Height ¼ in. With 4 or 5 whorls, fairly well-elevated spire. Aperture round, lip thin and sharp. Small but deep umbilicus. Volutions decorated with distinct vertical folds. Color deep gray.

Figure 49. Obscure Top Shell *Solariella obscura*

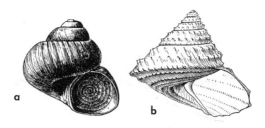

Figure 50. a) Little Ridged Top Shell *Solariella varicosa*
b) Otto's Spiny Margarite *Lischkeia ottoi*

●**Genus *Lischkeia* Fischer, 1879**

OTTO'S SPINY MARGARITE   **Fig. 50**
Lischkeia ottoi (Philippi, 1844)
  Range: Newfoundland to N. Carolina.
  Habitat: Moderately deep water.
  Description: Height about ³/₄ in. Stoutly top-shaped, with 5
rounded whorls tapering to a sharp apex. Aperture large and
nearly round, lip thin and sharp. Deep umbilicus. Each volution with sharp revolving spines on lower portion and
strongly beaded lines on upperpart. Color creamy white,
with pearly iridescence.
  Remarks: A handsome shell, seldom seen in collections. It
used to be known as *Margarites regalis* Verrill & Smith.

●**Genus *Synaptocochlea* Pilsbry, 1890**

PAINTED FALSE STOMATELLA
Synoptocochlea picta (Orbigny, 1842)
  Range: Bermuda; Florida; West Indies.
  Habitat: Moderately shallow water.
  Description: About ¹/₄ in. long. Only 2 or 3 whorls and mostly
all body whorl. Apex short, aperture large and flaring. Sculp-
ture of weak revolving lines. Color white, blotched with red-
dish brown. Columella white.

● Genus *Calliostoma* Swainson, 1840

ADELE'S TOP SHELL   Pl. 41
Calliostoma adelae Schwengel, 1951
   Range: Southeast Florida.
   Habitat: Moderately shallow water.
   Description: About ³/₄ in. high. Top-shaped, solid; 8 to 10 flat-sided whorls. Apex pointed. Volutions with beaded revolving lines, 2 larger ridgelike lines at suture, giving the shell a keeled appearance. Narrow umbilicus. Color pale brown, mottled with white.

SCULPTURED TOP SHELL   Pl. 41
Calliostoma euglyptum (A. Adams, 1854)
   Range: Cape Hatteras to Mexico.
   Habitat: Shallow water.
   Description: Strong and solid, height about 1 in. Top-shaped, apex well elevated, base flat. With 5 or 6 whorls, sutures rather indistinct. Ornamentation consists of revolving rows of beads. Columella oblique, thickened at base. Color dingy white, mottled with reds and browns.

CHOCOLATE-LINED TOP SHELL   Pl. 41
Calliostoma javanicum (Lamarck, 1822)
   Range: South Florida to the West Indies.
   Habitat: Moderately shallow water.
   Description: About 1¹/₄ in. high. Solid, top-shaped. With 9 or 10 flat-sided whorls, with sharp peripheral keel. Sutures indistinct. Sculpture of fine beaded ridges. Columella arched and twisted, umbilicus funnel-shaped. Color pale brownish, mottled with reds and orange.

JUBJUBE TOP SHELL   Pl. 41
Calliostoma jujubinum (Gmelin, 1791)
   Range: Cape Hatteras to Brazil.
   Habitat: Shallow water.
   Description: Height 1 in. Robust and conical, apex acutely pointed. With 8 to 10 whorls, sutures indistinct. Surface sculptured with revolving cords, those on the shoulders broken into beads. Umbilicus narrow and funnel-like. Color brownish with gray and white streaks.

NORTH ATLANTIC TOP SHELL   Pl. 41
Calliostoma occidentale (Mighels & Adams, 1842)
   Range: Nova Scotia to Massachusetts; Europe.

Habitat: Moderately shallow water.
Description: About $1^{1}/_{2}$ in. high, diameter about the same. Shell thin, acutely pointed, with flattened base. With 5 or 6 whorls, encircled by strong revolving ridges, the uppermost broken into a series of disjointed dots. Outer lip thin and made wavy by terminating ridges. No umbilicus. Creamy white to pearly white; aperture iridescent.

BEAUTIFUL TOP SHELL   Pl. 41
Calliostoma pulchrum (C. B. Adams, 1850)
   Range: N. Carolina to the West Indies.
   Habitat: Moderately shallow water, from 6 to 1,200 feet.
   Description: About $^{3}/_{4}$ in. high. Top-shaped, with flat sides. With 8 to 10 whorls, with angled keel at periphery. Sutures indistinct. Sculpture of finely beaded revolving lines. Color mottled with small reddish brown spots, rather evenly spaced, and with wavy vertical streaks of grayish.

● **Genus** *Cittarium* **Philippi, 1847**

WEST INDIAN TOP SHELL   Pl. 42
Cittarium pica (Linnaeus, 1758)
   Range: West Indies; rarely on lower Florida Keys.
   Habitat: Shallow water.
   Description: Height about 4 in. Large, solid, top-shaded. With 5 or 6 whorls and moderately sharp apex. Surface irregular, umbilicus deep, aperture roundish. Operculum leathery, with numerous whorls. Color dark green, heavily splashed with white zigzag markings.
   Remarks: This large and showy species is found as a dead shell in s. Florida. It is frequently found in old Indian shell heaps along the Florida coast, suggesting that the species may have been abundant on our shores in the past. It occurs quite commonly as a Pleistocene fossil in Florida and Bermuda. The shell is very pearly, and when the outer layer has been removed it can be given a high polish. Until recently it was listed as *Livona pica*.

●Genus *Tegula* **Lesson, 1832**

GREEN-BASE TEGULA   **Pl. 41**
Tegula excavata (Lamarck, 1822)
  Range: Southeast Florida to the West Indies.
  Habitat: Shallow water.
  Description: About ³/₄ in. high. With 4 or 5 flattish whorls,
  with no shoulders, but with sharply delineated sutures. Base
  concave. Aperture rather small, with umbilicus distinct.
  Color purplish brown or black, but most specimens are
  eroded in places to show the pearly layer. The excavated
  base and aperture often are greenish.

SMOOTH TEGULA *Tegula fasciata* (Born, 1778)   **Pl. 41**
  Range: South Florida to Brazil.
  Habitat: Shallow water.
  Description: About ¹/₂ in. high. Shell roundly pyramidal, consisting of 4 or 5 whorls, with smooth, sometimes shiny surface. Aperture oval, feebly toothed within, and there may be
  2 teeth at base of columella. White callus may extend partially over umbilicus. Operculum thin and horny. Color
  grayish pink, rather heavily mottled and marked with
  brownish or black. There is commonly a paler band on body
  whorl.

WEST INDIAN TEGULA   **Pl. 41**
Tegula lividomaculata (C. B. Adams, 1845)
  Range: Florida Keys to the West Indies.
  Habitat: Shallow water.
  Description: Height ³/₄ in., with 5 or 6 rather rounded whorls
  decorated with distinct revolving lines that are weakly
  beaded. Sutures well impressed. Deep umbilicus bordered
  by a pair of strong lines, or ridges. Aperture oval, operculum
  horny. Color gray, somewhat mottled with reds and blacks.
  Remarks: Formerly listed as *T. scalaris* Anton, 1844.

■ **TURBANS: Family Turbinidae**

  Shells generally heavy and solid, turbinate (top-shaped), and
  commonly brightly colored with pearly underlayers. The
  surface may be smooth, wrinkled, or spiny. There is a heavy

calcareous operculum, and no umbilicus as a rule. These are herbivorous gastropods, native to tropic seas throughout the world. Many are used for ornamental purposes. The famous cat's-eye of s. Pacific island jewelry is the colorful, shelly operculum of a member of this family (*Turbo petholatus* Linnaeus, 1758).

●**Genus *Arene* H. & A. Adams, 1854**

STAR ARENE *Arene cruentata* (Mühlfeld, 1829)   **Pl. 47**
   Range: Southeast Florida to the West Indies.
   Habitat: Shallow water.
   Description: About ¼ in. high, diameter ½ in. With 4 or 5 sharply angled whorls, each with a series of prominent triangular spines at the periphery. Spire low, aperture round, umbilicus small but deep. Color white, variously marked with red and brown.

GEM ARENE *Arene tricarinata* (Steams, 1872)
   Range: N. Carolina to the West Indies.
   Habitat: Shallow water.
   Description: Height ⅛ in. With 3 or 4 whorls, low spire, distinct sutures. Sculpture of 3 revolving ridges, beaded at the shoulders. Aperture round, umbilicus deep. Color whitish, blotched with reddish.
   Remarks: Formerly listed as *Liotia gemma* Toumey & Holmes, 1856.

●**Genus *Cyclostrema* Marryat, 1818**

CANCELLATE CYCLOSTREME   **Fig. 51**
Cyclostrema cancellatum Marryat, 1818
   Range: Southeast Florida to Brazil.
   Habitat: Shallow to moderately deep water.
   Description: Diameter ½ in., flat-topped, opaque white, and with a wide, deep umbilicus. Periphery squarish. Nodulose sculpture.
   Remarks: An uncommon species, usually found in small crevices or caves.

Figure 51. Cancellate Cyclostreme *Cyclostrema cancellatum*

●**Genus *Turbo* Linnaeus, 1758**

CHANNELED TURBAN   **Pl. 42**
Turbo canaliculatus Hermann, 1781
    Range: Southeast Florida to the West Indies.
    Habitat: Shallow water off the edges of reefs.
    Description: Height 2 to 3 in. About 5 well-rounded whorls, each sculptured on its upper half by deeply incised revolving lines. Aperture round, outer lip sharp, no umbilicus. Thick, round, calcareous operculum. A deep, smooth channel at suture. Surface smooth, often polished. Color greenish yellow, usually mottled and checked with green and brown; aperture pearly.
    Remarks: Formerly listed as *T. spenglerianus* Gmelin, 1791.

KNOBBY TURBAN *Turbo castaneus* Gmelin, 1791   **Pl. 42**
    Range: N. Carolina to Texas; West Indies.
    Habitat: Shallow water.
    Description: Height about 1½ in. Shell solid and roundly top-shaped, apex rather sharply pointed. With 5 or 6 whorls, decorated with revolving ridges of beads, those on the shoulders more pronounced. Aperture large and round, reflecting somewhat on columella. Operculum thick and calcareous. Color buffy brown, more or less blotched with darker brown; occasional specimens may be dull greenish.

FILOSE TURBAN   **Pls. 7, 42**
Turbo cailletii Fischer & Bernardi, 1856
    Range: Southeast Florida and the West Indies.
    Habitat: Offshore near coral reefs.
    Description: Length ¾ in., with a dozen, smooth spiral cords. Color bright red, rarely golden-yellow. Slightly umbilicate. Operculum shelly.
    Remarks: Formerly *T. filosus* Wood, 1828.

● Genus *Astraea* Röding, 1798

AMERICAN STAR-SHELL   Pl. 42
Astraea americana (Gmelin, 1791)
Range: Florida to the West Indies.
Habitat: Shallow water.
Description: About 1 in. high. With 7 or 8 whorls, apex bluntly
pointed. Solid and stony, with well-elevated spire. Volutions
decorated with vertical folds that terminate in knobs on the
shoulders. Outer lip crenulate, operculum calcareous. Color
greenish or grayish white.

CARVED STAR-SHELL   Pl. 42
Astraea caelata (Gmelin, 1791)
Range: South Florida to the West Indies.
Habitat: Shallow water.
Description: About 3 in. high. A large species, rugged and conical, sculptured with a series of strong, oblique ribs that become tubular at the periphery, and with equally prominent
revolving ribs. With 6 or 7 whorls. Aperture large and oblique, columella somewhat curved. Heavy calcareous operculum, dull white and finely pustulate. Color greenish
white, mottled with reds and brown.

LONG-SPINED STAR-SHELL   Pl. 42
Astraea phoebia Röding, 1798
Range: South Florida to the West Indies.
Habitat: Shallow water in grassy areas.
Description: Height about 1 in., diameter 2 in. or more. Shell
strong and solid, spire very low, base flat. With 6 or 7 whorls,
the margins sharply keeled. Ornamentation consists of a
series of triangular sawlike spines that project beyond the
periphery of shell. Color iridescent silvery white.
Remarks: Formerly listed as *A. longispina* (Lamarck, 1822).
The silvery color and ornate appearance make it a great favorite with collectors and manufacturers of shell jewelry,
but empty shells left on the beach soon lose their luster.
There is considerable variation in the length of the spines,
and those with short spines are often labeled *A. brevispina*
(Lamarck, 1822), but that name belongs to a West Indian
snail (Short-spined Star Shell) characterized by a small patch
of bright orange at the umbilicus.

GREEN STAR-SHELL *Astraea tuber* (Linnaeus, 1767)   Pl. 42
Range: Southeast Florida to the West Indies.
Habitat: Shallow water.

Description: About 2 in. high. A rugged and solid shell of about 5 whorls. Sculptured with strong obliquely vertical ribs swollen at the base and shoulders to present a double row of nodes on each volution. No umbilicus, operculum calcareous. Color green, with the pearly layer generally showing through in several places, especially at apex. Aperture very pearly, and there is a broad pearly area on the inner lip.

■ PHEASANT SHELLS: Family Phasianellidae

The shell is fairly high-spired, graceful in shape, porcelaneous, and shining. There is no periostracum. Tropical species attain a height of 2 or 3 inches and are among our most showy shells, usually brightly colored with pinks and browns. Only a few members of this family occur on our shores, and they all are small. The operculum is usually shelly, white, and smooth.

● Genus *Tricolia* Risso, 1826

CHECKERED PHEASANT SHELL   Pl. 43
Tricolia affinis (C. B. Adams, 1850)
   Range: Southeast Florida to the West Indies.
   Habitat: Shallow water.
   Description: About 1/4 in. high. With 4 or 5 whorls, the spire tapering gradually to a blunt apex. Sutures distinct. Surface polished. Color pale buff or gray, variously checkered and spotted with pink and reddish brown and often with a narrow encircling band of yellow or orange on body whorl.

UMBILICATE PHEASANT SHELL   Pl. 43
Tricolia thalassicola Robertson, 1958
   Range: Off N. Carolina and south through West Indies to Brazil.
   Habitat: Shallow water in turtle grass.
   Description: Height 1/4 in. With 5 whorls, sutures well impressed. Apex blunt. Tiny chinklike umbilicus. Shell polished, color creamy white, checkered and flecked with red and gray.
   Remarks: Formerly listed as *Phasianella umbilicata* Orbigny, 1842.

■ NERITES: Family Neritidae

Small, usually bright-colored shells, mostly globular in shape, and commonly with toothed apertures. They inhabit warm countries, where they are often found abundantly in shallow seas, in brackish waters, in fresh water, and in some cases even on dry land. The shelly operculum has a small, pointed hook at one end.

●Genus *Nerita* Linnaeus, 1758

ANTILLEAN NERITE *Nerita fulgurans* Gmelin, 1791   **Pl. 44**
Range: South Florida to the West Indies; Bermuda.
Habitat: Shallow, brackish water.
Description: Height about $^3/_4$ in., diameter about 1 in. With 4 or 5 whorls, little or no spire. Sculpture of close-set revolving lines. Aperture wide; broad shelf on inner lip, with feeble teeth. Two nublike teeth at top of outer lip. Color yellowish gray and mottled with brown. Operculum yellowish gray.
Remarks: This gastropod shows a marked preference for brackish water.

BLEEDING TOOTH *Nerita peloronta* Linnaeus, 1758   **Pl. 44**
Range: Bermuda; south Florida to the West Indies.
Habitat: Shallow water.
Description: Height 1 to $1^1/_2$ in. Shell thick and heavy, spire low. Surface bears several broadly rounded revolving ribs. Outer lip feebly toothed within, inner lip (columellar margin) sports 1 or 2 glistening white, strong central teeth surrounded by a rich red stain. Operculum shelly and reddish. Color yellowish white, marked with zigzag bars of red and black, the black predominating.
Remarks: Popular names are sometimes misleading or meaningless, but one has only to look into the aperture to see how perfectly the name Bleeding Tooth fits this snail. It is most active at night, when it roams about the rocks between tides feeding upon algae.

TESSELLATE NERITE *Nerita tessellata* Gmelin, 1791   **Pl. 44**
Range: Bermuda; Florida to Texas; West Indies.
Habitat: Shallow water.
Description: Diameter $^1/_2$ to $^3/_4$ in., height about same. With 4 or 5 whorls separated by indistinct sutures. Surface sculptured with some 12 rounded spiral ribs on each volution;

deep narrow grooves in between. Numerous small teeth on columellar margin. Color checkered black and white. Operculum bluish white.

FOUR-TOOTHED NERITE *Nerita versicolor* Gmelin, 1791   **Pl. 44**
Range: Florida to the West Indies.
Habitat: Shallow water.
Description: About 1 in. high. Shell thick and porcelaneous, semiglobose, with little if any spire. About 4 whorls, decorated with broad and rounded revolving ribs; narrow grooves in between. Outer lip toothed within; several robust teeth are present on inner lip. Color whitish, with zigzag bars of black and red. Operculum dark gray and with fine pimples.

● **Genus *Neritina* Lamarck, 1816**

CLENCH'S NERITE *Neritina clenchi* Russell, 1940   **Pl. 44**
Range: South Florida to the West Indies.
Habitat: Fresh or brackish water.
Description: Height about 1 in., glossy. With 3 to 4 whorls, apex moderately pointed. Less globular than many of the genus. Color and patterns quite variable. An area at the parietal wall is stained orange-yellow. Operculum black to pink.

OLIVE NERITE *Neritina reclivata* (Say, 1822)   **Pl. 44**
Range: Florida to Texas; West Indies.
Habitat: Brackish water.
Description: Height $1/2$ in., diam. about the same. Shell semiglobular, with 3 or 4 whorls; body whorl constitutes most of shell. Surface smooth, color greenish, commonly with tiny black lines; many examples are pure dark green. Columellar margin glistening white. Operculum black to dark brown.
Remarks: This snail should be looked for in the tidal areas of streams.

VIRGIN NERITE *Neritina virginea* (Linnaeus, 1758)   **Pls. 7, 44**
Range: Bermuda; Florida to Texas; West Indies.
Habitat: Brackish water, intertidal.
Description: Diameter usually less than $1/2$ in. Shell semiglobular, consists of 3 or 4 whorls, and body whorl makes up most of the shell. Aperture oval, lip thin. Whole shell highly polished. Color extremely variable — usually some shade of gray-green, tan, or yellow, scrawled all over with lines, circles, and dots of black; often shows banding. Operculum usually black.

Remarks: This colorful, abundant snail travels well up rivers and streams. Very similar species are found in tropic seas all around the world.

●Genus *Puperita* Gray, 1857

ZEBRA NERITE *Puperita pupa* (Linnaeus, 1767)　　　**Pl. 44**
　　Range: South Florida to the West Indies; Bermuda.
　　Habitat: Intertidal in rock pools.
　　Description: Diameter about $1/2$ in. Shell thin but sturdy, globular, no spire to speak of, and consists of 2 or 3 whorls. Sutures fairly distinct. Outer lip thin and sharp, and there is a broad, flat, polished area at base of columella. Operculum shelly, with flexible border. Color creamy white, spirally striped with fine, irregular black lines. Aperture varies from yellow to bright orange. Smooth operculum is light yellow.
　　Remarks: Formerly listed as a Neritina. Commonly found in splash pools just above the high-tide mark.

●Genus *Smaragdia* Issel, 1869

EMERALD NERITE　　　　　　　　　　　　　　**Pl. 43**
Smaragdia viridis (Linnaeus, 1758)
　　Range: Bermuda; south Florida to the West Indies.
　　Habitat: Shallow water.
　　Description: Diameter about $1/4$ in. With 2 or 3 whorls, practically no Spire. Aperture large, lip thin and sharp, broad polished area on inner lip. Surface highly polished. Color pale to brighter green, often with a few whitish streaks on the shoulders.
　　Remarks: Typical *S. viridis* is a Mediterranean snail. The West Indies form is considered the subspecies *viridemaris* Maury, 1917, by some workers.

■ CHINK SHELLS: Family Lacunidae

These snails are conical, stout, and thin-shelled. The aperture is half-moon-shaped, and the distinguishing character is a lengthened groove, or chink, alongside the columella. The thin operculum is chitinous and has few whorls.

● **Genus *Lacuna* Turton, 1827**

COMMON NORTHERN LACUNA   Pl. 43
Lacuna vincta (Montagu, 1803)
   Range: Labrador to New Jersey; Pacific Northwest.
   Habitat: Moderately shallow water.
   Description: About $^1/_3$ in. high. Shell thin and conical, about 5 rather stout whorls separated by moderately deep sutures. Apex pointed. Surface bears minute lines of growth. Aperture semilunar, outer lip thin and sharp; inner lip flattened and excavated by a smooth, elongated groove that terminates in a tiny umbilicus and forms a prominent chink beside the columella. Brownish white, commonly banded with purplish.

■ PERIWINKLES: Family Littorinidae

A large family of shore-dwelling snails found clinging to rocks and plants between the tides, sometimes well up beyond the high-tide limits. The shell is usually sturdy, has few volutions, and is without an umbilicus. Operculum chitinous, thin, and with few whorls. Distribution worldwide.

● **Genus *Littorina* Férussac, 1827**

ANGULATE PERIWINKLE   Pl. 44
Littorina angulifera (Lamarck, 1822)
   Range: Bermuda; south Florida to the West Indies.
   Habitat: Mangrove roots and leaves, coral walls.
   Description: About $1^1/_4$ in. high. With 6 or 7 whorls, sharp apex. Shell thin but strong. Sutures slightly channeled. Sculpture of minute spiral lines. Outer lip with central groove in lower part. Operculum horny. Color variable — may be gray, reddish, yellow, or purplish, with dark oblique markings.
   Remarks: Sometimes listed as *L. scabra* (Linnaeus, 1758), which is a closely allied species living in s. Pacific.

MARSH PERIWINKLE *Littorina irrorata* (Say, 1822)   Pl. 44
   Range: New Jersey to Florida and Texas.
   Habitat: Intertidal marshes in sedges.
   Description: Height about $^3/_4$ in. Heavy and robust, sharp apex. With 5 whorls, decorated with fine spiral ridges. Outer lip stout, tapering rapidly to a thin edge. Aperture oval, opercu-

lum horny. Color soiled white, with spiral rows of chestnut brown dots. Aperture commonly yellowish.

Remarks: In the past this periwinkle existed in the north, and fossil specimens (post-Pleistocene) are commonly washed ashore from peat beds on the Connecticut shore of Long Island Sound.

COMMON PERIWINKLE   Pl. 44
Littorina littorea (Linnaeus, 1758)

Range: Labrador to Maryland; Europe.
Habitat: Intertidal.
Description: Height $1/2$ to $1^1/4$ in. Shell solid and heavy, with 6 or 7 whorls. Outer lip thick, and black on inside, base of columella white. No umbilicus. Apex sharp, but shell appears rather squat. Surface fairly smooth, brownish olive to nearly black, usually spirally banded with dark brown.

Remarks: This snail, so common in Europe (where it is sold, roasted in its shell, from pushcarts in the city streets), was long believed to be a fairly recently introduced species. Apparently none of the early conchologists ever saw a specimen. The first one reported taken was at Halifax, Nova Scotia, in 1857. From there the species spread down the coast as far as New Jersey, where southward migration was halted, probably by water temperature and possibly by the sandy Jersey beaches, for this is a rock lover. Recent investigations of ancient Indian mounds in the vicinity of Halifax have brought to light unquestioned examples of this species, which may be more than 1,000 years old. It is likely that currents off Nova Scotia prevented the free-swimming larvae from reaching the New England shores until eventually a ship, possibly sailing from Halifax to Maine, inadvertently transported some eggs, perhaps in seaweeds used in packing. Once established in northern New England, this hardy snail had nothing to prevent its colonizing all of our Northeast.

WHITE-SPOTTED PERIWINKLE   Pl. 43
Littorina meleagris (Potiez & Michaud, 1838)

Range: South Florida to the West Indies.
Habitat: Intertidal.
Description: About $1/4$ in. high. With 3 or 4 whorls, the body whorl making up most of the shell. There is a respectable spire, however, with a pointed apex. Surface smooth and shining, color gray, with revolving lines of darker hue, the lines often broken into short dashes.

Remarks: Formerly listed as *L. guttata* Philippi, 1847.

DWARF BROWN PERIWINKLE   **Pl. 43**
Littorina mespillum Mühlfeld, 1824
  Range: South Florida to the West Indies.
  Habitat: Splash pools at high-water line.
  Description: Height ¹/₄ in. About 4 whorls, spire low. Surface
  smooth, white or pale brown, sometimes with rows of small
  round black dots. Aperture glossy brown. Tiny umbilicus.
  In life there is a thin brownish periostracum.

CLOUDY PERIWINKLE *Littorina nebulosa* Lamarck, 1822 **Pl. 44**
  Range: Florida to Texas to Brazil; Bermuda.
  Habitat: Intertidal.
  Description: Height about ³/₄ in. Fairly tall, with 5 whorls and
  a pointed apex. Sutures distinct, no umbilicus. Shell rather
  solid, smooth, and with a dull surface. Color bluish white to
  yellowish, often with reddish brown spots arranged in axial
  lines; aperture purplish.

NORTHERN YELLOW PERIWINKLE   **Pl. 44**
Littorina obtusata (Linnaeus, 1758)
  Range: Labrador to New Jersey; Europe.
  Habitat: Intertidal; commonly on seaweeds.
  Description: Height ¹/₃ in. Shell stout and globular, smooth and
  shining, with very faint revolving lines. About 4 whorls, the
  last large and the others scarcely rising above it. Aperture
  nearly circular, outer lip sharp. Operculum horny,
  umbilicus lacking. Color variable, usually yellow, but may
  be orange, whitish, or reddish brown. Some, especially
  juveniles, may be banded.
  Remarks: Formerly listed as *L. palliata* (Say, 1822).

NORTHERN ROUGH PERIWINKLE *Littorina saxatilis* (Olivi,
1792)   **Pl. 43**
  Range: Arctic Ocean to New Jersey; Europe; Alaska.
  Habitat: Intertidal.
  Description: About ¹/₂ in. high. Shell ovate, strong, and coarse.
  With 4 or 5 convex whorls, well-defined sutures. Moderately elevated spire, pointed apex. Sculpture of revolving
  grooves. Yellowish or ash-colored. Some young shells are
  smooth and variously mottled or spotted with yellow and
  black.
  Remarks: Formerly listed as *L. rudis* (Maton, 1797).

ZEBRA PERIWINKLE *Littorina ziczac* (Gmelin, 1791)   **Pl. 44**
  Range: South Florida to the West Indies.
  Habitat: Intertidal on rocks.

Description: About ½ in. high. Shell sturdy, sharply pointed, with well-defined keel near base of body whorl. Sculpture of very fine and widely spaced spiral grooves. Whorl count 5 or 6. Aperture oval and small, operculum horny. Color whitish; many wavy stripes of dark brown or black.

●**Genus _Nodilittorina_ von Martens, 1897**

PRICKLY PERIWINKLE   Fig. 52 & Pl. 44
Nodilittorina tuberculata (Menke, 1828)
    Range: Bermuda; south Florida to the West Indies.
    Habitat: Intertidal on shore rocks.
    Description: About ¾ in. high. About 5 whorls, sutures not very distinct. Aperture large, inner lip somewhat flattened at base. Sculpture of several revolving rows of pointed knobs. Color dark brown. Operculum chitinous with only a few whorls.

●**Genus _Echininus_ Clench & Abbott, 1942**

FALSE PRICKLY-WINKLE   Fig. 52 & Pl. 44
Echininus nodulosus (Pfeiffer, 1839)
    Range: South Florida to the West Indies.
    Habitat: Intertidal.
    Description: Just under 1 in. high. About 8 whorls, decorated with revolving rows of pointed knobs, larger and more pronounced along the sutures, which are generally lighter-colored than the rest of the shell. Aperture nearly round, lip moderately thick, no umbilicus. Color mottled gray and black. Operculum with many whorls.

    a _Nodilittorina_   b _Echininus_

Figure 52. a) Prickly Perwinkle _Nodilittorina tuberculata_ _operculum_ **b)** False Prickly-winkle _Echininus nodulosus_ _operculum_

●Genus *Tectarius* Valenciennes, 1833

BEADED PERIWINKLE   Pl. 44
Tectarius muricatus (Linnaeus, 1758)
   Range: Bermuda; south Florida to the West Indies.
   Habitat: Intertidal.
   Description: About $3/4$ in. high. Shell sturdy and top-shaped,
   with about 7 well-rounded whorls, slightly shouldered
   above, and with a sharp apex. Surface decorated with revolving rows of beads, about 5 rows to a volution. Aperture moderately small and oval. Outer lip somewhat thickened, and
   there is a small groove down the columella toward the base.
   Color yellowish gray.
   Remarks: This gastropod is often found on rocks well above
   the high-tide limits. It is able to survive for long periods out
   of water; indeed, Dr. Henry A. Pilsbry recorded a specimen
   that revived after being isolated in a cabinet for a year.

■ **SWAMP SNAILS: Family Hydrobiidae**

Shells very small, with several rounded whorls and a moderately tall spire. They inhabit both marine and nonmarine environments and are usually abundant in marshes and ditches
near the sea. Operculum chitinous and thin.

●Genus *Hydrobia* Hartman, 1840

MINUTE HYDROBIA *Hydrobia totteni* Morrison, 1954   **Fig. 53**
   Range: Labrador to New Jersey.
   Habitat: Salt-marsh pools.
   Description: About $1/8$ in. high. Shell thin and semitransparent,
   with about 5 rounded whorls, surface faintly marked and
   wrinkled by growth lines. Aperture oval, operculum horny.
   Surface shiny, color yellowish brown.
   Remarks: Formerly in the genus *Paludestrina* Orbigny, 1840.
   H. minuta Totten, 1834, is a synonym.

Figure 53. Minute Hydrobia *Hydrobia totteni*

● **Genus *Truncatella* Risso, 1826**

BEAUTIFUL TRUNCATELLA   **Pl. 45**
Truncatella pulchella Pfeiffer, 1839
  Range: Florida to the West Indies; Bermuda.
  Habitat: Under stones above high tide.
  Description: About 1/4 in. high. Approximately 6 whorls, each
  with 15 to 18 rather weak vertical lines. Sutures well im-
  pressed. Outer lip thin and sharp. Color white to pale yel-
  low.

LADDER TRUNCATELLA   **Pl. 45**
Truncatella scalaris (Michaud, 1830)
  Range: Florida; Bahamas; West Indies.
  Habitat: Under stones above high tide.
  Description: Height about 3/16 in. With 6 or 7 whorls; indented
  sutures suggest shoulders. With 7 to 10 rather coarse vertical
  lines, with minute revolving lines between. Outer lip thick-
  ened. Color yellowish orange.

■ **RISSOS: Family Rissoidae**

Very small shells, living for the most part on stones, shells,
and sponges. They are variable in structure and occur in
nearly all seas. Hundreds of species have been described.

● **Genus *Rissoina* Orbigny, 1840**

CARIBBEAN RISSO *Rissoina bryerea* (Montagu, 1803)   **Pl. 45**
  Range: Florida Keys to the West Indies.
  Habitat: Moderately shallow water.
  Description: About 1/4 in. high. A rather slender shell of 7 or 8

whorls, the sutures somewhat indistinct. Sculpture of weak vertical grooves. Aperture small, operculum horny. Surface shiny; color white.

CANCELLATE RISSO *Rissoina cancellata* (Philippi, 1847)   **Pl. 45**
Range: South Florida to the West Indies.
Habitat: Moderately shallow water.
Description: Height $1/4$ to nearly $1/2$ in. Elongate, with 8 whorls, well rounded and decorated with both vertical and revolving lines, so surface has a cancellate appearance. Aperture oval, lip rather thick. Color yellowish white.

DECUSSATE RISSO *Rissoina decussata* (Montagu, 1803)   **Pl. 45**
Range: N. Carolina to the West Indies.
Habitat: Moderately shallow water.
Description: About $1/4$ in. high. With 6 or 7 slightly rounded whorls, sutures indistinct. Aperture semilunar, lip thickened. Surface marked with very fine vertical striations. Color white.

MANY-RIBBED RISSO   **Pl. 45**
Rissoina multicostata (C. B. Adams, 1850)
Range: South Florida to the West Indies.
Habitat: Shallow water.
Description: Slightly more than $1/8$ in. high. With 7 or 8 whorls, sutures moderate. Sculpture of numerous fine vertical lines. Color yellowish white.

●**Genus** *Zebina* **H. & A. Adams, 1854**

SMOOTH RISSO *Zebina browniana* (Orbigny, 1842)   **Pl. 45**
Range: N. Carolina to the West Indies; Bermuda.
Habitat: Shallow water.
Description: About $1/8$ in. high. With 7 or 8 sloping whorls; sutures indistinct. Apex sharp. Surface smooth and polished, color white, occasionally with pale brownish encircling bands.
Remarks: Formerly in the genus *Rissoina*.

■ VITRINELLA SNAILS: Family Vitrinellidae

Small, rather flatly coiled snails, living chiefly in deep water. Shells are translucent and often polished. Small umbilicus, round aperture.

●Genus *Cyclostremiscus* Pilsbry & Olsson 1945

BEAU'S VITRINELLA   **Pl. 45**

Cyclostremiscus beaui (Fischer, 1857)
Range: Carolinas to the West Indies; Brazil.
Habitat: Moderately shallow water.
Description: Diameter about $\frac{1}{2}$ in. Flatly coiled, with 4 rounded whorls. Sculpture of prominent revolving lines, with relatively deep grooves in between. Umbilicus large. Color whitish or pale brown.
Remarks: Formerly in the genus *Vitrinella.*

■ CAECUMS: Family Caecidae

Very minute tubular shells; at first spiral-shaped but soon becoming cylindrical. The spiral portion is nearly always lost. The family contains but a single genus, with a great many species. Many live in sponges. Distributed in warm and temperate seas.

●Genus *Caecum* Fleming, 1813

COOPER'S ATLANTIC CAECUM

Caecum cooperi S. Smith, 1860
Range: Massachusetts to Florida.
Habitat: Moderately shallow water.
Description: About $\frac{1}{8}$ in. long. Tubular and slightly curved, marked with faint longitudinal lines. Sometimes there are a few rings at larger end, giving that portion a somewhat cancellate look. As with nearly all of this group, the spiral nuclear part is lost and the open tip is plugged with shelly material; in this species the tip is often distinctly prong-shaped. Color white or yellowish white.

BEAUTIFUL CAECUM

Caecum pulchellum Stimpson, 1851
Range: Massachusetts to Florida.
Habitat: Moderately shallow water.
Description: About $\frac{1}{10}$ in. long. Tubular, composed of a series of regular, rounded rings. Nuclear (initial) part generally lost,

open tip plugged with shelly material. Color yellowish white.

Remarks: This mollusk would be passed up by most searchers at the seashore, for it is so tiny that it could very easily be missed. Under a lens, however, it proves to be an attractive and unusual shell.

■ SKENEA SNAILS: Family Skeneopsidae

Very tiny flattish shells with few volutions, found under stones in moderately shallow to deep water.

● Genus *Skeneopsis* Iredale, 1915

FLAT-COILED SKENEOPSIS   **Fig. 54**
Skeneopsis planorbis (Fabricius, 1780)
  Range: Greenland to Florida.
  Habitat: Moderately shallow water.
  Description: A minute species, diameter no more than ⅛ in., with very low spire. Rather flatly coiled, 4 whorls, sutures well defined. Umbilicus relatively wide and deep. Surface smooth, color dull brown.
  Remarks: These diminutive snails may be found living on oysters, sponges, corals, and all sorts of objects offshore, but they are so tiny that they are usually overlooked.

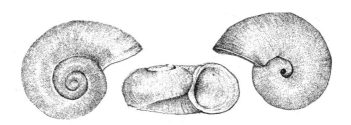

Figure 54. Flat-coiled Skeneopsis *Skeneopsis planorbis*

Figure 55. Atom Snail *Omalogyra atomus*

■ ATOM SNAILS: Family Omalogyridae

● Genus *Omalogyra* Jeffreys, 1867

ATOM SNAIL *Omalogyra atomus* (Philippi, 1841)   **Fig. 55**
   Range: Maine to Rhode Island; Europe.
   Habitat: Intertidal in lower rock pools.
   Description: The smallest New England marine snail known, reaching a diameter of 0.5 mm. Shell red-brown, flat, spire sunken; whorls round. Umbilicus very wide. Suture deep. Aperture round. Operculum with a few whorls.

■ TURRET-SHELLS: Family Turritellidae

Greatly elongated, many-whorled shells, generally turreted. A large family, living chiefly in Pacific waters. Relatively few representatives are present on our Atlantic coast.

● Genus *Turritella* Lamarck, 1799

BORING TURRET SHELL *Turritella acropora* Dall, 1889   **Pl. 47**
   Range: N. Carolina to the West Indies.
   Habitat: Moderately shallow water.
   Description: About 1 in. high. With 10 to 12 rather flat-sided whorls, the sutures not very distinct. Sculpture of fine revolving threadlike lines. Aperture small, squarish, operculum horny. Color yellowish or brownish red.

PLATES

PLATE 1

THE SHELL COLLECTION

A private shell collection

A museum study collection

…er trays, labels, and vials for shells

Minute shells in vial plugged with cotton

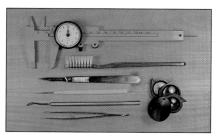

Calipers, hand lens, and dissecting equipment

PLATE 2

SHELL COLLECTING

Exposed sand and mud flats at low tide reveal a wealth of living mollusks. Collect in limited numbers.

Snorkeling opens up a rich world of underwater inhabitants. Return overturned rocks to their original position to protect snail eggs and young.

Dredging off the stern of a small boat can bring up many small uncommon species. Dry and sort sandy "grunge" later at home under a hand lens or microscope.

A small, 2-foot-wide metal frame with a net or wire bag can serve as an effective dredge in depths of 20 to 100 feet. Beware underwater cables and large rocks.

Amid the sandy coral rubble, dredge hauls may bring up unexpected treasures like these rare Murex shells. Sorting for minute shells is best done when sand is dry.

Large shells may be cleaned by boiling in water for 5 minutes. Save the "trap doors." Freezing overnight, later thawing, will work with smaller shells.

[Photos by Frank Frumar]

PLATE 3   **LIVING SCALLOPS**

BAY SCALLOP, *Argopecten irradians* subspecies *concentricus* (Say)   ×2   **p. 30**

LION'S PAW SCALLOP, *Nodipecten nodulosus* (Linnaeus)   ×1   **p. 29**

PLATE 4

LIVING SCALLOP AND COQUINAS

COQUINA CLAMS, *Donax variabilis* Say   Natural size   **p. 91**

CALICO SCALLOP, *Argopecten gibbus* (Linnaeus)   × ½   **p. 29**

ROUGH LIMA CLAM, *Lima scabra* form *tenera* Sowerby   **p. 32**

PLATE 5

SIPHONS OF BIVALVES

BLUE EDIBLE MUSSEL, *Mytilis edulis* (Linnaeus) ×½ **p. 14**

GREAT PIDDOCK, *Zirfaea crispata* (Linnaeus) ×2 **p. 108**

GIANT HEART COCKLE, *Dinocardium robustum* (Lightfoot) ×⅓ **p. 57**

PLATE 6

UNIVALVE EGG CAPSULES

LIGHTNING WHELK
Four chains, each one foot long
p. 228

LIGHTNING WHELK
Young ready to hatch from capsule
p. 228

BANDED TULIP
Clump of capsules on log
p. 232

APPLE MUREX
Community mass of egg capsules
p. 210
(photo by M. G. Harasewych)

NORTHERN BUCCINUM
Six-inch egg capsule mass
p. 222

FLORIDA HORSE CONCH
Female shell is 12 inches long
p. 233
(photo by Alice D. Barlow)

PLATE 7

LIVING TURBANS AND NERITES

(photo by Bob Lipe)

FILOSE TURBAN, *Turbo cailletii* F. & B.   Natural size   **p. 140**

(photo by Bob Lipe)

SOWERBY'S KEYHOLE LIMPET, *Lucapina sowerbii* Sby   ×2   **p. 128**

(photo by R. T. Abbott)

VIRGIN NERITE, *Neritina virginea* (Linnaeus)   ×2   **p. 144**

PLATE 8 **LIVING CONCHS AND OLIVES**

MILK CONCH, *Strombus costatus* Gmelin × ½ **p. 184**

FLORIDA FIGHTING CONCH, *Strombus alatus* Gmelin × ½ **p. 183**

LETTERED OLIVE, *Oliva sayana* Ravenel Natural size **p. 235**

PLATE 9

LIVING ALLIED COWRIES

COMMON WEST INDIAN SIMNIA, *Simnia acicularis* (Lamarck) ×3 **p. 197**

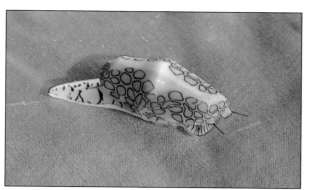

FLAMINGO TONGUE, *Cyphoma gibbosum* (Linn.) Nat. size **p. 197**

(Photo by Bob Lipe)

McGINTY'S FLAMINGO TONGUE ×2 **p. 198**

PLATE 10

LIVING COWRIES

ATLANTIC DEER COWRIE, *Cypraea cervus* Linnaeus × ½ **p. 194**

YELLOW COWRIE, *Cypraea acicularis* Gmelin Nat. size **p. 194**

Mouth of **MEASLED COWRIE** Natural size **p. 194**

PLATE 11   LIVING MOON, TRIVIA AND WHELK

(Bob Lipe photo)

COLORFUL ATLANTIC NATICA, *N. canrena* (L.)   ×1   **p. 190**

(Bob Lipe photo)

COFFEE BEAN TRIVIA, *Trivia pediculus* (L.)   ×2   **p. 195**

(Steven F. Barry photo)

COMMON NORTHERN BUCCINUM, *Buccinum undatum* (L.)   ×1   **p. 222**

PLATE 12

LIVING TRITONS

(Alice Barlow photo)

ATLANTIC HAIRY TRITON, *Cymatium pileare* (L.) ×1   **p. 203**

(Tom Honker photo)

DOG-HEAD TRITON, *Cymatium caribbaeum* C. & T.   **p. 201**

(Bob Lipe photo)

ATLANTIC TRITON, *Charonia variegata* (Lam.) ×¼   **p. 204**

PLATE 13

LIVING HELMET SHELLS

(Bob Lipe photo)

RETICULATED COWRIE-HELMET, *Cypraecassis testiculus* ×1 **p. 199**

(Frank Frumar photo)

SCOTCH BONNET, *Phalium granulatum* (Born) ×½ **p. 198**

(Bob Lipe photo)

ATLANTIC PARTRIDGE SHELL, *Tonna maculosa* (Dillwyn) ×1 **p. 206**

PLATE 14 **LIVING MOON-SHELLS AND JUNONIA**

NORTHERN MOON-SHELL, *Lunatia heros* (Say) × ⅓ **p.189**

(Steven F. Barry photo)

SHARK EYE, *Polinices duplicatus* (Say) × ½ **p. 188**

(Frank Frumar photo)

JUNONIA, *Scaphella junonia* (Lamarck) × ½ **p. 241**

(Bob Lipe photo)

PLATE 15   **LIVING CONE SHELLS**

(Bob Lipe photo)

FLORIDA CONE, *Conus floridanus* Gabb ×1   **p. 248**

(Tom Honker photo)

GLORY-OF-THE-ATLANTIC CONE, *C. granulatus* (L.) ×1   **p. 248**

(Bob Lipe photo)

ALPHABET CONE, *Conus spurius atlanticus* Clench ×1   **p. 250**

PLATE 16

LIVING CEPHALOPODS

COMMON SPIRULA, *Spirula spirula* (L.) Left: cross-section × 2   **p. 300**

(D. Opresko photo)

JOUBIN'S OCTOPUS, *Octopus joubini* Robson × 1 **p. 305**

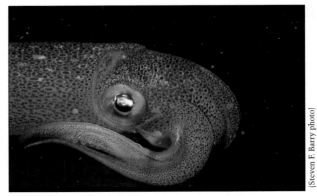

(Steven F. Barry photo)

Head of **LOLIGO SQUID** × ½ **p. 302**

PLATE 17

LIVING TUSKS AND CHITON

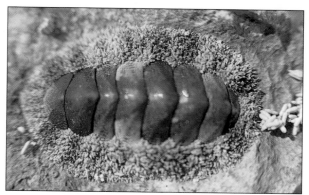

FUZZY CHITON, *Acanthopleura granulata* (Gmelin) × 1 **p. 296**

IVORY TUSK, *Dentalium eboreum* Conrad × 1 **p. 297**

(Bob Lipe photo)

MARGINELLAS feeding on dead cockle × ½ **p. 243**

PLATE 18

AWNING, NUT, AND ARK CLAMS

PLATE 19
ARK, NUT, AND BITTERSWEET CLAMS

PLATE 20

MUSSELS
(natural size)

PLATE 21

PEN SHELLS AND PEARL OYSTERS
(¹/₂ natural size)

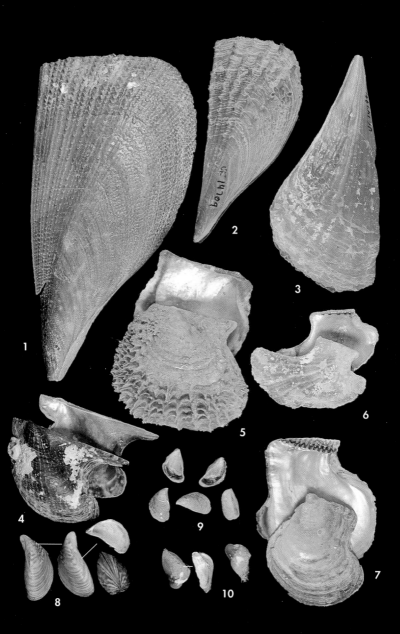

PLATE 22

SCALLOPS
(¹/₂ natural size)

1. **ATLANTIC DEEP-SEA SCALLOP**   p. 28
   Placopecten magellanicus (Gmelin, 1791)

2. **CALICO SCALLOP**   p. 29
   Argopecten gibbus (Linnaeus, 1758)

3. **PAPER SCALLOP**   p. 27
   Euvola papyraceam (Gabb, 1873)

4. **NUCEUS SCALLOP**   p. 30
   Argopecten nucleus (Born, 1778)

5. **ICELAND SCALLOP**   p. 27
   Chlamys islandica (Müller, 1776)

6. **LION'S PAW**   p. 29
   Nodipecten nodosus (Linnaeus, 1758)

7. **SENTIS SCALLOP**   p. 28
   Caribachlamys sentis (Reeve, 1853)

8. **RAVENEL'S SCALLOP** *Euvola raveneli* (Dall, 1898)   p. 26

9. **ROUGH SCALLOP**   p. 31
   Aequipecten muscosus (Wood, 1828)

10. **BAY SCALLOP**   p. 30
    Argopecten irradians (Lamarck, 1819)

11. **ZIGZAG SCALLOP** *Euvola ziczac* (Linnaeus, 1758)   p. 26

12. **ROUGH SCALLOP** rare yellow color form   p. 31

13. **SOUTHERN BAY SCALLOP**   p. 30
    Argopecten irradians concentricus (Say, 1822)

14. **LITTLE KNOBBY SCALLOP**   p. 27
    Caribachlamys imbricata (Gmelin, 1791)

15. **ORNATE SCALLOP**   p. 28
    Caribachlamys ornata (Lamarck, 1819)

PLATE 23

VENUS CLAMS, SCALLOPS, AND CORBULAS
(twice natural size)

PLATE 24

SCALLOPS, COCKLES, AND LUCINES

1. **SPATHATE SCALLOP** p. 31
   Cryptopecten phrygium Dall, 1886

2. **ANTILLEAN SCALLOP** p. 29
   Bractechlamys antillarum (Récluz, 1853)

3. **SPINOSE LUCINE** p. 50
   Phacoides muricata (Spengler, 1798)

4. **MORTON'S EGG COCKLE** p. 59
   Laevicardium mortoni (Conrad, 1830)

5. **RAVENEL'S EGG COCKLE** p. 59
   Laevicardium pictum (Ravenel, 1861)

6. **ATLANTIC DIPLODON** p. 46
   Diplodonta punctata (Say, 1822)

7. **LADY-IN-WAITING VENUS** p. 63
   Chione intapurpurea (Conrad, 1849)

8. **WHITE PYGMY VENUS** p. 64
   Chione pygmaea (Lamarck, 1818)

9. **WAVY CLAM** *Liocyma fluctuosa* (Gould, 1841) p. 73

10. **SHINING ERVILIA** p. 79
    Ervilia nitens (Montagu, 1806) Sometimes white.

11. **PIMPLED DIPLODON** p. 46
    Diplodonta semiaspersa (Philippi, 1836)

12. **FLORIDA MARSH CLAM** p. 53
    Cyrenoida floridana (Dall, 1896)

13. **LITTLE SURF CLAM** *Mulinia lateralis* (Say, 1822) p. 77

14. **DOMINGO CARDITA** p. 44
    Glans dominguensis (Orbigny, 1845)

15. **WOVEN LUCINE** p. 51
    Phacoides nassula (Conrad, 1846)

16. **THREE-TOOTHED CARDITA** p. 46
    Pleuromeris tridentata (Say, 1826)

PLATE 25

OYSTERS AND JINGLE SHELLS

1. **ATLANTIC THORNY OYSTER**   **p. 33**
   Spondylus americanus Hermann, 1781

2. **COMMON ATLANTIC OYSTER**   **p. 37**
   Crassostrea virginica (Gmelin, 1791)

3. **'COON OYSTER**   **p. 35**
   Dendostrea frons (Linnaeus, 1758)

4. **KITTEN'S PAW** *Plicatula gibbosa* Lamarck, 1801   **p. 34**

5. **McGINTY'S OYSTER**   **p. 36**
   Parahyotissa mcgintyi Harry, 1985

6. **SPONGE OYSTER**   **p. 36**
   Cryptostrea permollis (Sowerby, 1841)

7. **CRESTED OYSTER** *Ostreola equestris* (Say, 1834)   **p. 35**

8. **JINGLE SHELL** *Anomia simplex* Orbigny, 1842   **p. 38**

9. **FALSE JINGLE SHELL**   **p. 39**
   Pododesmus rudis (Broderip, 1834)

PLATE 26

ASTARTES AND LIMA CLAMS

PLATE 27

LUCINES AND CARDITAS

PLATE 28

LUCINES AND JEWEL BOXES

PLATE 29

COCKLES AND SPINY JEWEL BOXES

PLATE 30
VENUS CLAMS AND FALSE ANGEL WINGS

PLATE 31
VENUS CLAMS

PLATE 32

SURF CLAMS, PANDORAS, AND THRACIAS

PLATE 33

LARGE TELLINS AND MACOMAS

PLATE 34
SMALL TELLINS

PLATE 35
TELLINS, MACOMAS, AND SEMELES

PLATE 36

TAGELUS AND GARI CLAMS

PLATE 37
COQUINA CLAMS AND LYONSIAS

PLATE 38

ANGEL WING, RAZOR AND SOFT-SHELL CLAMS

PLATE 39

PLEUROTOMARIA SLIT-SHELLS
($\frac{1}{2}$ natural size)

PLATE 40
ABALONES AND KEYHOLE LIMPETS
(natural size)

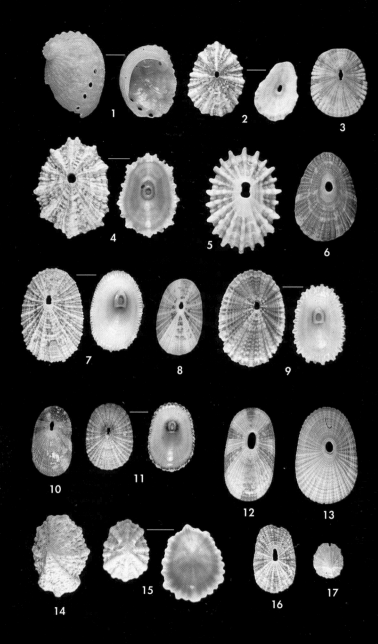

PLATE 41
LIMPETS AND TOP-SHELLS

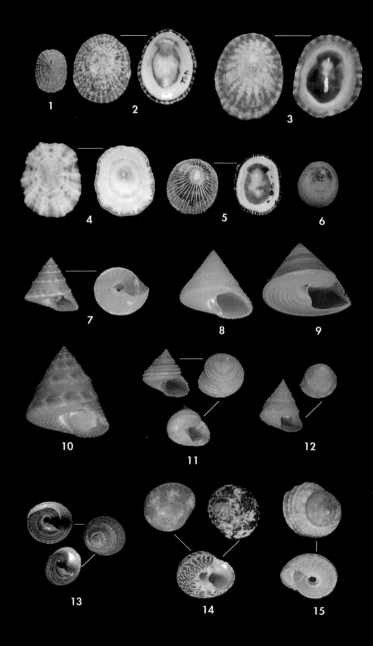

PLATE 42

TURBANS AND STAR-SHELLS

PLATE 43
PHEASANT SHELLS AND PERIWINKLES
(twice natural size)

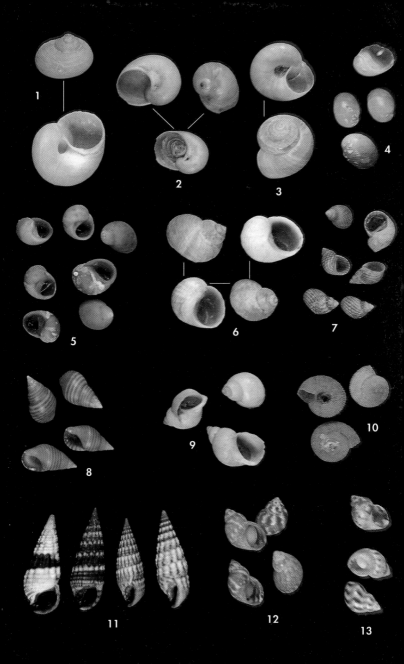

PLATE 44

PERIWINKLES AND NERITES
(natural size)

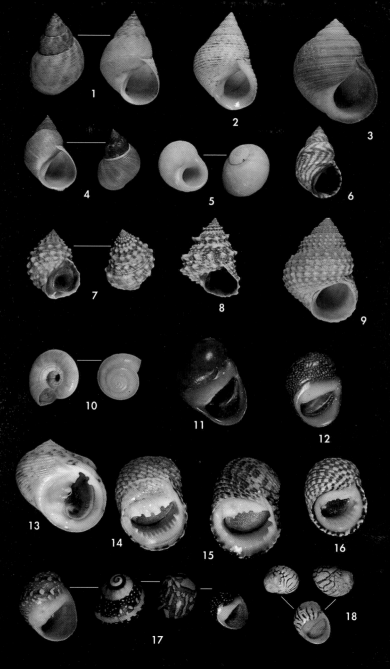

PLATE 45
RISSOIDS, BITTIUMS, AND TRIPHORAS
(twice natural size)

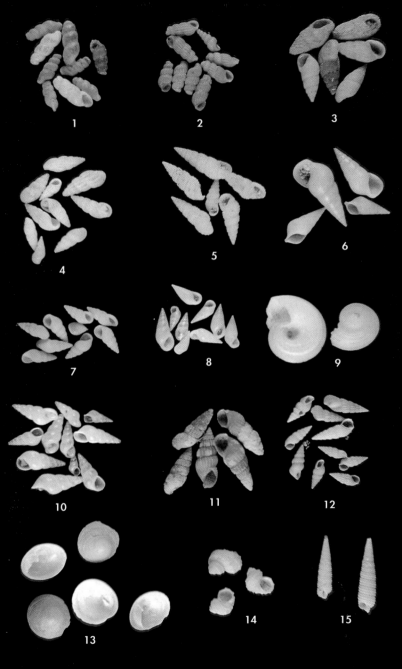

PLATE 46
CERITHS, PLANAXIS, AND BUTTON SHELLS

PLATE 47

TURRITELLAS, SUNDIALS, AND JANTHINAS

PLATE 48

WENTLETRAPS
(twice natural size)

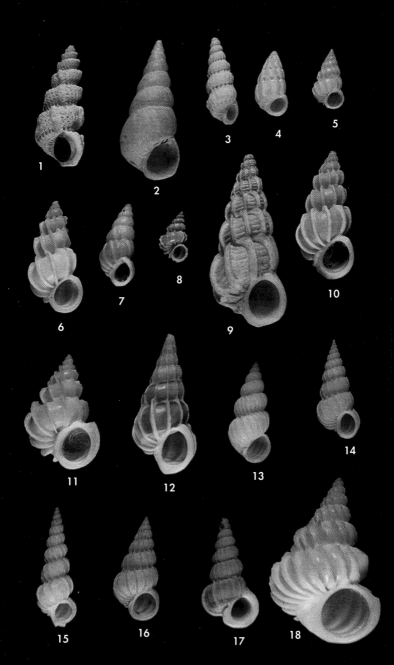

PLATE 49

FLAMINGO TONGUES AND SLIPPER-SHELLS
(natural size)

PLATE 50

STROMBUS CONCHS
(¹/₃ natural size)

1. **ROOSTER-TAIL CONCH**   p 184
   Strombus gallus Linnaeus, 1758

2. **PINK** or **QUEEN CONCH**   p. 184
   Strombus gigas Linnaeus, 1758. Immature at left.

3. **MILK CONCH** *Strombus costatus* Gmelin, 1791   p. 184

4. **HAWK-WING CONCH**   p. 185
   Strombus raninus Gmelin, 1791

5. **FLORIDA FIGHTING CONCH**   p. 183
   Strombus alatus Gmelin, 1791. Immature at right.

6. **FREAK-SPINED FIGHTING CONCH**
   form *sloani* Leach, 1814

7. **WEST INDIAN FIGHTING CONCH**   p. 185
   Strombus pugilis Linnaeus, 1758

PLATE 51
HELMETS, COWRIES, AND CARRIER-SHELLS
(¹/₂ **natural size**)

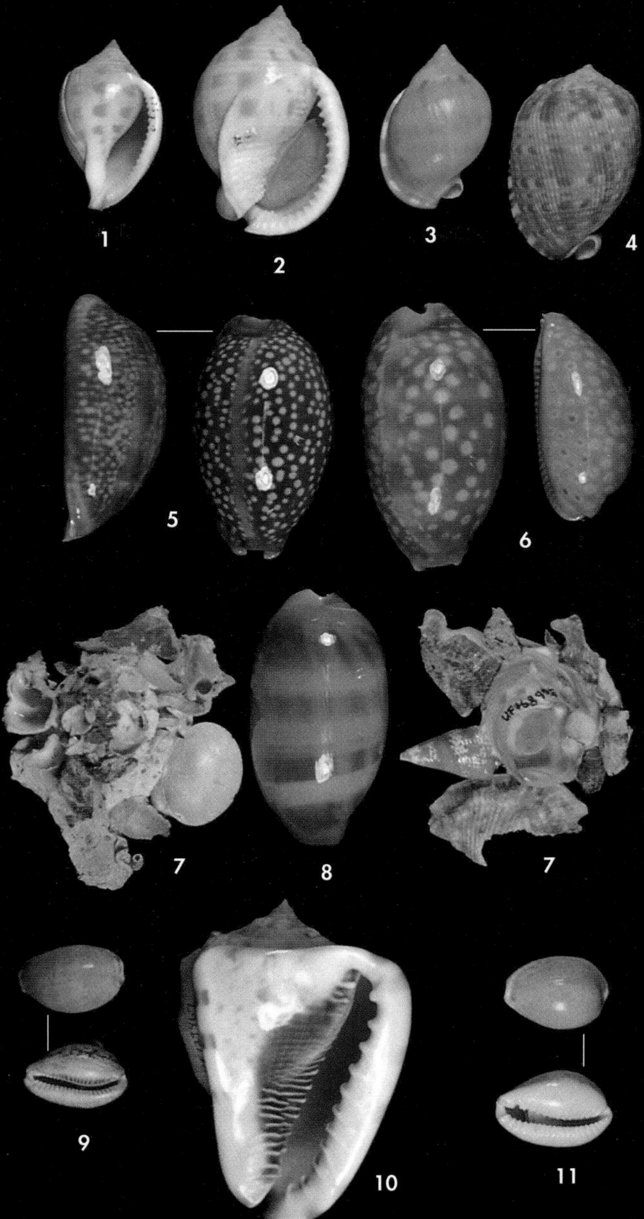
1
2
3
4
5
6
7
8
7
9
10
11

PLATE 52

HELMETS, HORSE CONCH, AND TRITONS
(¹/₃ natural size)

PLATE 53

TRIVIAS, SIMNIAS, AND ATLANTA

PLATE 54

MOON-SHELLS AND LAMELLARIAS
(¹/₂ natural size)

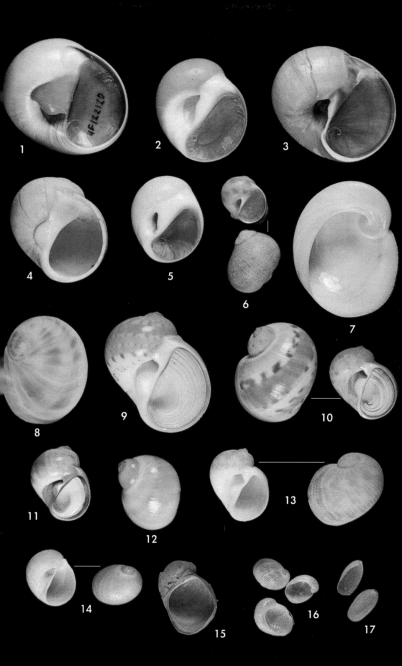

PLATE 55

TRITONS, FROG-SHELLS, AND TUNS
(¹/₂ **natural size**)

1. **ANGULAR TRITON**   p. 201
   Cymatium femorale (Linnaeus, 1758)

2. **NEAPOLITAN TRITON**   p. 202
   Cymatium parthenopeum (von Salis, 1793)

3. **DOG-HEAD TRITON**   p. 201
   Cymatium caribbaeum Clench & Turner, 1957

4. **ATLANTIC HAIRY TRITON**   p. 203
   Cymatium pileare (Linnaeus, 1758)

5. **POULSEN'S TRITON**   p. 203
   Cymatium cingulatum (Lamarck, 1822)

6. **GOLD-MOUTHED TRITON**   p. 202
   Cymatium nicobaricum (Röding, 1798)

7. **KNOBBED TRITON**   p. 202
   Cymatium muricinum (Röding, 1798)

8. **DWARF HAIRY TRITON**   p. 203
   Cymatium vespaceum (Lamarck, 1822)

9. **ST. THOMAS FROG-SHELL**   p. 205
   Bursa thomae (Orbigny, 1842)

10. **LIP TRITON**   p. 201
    Cymatium labiosum (Wood, 1828)

11. **GAUDY FROG-SHELL**   p. 204
    Bursa corrugata (Perry, 1811)

12. **ATLANTIC PARTRIDGE SHELL**   p. 206
    Tonna maculosa (Dillwyn, 1817)

13. **CUBAN FROG-SHELL**   p. 205
    Bursa cubaniana (Orbigny, 1842)

14. **ATLANTIC DISTORSIO**   p. 203
    Distorsio clathrata (Lamarck, 1816)

15. **McGINTY'S DISTORSIO**   p. 204
    Distorsio macgintyi Emerson & Puffer, 1953

16. **GIANT TUN SHELL** *Tonna galea* (Linnaeus, 1758)   p. 206

PLATE 56
TULIPS, SPINDLES, AND VASE SHELLS
(¹/₃ natural size)

PLATE 57

BUSYCON WHELKS AND FIG SHELLS
(¹/₃ **natural size**)

PLATE 58

MUREX SHELLS AND NEPTUNES
(¹/₂ natural size)

PLATE 59

ROCK SHELLS AND DRILLS

PLATE 60
OLIVES, AUGERS, AND TUSK SHELLS

PLATE 61
DWARF OLIVES AND MARGINELLAS
(natural size)

1. **JASPER DWARF OLIVE**   p. 236
   Jaspidella jaspidea (Gmelin, 1791)

2. **WEST INDIAN DWARF OLIVE**   p. 236
   Olivella nivea (Gmelin, 1791)

3. **VARIABLE DWARF OLIVE**   p. 235
   Olivella mutica (Say, 1822)

4. **COMMON RICE OLIVE**   p. 235
   Olivella floralia (Duclos, 1853)

5. **MINUTE DWARF OLIVE** *Olivella minuta* (Link, 1807) p. 235

6. **CARMINE MARGINELLA**   p. 244
   Marginella hematita Kiener, 1834

7. **DENTATE or TAN MARGINELLA**   p. 244
   Marginella eburneola Conrad, 1834

8. **COMMON MARGINELLA**   p. 244
   Prunum apicinum (Menke, 1824)
   (Rare sinistral specimen at right)

9. **BELL MARGINELLA**   p. 245
   Prunum bellum (Conrad, 1868)

10. **VELIE'S MARGINELLA**   p. 247
    Hyalina veliei (Pislbry, 1896)

11. **SPOTTED MARGINELLA**   p. 245
    Prunum guttatum (Dillwyn, 1817)

12. **ORANGE MARGINELLA**   p. 245
    Prunum carneum (Storer, 1837)

13. **ROOSEVELT'S MARGINELLA**   p. 245
    Prunum roosevelti Bartsch & Rehder, 1939)

14. **ORANGE-BANDED MARGINELLA**   p. 247
    Hyalina avena (Kiener, 1834)

15. **SHINY ATLANTIC AUGER**   p. 253
    Terebra hastata (Gmelin, 1791)

16. **COMMON AMERICAN AUGER**   p. 252
    Terebra dislocata (Say, 1822)

17. **GRAY ATLANTIC AUGER**   p. 252
    Terebra cinerea (Born, 1778)

18. **NASSULA AUGER** *Terebra nassula* Dall, 1889
    Gulf of Mexico. Not in text.

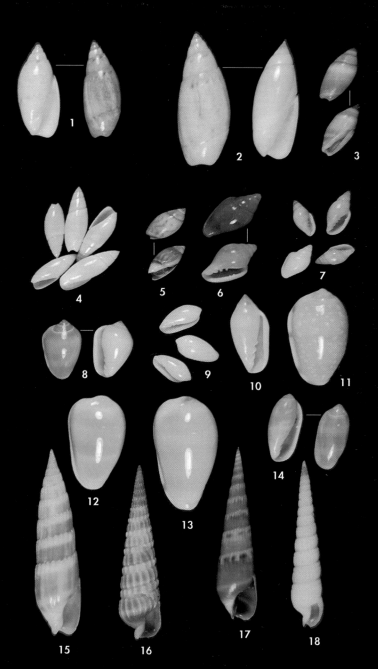

PLATE 62
MITERS, DOVES, AND MUD-SNAILS
(natural size)

PLATE 63

SCAPHELLA VOLUTES
(¹/₂ natural size)

PLATE 64

CONE SHELLS
(natural size)

PLATE 65

TURRIDS, BUBBLE SHELLS, AND PTEROPODS
(twice natural size)

1. **SANIBEL TURRID**   p. 254
   Crassispira sanibelensis Bartsch & Rehder, 1939

2. **TAMPA TURRID**   p. 254
   Crassispira tampaensis Bartsch & Rehder, 1939

3. **JANET'S TURRID** *Fenimorea janetae* Bartsch, 1934   p. 257

4. **KNOBBY DRILLIA**   p. 256
   Monilispira leucocyma (Dall, 1883)

5. **WHITE-BANDED DRILLA**   p. 255
   Monilispira albomaculata (Orbigny, 1842)

6. **VOLUTE TURRID**   p. 259
   Daphnella lymneiformis (Kiener, 1840)

7. **STAR TURRID** *Cochlespina radiata* (Dall, 1889)   p. 255

8. **GABB'S MANGELIA** *Glyphostoma gabbi* (Dall, 1889)   p. 255

9. **ELEGANT GLASSY BUBBLE**   p. 268
   Haminoea elegans (Gray, 1825)

10. **AMBER GLASSY BUBBLE**   p. 268
    Haminoea succinea (Conrad, 1846)

11. **COMMON CANOE SHELL**   p. 271
    Scaphander punctostriatus
    (Mighels & Adams, 1841)

12. **COMMON ATLANTIC BUBBLE**   p. 267
    Bulla striata Bruguière, 1792

13. **ANTILLEAN GLASSY BUBBLE**   p. 268
    Haminoea antillarum (Orbigny, 1841)

14. **STRIPED FALSE LIMPET**   p. 274
    Siphonaria pectinata (Linnaeus, 1758)

15. **COFFEE MELAMPUS**   p. 274
    Melampus coffeus (Linnaeus, 1758)

16. **WAVY CLIO** *Clio recurva* (Children, 1823)   p. 280

17. **SAY'S FALSE LIMPET**   p. 273
    Siphonaria alternata Say, 1826

18. **THREE-TOOTHED CAVOLINE**   p. 278
    Cavolina tridentata (Niebuhr, 1775)

19. **FLORIDA MELAMPUS**   p. 276
    Detracia floridana (Pfeiffer, 1856)

PLATE 66

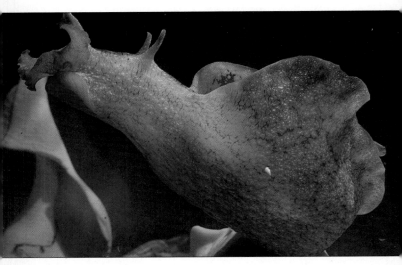

WILLCOX'S SEA-HARE, *Aplysia brasiliana* (Rang) ×½ **p. 283**

RAGGED SEA-HARE, *Bursatella leachi pleii* (Rang) ×½ **p. 284**

PLATE 67

UMBRELLA SHELL, *Umbraculum umbraculum* (Lft.) ×1 **p. 284**

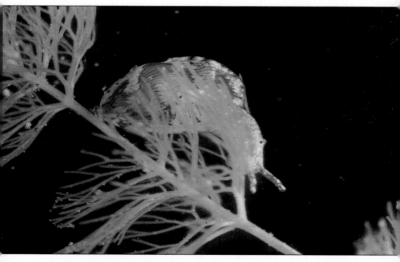

CARIBBEAN BIVALVED SNAIL, *Berthelinia caribbea* ×2 **p. 286**
(Ron J. Larson photo)

PLATE 68

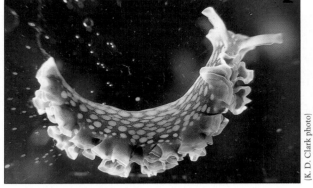

COMMON LETTUCE SLUG, *Tridachia crispata* (Mörch) ×2 **p. 286**

(K. D. Clark photo)

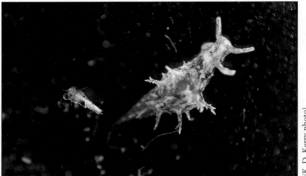

BLUE-SPOTTED SEA-HARE, *Stylocheilus longicauda* (Q. & G.) ×2 **p. 284**

(K. D. Kerry photo)

COMMON CLIONE, *Clione limacina* (Phipps) ×4 **p. 281**

(Norman Katz photo)

PLATE 69

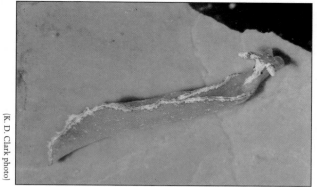

(K. D. Clark photo)

TUCA ELYSIA, *Elysia tuca* (Marcus & Marcus) ×2 **p. 285**

(K. D. Kerry photo)

PAPILLOSE ELYSIA, *Elysia papillosa* (Verrill) ×3 **p. 284**

(Alice D. Barlow photo)

FLORIDA ZEBRA DORIS, *Hypselodoris edenticulata* (White) ×2 **p. 287**

PLATE 70

(Steven F. Barry photo)

WHITE ATLANTIC DORIS, *Cadlina laevis* (L.)   ×3   **p. 287**

(K. D. Clark photo)

DUSKY STILIGER, *Stiliger fuscatus* Gould   ×3   **p. 285**

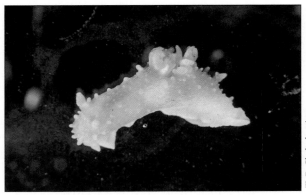

(K. D. Clark photo)

DUBIOUS POLYCERA, *Polycera dubia* (Sars)   ×3   **p. 288**

PLATE 71

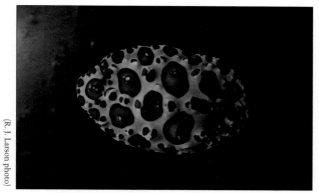

(R. J. Larson photo)

PAPILLOSE DORIS, *Phillidiopsis papilligera* Bergh ×2 **p. 288**

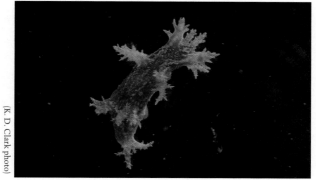

(K. D. Clark photo)

FROND EOLIS, *Dendronotus frondosus* (Ascanius) ×3 **p. 291**

(R. J. Larson photo)

BAYER'S TRITONIA, *Tritonia bayeri* Marcus, 1967 ×4 **p. 288**

PLATE 72

CORONATE DOTO, *Doto coronata* (Gmelin) ×4 **p. 289**

(K. D. Clark photo)

BOSTON FACELINA, *Facelina bostoniensis* (Couthouy) ×3 **p. 289**

(George M. Moore photo)

AIRY FAVORINUS, *Favorinus auritulus* Marcus ×4 **p. 290**

(K. D. Clark photo)

PLATE 73

(Norman Katz photo)

PAPILLOSE EOLIS, *Aeolidia papillosa* (L.) ×3 **p. 290**

(K. D. Clark photo)

WESTERN ATLANTIC DONDICE, *Dondice occidentalis* (Engel) ×2 **p. 290**

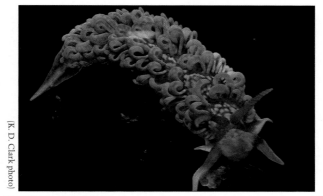

(K. D. Clark photo)

NEAPOLITAN SPURILLA, *S. neapolitana* (Delle Chiaje) ×2 **p. 290**

PLATE 74

CHITONS AND ARGONAUTS

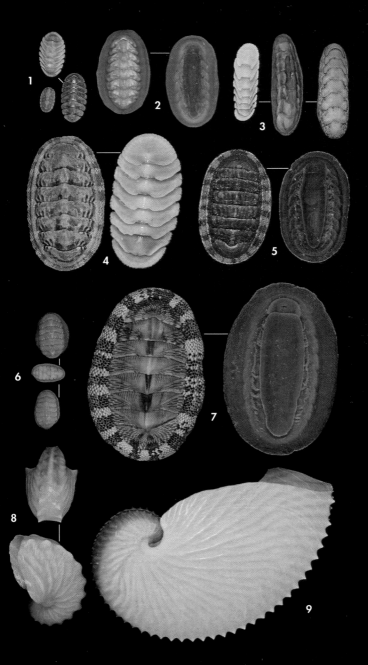

EASTERN TURRET SHELL   **Pl. 47**
Turritella exoleta (Linnaeus, 1758)
  Range: Southern Florida to West Indies.
  Habitat: Moderately shallow to deep water.
  Description: Height to 3 in., with 16 to 18 whorls. Shell slender and tall, with sharp apex. Sutures distinct. Upper few volutions, which are not occupied by the animal, divided by a septum at each half turn. Volutions decidedly concave at center, sculptured with fine revolving lines. Aperture squarish, lip thin. Color creamy white, usually splashed with chocolate-brown.

VARIEGATED TURRET SHELL   **Pl. 47**
Turritella variegata (Linnaeus, 1758)
  Range: Texas; West Indies.
  Habitat: Moderately shallow water.
  Description: Height 2 to 4 in. A gracefully elongated, spike-like species. About 12 rather flattish whorls, sutures well impressed. Sculpture of revolving lines. Aperture squarish, operculum horny. Color whitish or purplish, with reddish vertical streaks.

●**Genus** *Tachyrhynchus* **Mörch, 1868**

ERODED TURRET SHELL   **Pl. 42**
Tachyrhynchus erosum (Couthouy, 1834)
  Range: Labrador to Massachusetts; Alaska to Br. Columbia.
  Habitat: Moderately deep water.
  Description: About ³/₄ in. high. An elongate, high-spired shell of 9 or 10 whorls, each grooved with 5 blunt furrows that give the surface a spiral ornamentation. Aperture nearly round, operculum horny. Color chalky white, with a brown periostracum.
  Remarks: Apex commonly eroded or broken in majority of adults.

●**Genus** *Vermicularia* **Lamarck, 1799**

FARGO'S WORM SHELL   **Pl. 42**
Vermicularia fargoi Olsson, 1951
  Range: Western Florida to Texas.
  Habitat: Shallow water.
  Description: Length 3 to 5 in. In its youthful stages the shell is

tightly coiled and looks like a small Turritella, but as it grows older it becomes free and wanders off in an irregular and seemingly aimless fashion. Surface with longitudinal keels, rendering the aperture somewhat square. Color reddish brown.

Remarks: This genus used to be placed in the family Vermetidae. See next species for differences.

KNORR'S WORM SHELL   Pl. 42
Vermicularia knorri Deshayes, 1843
  Range: N. Carolina to West Indies; Bermuda.
  Habitat: Chiefly in sponges.
  Description: Length 2 to 3 in. Very much like Fargo's Worm Shell, but the tip and first few volutions are pure white, the rest of the shell buffy brown.
  Remarks: This genus used to be placed in the family Vermetidae.

COMMON WORM SHELL   Pl. 42
Vermicularia spirata Philippi, 1836
  Range: Florida to West Indies; Bermuda.
  Habitat: Shallow water.
  Description: Length to 6 in., possibly more. First few whorls tightly coiled, most of shell tubular and unpredictable; several individuals often found growing together in an intricate, tangled mass. Prominent longitudinal ridges. Color yellowish brown.
  Remarks: This curious creature appears more like a worm than a mollusk, but it is a true gastropod. The body is greatly elongated, and the head bears tentacles, eyes, and a toothed tongue (radula) that is thoroughly snail-like. The shell has been likened to a petrified angleworm. Some authorities believe that this species does not occur north of Florida, and that the usually smaller specimens found off Massachusetts should be called *V. radicula* Stimpson.

■ SUNDIALS: Family Architectonicidae

SHELL solid, circular, and slightly elevated. The umbilicus is broad and deep, commonly bordered by a knobby keel. Confined chiefly to warm seas.

● **Genus** *Architectonica* **Röding, 1798**

COMMON SUNDIAL   Pl. 47
Architectonica nobilis Röding, 1798
   Range: N. Carolina to Texas; West Indies; Brazil.
   Habitat: Shallow water.
   Description: Diameter about 1½ in., height about ¾ in. Shell
   circular and somewhat flattened, with 6 or 7 whorls and
   rather distinct sutures. Base flat. Surface finely checked by
   crossing spiral lines and radiating ridges that produce a pattern of raised granules. Umbilicus wide and deep and strongly crenulate. Aperture round, lip thin and sharp. Color
   white or gray, spotted and marbled with brown and purple.
   Remarks: Formerly in the genus *Solarium* Lamarck, it has
   been listed as *S. granulatum* (Lamarck, 1816). Related species, some of them much larger but otherwise similar, are
   found in the Pacific and Indian oceans.

● **Genus** *Heliacus* **Orbigny, 1842**

ORBIGNY'S SUNDIAL   Pl. 43
Heliacus bisulcatus Orbigny, 1842
   Range: N. Carolina to Brazil; Bermuda.
   Habitat: Moderately deep water.
   Description: Diam. about ½ in. With 4 or 5 whorls, low spire.
   Sculptured with prominent beaded cords. Umbilicus wide
   and deep, crenulate at edge. Color yellowish brown. Opercu-
   lum corneous and conical.

ATLANTIC CYLINDER SUNDIAL   Pl. 47
Heliacus cylindricus (Gmelin, 1791)
   Range: Southern Florida to Brazil; Bermuda.
   Habitat: Moderately shallow water.
   Description: Diameter about ½ in., height approximately the
   same. With 4 or 5 whorls, spire moderately elevated. Sculpture of revolving lines, cut by sharp vertical heads. Umbilicus narrow but deep, the edges crenulate. Color brownish to
   black, commonly dotted with white.
   Remarks: Feeds and lives on the colonial zoanthid coelenter-
   ate, Palythoa. Uncommon.

● **Genus** *Philippia* **Gray, 1847**

KREBS' SUNDIAL *Philippia krebsi* (Mörch, 1875)   Pl. 44
   Range: N. Carolina to Brazil; Bermuda.

Habitat: Moderately deep water.
Description: Diameter about $\frac{1}{2}$ in. A rather flatly coiled shell of 4 or 5 whorls. Spire low. Surface smooth and polished. Umbilicus moderate-sized, bordered by 2 beaded lines. Color yellowish white, with brownish spots at periphery.

■ WORM SHELLS: Family Vermetidae

Wormlike mollusks usually attached to some firm substrate, such as rocks or other shells and sometimes on sponges. The early whorls are similar to those of other young gastropods but the later whorls are nonattached to one another and sometimes become considerably elongated. Worldwide, generally in warm seas. Operculum chitinous and with many whorls.

● **Genus** *Petaloconchus* **Lea, 1843**

ERECT WORM SHELL   **Fig. 56**
Petaloconchus erectus (Dall, 1888)
Range: South Florida to the West Indies.
Habitat: Moderately shallow water; on dead shells.
Description: Diameter of each tube $\frac{1}{8}$ in. Spreads out over the surface of corals or some dead shell, occasionally one tube growing over another; the last half inch or so usually stands straight up. Color whitish.

Figure 56. Erect Worm Shell *Petaloconchus erectus*

IRREGULAR WORM SHELL **Pl. 42**
Petaloconchus irregularis (Orbigny, 1842)
  Range: South Florida to the West Indies.
  Habitat: Moderately shallow water; on stones.
  Description: Diameter of each tube nearly $1/4$ in. A tangled mass of reddish brown, twisted and coiled tubelike shells. Surface roughened by coarse revolving ridges.

BLACK WORM SHELL **Pl. 42**
Petaloconchus nigricans (Dall, 1884)
  Range: West Florida.
  Habitat: Shallow water.
  Description: Diameter of each tube $1/8$ in. Individually a loosely coiled, twisted, elongated tubelike shell growing in almost any contorted manner, but it is usually intertwined with others of its kind to form an intricate mass. Shell ribbed horizontally and roughened by wrinkles and lines of growth. Color reddish brown to black.
  Remarks: This wormlike gastropod often forms reefs just off shore with the accumulation of its twisted shells. It is considered a subspecies of the West Indian *P. varians* (Orbigny, 1841) by some workers.

● **Genus** *Serpulorbis* **Sasso, 1827**

DECUSSATE WORM SHELL **Pl. 42**
Serpulorbis decussata (Gmelin, 1791)
  Range: N. Carolina to the West Indies.
  Habitat: Shallow water.
  Description: Diameter of tube about 5 mm., sometimes a little more. A wormlike gastropod living singly and attached to a stone or dead shell; adhering surface is flat, generally in a coiled position. Surface decorated with longitudinal lines or ridges. Color yellowish brown. Operculum absent.
  Remarks: The form, *Serpulorbis riisei* (Mörch, 1862) from the West Indies, is more pebbly.

■ **SLIT WORM SHELLS: Family Siliquariidae**

  Shell tubular, irregular, often spiral at first. Tube with continuous longitudinal slit. Attached to stones and dead shells.

● **Genus** *Siliquaria* **Bruguière, 1789**

SLIT WORM SHELL *Siliquaria squamata* Blainville, 1827 **Pl. 42**
  Range: Off N. Carolina to Brazil; Bermuda.

Habitat: Shallow water.
Description: Diameter about 17, in., length of shell may be as much as 6 in. A loosely coiled snail living unattached. Noticeable slit along upper surface of shell. Ornamentation of weak longitudinal ridges. Early whorls smooth and white, later whorls becoming spinose and stained with brown.

■ PLANAXIS: Family Planaxidae

Small brownish snails living under stones in shallow water and characterized by a spirally grooved ornamentation. The aperture is oval, well-notched below. The operculum is soft, chitinous and brown. Common in warm seas.

● Genus *Angiola* Dall, 1926

DWARF ATLANTIC PLANAXIS   **Pl. 43**
Angiola lineata (da Costa, 1778)
   Range: South Florida to the West Indies; Bermuda.
   Habitat: Shallow water; under stones.
   Description: About ¼ in. high. Quite solid and well inflated. With 3 or 4 whorls, decorated with evenly spaced spiral grooves. Aperture oval, notched at lower margin. Outer lip thick. Yellowish brown, with spiral brown bands.
   Remarks: Common from the mid-tide line to a few feet in quiet areas amid small stones. Formerly in the genus *Planaxis*.

● Genus *Supplanaxis* Thiele, 1929

BLACK PLANAXIS *Supplanaxis nucleus* (Bruguière, 1789) **Pl. 46**
   Range: Southeast Florida to the West Indies; Bermuda.
   Habitat: Shallow water; under stones.
   Description: Height about ¼ in. A stubbier shell than Lined Planaxis. With 3 or 4 whorls, the last one making up most of the shell, sutures distinct. Aperture large and oval, notched below, with shiny area on columella. Outer lip strongly crenulate within. Color rich brown, with rather thick grayish periostracum.
   Remarks: This genus has a large brood pouch on each side of the head.

■ MODULUS: Family Modulidae

Flattish, top-shaped shells, the whorls grooved and tuberculated. There is a narrow umbilicus. The columella ends below in a sharp tooth. There is but a single genus in this family. Found in warm seas.

● Genus *Modulus* Gray, 1842

ANGLED MODULUS
Modulus carchedonius (Lamarck, 1822)
Range: Caribbean.
Habitat: Shallow water.
Description: Height about $1/2$ in. With 4 or 5 whorls, rather pointed apex. Periphery sharply angled. Small umbilicus, distinct tooth on lower columella. Sculpture of revolving beaded lines. Color yellowish tan, beaded lines reddish brown.

ATLANTIC MODULUS   Pl. 46
Modulus modulus (Linnaeus, 1758)
Range: Off N. Carolina to Brazil; Bermuda.
Habitat: Shallow water; among weeds and turtle grass.
Description: A knobby little shell about $1/2$ in. high and about the same in diameter. Spire rather low. With 3 or 4 whorls, body whorl large, with sloping shoulders. Periphery keeled. Sculpture of low revolving ridges and stout vertical ribs separated by deep grooves. Aperture nearly round, outer lip thin and crenulate. Operculum horny, small umbilicus. Color yellowish white, spotted and marked with brown.
Remarks: A somewhat more knobby form used to be called a subspecies, *M. m. floridanus* Conrad, 1869, but now all of the specimens found in Florida are considered as one single, somewhat variable species.

■ HORN SHELLS: Family Potamididae

These are mud dwellers, with elongated, many-whorled shells, usually with vertical ribs or grooves. The aperture is round, the lip commonly flaring. Distributed in warm seas. Operculum horny, thin, with a few whorls and the nucleus at the center.

● **Genus Cerithidea Swainson, 1840**

COSTATE HORN SHELL   **Pl. 46**
Cerithidea costata (da Costa, 1778)
  Range: South Florida to the West Indies.
  Habitat: Shallow water.
  Description: Height 1/2 in. About 12 rounded whorls, sutures well defined. Each volution sculptured with rather thin and sharp vertical ribs, which tend to fade somewhat on body whorl. Aperture nearly round, lip thin. Color yellowish brown.
  Remarks: The subspecies *turrita* Stearns, 1873, from Tampa to Sanibel, has 15 to 20 (instead of 25 to 30) axial ribs on the next to the last whorl.

PLICATE HORN SHELL
Cerithidea pliculosa (Menke, 1829)
  Range: Louisiana to Texas; Cuba.
  Habitat: Shallow water.
  Description: Height 1 in. From 10 to 12 well-rounded whorls, sutures well defined. Sculpture is of curved vertical ribs crossed by fine spiral lines; usually 1 or 2 pronounced varices. Color brown, sometimes with paler band midway of each volution.

LADDER HORN SHELL   **Pl. 46**
Cerithidea scalariformis (Say, 1825)
  Range: S. Carolina to the West Indies; Bermuda.
  Habitat: Shallow water.
  Description: About 1 in. high. With 10 to 13 well-rounded whorls, sutures very distinct. Sculptured with closely spaced vertical ribs, no varices. Base of body whorl bears spiral riblets. Aperture large and circular, outer lip partially reflected. Operculum horny. Color pale to buffy gray.

● **Genus Batillaria Benson, 1842**

FALSE CERITH *Batillaria minima* (Gmelin, 1791)   **Pl. 43**
  Range: South Florida to Brazil; Bermuda.
  Habitat: Shallow water; mud flats.
  Description: About 1/2 in. high. Elongate, with 6 to 8 whorls, sutures distinct. Apex sharp. Sculpture of low vertical ribs, broken by unequally knobby ridges. Aperture oval, canal

short and turned to left. Black or deep brown, commonly with a paler band encircling each volution just below the suture.

Remarks: An extremely variable shell in its markings. Many individuals are sharply black and white. A jet-black form is sometimes listed as a form *nigrescens* (Menke, 1828).

■ CERITHS: Family Cerithiidae

A large family of generally elongate, many-whorled snails living in moderately shallow water, mostly on grasses and seaweeds, in tropical and semitropical seas. The aperture is small and oblique, and there is a short anterior canal, commonly somewhat twisted.

● Genus *Cerithium* Bruguière, 1789

IVORY CERITH *Cerithium eburneum* Bruguière, 1792   **Pl. 46**
Range: Southeast Florida to the West Indies.
Habitat: Shallow water.
Description: About 1 in. high. Elongate, spire tapering to sharp apex. With 6 or 7 whorls, sutures distinct. Sculpture of revolving bands of small tubercles gives surface a beaded appearance. Aperture oval, canal short and turned to left. White to deep brown, usually with reddish brown blotches.
Remarks: The form *algicola* C. B. Adams, 1845, has extra long pointed beads in the middle of the whorl. More common in the West Indies.

FLORIDA CERITH *Cerithiurn atratum* (Born, 1778)   **Pl. 46**
Range: N. Carolina to Florida to Brazil.
Habitat: Shallow water.
Description: Height to 1½ in. Sturdy, apex sharp, about 10 whorls with distinct sutures. Sculpture of elevated, nodular ribs, sharply angled at edge of volutions, and many unequal ridges and fine lines spiraling over entire shell. Aperture small, oval, oblique. White or gray, with spiral pattern of brown.
Remarks: *C. floridanum* Mörch, 1876, is a synonym.

Figure 57. a) Cerith *Batillaria* **b)** Cerith *Cerithium*

STOCKY CERITH *Cerithium litteratum* Born, 1778   **Pl. 46**
Range: Bermuda; south Florida to Brazil.
Habitat: Shallow water.
Description: About 1 in. high. Shell stout, apex sharply pointed. With 7 whorls, sutures somewhat indistinct. Two rows of prominent knobs encircle each volution (those on shoulders the largest), and between them are spiral lines more or less beaded. Aperture moderately large and oval, lip thickened. Canal short and only partially recurved. Color varies from white to gray, checked with brownish black.

FLY-SPECKED CERITH *Cerithium muscarum* Say, 1832   **Pl. 46**
Range: South Florida to the West Indies.
Habitat: Shallow brackish water.
Description: Height 1 in. Elongate-conical, apex sharp. With 9 or 10 whorls, sutures rather distinct. Sculpture of prominent vertical ribs, about 11 on body whorl, crossed by impressed revolving lines. Aperture oval and oblique, canal short and turned to left. Color grayish white, with small chestnut dots.

DWARF CERITH *Cerithium lutosum* Menke, 1828   **Pl. 46**
Range: Florida to the West Indies; Texas; Bermuda.
Habitat: Shallow water.
Description: Generally less than $1/2$ in. high. Stoutly conical, apex sharp. With 7 or 8 whorls, sutures indistinct. Revolving rows of beads decorate volutions, and a varix on the last whorl is common. Color varies from dark brown to whitish with darker mottlings.
Remarks: *C. variabile* C. B. Adams, 1845, is a synonym of the common species.

SCHWENGEL'S CERITH
Pl. 46
Cerithium guinaicum Philippi, 1849
Range: Florida and the Caribbean; West Africa.
Habitat: On reef flats, clinging to rocks.
Description: From 1 to 1¹/₂ in., somewhat stubby, with 9 or 10 large, rounded, elongate ribs or nodes per whorl which on the last whorl are limited to the upper third portion. Color cream with burnt smudges of brown. Fine spiral thread encircle the whorls. Aperture white, with a blackish smudge inside the outer wall.

● **Genus *Bittium* Gray, 1847**

ALTERNATE BITTIUM *Bittium alternatum* (Say, 1822) Pl. 45
Range: Massachusetts to Virginia.
Habitat: Shallow water.
Description: Height about ¹/₅ in. With 6 to 8 rounded whorls, well-impressed sutures. Sculpture a granulated network of elevated spiral lines crossed by rounded vertical folds. Aperture obliquely rounded, lip sharp. Canal a mere notch or fissure. Operculum horny. Color bluish black or slate-gray, the lower whorls sometimes paler in tone. See next species for differentiation.
Remarks: Young specimens are reddish brown and sometimes occur in such numbers that the sand appears to be alive with them.

VARIABLE BITTIUM *Bittium varium* (Pfeiffer, 1840) Pl. 45
Range: Maryland to Texas.
Habitat: Shallow water; on eelgrass.
Description: Much like *B. alternatum,* but a trifle smaller and slimmer, usually with a thickened rib (varix) on the body whorl. Sculpture of weak vertical folds and spiral lines. Grayish or slate-colored.

● **Genus *Litiopa* Rang, 1829**

SARGASSUM SNAIL *Litiopa melanostoma* Rang, 1829 Pl. 53
Range: Massachusetts to the West Indies; Bermuda.
Habitat: Pelagic in floating sargassum weed.
Description: About ¹/₄ in. high. A thin and delicate shell, its shape rather stoutly conic. With 6 or 7 roundish whorls, sutures well impressed. Sharply pointed apex, elongate-oval

aperture, lip thin and sharp. Volutions bear weak revolving lines, but surface appears smooth and glossy. Color pale yellowish gray, often with rows of small brownish dots.
Remarks: This is a pelagic gastropod living in floating masses of sargassum weed, and specimens are often found in clumps blown ashore. *L. bombyx* "Rang" is a synonym.

● **Genus *Alaba* H. & A. Adams, 1853**

VARICOSE ALABA SHELL   **Fig. 58 & Pl. 45**
Alaba incerta (Orbigny, 1842)
    Range: Florida Keys to the West Indies.
    Habitat: Shallow water; weeds.
    Description: About ¼ in. high. A slender elongate shell of about 7 whorls, sutures fairly well indented. Aperture oval, lip thin. Surface glossy, color white or gray.
    Remarks: Formerly listed as *A. tervaricosa* C. B. Adams, 1845.

● **Genus *Cerithiopsis* Forbes & Hanley, 1849**

CRYSTAL MINIATURE CERITH
Cerithiopsis crystallinum Dall, 1881
    Range: Gulf of Mexico.
    Habitat: Deep water, 18 to 2,500 feet.
    Description: A slender spikelike shell ½ in. high. With 9 or 10 whorls, sutures moderately distinct. Decorated with revolving rows of tubercles. Lower portion of body whorl bears spiral grooves. Aperture small. Color white.

Figure 58. Varicose Alaba Shell *Alaba incerta*

AWL MINIATURE CERITH
Cerithiopsis emersoni (C. B. Adams, 1838)
Range: Massachusetts to Brazil.
Habitat: Moderately shallow water.
Description: About ¹/₂ in. high. A slender shell of 10 to 14 flattish whorls, sutures indistinct. Sculpture of spiraling rows of tiny beads, base of last whorl smooth, with cordlike ridges. Aperture quite small, outer lip somewhat thickened, inner lip slightly twisted. Color chocolate-brown.
Remarks: Erroneously thought to be *C. subulata* (Montagu, 1808).

GREEN'S MINIATURE CERITH
Cerithiopsis greeni (C. B. Adams, 1839)
Range: Massachusetts to Brazil; Bermuda.
Habitat: Shallow water.
Description: Nearly ¹/₄ in. high. A shiny shell of about 8 whorls. Volutions rather flat, sutures indistinct. Ornamented by revolving rows of tiny beads. Aperture quite small, with smooth area on the slightly arched inner lip. Color brown.

● **Genus** *Seila* **A. Adams, 1861**

ADAMS' MINIATURE CERITH   Pl. 53
Seila adamsi (H. C. Lea, 1845)
Range: Massachusetts to the West Indies; Texas.
Habitat: Shallow water to 240 ft.
Description: Height about ¹/₂ in. Slender, elongate, with about 12 whorls, sutures indistinct. Sculpture of 3 or 4 elevated revolving ridges on each volution, with fine vertical lines between them. Aperture small, canal short and twisted. Color brown.
Remarks: Formerly listed as *Cerithiopsis terebralis* (C. B. Adams, 1840), not Lamarck, 1804. Common.

■ TRIPHORAS: Family Triphoridae

An interesting family of very small, elongate, left-handed (sinistral) gastropods. There are many whorls. Widely distributed in warm seas.

● Genus *Triphora* Blainville, 1828

WHITE TRIPHORA   Pl. 45
Triphora melanura (C. B. Adams, 1850)
  Range: Off N. Carolina to Brazil; Bermuda.
  Habitat: Shallow water to 300 ft.
  Description: About ¹/₄ in. high. A slender shell of some 12 rather flat whorls, decorated with revolving rows of small beads. Apex sharp, aperture small. Sinistral (left-handed). Color white, sometimes with a few scattered reddish brown marks.

BLACK-LINED TRIPHORA   Fig. 59
Triphora nigrocinta (C. B. Adams, 1850)
  Range: Massachusetts to Brazil; Bermuda.
  Habitat: Shallow water; weeds.
  Description: About ¹/₄ in. high. Shell elongate, 10 to 12 whorls, sutures slightly excavated. Surface bears revolving rows of beadlike tubercles, 4 rows on body whorl. Spiral turns to left (sinistral) instead of to right as with most gastropods. Color pale brown, occasionally with lighter band near suture.
  Remarks: Sometimes considered a subspecies of the European *T. perversa* (Linnaeus).

BEAUTIFUL TRIPHORA   Fig. 59
Triphora pulchella (C. B. Adams, 1850)
  Range: South Florida to Brazil.
  Habitat: Moderately shallow water.
  Description: Nearly ¹/₄ in. high. As many as 15 moderately rounded whorls, sutures indistinct. Spiral turns to left (sinistral). Sculpture consists of 3 rows of tiny beads on each whorl, the beads connected by threadlike lines. Upper portions of each volution rich brown, lower part white

● Genus *Triforis* Jousseaume, 1884

THOMAS' TRIPHORA   Fig. 59
Triforis turristhomae (Holten, 1802)
  Range: N. Carolina to Brazil; Bermuda.
  Habitat: Shallow water to 30 ft. in sand.
  Description: Height ¹/₄ in. Slender and high-spired, 12 to 16 whorls. Sinistral sculpture of 2 revolving rows of heads, upper row white, the lower with a brownish band.

Figure 59. a) Black-lined Triphora *Triphora nigrocincta* **b)** Beautiful Triphora *Triphora pulchella* **c)** Thomas' Triphora *Triforis turristhomae*

■ WENTLETRAPS: Family Epitoniidae

These are predatory, carnivorous snails, occurring in all seas, and popularly known as wentletraps or staircase shells. They are high-spired, usually white and polished, and consist of many rounded whorls. The outer lip is thickened considerably during rest periods in shell growth, and this thickened lip becomes a new varix as the mollusk increases in size. Among the most delicately graceful of all marine shells and great favorites with collectors.

● Genus *Cirsotrema* Mörch, 1852

DALL'S WENTLETRAP *Cirsotrema dalli* Rehder, 1945   **Pl. 48**
Range: N. Carolina to West Indies and south to Brazil.
Habitat: Deep water; from 80 to 300 ft.
Description: About 1 in. high. A slender, high-spired shell of about 8 whorls, sutures well indented. Aperture round, bordered by a thickened lip, and as growth takes place successive varices are left on the earlier whorls at regular intervals in the form of thickened ribs. Surface between varices heavily pitted. Color dusky white.

● **Genus *Acirsa* Mörch, 1857**

NORTHERN WENTLETRAP   **Pl. 48**
Acirsa borealis (Lyell, 1842)
  Range: Arctic Ocean to Massachusetts.
  Habitat: Moderately shallow water.
  Description: Height to $1\frac{1}{4}$ in. With 8 or 9 whorls, surface smooth except for very tiny revolving lines. This wentletrap completely lacks the characteristic vertical ribs of this group. Aperture circular, outer lip thin. Color yellowish to grayish white.
  Remarks: Formerly listed as *A. costulata* (Mighels & Adams, 1842).

● **Genus *Opalia* H. & A. Adams, 1853**

HOTESSIER'S WENTLETRAP   **Pl. 48**
Opalia hotessieriana (Orbigny, 1842)
  Range: South Florida to the West Indies; Bermuda.
  Habitat: Moderately shallow water.
  Description: About $\frac{3}{4}$ in. high. With 7 whorls, the vertical ribs only faintly present, but along the top of each whorl is a series of large squarish indentations, or notches. Aperture round. Color grayish white.

PUMILIO WENTLETRAP *Opalia pumilio* (Mörch, 1874)   **Pl. 48**
  Range: Florida to the West Indies; Brazil; Bermuda.
  Habitat: Moderately shallow water.
  Description: About $\frac{1}{2}$ in. high. With 7 or 8 whorls, sutures distinct. Sculpture of curving vertical ribs, about 15 on body whorl. Aperture round, lip thickened. Color white or yellowish.

● **Genus *Amaea* H. & A. Adams, 1853**

MITCHELL'S WENTLETRAP *Amaea mitchelli* Dall, 1896   **Pl. 47**
  Range: Texas coast to Panama.
  Habitat: With sea anemonies in sand in shallow water. Uncommon.
  Description: Length 2 in., thin but strong; without an umbilicus. With about 15 rather strongly convex, pale ivory whorls which have a dark brownish band at the periphery and a solid brown area below the basal ridge. With 22 low

ribs per whorl. Numerous spiral threads are fine and produce a weak, reticulated pattern.

● **Genus *Epitonium* Röding, 1798**

BLADED WENTLETRAP   **Pl. 48**
Epitonium albidum (Orbigny, 1842)
   Range: South Florida to Argentina; Bermuda.
   Habitat: Moderately shallow water.
   Description: Height about ³/₄ in. A stocky shell with 7 or 8 rounded whorls, sutures distinct. Sculpture of sharp blade-like ribs, about 12 on body whorl. Substance thin, the ribs visible through shell in aperture. Color white.

ANGULATE WENTLETRAP   **Pl. 48**
Epitonium angulatum (Say, 1830)
   Range: Long Island to Texas; Bermuda.
   Habitat: Moderately shallow water; common.
   Description: About ³/₄ in. high. Stoutly elongate, some 6 whorls that do not touch each other in the coil. About 10 vertical bladelike varices on each volution, each with a more or less blunt angle (shoulder) above, near the suture. Color white.

CHAMPION'S WENTLETRAP   **Pl. 48**
Epitonium championi Clench & Turner, 1952
   Range: Massachusetts to N. Carolina.
   Habitat: Shallow water.
   Description: Height about ¹/₂ in. About 10 whorls that are not as convex as in most of the wentletraps. Volutions bear thickened varices, about 9 to a whorl, and between them the surface is marked with distinct revolving lines. No ridge at base of body whorl. Color dull white.
   Remarks: This species was not discovered and named until 1951. Specimens seen before that time were thought to be young examples of the Greenland Wentletrap (below)

WIDELY-COILED WENTLETRAP   **Pl. 48**
Epitonium echinaticostum (Orbigny, 1842)
   Range: Bermuda; south Florida to Brazil.
   Habitat: Moderately deep water.
   Description: Less than ¹/₂ in. high. About 8 very convex whorls, sculptured with sharp varices, about 7 on body whorl. Varices thin, commonly waved or fluted, so that the

shell has an elaborate appearance. Aperture round, bordered by thickened lip. Small but well-defined umbilicus. Color pure white.

Remarks: In occasional specimens the last few whorls become free and well separated.

GREENLAND WENTLETRAP   Pl. 48
Epitonium greenlandicum (Perry, 1811)
   Range: Circumpolar; south to Long Island; Alaska; Norway.
   Habitat: Deep water.
   Description: A large wentletrap, attaining a height of nearly 2 in., although most are closer to 1 in. Shell elongate, tapering regularly to a rounded point. About 12 moderately rounded whorls, barred with about 12 stout, rather flat varices. Spaces between varices sculptured with rounded revolving ridges. Generally a well-marked spiral ridge at base. Aperture circular, bordered by a stoutly thickened lip. Color dull yellowish white.
   Remarks: This is one of the showy shells of the n. Atlantic, making up in bizarre sculpture what it lacks in size.

HUMPHREY'S WENTLETRAP   Pl. 48
Epitonium humphreysi (Kiener, 1838)
   Range: Massachusetts to Texas.
   Habitat: Moderately shallow water.
   Description: About ³/₄ in. high. With 8 or 9 rounded whorls, decorated with well-spaced thickened varices; spaces between are smooth and glossy, sometimes showing faint spiral lines. Color pure white.
   Remarks: Formerly listed as *Scalaria sayana* Dall, 1889.

KREBS' WENTLETRAP *Epitonium krebsii* (Mörch, 1874)   Pl. 48
   Range: S. Carolina to Brazil; Bermuda.
   Habitat: Moderately shallow water.
   Description: About ¹/₂ in. high. With 5 or 6 convex whorls that are hardly joined at sutures. Body whorl relatively large, giving shell a somewhat squat appearance; there is a noticeable umbilicus. About 10 varices to a volution, slightly toothed at upper ends. Color white.

LAMELLOSE WENTLETRAP   Pl. 48
Epitonium lamellosum (Lamarck, 1822)
   Range: South Florida to the West Indies; Bermuda.
   Habitat: Moderately shallow water.
   Description: Height to 1¹/₄ in. With 7 or 8 whorls, each with

about 11 thin bladelike varices, spaces between them smooth and polished. Single revolving line at base. Shell elongate, rather stout at base. Creamy to pure white, sometimes with irregular markings of pale brown.
Remarks: Formerly listed as *E. clathrum* (Linnaeus, 1758).

MANY-RIBBED WENTLETRAP   Pl. 48
Epitonium multistriatum (Say, 1826)
   Range: Massachusetts to Texas; Bermuda.
   Habitat: Moderately deep water.
   Description: About $1/2$ in. high. Well elevated and sharply pointed, with 7 or 8 convex whorls, sutures well indented. Varices closely crowded, particularly on earlier whorls; about 19 on last volution, but on a section 2 or 3 volutions away from apex there may be as many as 40. Color dull white.

NEW ENGLAND WENTLETRAP   Pl. 48
Epitonium novangliae (Couthouy, 1838)
   Range: Virginia; West Indies south to Brazil.
   Habitat: Moderately shallow water.
   Description: About $1/2$ in. high. A delicate shell of 8 or 9 whorls. Some 12 robust varices to a volution, the spaces between marked with weak spiral lines, and still weaker crosslines, exhibiting a faint network pattern. Color white, sometimes lightly banded on later whorls.
   Remarks: The first specimen (type) of this species was taken from the stomach of a cod in New England — hence the name *novangliae*; however, no specimens have ever been taken alive north of Virginia.

WESTERN ATLANTIC WENTLETRAP   Pl. 48
Epitonium occidentale (Nyst, 1871)
   Range: S. Carolina to Brazil; Bermuda.
   Habitat: Deep water.
   Description: Nearly 1 in. high. With 7 or 8 rounded whorls, sutures deep. About 14 thin varices on body whorl, well angled at suture. Surface between varices smooth and glossy. Color white.

BROWN-BANDED WENTLETRAP   Pl. 48
Epitonium rupicola (Kurtz, 1860)
   Range: Massachusetts to Texas.
   Habitat: Moderately shallow to deep water.
   Description: Height $1/2$ in. About 10 rounded whorls, each with some 10 to 16 delicate varices, spaces between smooth and

polished. Sutures distinct. Color pinkish white, often with 1 or 2 brownish bands on later volutions.
Remarks: Formerly listed as *E. lineatum* (Say, 1822).

TOLLIN'S WENTLETRAP   Pl. 48
Epitonium tollini Bartsch, 1938
   Range: Gulf of Mexico.
   Habitat: Moderately shallow water.
   Description: About $1/2$ in. high. With 8 to 10 rounded whorls, each with about 12 varices that are rounded at the shoulders, spaces between them smooth and polished. Color pure white.

● **Genus *Sthenorhytis* Conrad, 1862**

NOBLE WENTLETRAP   Pl. 48
Sthenorhytis pernobilis (Fischer & Bernardi, 1857)
   Range: N. Carolina to the West Indies.
   Habitat: Deep water.
   Description: Height to $1^3/_4$ in. A sturdy shell of 6 or 7 rounded whorls, sutures well indented. Taper rapid, body whorl wide. Sculpture of strong curving bladelike varices, 12 on last volution; surface in between with weak revolving lines. Aperture round. Color white.
   Remarks: Probably our largest wentletrap, but unfortunately quite rare. *Sthenorytis* is a misspelling.

■ PURPLE SEA-SNAILS: Family Janthinidae

These are floating pelagic mollusks (living miles from land). They are very delicate lavender or purple shells, shaped much like land snails. There is no operculum. The animal is capable of ejecting a purplish fluid when disturbed. The mollusk is fastened to a raft of frothy bubbles of its own making, to which the eggs are attached. These snails float about in tremendous quantities; sometimes huge numbers are blown ashore, where the purple color may stain the beach for considerable distances.

● **Genus *Janthina* Röding, 1798**

ELONGATE PURPLE SEA-SNAIL   Pl. 47
Janthina globosa Swainson, 1822
   Range: Both coasts of U.S.

Habitat: Pelagic; warm waters.
Description: Diameter about $3/4$ in. Shell globular, thin, very fragile, with about 3 whorls. Aperture large and moderately elongate. Color pale violet all over, usually darker toward base.
Remarks: Despite its scientific name, this is not the most globose species.

COMMON PURPLE SEA-SNAIL   Pl. 47
Janthina janthina (Linnaeus, 1758)
    Range: Both coasts of U.S.
    Habitat: Pelagic; warm waters.
    Description: Diameter about $1^1/_2$ in. This graceful shell is thin and fragile and consists of 3 or 4 sloping whorls. Surface bears very fine lines (striae). Aperture large, lip thin and sharp. No operculum or umbilicus. A two-toned shell: pale violet above, deep purple below.

DWARF PURPLE SEA-SNAIL   Pl. 47
Janthina exigua Lamarck, 1816
    Range: Both coasts of U.S.
    Habitat: Pelagic; warm waters.
    Description: About $1/4$ in. in size. Whorls slightly flattened from above. Outer lip with a prominent notch. Light-violet, banded at the suture.

PALLID PURPLE SEA-SNAIL   Pl. 47
Janthina pallida (Thompson, 1840)
    Range: Worldwide.
    Habitat: Pelagic; warm seas.
    Description: About $3/4$ to 1 in., globose; base of aperture rounded. Color whitish violet, not glossy.
    Remarks: Despite its scientific name, this common shell, occasionally washed ashore, is the most globose of our four species.

● **Genus *Recluzia* Petit, 1853**

RECLUZIA SNAIL *Recluzia rollandiana* Petit, 1853
    Range: Florida to Texas; Brazil.
    Habitat: Pelagic; associated with the floating sea anemone, Minyas. Rare.
    Description: Size 1 in. Resembles a freshwater pond snail, Lymnaea; thin-shelled, but strong. Whorls globose, chocolate-brown. Float of brown bubbles is 2–3 in. long

■ HOOF SHELLS: Family Hipponicidae

Shell obliquely conical and generally thick and heavy, the apex hooked backward but not spirally. Surface usually rough, wrinkled, and yellowish or grayish white. The animal secretes a shelly plate between itself and the object on which it lives. This plate was once believed to be a second valve, and several species were described as bivalve mollusks.

● Genus *Hipponix* Defrance, 1819

HOOF SHELL *Hipponix antiquatus* (Linnaeus, 1767) **Pl. 49**
Range: Florida to the West Indies; west Mexico.
Habitat: Shallow water; on stones.
Description: Height $1/2$ to $3/4$ in. Shell thick, conical, cap-shaped, concave at base. Apex bluntly pointed and curved backward. Surface variable, sometimes fairly smooth but often wrinkled by coarse laminations. Variable in shape too, since it lives attached to a rock or shell and grows to conform to its particular shape of seat; secretes a calcareous plate between itself and object to which it adheres. Color white or yellowish white.

■ FOSSARUS: Family Fossaridae

Small, short, and stubby shells, the surface strongly sculptured. Occur in cold seas, generally at considerable depths.

● Genus *Fossarus* Philippi, 1841

ELEGANT FOSSARUS **Pl. 45**
Fossarus elegans Verrill & Smith, 1882
Range: Massachusetts to Florida.
Habitat: Deep water.
Description: Height $1/8$ in. Shell ovate, stout, and rugged, with acutely pointed spire. With 5 sharply carinated whorls, elegantly latticed with sharp bladelike lines between the keels (carinae). Aperture nearly round, outer lip thickened, with projections where the carinae terminate. Color white.

■ HAIRY-KEELED SNAILS: Family Trichotropidae

Small thin shells with widely flaring outer lips. The angles of the whorls are keeled, and there is a small umbilicus. Found in cool seas.

● **Genus *Trichotropis* Broderip & Sowerby, 1829**

NORTHERN HAIRY-KEELED SNAIL
Trichotropis borealis Broderip & Sowerby, 1829
  Range: Labrador to Massachusetts; n. Pacific.
  Habitat: Moderately shallow water.
  Description: About ¹/₂ in. high. With 4 whorls with deeply channeled sutures. Body whorl relatively large, encircled by 2 prominent keels, as well as 2 or 3 less conspicuous ones. Aperture broad and rounded above and somewhat pointed below. Outer lip flares considerably. Color brown, with yellowish periostracum that rises like a bristly fringe along the keels.
  Remarks: A common shell collected from the stomachs of fishes taken off the New England coast.

■ CAP SHELLS: Family Capulidae

Shell conical, cap-shaped, without internal plate or cup. The apex is spiral, the base open, and the whole shell is considerably curved.

● **Genus *Capulus* Montfort, 1810**

INCURVED CAP SHELL   **Pl. 49**
Capulus incurvatus (Gmelin, 1791)
  Range: N. Carolina to Brazil.
  Habitat: Shallow water; on stones.
  Description: Height ¹/₂ in. Caplike, nearly all body whorl. Apex incurved. Aperture large and round. Sculpture of revolving and vertical lines, producing a cancellate pattern. Color glossy white.

CAP SHELL *Capulus ungaricus* (Linnaeus, 1767)   **Pl. 47**
  Range: Greenland to the West Indies.
  Habitat: Deep water; 90 to 2,500 ft.
  Description: Height 1 to 1¹/₂ in. and about 1 in. across at base.

Conical, apex coiled and curved forward. Surface bears fine lines that radiate, and these are crossed by less frequent lines of growth. Open base shaped to fit the object to which the gastropod is attached, for the cap shell is limpetlike in habits. It forms a shallow excavation at the place of attachment and sometimes deposits a shelly floor. Whitish, with grayish periostracum.

Remarks: The conical shell reminds one of a jester's hat. It is a modern representative of a very ancient group, fossil specimens of the same genus being found in rocks of Silurian age some 300,000,000 years old.

■ CUP-AND-SAUCER LIMPETS AND SLIPPER SHELLS: Family Crepidulidae

Limpetlike gastropods, cap-shaped, with a shelly plate (platform) or cup-shaped process on inner side of shell. They live attached to other shells or to stones. Found in nearly all seas, from shallow water to moderate depths.

● Genus *Cheilea* Modeer, 1793

FALSE CUP-AND-SAUCER LIMPET   **Pl. 49**
Cheilea equestris (Linnaeus, 1758)
  Range: South Florida to the West Indies.
  Habitat: Shallow water.
  Description: Diameter about 1 in. Orbicular at base, although circumference may be irregular because of wavy rim; outer edge rises to a blunt point situated somewhat to the rear and directed backward. Exterior with rough corrugated appearance, interior with thin horseshoe-shaped plate. Color dull grayish white.
  Remarks: This snail lives attached to other shells and usually excavates a shallow cavity at the place of attachment.

● Genus *Calyptraea* Lamarck, 1799

CIRCULAR CUP-AND-SAUCER LIMPET   **Pl. 45**
Calyptraea centralis (Conrad, 1841)
  Range: Cape Hatteras to the West Indies.
  Habitat: Moderately shallow water.
  Description: Diameter about $1/2$ in. Cap-shaped, circular at

base. Apex blunt, centrally situated, only moderately elevated. Small shelflike plate on inside. Color pure white.

● Genus *Crucibulum* Schumacher, 1817

ROSY CUP-AND-SAUCER LIMPET   Pl. 49
Crucibulum auricula (Gmelin, 1791)
   Range: South Florida to Texas and Brazil.
   Habitat: Moderately shallow water.
   Description: Cap-shaped, diameter at base about 1 in. Summit moderately elevated, rim of aperture wavy. Inner cup stands nearly free, whereas in the Cup-and-Saucer Limpet that structure is fastened by almost half of its area. Color grayish; interior usually pinkish.

STRIATE CUP-AND-SAUCER   Pl. 49
Crucibulum striatum Say, 1824
   Range: Nova Scotia to Florida.
   Habitat: Moderately shallow water.
   Description: Moderately solid and cap-shaped, diameter at base 1 in. Surface bears numerous slightly elevated radiating lines. Summit usually smooth and bluntly pointed. Inner partition cup-shaped and attached by one side to shorter end of shell. Color pinkish white, generally streaked with brown.

● Genus *Crepidula* Lamarck, 1799

SPINY SLIPPER SHELL   Pl. 49
Crepidula aculeata (Gmelin, 1791)
   Range: N. Carolina to the West Indies; Bermuda; Pacific.
   Habitat: Shallow water.
   Description: About 1 in. long. Apex turned considerably to one side. Outer surface bears irregular thorny or spiny ridges, radiating from apex. Inner cavity with shelflike shelly plate. Color brownish or grayish, quite variable in its markings; commonly there are broad rays of paler tint. Interior polished and often rayed with brown, shelly plate white.

CONVEX SLIPPER SHELL   Pl. 49
Crepidula convexa Say, 1822
   Range: Massachusetts to the West Indies; Texas.
   Habitat: Shallow water.
   Description: Length about ½ in. Shell obliquely oval and

deeply convex. Apex prominent and separate from the body whorl, turning down nearly to the plane of the aperture, occasionally beyond it. Shelly plate deeply situated. Outer surface minutely wrinkled. Color ashy brown, with streaks or dots of reddish brown.

COMMON SLIPPER SHELL   Pl. 49
Crepidula fornicata (Linnaeus, 1758)
Range: Nova Scotia to Gulf of Mexico.
Habitat: Shallow water.
Description: Length 1½ in. Shell obliquely oval, apex prominent and turned to one side, not separate from body of shell. Moderately convex, according to the object on which it is seated. Cavity partially divided by a horizontal white plate (platform). Color pale gray, flecked with purplish chestnut. See next species for differentiation.
Remarks: Also called Boat Shell and Quarterdeck. These are among the first objects collected by children at the seashore, since they make excellent miniature boats to sail in tide pools and also serve as tiny scoops for digging in the sand. The empty shells have a commercial value; under the name Quarterdecks many tons are annually scattered over the ocean floor for embryo oysters to settle upon.

SPOTTED SLIPPER SHELL   Pl. 49
Crepidula maculosa Conrad, 1846
Range: Florida to Mexico; Bahamas.
Habitat: Shallow water.
Description: This slipper shell is much like the Common Slipper Shell, but the edge of the shelly plate is straight instead of convex. The exterior is usually checked with small brown or chocolate marks. There is a circular scar under the right edge of the shelf.

EASTERN WHITE SLIPPER SHELL   Pl. 49
Crepidula plana Say, 1822
Range: Nova Scotia to Brazil; Bermuda.
Habitat: Shallow water; on shells.
Description: Length 1 in. General shape may be flat, slightly curved, or even concave, according to the outline of the object to which it is attached. Platform less than half the length of shell. Outer surface wrinkled by concentric lines of growth, inner surface highly polished, sometimes iridescent. Color pure white, semitransparent when young.
Remarks: Generally found flattened against the inside of the aperture of dead shells, particularly large examples of *Busy-*

con and *Polinices.* Often a large king (horseshoe) crab *(Limulus),* will be found to have several dozen on the lower side of its domelike shell.

■ CARRIER SHELLS: Family Xenophoridae

Shell top-shaped, somewhat flattened. All but the deep-sea forms camouflage their shells by cementing pebbles and broken shell fragments to them. From above they look like small piles of debris. Early in life the snail fastens a bit of shell or a tiny pebble to its back, at the upper edge of its aperture. As the shell grows the foreign object is firmly anchored in place, and a larger piece is then added. This results in a spiral of foreign material following the suture line. The snail usually sticks to one kind of object, rarely mixing them. Fossil specimens of this genus are found as far back as the Cretaceous period (100,000,000 years), showing that this curious habit of self-ornamentation has persisted for countless thousands of generations.

● **Genus *Xenophora* Fischer, 1807**

ATLANTIC CARRIER SHELL   **Pl. 51**
Xenophora conchyliophora (Born, 1780)
    Range: N. Carolina; West Indies south to Brazil.
    Habitat: Moderately shallow water.
    Description: Diameter about 2 in. Shell top-shaped, apex low but sharp. With 6 or 7 whorls, rather flattened. Surface bears prominent growth lines, although they may be visible only from below. Aperture large and oblique, lip thin. No umbilicus, operculum horny. Color yellowish brown.
    Remarks: This species does a good job in concealing the upperpart of its shell with marine trash. It appears to prefer bivalve shells, particularly those of the Cross-barred Chione, *Chione cancellata,* and it is noteworthy that the bits of shell are so disposed as not to curve downward beyond edge of the shell (this would impede progress of the animal) but are almost invariably placed with their concave sides uppermost. Formerly called *trochiformis* (Born, 1778).

■ PELICAN'S FOOT SHELLS: Family Aporrhaidae

Strong and solid shells, with a high spire and a long and narrow aperture. The outer lip is greatly thickened and flaring, forming a winglike expansion. The best-known example of this family is the Pelican's Foot, *Aporrhais pespelicani* (Linnaeus), of European waters.

● Genus *Aporrhais* da Costa, 1778

AMERICAN PELICAN'S FOOT   **Pl. 47**
Aporrhais occidentalis Beck, 1836
Range: Labrador to N. Carolina.
Habitat: Moderately deep water.
Description: About 2 in. high. Shell thick and strong, with 8 to 10 whorls, each decorated with numerous smooth, rounded, crescent-shaped folds, about 20 on body whorl. Surface ornamented by closely spaced revolving lines. Aperture semilunar; outer lip expanded into a wide 3-cornered wing. Color white or yellowish white.

■ CONCHS: Family Strombidae

An interesting family of active snails, widely distributed in warm seas. The shells are thick and solid, with greatly enlarged body whorls. The aperture is long and narrow, with a notch at each end, and the outer lip in adults is usually thickened and expanded. The operculum is clawlike and does not close the aperture.

● Genus *Strombus* Linnaeus, 1758

FLORIDA FIGHTING CONCH   **Pls. 8, 50**
Strombus alatus Gmelin, 1791
Range: N. Carolina to Texas and northeast Mexico.
Habitat: Shallow water.
Description: Height 3 to 4 in. Shell solid, about 7 whorls, spire pointed. Early volutions decorated with revolving ribs, body whorl smooth. Shoulders of later whorls may or may not bear blunt spines. Aperture long, lip thickened and flaring, notched below. Operculum clawlike. Color yellowish

brown, clouded and sometimes striped with orange and purple. Interior commonly dark brown. Juvenile, or half-grown
individuals, do not have the flaring lip, and look considerably like cone shells *(Conus)*.

Remarks: There has been some confusion regarding the iden-
tity of this species and the West Indian Fighting Conch, *S.
pugilis* (below). Since the original figure of *S. alatus* showed
a specimen without shoulder spines, it is commonly
believed that the spineless form is *S. alatus* and the form
with well-developed spines is *S. pugilis*. However, *S. alatus*
also has spines in many cases. It is very common in Florida
and is usually quite mottled; the shoulder spines, when
present, are confined to the last whorl, whereas the typical
S. pugilis is a West Indies form, uncommon in Florida, with
prominent spines on the last 2 whorls. Furthermore, *S. pugilis* is a somewhat heavier shell and is generally of a more
solid, orange color.

MILK CONCH *Strombus costatus* Gmelin, 1791   **Pls. 8, 50**
  Range: Florida to Brazil; Bermuda.
  Habitat: Shallow water.
  Description: A large and solid shell, 4 to 6 in. high. About 10
  whorls, producing a fairly tall spire. Body whorl greatly expanded. A series of large blunt nodes on last whorl, with a
  series of smaller ones twisting up the spire. There are also a
  number of rather distinct horizontal corrugations on the
  body whorl. Aperture long and narrow, outer lip expanded
  and much thickened in old specimens. Color yellowish
  white, somewhat mottled; interior pure white, with a noticeable aluminumlike glaze on columella and outer lip.

ROOSTER-TAIL CONCH *Strombus gallus* Linnaeus, 1758   **Pl. 50**
  Range: South Florida to Brazil; Bermuda.
  Habitat: Moderately shallow water.
  Description: Height 4 to 7 in. Strong and solid, with sharp
  spire of about 7 whorls. Sculpture of strong revolving ribs;
  body whorl bears blunt spines, or nodes, at shoulders. Outer
  lip expanded, its upper tip extending above top of spire.
  Color a mottled brown, white, and orange.
  Remarks: Relatively uncommon throughout its range.

PINK CONCH, QUEEN CONCH   **Pl. 50**
Strombus gigas Linnaeus, 1758
  Range: Bermuda; south Florida to the West Indies.
  Habitat: Shallow water.

Description: Height 8 to 12 in. Heavy and solid, with short conical spire. Mostly body whorl, the aperture moderately narrow and channeled at both ends. Outer lip thickened and greatly flaring when mollusk is fully grown. With 8 to 10 whorls, with blunt nodes on shoulders. Operculum clawlike, horny. Color yellowish buff; interior bright rosy pink; young specimens have zigzag axial strips of brown.

Remarks: This is the shell that for generations has been used by families of seafaring men as a doorstop or for decorating the borders of flower beds. It is one of our largest and heaviest gastropods, individuals sometimes weighing more than 5 lbs. It is a commercial shell and large numbers are exported from the Bahamas for cutting into cameos; the scrap material is ground into powder for manufacturing porcelain. The flesh is eaten in the West Indies, where the aborigines formerly made scrapers, chisels, and various other tools from the shell. Semiprecious pearls are occasionally found within the mantle fold. When traveling through Florida one often sees huge piles of this shell heaped up beside a gas station or tourist lodge. They make popular Florida souvenirs, even though all of them are imported from one of the West Indian islands.

WEST INDIAN FIGHTING CONCH   Pl. 50
Strombus pugilis Linnaeus, 1758

Range: Southeast Florida (uncommon); West Indies south to Brazil.

Habitat: Shallow water.

Description: A robust shell of 7 whorls, maximum height about 5 in. and most specimens between 3 and 4 in. Early whorls sculptured with revolving ribs. Prominent spines on later whorls. Body whorl enlarged, aperture quite narrow, outer lip widely flaring and deeply notched below. Operculum clawlike. Color deep yellowish brown, commonly with a paler band midway of body whorl. Aperture deep orange.

HAWK-WING CONCH *Strombus raninus* Gmelin, 1791   Pl. 50

Range: South Florida to Brazil; Bermuda.

Habitat: Shallow water.

Description: Height 4 to 5 in. About 8 whorls, well-developed spire. Shoulders of body whorl bear small knobs, and there is a single large knob on the back, with a smaller knob between it and the margin. Outer lip thick and flaring, deeply notched below. Color yellowish white, streaked and blotched with brown and black.

Remarks: Formerly listed as *S. bituberculatus* Lamarck, 1822. Dwarf specimens were named *nanus* Bales, 1938.

■ LAMELLARIA SNAILS: Family Lamellariidae

Small, thin-shelled mollusks living chiefly in cold seas, commonly at considerable depths. Most of them feature a very heavy periostracum.

● **Genus** *Lamellaria* **Montagu, 1815**

TRANSPARENT LAMELLARIA
Lamellaria perspicua (Linnaeus, 1758)
   Range: Florida; Gulf of Mexico to Brazil.
   Habitat: Moderately deep water to 180 ft.
   Description: Diameter about ¹/₂ in. Thin and delicate, about 8 whorls, the body whorl making up most of the shell. Very fine growth lines the only sculpture. Aperture flaring. Color white. Enveloping soft parts reddish. No operculum.
   Remarks: In life the shell is covered by the soft parts. Synonyms are *rangi* Bergh, 1853, and *cochinella* Louise Perry, 1939.

● **Genus** *Velutina* **Fleming, 1821**

SMOOTH VELUTINA *Velutina velutina* Müller, 1776
   Range: Labrador to Massachusetts; also Alaska to California.
   Habitat: Moderately deep water, 18 to 300 ft.
   Description: A thin and fragile shell of 3 whorls, diameter about ¹/₂ in. Very large body whorl, no spire. Aperture large and flaring. Surface shows minute revolving threadlike lines, and there is a thick brownish periostracum that is usually ragged and frayed. Color brown or light tan.
   Remarks: This snail gives the impression that it is made up of periostracum with a thin layer of shell on the inside. Often found in fish stomachs. Common. *Helix laevigata* Linnaeus is a rejected name.

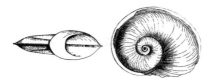

Figure 60. Peron's Atlanta *Atlanta peroni*

■ ATLANTAS: Family Atlantidae

Small flatly coiled shells, thin and translucent. They are pelagic snails, living a floating life in tropical and semitropical seas. Referred to as "heteropods."

● Genus *Atlanta* Lesueur, 1827

PERON'S ATLANTA   Fig. 60 & Pl. 53
Atlanta peroni Lesueur, 1817
   Range: Massachusetts to West Indies; West Coast.
   Habitat: Pelagic.
   Description: Diameter ¹/₂ in. A fragile and glassy shell of 3 whorls. It is very flatly coiled, like a compressed ram's horn, with fairly large aperture. There is a thin bladelike keel, or fin, around the periphery of last whorl. Color white.
   Remarks: Specimens are now and then washed up on beaches after storms

■ CARINARIAS: Family Carinariidae

A pelagic group, cigar-shaped, swimming upside down with a delicate, glassy, cap-shaped shell on the underside. Rarely captured.

LAMARCK'S CARINARIA   Fig. 61 & Pl. 47
Carinaria lamarcki Peron & Lesueru, 1810
   Range: Caribbean; Bermuda; Indo-Pacific; Eastern Pacific.
   Habitat: Pelagic in warm seas.
   Description: Up to 10 in. long. Proboscis large and purple. Shell ¹/₅ size of animal, very thin and fragile. Apex hooked.
   Remarks: Very rare in collections.

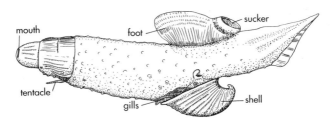

Figure 61. Lamarck's Carinaria *Carinaria lamarcki*

■ MOON SHELLS: Family Naticidae

These are carnivorous snails, found in all seas. The shell is usually globular, sometimes depressed, smooth, and often polished. The snails burrow into the sand and have no eyes. Foot of the animal very large and often conceals entire shell when mollusk is extended. Operculum may be calcareous or horny. Females lay a circular band of jelly eggs covered with sand.

● Genus *Polinices* Montfort, 1810

SHARK EYE *Polinices duplicatus* (Say, 1822)　　**Pls. 14, 54**
　Range: Massachusetts to Florida and Gulf of Mexico.
　Habitat: Sand and mud flats.
　Description: About 2 in. high, diameter nearly 3 in. Shell solid, 4 or 5 whorls, their upper portions compressed so as to give the shell a somewhat pyramidal outline. Umbilicus irregular and covered wholly or in part by a thick, chestnut brown lobe. Operculum horny. Color grayish brown, tinged with bluish.

BROWN MOON SHELL　　　　　　　　　　　　　**Pl. 54**
Polinices hepaticus (Röding, 1798)
　Range: Southeast Florida to the West Indies.
　Habitat: Shallow water.
　Description: About 1¹/₂ in. high. An ovate shell of some 4 whorls, the body whorl constituting mostly of shell. Polished white callus over the umbilicus. Operculum horny. Color yellowish tan, aperture white.
　Remarks: Formerly listed as *P. brunneus* (Link, 1807). Uncommon.

IMMACULATE MOON SHELL   Pl. 53
Polinices immaculatus (Totten, 1835)
Range: Gulf of St. Lawrence to N. Carolina.
Habitat: Moderately shallow water.
Description: Not quite $1/2$ in. high. With 3 or 4 whorls, short pointed apex. Surface smooth and shiny. Thickened callus does not block the umbilicus. Operculum horny. Color white, with thin yellowish periostracum.

MILK MOON SHELL *Polinices lacteus* (Guilding, 1834)   Pl. 54
Range: Florida to the West Indies; Texas.
Habitat: Shallow water.
Description: About 1 in. high. Shell obliquely oval, smooth and polished. With 3 or 4 whorls, less flattened than with most of the genus. Umbilicus partly filled by a callus. Operculum horny, the color amber or claret. Shell milky white.
Remarks: Common in sandy, intertidal areas. See next species for similarities.

● **Genus** *Lunatia* **Gray, 1847**

PALE NORTHERN MOON SHELL
Lunatia pallida (Broderip & Sowerby, 1829)
Range: Greenland to New Jersey; Alaska to California.
Habitat: Moderately deep water.
Description: About 1 in. high. Approximately 5 well-rounded whorls, apex blunt. Small umbilicus, nearly closed by an enlargement at upperpart of inner lip. Operculum horny. Color gray or white, with thin greenish yellow periostracum. Aperture white.
Remarks: *P. groenlandica* (Moller, 1842) and *P. borealis* Gray, 1834, are synonyms.

NORTHERN MOON SHELL *Lunatia heros* (Say, 1822) Pls. 14, 54
Range: Gulf of St. Lawrence to N. Carolina.
Habitat: Sand and mud flats.
Description: Height about 4 in. With 5 very convex whorls, somewhat flattened at the top. Aperture large and oval, operculum horny. Umbilicus large, rounded, coarsely wrinkled, and extending through to top of shell. Outline somewhat globular. Color ashy brown, with thin yellowish periostracum. See also the next species.
Remarks: This is a voracious feeder, drilling into and sucking the contents from many a luckless bivalve encountered in

its subterranean wanderings. The eggs of this and most moon shells are laid in a mass of agglutinated sand grains that is molded over the shell, and, upon hardening, form the fragile "sand collars" often found lying on the beach during the summer months.

SPOTTED NORTHERN MOON SHELL   Pl. 54

Lunatia triseriata (Say, 1826)
Range: Gulf of St. Lawrence to N. Carolina.
Habitat: Shallow water.
Description: Less than 1 in. high. With 4 or 5 whorls, general shape almost exactly like a miniature specimen of Northern Moon Shell. Color yellowish gray, sometimes uniformly so and sometimes with oblique chestnut brown squarish spots arranged in bands.
Remarks: Some writers have contended that this is indeed merely the juvenile stage of the Northern Moon Shell; but certain characters, particularly a relatively thick callus on the inner lip, seem to indicate a mature shell.

● **Genus *Amauropsis* Morch, 1857**

ICELAND MOON SHELL

Amauropsis islandica (Gmelin, 1791)
Range: Arctic Ocean to Virginia.
Habitat: Moderately deep water.
Description: About 1 in. high. A rather plump shell of 4 whorls. Shell thin in substance but well inflated. Aperture semicircular, outer lip thin and sharp. Inner lip overspread with white callus. A small slitlike umbilicus. Operculum horny. Yellowish white, with orange-brown periostracum.

● **Genus *Natica* Scopoli, 1777**

COLORFUL ATLANTIC NATICA   Pls. 11, 54

Natica canrena (Linnaeus, 1758)
Range: N. Carolina to Brazil; Bermuda.
Habitat: Shallow water in sand.
Description: Height 1 to 2 in. Shape globular, somewhat flattened at the top. About 4 whorls, body whorl large and expanded, apex small. Operculum calcareous, thick, white, with deeply cut grooves or channels following its outside

curvature. Surface smooth and polished. Color pale bluish gray, with spiral chestnut bars or stripes and zigzag markings, along with various mottlings of dark brown and purple.

FLORIDA NATICA *Natica tedbayeri* Rehder, 1986   **Pl. 54**
Range: Southeast Florida to Panama; Brazil.
Habitat: In sand, shore to 48 ft. Uncommon.
Description: Height ³/₄ in., resembling the Colorful Natica, but with a thicker, rough, axially fimbriated periostracum. Without axial streaks of brown; possesses 2 broad, irregular, spiral bands of light brown, each bounded above and below by oblong (not arrow-shaped) small, brown spots. Operculum with 2 broad and 2 small ribs.
Remarks: Synonyms are *floridana* Rehder and *bayeri* Rehder, 1986.

ARCTIC NATICA   **Pl. 54**
Natica clausa Broderip & Sowerby, 1929
Range: Circumpolar; to N. Carolina; also from Arctic Ocean to California.
Habitat: Moderately deep water in sand.
Description: Height 1¹/₂ in. at times but usually smaller. Shell nearly spherical, and consists of 4 or 5 whorls, spire only slightly elevated. Aperture oval, lip sharp, thickened, and rounded as it ascends to umbilicus, which is completely closed by a shiny ivory-white callus. Operculum calcareous, bluish white. Shell pale brown.

LIVID NATICA *Natica livida* Pfeiffer, 1840   **Pl. 54**
Range: Bermuda; south Florida to Brazil.
Habitat: Shallow water in sand.
Description: About ¹/₂ in. high. A smooth and shiny shell of 3 or 4 whorls, apex rounded. Lip thin and sharp. Umbilicus deep, partly shielded by a deep brown callus. Operculum calcareous. Color pearl-gray, often with faint darker markings; brownish around aperture.

MOROCCO NATICA   **Pl. 54**
Natica marochiensis Gmelin, 1791
Range: Bermuda; Florida to Brazil.
Habitat: Shallow water in sand.
Description: About 1 in. high. With 4 rounded whorls. Umbilicus deep, with sturdy white plug. Operculum shelly. Surface smooth, color grayish brown, with encircling rows of obscure reddish brown spots.

SOUTHERN MINIATURE NATICA *Natica pusilla* Say, 1822
Range: Maine to Florida to Brazil.
Habitat: Shallow water to moderately deep water.
Description: About $1/4$ in. high. A small but sturdy shell of about 3 whorls, the body whorl making up most of the shell. Umbilicus a slit in back of rolled callus. Operculum calcareous. Color white or gray, sometimes faintly spotted or banded with brown.

● **Genus *Sigatica* Mayer & Aldrich, 1886**

SEMISULCATE MOON SHELL   **Pl. 54**
Sigatica semisulcata (Gray, 1839)
Range: North Carolina to the West Indies.
Habitat: Offshore in sand in moderately deep water.
Description: About $1/4$ in., ovate, fairly thin-shelled, glossy white in color. Umbilicus deep, round, without a callus. Characterized by 2 smooth nuclear whorls, followed by 3 whorls which are finely grooved by about 20 spiral lines. Suture channeled. Operculum corneous and with few whorls.
Remarks: This is a small uncommon species. *S. holograpta* McGinty, 1940, is probably a synonym or minor form from the Lower Florida Keys.

● **Genus *Stigmaulax* Mörch, 1852**

SULCATE NATICA *Stigmaolax sulcata* (Born, 1778)   **Pl. 54**
Range: Southeast Florida to Brazil.
Habitat: Moderately shallow water.
Description: Height $3/4$ in. With 3 or 4 rounded whorls, short spire. Aperture large and high, umbilicus broad and deep, with strong plug. Sculpture of revolving ridges cut by vertical lines. Color yellowish, with pale brown blotches; base white.

● **Genus *Sinum* Röding, 1798**

MACULATED BABY'S EAR *Sinum maculatum* (Say, 1831)   **Pl. 54**
Range: N. Carolina to Florida; West Indies.
Habitat: Shallow water.
Description: This species is very much like the Common Baby's Ear, but the top is slightly more elevated and the shell is not quite so flat; also, the sculpture is more delicate. Color white or buffy white, somewhat spotted with weak yellowish brown marks.

COMMON BABY'S EAR *Sinum perspectivum* (Say, 1831)   **Pl. 54**
Range: Maryland to Brazil; Bermuda.
Habitat: Shallow water in sand.
Description: Diameter about $1^1/_2$ in., height less than $^1/_2$ in.
Shell elongate-ovate, greatly depressed. With 3 or 4 whorls,
the enormously expanded body whorl makes up more than
$^3/_4$ of entire shell; aperture wide and flaring. Surface sculptured with numerous impressed, transverse, slightly undulating lines. No umbilicus, operculum rudimentary. Color
milky white. See Spotted Ear Shell for comparisons.
Remarks: This curious gastropod looks like a moon shell that
has been squeezed flat. In life the shell is almost buried in
the soft mantle and foot of the mollusk.

● **Genus *Haliotinella* Sowerby, 1875**

FINGERNAIL SINUM   **Pl. 54**
Haliotinella patinaria Guppy, 1876
Range: Southeast Florida and the Caribbean.
Habitat: Shallow water in muddy sand in turtle grass.
Description: Length $^1/_2$ in., elongate, fragile, narrow with the
aperture as large as the shell itself. Periostracum thin and
yellow. Operculum chitinous, oval, and with few whorls.
Animal 2 in. long, whitish, and envelopes the shell.

■ **COWRIES: Family Cypraeidae**

Cowries are a large family of brightly polished and often brilliantly colored snails that have always been great favorites
with collectors. The shell is more or less oval, well inflated,
with the spire usually covered by the body whorl, and the
aperture — lined with teeth on both sides — running the full
length of the shell. There is no operculum. This is predominantly a tropical family, with scores of richly colored representatives distributed all around the world. Only a few species, however, are hardy enough to live as far north as
Florida.

   The genus *Cypraea* has been split into numerous subgenera, and some authorities believe that some are deserving of
full generic rank. Most collectors prefer to use the name
Cypraea for all of their species, and that system is followed
here.

● Genus *Cypraea* Linnaeus, 1758

ATLANTIC DEER COWRIE   Pls. 10, 51
Cypraea cervus Linnaeus, 1771
Range: Off N. Carolina to Cuba; Bermuda.
Habitat: Shallow to moderately deep water.
Description: Our largest cowrie, length up to 5 in. Once re-
garded as a subspecies of the Measled Cowrie (below), but
thinner and more inflated, and more heavily spotted with
smaller whitish spots, which are never in rings.

ATLANTIC GRAY COWRIE *Cypraea cinerea* Gmelin, 1791 Pl. 51
Range: South Florida to the West Indies.
Habitat: Shallow water under rocks.
Description: About $1^1/_2$ in. long. A plump cowrie, grayish
brown on top, with lower portions shading to lilac. With 2
paler bands commonly encircle the shell, and the sides are
often decorated with black dots and sometimes streaks. Bottom creamy white, the apertural teeth rather small.

YELLOW COWRIE   Pls. 10, 51
Cypraea spurca acicularis Gmelin, 1791
Range: Off N. Carolina to Brazil; Bermuda.
Habitat: Shallow water under rocks.
Description: About 1 in. long. Shell oval and solid; a tiny spire
present in juveniles but concealed in adults. Aperture long
and narrow, slightly curved and evenly toothed. Surface
highly polished. Color yellowish tan, spotted with yellow;
violet spots along sides.
Remarks: Typical *C. spurca* Linnaeus, 1758, is a Mediterranean species.

MEASLED COWRIE *Cypraea zebra* Linnaeus, 1758   Pls. 10, 51
Range: South Florida to the West Indies.
Habitat: Shallow water under bridges.
Description: About 3 to 4 in. long. Shell moderately inflated
and oval, spire completely concealed by last whorl. Highly
polished. Aperture narrow, notched at both ends. Lips
toothed and dark brown. Color of shell purplish brown,
with round whitish spots, often in rings. Young specimens
are strongly banded with broad streaks of brown, and these
streaks often persist in adult shells, occasional examples
having their backs practically unspotted.
Remarks: Formerly listed as *C. exanthema* Linnaeus, 1767.
This species and the Atlantic Deer Cowrie are being over-
collected in the Lower Florida Keys.

■ ERATO SNAILS: Family Eratoidae

Shells somewhat like miniature cowries, many characterized by wrinkles or small ribs running around the shell from
the narrow aperture to the middle of the back. Chiefly confined to warm seas.

● Genus *Erato* Risso, 1826

MAUGER'S ERATO *Erato maugeriae* Gray, 1832   **Pl. 53**
  Range: N. Carolina to Florida; to Brazil.
  Habitat: Moderately shallow water.
  Description: About ¼ in. high. A tiny pear-shaped shell resembling one of the *Marginella* shells but its rolled-in outer lip
  bears a row of distinct teeth. Rounded and wide at blunt
  apex and tapering to a bluntly rounded base. Aperture narrow, running full length of shell. Surface smooth and polished. Color pale tan, often with a rosy tint.

● Genus *Trivia* Broderip, 1837

ANTILLEAN TRIVIA *Trivia antillarum* Schilder, 1922   **Pl. 53**
  Range: N. Carolina to Brazil.
  Habitat: Moderately shallow water.
  Description: About ¼ in. long. Oval, well arched. Narrow
  lines over upper surface, crossing weak median groove and
  continuing on base to curved aperture. Color dark purplish.
  Remarks: This is a relatively rare species.

WHITE GLOBE TRIVIA *Trivia nix* (Schilder, 1922)   **Pl. 53**
  Range: South Florida to Brazil.
  Habitat: Moderately shallow water.
  Description: About ½ in. long. Nearly globular. Marked me-
  dial groove. Sculpture of strong ridges that sometimes fork
  at the sides. Color white.

COFFEE BEAN TRIVIA   **Pls. 11, 53**
Trivia pediculus (Linnaeus, 1758)
  Range: Florida to Brazil; Bermuda.
  Habitat: Shallow water.
  Description: Length ½ in. Shell solid, nearly spherical, the nar-
  row aperture running full length of lower side, and strongly
  toothed within. Upper surface bears an impressed median
  furrow, with strong radiating ridges that extend around and

into the aperture. Surface not polished. Color tan to violet-brown, with patches of chócolate.

Remarks: Shells of this genus resemble those of *Cypraea*, but the animal is quite different. This species is the largest form on our coast.

FOUR-SPOTTED TRIVIA   Pl. 53
Trivia quadripuntata (Gray, 1827)

Range: Southeast Florida to the West Indies; Bermuda.

Habitat: Shallow water.

Description: About ¼ in long. Shell nearly globular, with strong dorsal furrow. Fine but distinct ridges radiate from this to the elongate aperture. Color pale pink; upper surface bears 4 brownish spots, 2 on each side of the median furrow.

Remarks: The body of this gastropod is vivid scarlet and surprisingly large when fully extended; one marvels that it can all be packed away in such a tiny shell.

LITTLE WHITE TRIVIA   Pl. 53
Trivia candidula (Gaskoin, 1836)

Range: N. Carolina to Florida and to the Lesser Antilles.

Habitat: Shallow water near reefs.

Description: About ¼ in., fairly globulus, pure white, somewhat rostrate and with 17 to 24 riblets. There is no dorsal furrow, as in *T. nix.*

Remarks: *T. leucosphaera* Schilder, 1931, is a synonym.

SUFFUSE TRIVIA *Trivia suffusa* (Gray, 1832)   Pl. 53

Range: South Florida to the West Indies to Brazil.

Habitat: Shallow water offshore.

Description: Usually less than ¼ in. long. Upper surface sculptured with numerous transverse lines divided along the median line by a longitudinal furrow. Lines weakly beaded and continue around the shell and into the narrow aperture. Color rosy pink, sometimes a little darker at the side; generally there is a faint suggestion of spotting.

■ SIMNIAS: Family Ovulidae

Shells usually long and slender, with a straight aperture notched at each end. Occurring in warm seas, the mollusks attach themselves to sea fans and various marine growths and are usually colored to match their environment.

● **Genus Simnia Risso, 1826**

COMMON WEST INDIAN SIMNIA   Pls. 9, 53
Simnia acicularis (Lamarck, 1810)
Range: N. Carolina to Brazil; Bermuda.
Habitat: Shallow water; on sea fans *(Gorgonia)*.
Description: About ³/₄ in. long, a rather thin and elongate shell.
Aperture extends entire length of shell, lip thin and sharp.
Surface smooth and shiny. Columella bears a paler ridge.
Color yellowish or purplish, according to shade of the sea
fan on which it lives.

SINGLE-TOOTHED SIMNIA   Pl. 53
Simnia uniplicata (Sowerby, 1848)
Range: N. Carolina to the West Indies.
Habitat: Shallow water; on sea fans *(Gorgonia)*.
Description: Length about ³/₄ in. Shell thin, elongate, somewhat cylindrical, the aperture a narrow slit running full
length of shell; ends bluntly pointed. Surface smooth and
polished. Color usually some shade of pink or purple,
although it may be white or yellowish.
Remarks: Like the Common West Indian Simnia, it lives
attached to stems of some marine growth, usually sea fans,
and is nearly always colored to harmonize with its surround-
ings. The genus *Neosimnia* Fisher, 1884 is the same.

● **Genus *Cyphoma* Röding, 1798**

FLAMINGO TONGUE   Pls. 9, 49
Cyphoma gibbosum (Linnaeus, 1758)
Range: N. Carolina to Brazil; Bermuda.
Habitat: Shallow water; on sea fans *(Gorgonia)*.
Description: About 1 in. long. Shell solid and durable, with a
dorsal ridge, or hump, near center of shell and extending
squarely across it; see McGinty's Flamingo Tongue for differentiation. Aperture long and narrow, running full length of
lower side. Inner and outer lips without teeth. Color white
or yellowish, highly polished.
Remarks: The humpbacked Flamingo Tongue is generally
found living on the sea fan or some other branching aquatic
growth, where it clings tightly to one of the stems. In life the
shell is covered by the mantle, which is pale flesh color
with squarish black rings. This species is being over-col-
lected.

McGINTY'S FLAMINGO TONGUE   Pls. 9, 49
Cyphoma macgintyi Pilsbry, 1939

Range: Florida Keys and Bahamas to Texas; Bermuda.

Habitat: Shallow water; on sea fans *(Gorgonia)*.

Description: About 1 in. long. Shell very much like Flamingo Tongue, though slightly more elongate and with a somewhat narrower hump. The animal itself is colored quite differently. In Flamingo Tongue the mantle is flesh color decorated with squarish black rings; in McGinty's Flamingo Tongue the color is pinkish lavender, with marginal rows of round black dots.

■ HELMET SHELLS: Family Cassidae

These are mostly large and heavy shells, many of them used for cutting cameos. The shells are thick and commonly 3-cornered when viewed from below. The aperture is long and terminates in front in a recurved canal. The outer lip is generally thickened and toothed within, and the inner lip commonly bears teeth, wrinklelike ridges, or pustules. Common on sandy bottoms in warm seas. The family name was once spelled Cassididae. The genus *Morum* has now been placed in the family Harpidae (see p. 242).

● Genus *Sconsia* Gray, 1847

ROYAL BONNET *Sconsia striata* (Lamarck, 1816)   Pl. 51

Range: Bermuda; Florida; Bahamas south through West Indies to n. Brazil.

Habitat: Deep water.

Description: About 2 in. high. A solid shell of about 5 whorls. There is a short and pointed spire, but most of the shell is body whorl. Aperture elongate, outer lip thickened and toothed within. Inner lip broadly reflected and polished. Surface bears fine revolving lines, usually with 1 or 2 varices on last volution. Operculum horny. Color buffy gray with squarish spots of chestnut, the latter sometimes obscure.

● Genus *Phalium* Link, 1807

SCOTCH BONNET   Pls. 13, 51
Phalium granulatum (Born, 1778)

Range: N. Carolina south to Brazil; Bermuda.

Habitat: Moderately shallow water.
Description: Height 2 to 4 in. Shell moderately solid, about 5 whorls, spire short, sutures indistinct. Surface bears deeply incised transverse lines. Aperture large, outer lip thickened and toothed within, canal strongly curved. One or more varices commonly present. Inner lip broadly reflected, pustulate on lower part. Color pale yellow or whitish, with squarish pale brown spots distributed over the shell with considerable regularity. See Polished Scotch Bonnet for similarity.
Remarks: Spots may be faded or obliterated over the shell in beach specimens. Formerly listed as *Semicassis inflata* (Shaw) and *S. abbreviata* (Lamarck). The smooth Polished Scotch Bonnet, *P. cicatricosum* (Gmelin, 1791) is merely a minor genetic form of this species (see Pl. 51).

● **Genus *Cypraecassis* Stutchbury, 1837**

RETICULATED COWRIE-HELMET   **Pls. 13, 51**
Cypraecassis testiculus (Linnaeus, 1758)
    Range: Bermuda; Florida; West Indies south to Brazil.
    Habitat: Moderately shallow water.
    Description: About 2 to 3 in. high. Shell solid, with very short spire. Some 5 whorls, the body whorl comprising most of shell. Aperture long and narrow, inner lip with a shield on body whorl and plicate (folded) for entire length along the aperture; outer lip rolled back and strongly toothed within. No operculum. Canal twisted to left and folded against shell. Sculpture of sharp vertical lines, crossed by strong revolving indentations. Color pinkish buff, mottled with orange and brown.
    Remarks: Feeds on sea-urchins. Some specimens may have strong axial plications on the shoulder of the body whorl. Likeness appears on a 22 cent U.S. postage stamp.

● **Genus *Cassis* Scopoli, 1777**

FLAME HELMET *Cassis flammea* (Linnaeus, 1758)   **Pl. 52**
    Range: Bahamas and south to Lesser Antilles.
    Habitat: Shallow water.
    Description: Height 3 to 6 in. About 6 whorls, small pointed spire. Body whorl large, ornamented with encircling knobs but lacking reticulate sculpture of King Helmet (below). Aperture elongate, outer lip strongly toothed within. Inner lip

reflected on last volution and decorated with distinct wrinkles. Canal strongly recurved. Surface generally polished, color yellowish, with brown streaks and splashes. Outer lip with no brown spots between the teeth but with heavy brown bars on outer margin. Operculum chitinous, elongate and narrow.

CLENCH'S HELMET   **Pl. 52**
Cassis madagascariensis spinella Clench, 1944
    Range: N. Carolina to West Indies; Bermuda.
    Habitat: Shallow water.
    Description: Our largest helmet shell attains a height of 14 in. Heavy and ponderous, practically no spire, the greatly enlarged body whorl constituting most of the shell. This body whorl bears 3 spiral ridges with blunt knobs. The thickened outer lip has a few well-separated large teeth and the inner lip bears many riblike smaller teeth, or plications. These are pale buff, the area between them dark brown. Front of aperture recurved and folded back on shell. Color grayish yellow, clouded with brown markings. Operculum narrow.
    Remarks: The Emperor Helmet, *C. madagascariensis* Lamarck, 1822, is smaller, proportionately heavier, and has one or more knobs larger than the others. Occurs in the West Indies.

KING HELMET *Cassis tuberosa* (Linnaeus, 1758)   **Pl. 51**
    Range: South Florida to Brazil; Bermuda.
    Habitat: Shallow water.
    Description: This shell is much like the Flame Helmet (above), but more triangular when viewed from below. Color buffy or rufous yellow, mottled and blotched with various shades of brown. In addition to the brown stain between the folds of the inner lip, and the strong teeth lining the outer lip, there is a conspicuous patch of bright chestnut toward the posterior end of the aperture. Outer lip rolled over and strongly marked with brown patches.
    Remarks: This species is preferred for cameo cutting: there is a very dark coat beneath the outer layer, so the figure stands out well against the "onyx" background. The shell is sometimes known as the Sardonyx Helmet. Most of the helmet shells yield a cameo with a reddish orange or pink background. This species is sometimes confused with the Flame Helmet, *C. flammea,* which has a smooth, almost polished surface; *C. tuberosa* is marked with fine but sharp longitudinal lines.

■ TRITONS: Family Ranellidae

These are rather decorative shells, rugged and strong, with no more than 2 varices to a volution. The closely related *Murex* shells have 3. The canal is prominent, and teeth are usually present on the lips. They are distributed in warm and temperate seas. The name Cymatiidae was formerly used for this family.

● Genus *Cymatium* Röding, 1798

DOG-HEAD TRITON   Pls. 12, 55
Cymatium caribbaeum Clench & Turner, 1957
Range: S. Carolina to the West Indies; Bermuda.
Habitat: Moderately shallow water.
Description: Height 2 to 3 in. About 5 whorls, a low spire, and a long, somewhat curved canal nearly closed at its upper end. Surface bears very heavy revolving ribs, and there are 2 or 3 robust varices. Aperture large, inner lip reflected on last whorl; outer lip strongly crenulate within. Color pale yellow, variously clouded with gray and white.
Remarks: Formerly listed as *C. cynocephalum* (Lamarck, 1816). This is an uncommon species.

ANGULAR TRITON   Pl. 55
Cymatium femorale (Linnaeus, 1758)
Range: South Florida; West Indies south to Brazil.
Habitat: Shallow water.
Description: A large and spectacular species, to 7 in. high. The 7 or 8 whorls are well shouldered. Sculpture consists of revolving ribs of two sizes, the larger ones studded with coarse knobs at regular intervals; 2 prominent varices stand out on each volution. Outer lip rolled inward at margin and decorated with large nodules at ends of ribs, the top one curving upward in direction of the spire. Canal moderately long, partly reflected, and nearly closed. Pale yellowish brown, with bands of darker shade. Aperture white.
Remarks: A common West Indies shell, infrequently taken in the Lower Florida Keys.

LIP TRITON *Cymatium labiosum* (Wood, 1828)   Pl. 55
Range: Florida Keys to the West Indies and Brazil.
Habitat: Moderately shallow water.
Description: Height ³/₄ in. A small squat shell of 4 or 5 stout

whorls, each decorated with coarse vertical and revolving ribs. Aperture small and notched above, canal short, outer lip greatly thickened and ornamented with sharp transverse lines. Color yellowish white.

KNOBBED TRITON   Pl. 55
Cymatium muricunum (Röding, 1798)
   Range: Bermuda; south Florida to Brazil.
   Habitat: Shallow water.
   Description: About 2 in. high. Rugged and strong, with 5 whorls and a sharp spire. Surface sculptured with revolving nodular ribs, and usually with 2 varices prominently displayed on each volution. Aperture large, notched at upper end, canal moderately long and open. Inner lip reflected on body whorl. Color gray, marked and sometimes mottled with brown. Aperture white.
   Remarks: Formerly listed as *C. tuberosum* (Lamarck, 1822) and also called the White-mouthed Triton.

GOLD-MOUTHED TRITON   Pl. 55
Cymatium nicobaricum (Röding, 1798)
   Range: Bermuda; south Florida to the West Indies.
   Habitat: Moderately shallow water.
   Description: Usually 2 to 3 in. high. Rugged and solid, about 5 whorls, a short spire, and 2 stout varices on each volution. Surface divided into squares by the crossing of horizontal and vertical ribs. Outer lip thick and heavy, with double row of teeth inside. Canal short and curved. Color gray or whitish, clouded and mottled with brown. Inside of aperture usually orange or bright yellow, the white teeth standing out vividly.
   Remarks: Formerly listed as *C. chlorostomum* (Lamarck, 1822). A common sand-dwelling species.

NEAPOLITAN TRITON   Pl. 55
Cymatium parthenopeum (von Salis, 1793)
   Range: Bermuda; Florida to the West Indies.
   Habitat: Moderately shallow water.
   Description: Height 3 to 4 in. About 5 whorls, sutures indistinct. Sculpture consists of prominent revolving ribs, those on shoulders somewhat wavy. Aperture moderately large, outer lip thick and made knobby by the terminating ribs. Color yellowish brown, somewhat mottled with darker hues. In life there is a hairy periostracum.
   Remarks: Formerly listed as *C. costatum* (Born).

ATLANTIC HAIRY TRITON   Pls. 12, 55
Cymatium pileare (Linneaus, 1758)
Range: South Florida; West Indies south to Brazil; Bermuda.
Habitat: Moderately shallow water.
Description: About 3 to 5 in. high. Strong and solid, 5 or 6 whorls, rather pointed spire. Surface crosshatched with lines running in 2 directions, the shoulders somewhat nodulous, and there are 2 robust varices on each volution. Aperture large, both lips wrinkled into small teeth. Color pale brown, banded with gray and white.
Remarks: Formerly listed as *C. aquitila* (Reeve) and *C. martinianum* (Orbigny).

POULSEN'S TRITON   Pl. 55
Cymatium cingulatum (Lamarck, 1822)
Range: Florida and Texas south through West Indies; Bermuda.
Habitat: Moderately deep water.
Description: About 2¹/₂ in. high. With 4 or 5 whorls, a moderately short acute spire, a moderate canal, and a wide aperture. Whorls well shouldered, decorated with revolving ribs that alternate in size. Color yellowish white.

DWARF HAIRY TRITON   Pl. 55
Cymatium vespaceum (Lamarck, 1822)
Range: N. Carolina to Brazil; Bermuda.
Habitat: Moderately deep water.
Description: About 1¹/₂ in. high. With 5 or 6 shouldered whorls, pointed apex, sutures distinct. Sculpture of strong revolving lines, prominent varices. Aperture small, toothed within on both lips, canal long and nearly closed. Color yellowish white, varices brown and white.

● Genus *Distorsio* Röding, 1798

ATLANTIC DISTORSIO *Distorsio clathrata* (Lamarck, 1816) Pl.55
Range: Off N. Carolina to Brazil.
Habitat: Moderately deep water.
Description: About 1 to 2 in. high. With 6 or 7 whorls, sculptured by strong revolving and vertical ribs, giving the surface a checkered appearance. Aperture small, constricted, with deep notch on inner lip. Both lips toothed. Columella strongly reflected on body whorl. Canal open and moderately long. Color yellowish white.
Remarks: This and the following species are often found in scallop dumps near shellfish factories.

McGINTY'S DISTORSIO Pl. 55
Distorsio macgintyi Emerson & Puffer, 1953
Range: Off N. Carolina to Brazil; Bermuda.
Habitat: Deep water.
Description: Height 1 to 1½ in. About 6 whorls, the last bulges noticeably. Sculpture of revolving cords and vertical ridges. Aperture small and constricted, outer lip strongly toothed, and columella with distinct gouge. Canal short. Color yellowish white.

● Genus *Charonia* Gistel, 1848

ATLANTIC TRITON Pls. 12, 52
Charonia variegata (Lamarck, 1816)
Range: Southeast Florida to Brazil; Bermuda.
Habitat: Moderately shallow water.
Description: Height 10 to 15 in. Shell strong and solid, gracefully elongate, apex bluntly pointed. With 8 or 9 whorls, sutures plainly marked; body whorl shows distinct shoulders. Widely separated round ribs encircle the shell, and each volution bears 2 rather obscure varices. Inner lip reflected, and stained a dark purplish brown, crossed by whitish wrinkles. Shell richly variegated with buff, brown, purple, and red, in crescentic patterns suggestive of pheasant plumage. Aperture pale orange.
Remarks: Formerly considered a subspecies of the Pacific Trumpet Shell, and erroneously listed as *C. tritonis nobilis* (Conrad, 1848). Feeds on the smooth-armed starfish, *Linckia*.

■ **FROG-SHELLS: Family Bursidae**

Shells ovate or oblong, somewhat compressed laterally, with 2 varices of continuous nature, 1 on each side. Deepwater forms have the varices thin and bladelike, whereas those living among the rocks and on coral reefs closer to shore are more nodular. They inhabit warm seas.

● Genus *Bursa* Röding, 1798

GAUDY FROG-SHELL *Bursa corrugata* (Perry, 1811) Pl. 55
Range: South Florida to the West Indies.
Habitat: Moderately shallow water.

Description: Height 2 to 3 in. About 5 whorls, somewhat flattened laterally. Each volution bears a series of encircling knobs and a pair of knobby varices. Outer lip broad and toothed within, inner lip strongly reflected. Aperture with deep notch at upper angle. Canal short and nearly closed. Color yellowish brown, more or less clouded with darker hues.

Remarks: Also once called *B. caelata* Broderip, 1833, and the Corrugated Frog-shell.

CUBAN FROG-SHELL *Bursa cubaniana* (Orbigny, 1842)   **Pl. 55**
Range: South Florida to the West Indies.
Habitat: Moderately deep water.
Description: Height 2 in. About 7 whorls, a moderately tall spire with pointed apex. Whorls well inflated but somewhat compressed laterally. With 2 prominent varices on each whorl; they are directly opposite each other, so there is a nearly continuous ridge running up each side of shell. Surface decorated with revolving lines, some of them beaded; a row of larger beads, or nodes, on the shoulders. Aperture oval, outer lip thickened and toothed within, inner lip plicate. Short anterior canal, strong notch at upper angle of aperture. Color reddish brown, blotched with white.

Remarks: Formerly listed as *B. granularis* (Röding), of which it may be a subspecies.

ST. THOMAS FROG-SHELL   **Pl. 55**
Bursa thomae (Orbigny, 1842)
Range: Southeast Florida; West Indies south to Brazil.
Habitat: Moderately shallow water.
Description: About 1 in. high. A rather squat shell of 4 or 5 whorls. Varices along each side knobby and prominent, and the volutions themselves bear many rounded tubercles and beadlike knobs. Aperture moderate in size, strongly notched above. Color yellowish white, sometimes spotted with reddish.

■ TUN SHELLS: Family Tonnidae

A small group of large or medium-sized gastropods, chiefly of the tropics. The shell is thin and nearly spherical (subglobular) usually with a greatly swollen body whorl. They are sometimes called cask shells or wine jars.

● **Genus** *Tonna* **Brünnich, 1772**

GIANT TUN SHELL *Tonna galea* (Linnaeus, 1758) **Pl. 55**
Range: N. Carolina to Brazil.
Habitat: Moderately deep water.
Description: Averages 6 in. high, but 10 in. specimens have been recorded. Shell thin but quite sturdy and greatly inflated, being almost as broad as tall. About 5 whorls, sutures somewhat sunken. Very low spire. Surface with widely spaced encircling grooves. Aperture very large, outer lip thickened in mature examples, thin and sharp in partly grown individuals. Columella strongly twisted. Juvenile specimens possess a small horny operculum, but this structure is lacking in adults. Color yellowish white, blotched or banded with brown.
Remarks: Very similar shells, now believed by some authorities to belong to this species, are found in the eastern Atlantic along the African coast, and in both the Pacific and Indian oceans.

ATLANTIC PARTRIDGE SHELL **Pls. 13, 55**
Tonna maculosa (Dillwyn, 1817)
Range: South Florida to Brazil; Bermuda.
Habitat: Moderately deep water.
Description: About 5 or 6 in. high. With 4 or 5 whorls, sutures impressed. Shell thin and inflated, spire short and with pointed apex. Aperture large, outer lip thin and sharp, slightly crenulate at edge. Sculpture of widely spaced encircling grooves. Color pale to rich brown, heavily mottled with darker shades and bearing crescent-shaped patches of white, so the surface does indeed remind one of the plumage of a partridge.
Remarks: This shell has long been considered a subspecies of the Indo-Pacific *Tonna perdix* (Linn.) and has been listed as *T. perdix pennata* (Mörch), but it is now recognized as a distinct species, entitled to full specific rank. It has been given the earliest available name, *maculosa*, proposed by Lewis Dillwyn in 1817.

■ **FIG SHELLS: Family Ficidae**

Thin and light in substance but surprisingly strong. In life, when the mollusk is crawling the shell appears to be almost buried in the mantle. There is no operculum in the adults. Occur in warm seas around the world.

● Genus *Ficus* Röding, 1798

PAPER FIG SHELL *Ficus communis* Röding, 1798   Pl. 57
   Range: N. Carolina to Gulf of Mexico.
   Habitat: Moderately deep water.
   Description: About 3 to 4 in. high. Shell thin and pear-shaped,
   flat on top, no spire. About 4 whorls, the body whorl enlarged above and narrowing to a long, straight canal. Surface
   sculptured with fine growth lines crossed by small revolving, cordlike ribs. Aperture large, lip thin and sharp. No
   operculum. Color pinkish gray, with widely spaced pale
   brown dots that are sometimes scarcely discernible. Interior
   polished orange-brown.
   Remarks: This snail is uncommon on the colder Atlantic
   coast but quite abundant on the western coast of Florida. It
   was formerly listed as *Ficus* (or *Pyrula*) *papyratia* (Say, 1822).
   Carol's Fig Shell, *Ficus carolae* Clench, 1945 (Pl. 57) may be
   only a deep water form of *communis*.

■ **ROCK OR DYE SHELLS: Family Muricidae**

   Shells thick and solid, generally more or less spiny. There
   are usually 3 varices to a volution. These are active, carnivorous snails, preferring a rocky or gravelly bottom and moderately shallow water. They are found in all seas, but are
   most abundant in the tropics. The famous Tyrian purple of
   the ancients was a dye obtained by crushing the bodies of
   certain Mediterranean species of this group and skimming
   the dye off the water surface.

● Genus *Siratus* Jousseaume, 1880

BEAU'S MUREX   Pl. 58
Siratus beaui Fischer & Bernardi, 1857
   Range: South Florida to the West Indies.
   Habitat: Deep water.
   Description: Height 3 to 4 in. Wtih 6 or 7 rounded whorls, a
   rather tall spire, and a long canal. The 3 varices are armed
   with spines, and in addition they often bear thin bladelike
   webs. Surface of shell decorated with several rows of encircling beads. Color creamy yellowish or brownish.
   Remarks: One of the handsomest members of its group in our
   waters, and one of the rarest. Considered a collector's item.

●**Genus** *Murex* **Linnaeus, 1758**

CABRIT'S MUREX   **Pl. 58**
Murex cabritii Bernardi, 1859
  Range: Florida to the West Indies.
  Habitat: Moderately deep water.
  Description: Height to 3 in. Shell quite sturdy, generally
  spiny, with about 6 whorls, sutures indistinct. Surface bears
  revolving ridges. Aperture small, canal narrow and much
  elongated, being fully twice as long as rest of shell. With 3
  varices on each volution, decorated with slender spines that
  continue on down the canal. Color pinkish buff.
  Remarks: In number and length of spines there is considerable
  variation, and in some individuals they may be completely
  lacking.

RED MUREX   **Pl. 58**
Murex recurvirostris rubidus Baker, 1897
  Range: Off N. Carolina to the Bahamas.
  Habitat: Shallow water.
  Description: Height 1½ in. Small but stocky, has 5 whorls
  sculptured with revolving ribs. With 3 rounded varices, and
  with 2 or 3 vertical ridges between them. Varices may bear
  short spines or they may be spineless. Aperture round, canal
  long and nearly closed. Mottled gray, brown, pink, or reddish, sometimes showing weak bands. Horny operculum
  pale yellow.
  Remarks: Typical *M. recurvirostris* Broderip is an eastern Pacific shell.

●**Genus** *Favartia* **Jousseaume, 1880**

PITTED MUREX   **Pl. 59**
Favartia cellulosus (Conrad, 1846)
  Range: N. Carolina to Brazil; Bermuda.
  Habitat: Shallow water on oyster beds.
  Description: About ¾ in. high. A solid and rough shell of
  about 6 whorls. The 5 or 6 poorly defined varices have strong
  wrinkled lines between them. Aperture round, canal moderate, closed, and termination of the varices at that point pro-
  duces a forked appearance. Color grayish; aperture purplish
  within.
  Remarks: Formerly listed as *Tritonalia cellulosa* (Conrad).

● Genus *Chicoreus* Montfort, 1810

WEST INDIAN MUREX   Pl. 58
Chicoreus brevifrons (Lamarck, 1822)
Range: South Florida to the West Indies.
Habitat: Moderately shallow water.
Description: Height 5 in. Shell rough and strong, with about 5 whorls having rather indistinct sutures. Surface roughened by many transverse wrinkles. With 3 varices, decorated with spines and hollow fronds, those near the shoulders curving upward. Aperture oval, canal fairly long and partially closed. Color grayish, mottled with white and brown.

LACE MUREX   Pl. 58
Chicoreus florifer subsp. *dilectus* (A. Adams, 1855)
Range: Florida to N. Carolina
Habitat: Shallow water.
Description: Height 2 to 3 in. Shell rough, sturdy, and ornate, with about 7 whorls. Three prominent varices, decorated with frondlike spines. Sculpture of revolving cords. Canal curved backward, nearly closed, and flattened below. Operculum horny. Color deep brownish black, the aperture and apex pink. Young specimens are commonly pink all over.
Remarks: Typical *florifer* (Reeve, 1846) from the West Indies is darker and larger.

● Genus *Hexaplex* Perry, 1810

GIANT EASTERN MUREX   Pl. 58
Hexaplex fulvescens Sowerby, 1834
Range: N. Carolina to Florida; Texas.
Habitat: Moderately shallow water.
Description: To 7 in. high, the largest member of this genus on our shores. Body whorl quite large, giving the shell a somewhat globular look. With 7 or 8 whorls, 3 prominent varices with what might be termed subvarices between them. Apex sharp, canal broadly thickened and nearly closed. Outer lip and canal supplied with spines; shorter spines are usually present on varices as well. Color buffy white.
Remarks: Formerly listed as *M. spinicostatus* Kiener, 1843. Feeds on oysters.

● **Genus** *Phyllonotus* **Swaianson, 1833**

APPLE MUREX   **Pl. 58**
Phyllonotus pomum (Gmelin, 1791)
  Range: N. Carolina to the West Indies and south to Brazil.
  Habitat: Shallow water.
  Description: Height 2 to 3 in. Shell rough and heavy, spire well
  developed, body whorl large. With 5 or 6 whorls, sutures indistinct. Surface nodular and sculptured with revolving
  ridges and cordlike ribs. With 3 prominent varices on each
  volution. Aperture large and round, outer lip thickened, columellar callus plastered on body whorl. Canal short, nearly
  closed, and curving backward. Operculum horny. Color yellowish brown, with broad stripes and mottlings of darker
  shades. Aperture tinged with rose and marked with brownish on inner lip.
  Remarks: In Jamaica this species grows to a height of nearly 5
  in. Bores holes into and feeds upon oysters.

● **Genus** *Muricopsis* **Bucquoy, Dautzenberg, & Dollfus 1882**

HEXAGONAL MUREX   **Pl. 59**
Muricopsis oxytatus M. Smith, 1936
  Range: South Florida to the West Indies.
  Habitat: Moderately shallow water.
  Description: About 1¼ in. high. Some 6 whorls, rather
  indistinct sutures. Well-developed spire, short open canal.
  Surface somewhat spiny, with about 5 rows of short spines
  on body whorl. Outer lip margined with frondlike
  protuberances. Color grayish white, tinged with reddish,
  especially on apex.
  Remarks: Formerly listed as *Muricidea hexagona* (Lamarck,
  1816).

● **Genus** *Calotrophon* **Hertlein & Strong, 1951**

MAUVE-MOUTHED DRILL   **Pl. 46**
Calotrophon ostrearum (Conrad, 1846)
  Range: West Florida.
  Habitat: Shallow water.
  Description: About 1 in. high. A spindle-shaped shell of 6
  whorls, sutures rather indistinct. Spire well elevated, canal
  long and open. Sculpture consists of strong revolving riblets
  crossed by sharp vertical lines, and there is a series of nodes
  at the shoulders. Color grayish; aperture commonly mauve.

● **Genus *Dermomurex* Monterosato, 1890**

LITTLE ASPELLA   **Pl. 59**
Dermomurex pauperculus (C. B. Adams, 1850)
   Range: South Florida to the West Indies.
   Habitat: Moderately deep water; on rocks.
   Description: Height $1/2$ in. With 7 or 8 whorls, sutures fairly
impressed. Shell decorated with thin varices and vertical
knobs. Aperture small, canal short and closed. Color grayish,
clouded with brown or black.

● **Genus *Urosalpinx* Stimpson 1865**

OYSTER DRILL *Urosalpinx cinerea* (Say, 1822)   **Pl. 59**
   Range: Nova Scotia to northeast Florida.
   Habitat: Shallow water on oyster beds.
   Description: About $1^1/4$ in. high. A rugged shell of approximately 5 whorls that are rather convex. Shell coarse and
quite solid, surface sculptured with raised revolving lines,
made wavy by rounded vertical folds. Aperture oval, lip thin
and sharp, canal short. Operculum horny. Color dingy gray;
aperture dark purple. See Gulf Oyster Drill, which is similar.
   Remarks: Next to the starfish, this snail is the worst enemy
the oystermen have to contend with. In some localities, no-
tably the Chesapeake Bay area, their depredations sometimes exceed those of the starfish. Settling upon a young bivalve, the Oyster Drill quickly bores a neat round hole
through a valve, making expert use of its sandpaperlike radula. Through this perforation the Drill is able to insert its
long proboscis and consume the soft parts of the oyster.

GULF OYSTER DRILL   **Pl. 59**
Urosalpinx perrugata (Conrad, 1846)
   Range: Both sides of Florida to Texas and Yucatan.
   Habitat: Shallow water.
   Description: Height about 1 in. A sturdy shell much like the
Oyster Drill, but with vertical folds more prominent and
with a coarser sculpture of revolving lines; also a somewhat
slimmer shell. Outer lip thickened and weakly toothed
within. Operculum horny. Color yellowish gray. It feeds on
oysters and *Brachidontes* mussels.

TAMPA OYSTER DRILL   Pl. 59
Urosalpinx tampaensis (Conrad, 1846)
   Range: West Florida.
   Habitat: Mudflats.
   Description: Height 1 in. Shell rugged, 5 or 6 broadly rounded, well-shouldered whorls with distinct sutures. About 10 vertical ridges to a volution, cut by strongly sculptured revolving cords. Ridges generally paler-colored than spaces in between. Canal short and open, slightly curved. Operculum horny and yellow. Shell grayish brown, rather mottled with white.

● **Genus *Eupleura* H. & A. Adams 1853**

THICK-LIPPED OYSTER DRILL   Pl. 59
Eupleura caudata (Say, 1822)
   Range: Massachusetts to Florida.
   Habitat: Shallow water.
   Description: Height $^3/_4$ in. Shell solid, with about 5 distinctly shouldered whorls. Surface bears about 11 stout vertical ribs, the one bordering the aperture and one directly opposite (on left side of body whorl) enlarged into stout knobby ridges. Numerous revolving lines. Outer lip thick and bordered within by raised granules. Canal short and nearly closed, operculum horny. Color varies from reddish brown to bluish white.
   Remarks: This little snail also drills into bivalve shells, but it is not numerous enough to be as much a pest as the common Oyster Drill, *Urosalpinx cinerea.*

SHARP-RIBBED DRILL   Pl. 59
Eupleura sulcidentata Dall, 1890
   Range: West coast of Florida; Bahamas.
   Habitat: In shallow grass and sandy mud areas.
   Description: About $^1/_2$ to $^3/_4$ in., similar to the Thick-lipped Oyster Drill, but smaller, more delicate, with the upper whorls more shelved and spiny. Spiral sculpture almost absent. There are only 2 or 3 axial nodes between the last 2 thin, side varices. Color gray or brownish, rarely pinkish, and sometimes with narrow spiral brown bands.
   Remarks: A common shallow-water species whose soft parts are white with opaque-chalk mottlings. The egg capsules, shaped like narrow, stalked urns, are laid on dead shells from February to April.

● Genus *Boreotrophon* Fischer 1884

CLATHRATE TROPHON
Boreotrophon clathratus (Linnaeus, 1758)
  Range: Arctic Ocean to Maine.
  Habitat: Moderately deep water.
  Description: Height 1 to 2 in. A sturdy shell of 5 or 6 whorls, sutures distinct and shoulders angled. Sculpture of sharp vertical ridges. Aperture oval, canal open and moderately long. Color chalky white.
  Remarks: A variable shell, and several forms have been described.

■ **CORAL SNAILS: Family Magilidae**

Rather small but thick and solid shells, living on corals and on stony bottoms. Shells may be spiny or relatively smooth, with close lines of growth. The aperture is generally pinkish or purplish. The family Coralliophilidae is the same.

● Genus *Coralliophila* H. & A. Adams 1853

SHORT CORAL SNAIL   **Pl. 59**
Coralliophila abbreviata (Lamarck, 1816)
  Range: South Florida to Brazil; Bermuda.
  Habitat: At bases of sea fans.
  Description: About 1 in. high, sometimes a little more. A solid shell of 5 or 6 shouldered whorls, the last making up most of shell. Sculpture of weak vertical folds and closely spaced encircling threadlike lines. Aperture flaring, outer lip simple, and inner lip rolled over to form a distinct umbilicus. Color grayish white; aperture pinkish or violet.

GLOBULAR CORAL SNAIL   **Pl. 59**
Coralliophila aberrans (C. B. Adams, 1850)
  Range: West Indies.
  Habitat: Shallow water.
  Description: Height $1/2$ in. About 4 whorls, slightly shouldered. Moderate spire. Strong nodes at shoulders. Sculpture of revolving ridges. Aperture pear-shaped. Color white; aperture purple.

CARIBBEAN CORAL SNAIL   **Pl. 59**
Coralliophila caribaea Abbott, 1958
  Range: South Florida to Brazil; Bermuda.
  Habitat: Shallow water.
  Description: Height ³/₄ in. With 5 whorls, angled at shoulder,
  so spire appears turreted. Apex pointed. Sculpture of slanting
  vertical folds and weak revolving lines. Color whitish; aper-
  ture purplish.
  Remarks: Formerly called *Coralliophila plicata* Wood.

■ **ROCK SHELLS AND DOGWINKLES: Family Thaididae**

Stout shells with an enlarged body whorl, wide aperture, and
usually a short spire. These are predatory mollusks living
close to shore in rocky situations. The popular name dye
shells derives from the fact that the body secretes a colored
fluid that may be green, scarlet, or purple. This family is
considered to be a subfamily of the Muricidae by some
workers. The subfamily purpurinae is a synonym.

● **Genus *Morula* Röding 1798**

BLACKBERRY SNAIL   **Pl. 59**
Morula nodulosa (C. B. Adams, 1845)
  Range: South Florida to Brazil; Bermuda.
  Habitat: Shallow water; under stones.
  Description: A bumpy little shell about ¹/₂ in. high. Shell
  strong and solid, moderately high spired, with 5 or 6 whorls.
  Surface sculptured with spiral rows of prominent nodules,
  about 5 rows on body whorl and 3 on each of the early volutions. Aperture long and rather narrow, rather constricted
  by teeth on both lips. Color grayish green, the nodules shiny
  black.
  Remarks: This common species has been placed in the subgenus *Trachipollia* Wooding, 1928.

● **Genus *Purpura* Bruguière 1789**

WIDE-MOUTHED PURPURA   **Pl. 59**
Purpura patula (Linnaeus, 1758)
  Range: Florida to the West Indies on shore rocks.
  Habitat: Intertidal.

Description: Attains height of about 3 in. Rough and solid, body whorl greatly enlarged and makes up most of shell. Surface bears revolving lines and numerous nodules, very pronounced in partly grown specimens but often worn and indistinct in old individuals. Aperture very large, outer lip thin and sharp, a broad polished area on inner lip. Small horny operculum, too small to close the aperture. Color grayish green or brown; interior often salmon pink.
Remarks: Gives off a permanent purple dye.

● Genus *Thais* Röding 1798

DELTOID ROCK SHELL *Thais deltoidea* (Lamarck, 1822)   **Pl. 59**
    Range: Bermuda; Florida to Brazil.
    Habitat: Intertidal on rocks.
    Description: About 1^1/$_2$ in. high. A squat shell, 3 or 4 whorls; sutures quite indistinct. With 3 series of nodules on body whorl, those on shoulders forming pronounced knobs. Aperture large, lip simple and thin. Columella with fold at lower part. Grayish or pinkish white, blotched with brown and purple, typically in form of broad bands encircling shell.
    Remarks: Usually common on rocks at low tide, although its shell is often so covered with encrustations that it matches the rock and therefore is not easily seen.

FLORIDA ROCK SHELL   **Pl. 59**
Thais haemastoma floridana (Conrad, 1837)
    Range: N. Carolina to West Indies; Gulf of Mexico south to Brazil.
    Habitat: Intertidal.
    Description: About 2 in. high. Strong and solid, large body whorl, pointed apex. About 5 whorls, sutures indistinct. Shoulders sloping, surface decorated with sharp revolving lines and a double row of tubercles on last volution. Outer lip thick, crenulate within, short canal. Columella folded at base to form polished area. Color grayish, somewhat blotched with brown; aperture pinkish flesh color.
    Remarks: Typical *T. haemastoma* (Linnaeus, 1767) is a Mediterranean snail.

HAYS' ROCK SHELL
Thais haemastoma canaliculata (Gray, 1839)
    Range: West Florida to Texas.
    Habitat: Shallow water.
    Description: Nearly 5 in. high. This snail is considerably larger

than Florida Rock Shell, with a taller spire and sharper revolving lines. Sutures rather deeply channeled. Color grayish, clouded with brown; aperture pinkish flesh color.

Remarks: This subspecies is very destructive to oyster beds in the Gulf of Mexico. *T. haysae* Clench, 1927, is a synonym.

RUSTIC ROCK SHELL *Thais rustica* (Lamarck, 1822)　　**Pl. 59**
　　Range: Bermuda; Florida to the West Indies.
　　Habitat: Intertidal.
　　Description: Height $1^1/_2$ in. About 5 whorls with sloping shoulders, a sharply pointed apex, and a long and wide aperture. Sculpture of revolving riblets and vertical lines, plus a row of nodes at shoulders and a second row of weaker nodes midway on body whorl. Color gray or brown, sometimes banded with white; aperture whitish.
　　Remarks: Formerly listed as *T. undata* (Lamarck) but that name rightfully belongs to an Indo-Pacific species.

● **Genus *Nucella* Roding, 1798**

DOGWINKLE *Nucella lapillus* (Linnaeus, 1758)　　**Pl. 59**
　　Range: Labrador to New York; Europe.
　　Habitat: Intertidal on rocks.
　　Description: Height 1 to $1^1/_2$ in. Shell thick and solid, with 5 whorls, a short spire, and bluntly pointed apex. Surface sculptured with deep revolving ridges and furrows, as well as many transverse wrinkles. Aperture oval, lip arched, operculum horny. Very short, open canal. Variable color ranges from white to lemon yellow and purplish brown. Some individuals are banded with white or yellow.
　　Remarks: There is considerable variation in the shells aside from color: some are more angular than others, some larger, and some stouter. In a series of several dozen shells it is often possible to find extremes that if studied alone would almost seem to represent different species.

● **Genus *Ocenebra* Gray 1847**

FRILLY DWARF ROCK SHELL
Ocenebra alveata (Kiener, 1842)
　　Range: Florida Keys to Brazil; Bermuda.
　　Habitat: Moderately shallow water.

Description: Height 1 in. With 5 or 6 whorls, elongate spire. Sculpture of robust revolving ridges and strong frilly varices. Aperture small, outer lip thickened. Canal short and closed. Color white, occasionally banded with pale brown.

Remarks: Formerly known as *intermedia* C.B. Adams, 1850.

■ DOVE SHELLS: Family Columbellidae

Small fusiform shells, with an outer lip commonly thickened in the middle. The inner lip has a small tubercle at its lower end. The shells are sometimes quite colorful, and often shiny. Chiefly inhabitants of temperate and warm seas. Operculum horny.

● Genus *Columbella* Lamarck 1799

COMMON DOVE SHELL   Pl. 62
Columbella mercatoria (Linnaeus, 1758)

Range: Florida to Brazil; Bermuda.

Habitat: Shallow water in weeds.

Description: Height ¹/₂ in., sometimes slightly more. Sturdy, solid, 5 or 6 whorls, short and blunt spire. Surface bears numerous revolving grooves. Aperture long and narrow, outer lip thickened, particularly in the middle, and strongly toothed within. Inner lip with series of fine teeth on lower part. Tiny horny operculum. Color very variable, usually gray, clouded and spotted with purplish brown, rusty red, and white, often in the form of encircling bars.

RUSTY DOVE SHELL   Pl. 62
Columbella rusticoides Heilprin, 1887

Range: West Florida and northwest Cuba.

Habitat: Shallow water.

Description: Height about ³/₄ in. Shell oval, 6 or 7 whorls, well-elevated spire with pointed apex. Surface smooth, often polished. Aperture long and narrow, outer lip thickened at center, toothed within. A few teeth on lower portion of inner lip. Color yellowish or whitish, heavily marked with chestnut brown.

● **Genus *Anachis* H. & A. Adams 1853**

GREEDY DOVE SHELL *Anachis avara* (Say, 1822)
Range: Massacusetts to Texas and Yucatan.
Habitat: Shallow water.
Description: Less than $1/2$ in. high. Shell thick and strong, spire elevated and acute. With 6 or 7 whorls, sculptured with impressed spiral lines and prominent vertical folds. The folds usually do not extend beyond middle of last whorl, leaving only revolving lines on that portion of shell. Outer lip feebly toothed within. Color brownish yellow.
Remarks: See Well-ribbed Dove Shell (below) for similarity.

CHAIN DOVE SHELL
Anachis catenata (Sowerby, 1844)
Range: Southeast Florida to the West Indies.
Habitat: Shallow water in weeds.
Description: Height $1/4$ in. About 5 whorls, sutures plainly marked. Apex rather blunt. Sculpture of well-developed vertical ribs with faint encircling lines. Color yellowish white, with scattered brown dots.

FAT DOVE SHELL *Anachis obesa* (C. B. Adams, 1845)
Range: Virginia to Uruguay; Bermuda.
Habitat: Shallow water.
Description: Height about $1/4$ in. A stocky shell of 5 whorls, sutures not very distinct. Numerous vertical folds and fine revolving lines. Outer lip with a few small teeth on inner margin. Color yellowish gray.

BEAUTIFUL DOVE SHELL
Anachis pulchella (Blainville, 1829)
Range: South Florida to the West Indies.
Habitat: Shallow water.
Description: Nearly $1/2$ in. high. With 6 whorls, sutures indistinct. Fusiform (spindle-shaped) in outline, pointed apex. Sculpture of weak vertical ribs and revolving lines. Aperture elongate. Color yellowish white, with reddish brown scrawls.
Remarks: Sowerby also named this species in 1844.

WELL-RIBBED DOVE SHELL   **Pl. 62**
Anachis lafresnayi (Fischer & Bernardi, 1856)
Range: Maine to Florida and east Mexico.
Habitat: Shallow water.

Description: About $1/2$ in. high. This species closely resembles Greedy Dove Shell (above), and was once considered a subspecies. It is slightly stouter, and the vertical folds are more numerous, occasionally running the full height of each volution. Color brown, sometimes weakly banded with darker.

Remarks: Abundant on shelly bottoms. *A. translirata* (Ravenel, 1861) is a synonym.

● Genus *Nitidella* Swainson 1840

SMOOTH DOVE SHELL
Nitidella laevigata (Linnaeus, 1758)
   Range: Florida Keys to the West Indies; Bermuda.
   Habitat: Shallow water.
   Description: About $1/2$ in. high. With 4 or 5 whorls, sutures well impressed. Apex pointed, aperture rather wide. Surface smooth and glossy as a rule. Color variable; usually yellowish orange, with vertical white streaks and a broken band of brown at middle of body whorl.

GLOSSY DOVE SHELL *Nitidella nitida* (Lamarck, 1822)
   Range: Southeast Florida to Brazil; Bermuda.
   Habitat: Shallow water.
   Description: Height $1/2$ in. A fusiform (spindle-shaped) shell of about 5 whorls, sutures fairly distinct. Aperture long and narrow, lip smooth. Surface of shell polished. Color pale yellow, heavily mottled with chestnut brown.
   Remarks: Formerly listed as *N. nitidula* (Sowerby).

● Genus *Mitrella* Risso 1826

CRESCENT MITRELLA *Mitrella lunata* (Say, 1826)
   Range: Massachusetts to Florida and Texas; West Indies to Brazil.
   Habitat: Shallow water.
   Description: Height $1/5$ in. Shell rather stoutly fusiform, 6 whorls separated by shallow sutures. Surface smooth except for a single revolving line below the sutures and a few at base. Aperture oval and narrow, outer lip simple, a few teeth on inner margin. Color yellowish tan, with reddish brown crescent-shaped markings.

WHITE-SPOTTED DOVE SHELL
Mitrella ocellata (Gmelin, 1791)
Range: Bermuda; south Florida to the West Indies.
Habitat: Shallow water.
Description: Nearly $1/2$ in. high. A spindle-shaped shell of about 7 sloping whorls, no shoulders. Aperture long and narrow, outer lip thickened and feebly toothed within. Surface smooth and shining. Color yellowish tan to nearly black, round white spots variable. In life there is a dark brown periostracum.
Remarks: Formerly listed as *Nitidella cribraria* (Lamarck, 1822).

■ NASSA MUD SNAILS: Family Nassariidae

Small carnivorous snails, present in all seas. The shells are rather stocky, with pointed spires. The aperture is strongly notched at both ends, and commonly there is a marked columellar callus (calcareous deposit). Mostly inhabitants of shallow water.

● Genus *Ilyanassa* Stimpson, 1865

EASTERN MUD NASSA *Ilyanassa obsoleta* (Say, 1822)   **Pl. 62**
Range: Gulf of St. Lawrence to Florida.
Habitat: Mudflats.
Description: Nearly 1 in. high, with 6 whorls and a moderately elevated spire. Apex blunt. Surface marked with numerous unequal revolving lines crossed by minute growth lines and rather oblique folds, especially on early volutions. Aperture oval, outer lip thin and sharp, inner lip strongly arched, with fold at front. Canal a mere notch. Color dark reddish purple to almost black.
Remarks: This dark and unattractive mollusk is one of the most abundant univalves to be found along the Atlantic Coast. It is a scavenger, and a dead fish or a crushed clam thrown into shallow water will quickly attract hundreds of individuals. Adult specimens very commonly have the apex somewhat eroded. Formerly put in the genus *Nassarius*.

● Genus *Nassarius* Duméril 1806

VARIABLE NASSA *Nassarius albus* (Say, 1829)   **Pl. 62**
 Range: N. Carolina to the West Indies.
 Habitat: Shallow water.
 Description: Height ½ in. Shell stout and well elevated, apex
 sharp. About 5 whorls, well shouldered and decorated with
 vertical ribs (suture to suture) crossed by ridges that vary in
 size. Aperture small, outer lip thickened, inner lip twisted at
 base. Variable in color but predominantly white, often spotted with brown.
 Remarks: Formerly listed as *N. ambiguus* (Pulteney, 1799).

NEW ENGLAND NASSA   **Pl. 62**
Nassarius trivittatus (Say, 1822)
 Range: Nova Scotia to S. Carolina.
 Habitat: Shallow water.
 Description: About ¾ in. high. A robust shell with an acute
 apex. With 6 or 7 whorls, each slightly flattened at the
 shoulder. A series of spiral grooves cuts across a series of
 beaded lines, giving surface a pimpled appearance. Outer lip
 sharp and scalloped by the revolving lines. Inner lip strongly
 arched, aperture notched at both ends. Color white or yellowish white, sometimes banded with brown.

COMMON EASTERN NASSA   **Pl. 62**
Nassarius vibex (Say, 1822)
 Range: Massachusetts to the West Indies.
 Habitat: Shallow water.
 Description: About ½ in. high. Shell short and heavy, with
 about 5 whorls. Sutures well defined, apex pointed. Surface
 bears strong vertical folds crossed by indistinct revolving
 lines. Aperture notched at both ends, outer lip thick, and
 there is a heavy patch of enamel on inner lip. Color white,
 variously mottled and marked with brown and gray.
 Remarks: This is a variable species, and individuals from different beaches are apt to show different color patterns. Very
 abundant in the South, uncommon north of Cape Hatteras.

■ **WHELKS: Family Buccinidae**

 Shells generally large, with convex whorls. The aperture is
 large and usually notched below. These carnivorous snails
 occur in northern seas all around the world. Certain species
 are used for food in some countries.

● **Genus** *Bailya* **M. Smith 1944**

INTRICATE BAILY SHELL *Bailya intricata* (Dall, 1884)   **Pl. 46**
Range: South Florida to the Bahamas.
Habitat: Intertidal; under stones.
Description: Height ¹/₂ in. About 6 shouldered whorls, pointed apex, elongate aperture, weakly notched above. Outer lip thickened. Sculpture of strong revolving lines and weaker vertical ribs. Color grayish white.

LITTLE BAILY SHELL
Bailya parva (C. B. Adams, 1850)
Range: West Indies.
Habitat: Shallow water.
Description: Height ³/₄ in. About 6 whorls, no shoulders. Sutures well indented. Sculpture of strong vertical ribs and weaker revolving lines. Aperture notched above. Color yellowish white, with orange-brown bands.

● **Genus** *Buccinum* **Linnaeus 1758**

COMMON NORTHERN BUCCINUM   **Pls. 11, 58**
Buccinum undatum Linnaeus, 1758
Range: Arctic Ocean to New Jersey; Europe.
Habitat: Moderately shallow water.
Description: Height 3 to 4 in. Moderately solid, regularly convex, sharp apex. About 6 whorls, decorated with distinct revolving lines, and wavy vertical folds. Aperture large, lip sharp, canal notched. Operculum horny. Color pale reddish or yellowish brown. Aperture yellow in fresh specimens.
Remarks: This is the edible whelk of Scotland and Ireland. It is common in New England waters.

● **Genus** *Colus* **Röding 1798**

PYGMY WHELK *Colus pygmaeus* (Gould, 1841)
Range: Gulf of St. Lawrence to N. Carolina.
Habitat: Moderately deep water.
Description: About 1 in. high. Shell fusiform (spindle-shaped), with 7 or 8 whorls. Surface marked with numerous revolving lines, but these can be seen only after the periostracum has been removed. Aperture oval, canal rather short. Operculum horny. Color grayish; periostracum greenish gray.

Remarks: This snail occurs with Stimpson's Whelk (below), but it may be distinguished from young specimens of the latter by the number of volutions when compared with a shell of the same size. Generally the word *Colus* has been considered masculine in conchology.

SPITSBERGEN WHELK
Colus spitzbergensis (Reeve, 1855)
Range: Arctic Ocean to Nova Scotia; Europe.
Habitat: Deep water.
Description: Height nearly 4 in. With 7 or 8 well-rounded whorls, sutures deep. Apex sharp, canal short. Sculpture of prominent revolving ribs, about 20 to a volution. Aperture roundish, lip thin and sharp. Color yellowish gray.

STIMPSON'S WHELK *Colus stimpsoni* (Mörch, 1867)   Pl. 58
Range: Labrador to Cape Hatteras.
Habitat: Deep water.
Description: Height 3 to 4 in. Spindle-shaped (fusiform) and elongate, with 7 or 8 rather flat whorls, sutures indistinct. Surface bears weak revolving lines beneath the tough periostracum. Aperture oval, white within, canal moderately long, open, and inclined to turn backward. Color bluish white; velvety periostracum dark greenish brown.
Remarks: See Remarks under Pygmy Whelk (above).

● Genus *Neptunea* Roding 1798

NEW ENGLAND NEPTUNE   Pl. 58
Neptunea decemcostata (Say, 1826)
Range: Nova Scotia to Massachusetts.
Habitat: Moderately shallow water.
Description: About 3 to 4 in. high. Shell large and stout, composed of 6 or 7 whorls, spirally ribbed with raised keels, or ridges. There are 10 of these on body whorl, 3 on upper whorls. Short open canal, operculum horny. Color yellowish gray, ridges reddish brown. Aperture white within, the darker ridges faintly showing through.
Remarks: Quite colorful for a mollusk of northern seas. Albino shells are very rare. Fishermen often bring them up in their nets and the snail frequently manages to get into lobster traps, but good specimens are not commonly found on the shore. It may be considered a subspecies of *Neptunea lyrata* (Gmelin, 1791).

● Genus *Antillophos* Woodring 1928

CANDÉ'S PHOS *Antillophos candei* (Orbigny, 1842)   **Pl. 46**
    Range: N. Carolina to Brazil.
    Habitat: Moderately deep water.
    Description: About 1 in. high. With 8 or 9 whorls, an elevated spire, and a sharply pointed apex. Sculpture of sharp vertical ribs, about 15 to a volution, and these are crossed by distinct revolving lines, so the surface has a beaded appearance. Aperture oval and quite long, outer lip somewhat thickened, inner lip with a few folds at lower end. Operculum small, clawlike, and horny. Color pale brownish yellow, sometimes almost white; occasionally lightly banded with pale orange.
    Remarks: Formerly in the genus *Phos* Montfort 1810.

● Genus *Nassarina* Dall, 1889

MANY-SPOTTED DOVE SHELL
Nassarina monilifera (Sowerby, 1844)
    Range: Florida to the West Indies; Bermuda.
    Habitat: Shallow water.
    Description: About 1/4 in. high. About 6 whorls, sutures faint. Shell elongate, apex rather blunt. Aperture small, outer lip toothed within. Sculpture of strong revolving ridges and vertical folds. Color whitish, with broken bands of brown.

● Genus *Engina* Gray 1839

WHITE-SPOTTED ENGINA   **Pl. 62**
Engina turbinella (Kiener, 1835)
    Range: South Florida to Brazil.
    Habitat: Moderately shallow water; reefs.
    Description: About 1/2 in. high. A stoutly fusiform (spindle-shaped) shell of 6 whorls. Aperture elongate, lip somewhat thickened and toothed within. Columella with slight twist. A number of white knobs encircle each volution; rest of shell is purplish brown.

● Genus *Pisania* Bivona 1832

MINIATURE TRITON TRUMPET   **Pl. 60**
Pisania pusio (Linnaeus, 1758)
   Range: South Florida to Brazil; Bermuda.
   Habitat: Moderately shallow water; reefs.
   Description: About 1½ in. high. With 5 or 6 sturdy and strong whorls, sutures indistinct. Well-developed spire, sharp apex. Aperture oval, outer lip toothed within, inner lip with prominent tooth at upper angle. Canal short and straight. Surface smooth and polished, purplish brown with bands of irregular dark and light spots often resembling chevrons.

GAUDY CANTHARUS *Pisania auritula* (Link, 1807)   **Pl. 58**
   Range: South Florida to Brazil; Bermuda.
   Habitat: Shallow water.
   Description: About 1 in. high, stout and solid. With 5 or 6 whorls decorated with strong vertical folds and weaker revolving lines. Whorls somewhat shouldered and knobby. Outer lip thickened, canal short. With 2 teeth at upper angle of the aperture. Color mottled gray, brown, and black.

TINTED CANTHARUS *Pisania tincta* (Conrad, 1846)   **Pl. 60**
   Range: N. Carolina to Brazil; Bermuda.
   Habitat: Shallow water.
   Description: About 1 in. high. Shell solid and fusiform, with 5 or 6 whorls. Shoulders slightly constricted to form small nodules. Ornamentation of low vertical folds crossed by revolving ridges. Aperture oval, outer lip thickened, inner lip with prominent tooth above. Canal very short. Color reddish brown, mottled with white. The smooth subspecies *grandana* Abbott, 1989, is illustrated on Pl. 46.

● Genus *Cantharus* Röding 1798

CANCELLATE CANTHARUS   **Pl. 58**
Cantharus cancellarius (Conrad,1846)
   Range: Florida to Texas.
   Habitat: Shallow water.
   Description: Height 1¼ in. Shell spindle-shaped, elongate, with 5 or 6 whorls. Sculpture of rather indistinct vertical folds crossed by wavy encircling lines. Aperture elongate-oval, outer lip thickened, inner lip with tooth at upper angle, pleat at bottom of columella. Color reddish brown, somewhat mottled with white.

Figure 62. False Drill *Cantharus multangulus*

FALSE DRILL *Cantharus multangulus* (Philippi, 1848)   **Fig. 59**
Range: N. Carolina to the West Indies; Texas.
Habitat: Moderately shallow water.
Description: About 1 in. high. With 6 whorls, body whorl large, sutures distinct. Sculpture of 7 prominent vertical ribs interrupted at the sutures and crossed by numerous revolving threadlike lines. Aperture oval, lip thin, canal short, operculum horny. Color variable, usually creamy white flecked with brown, but occasional specimens are solid brown or orange. Aperture commonly rosy pink.

■ CROWN CONCHS: Family Melongenidae

Moderately large and solid shells, living from shoreline to moderate depths. They are carnivorous and predacious, and they occur in tropical and temperate seas.

● Genus *Melongena* Schumacher 1817

CROWN CONCH *Melongena corona* (Gmelin 1791)   **Pl. 58**
Range: Florida to Mexico.
Habitat: Shallow water.
Description: About 2 to 5 in. high. Shell roughly pear-shaped, with short spire and large inflated body whorl. With 5 or 6

whorls, the last few bearing a single or double row of short but sharp spines. An additional row or two of blunter spines encircles base of shell, or may be lacking. Aperture oval and wide, outer lip simple, with notch at base, columella twisted. Operculum clawlike, horny. Color dark brown to black, spirally banded with bluish white or yellow, in various shades and irregular arrangements.

Remarks: Several subspecies have been named, such as the High-spired Crown Conch, *M. c. altispira* Pilsbry & Vanatta, 1934. The separations are based on the shell's differences in height, spine size, and general sturdiness, but since it is possible to find all gradations, most authorities do not believe that the rank of subspecies is valid and prefer to call them forms or varieties. Sinistral specimens are very rare. However, *bicolor* (Say, 1826) from the Lower Florida Keys seems to be good dwarf subspecies with numerous erect spines on the shoulder.

● **Genus** *Busycotypus* **Wenz, 1943**

CHANNELED WHELK   **Pl. 57**
Busycotypus canaliculatus (Linnaeus, 1758)
Range: Massachusetts to east Florida.
Habitat: Shallow water.
Description: About 4 to 7 in. high. A large pear-shaped shell with 5 or 6 turreted whorls. Body whorl very large above, gradually diminishing downward and terminating in a long, nearly straight canal. A broad and deep channel at the suture forms a winding terrace up the spire. Shoulders bear weak knobs. Sculpture of fine revolving lines. Color buffy gray; aperture yellowish. In life there is a yellowish brown periostracum bristling with stiff hairs.
Remarks: Indian wampum was made from the twisted columellas of this and the next species, cut into elongate beads.

● **Genus** *Busycon* **Röding 1798**

KNOBBED WHELK *Busycon carica* (Gmelin, 1791)   **Pl. 57**
Range: Massachusetts to northwest Florida.
Habitat: Shallow water.
Description: Height 4 to 9 in. Shell thick and solid, pear-shaped (see Lightning Whelk, below). About 6 whorls, body whorl large and broad, crowned by a series of blunt spines or

nodes. Spire low, with series of nodules encircling the shoulders of each volution. Aperture long and oval, canal long and open. Operculum horny. Color yellowish gray; interior orange-red. Young specimens often streaked with violet.

Remarks: The largest gastropod found north of Cape Hatteras. Most visitors at the seashore have noted the egg ribbons of the mollusks of this genus. The strings of curiously flattened, disklike capsules may be picked up alongshore during the summer months and are popularly called Venus necklaces.

KIENER'S WHELK   Pl. 57
Busycon carica subsp. *eliceans* (Montfort, 1810)
Range: N. Carolina to central east Florida.
Description: About 6 in., with prominent shoulder spines and a fairly heavy swelling around the center girth of the body whorl.

TURNIP WHELK *Busycon coarctatum* (Sowerby, 1825)   Pl. 57
Range: Yucatan, Mexico.
Habitat: Moderately shallow water.
Description: About 6 in. high. Rather solid, a short sloping spire, a somewhat bulbous body whorl, and a long open canal. Whorl count about 5. A few short spines may be present on shoulders. Buffy gray, decorated with vertical streaks of purplish brown. Aperture orange-yellow, ribbed within.
Remarks: This species was first described by Sowerby in 1825. A very similar shell, *B. rapum* (Heilprin), occurs as a fossil in the Pliocene of Florida, and *B. coarctatum* is believed to be a modern descendant of that ancient gastropod. Very few examples were known, none had been collected for about a century, and the species was generally regarded as being extinct. Since 1950 the shrimp fishermen, dredging in Campeche Bay, Mexico, have been bringing them up occasionally, but it is still considered a rare and coveted shell.

LIGHTNING WHELK   Pl. 57
Busycon contrarium (Conrad, 1840)
Range: S. Carolina to Florida.
Habitat: Shallow water.
Description: Height 7 to 10 in., but 15 in. specimens are recorded. Shell thick and strong, shaped very much like the Knobbed Whelk (above), except that the spiral turns to the left. In other words, this is a left-handed (sinistral) snail and the Knobbed Whelk is right-handed (dextral). Spire rather flatter, and whole shell more graceful. Fawn color, vertically

streaked with violet-brown. Young specimens are brightly colored, but after the shell grows to 8 or 9 in. the colors fade, and the shell becomes dull grayish white.

Remarks: This species is also called *B. sinistrum* (Hollister, 1958)

PERVERSE WHELK   **Pl. 57**
Busycon perversum (Linnaeus, 1758)
 Range: Southwestern Gulf of Mexico; offshore.
 Habitat: Moderately shallow water.
 Description: Height 6 to 8 in. A heavy and rugged shell of 5 or 6 whorls. Body whorl very thick and swollen, particularly in region of canal. Color grayish, somewhat streaked with violet-brown.
 Remarks: Found only in offshore waters in the southwest section of the Gulf of Mexico.

PEAR WHELK *Busycon spiratum* (Lamarck, 1816)   **Pl. 57**
 Range: N. Carolina to Florida and Gulf states.
 Habitat: Shallow water.
 Description: Height 3 to 5 in. With 4 or 5 whorls, body whorl very large. Sutures wide and deeply channeled. Shell thin but sturdy, spire very short. Aperture wide and prolonged into a straight, open canal. Operculum horny. Surface sculptured with weak revolving lines. Flesh-colored, with reddish brown streaks.
 Remarks: Formerly listed as *B. pyrum* (Dillwyn, 1817). Say's Pear Whelk, *Busycon spiratum* subspecies *pyruloides* (Say, 1822) from North Carolina to both sides of Florida is more elongate, thinner-shelled, has very weak spiral threads on the outside, and flames of purple-brown. Sinistral specimens are very rare. The subspecies *plagosum* (Conrad 1863) offshore from Alabama to Mexico has a strong ridge of the upper part of the whorl. Synonyms of this subspecies are *galvestonense* Hollister, 1958, and *texanum* Hollister, 1958.

■ TULIP SHELLS: Family Fasciolariidae

Large snails, with strong, thick, fusiform (spindle-shaped) shells. The spire is elevated and sharply pointed, and there is no umbilicus. Inner lip usually decorated with a few oblique folds. These are predatory mollusks, slow and deliberate in their movements. Generally distributed in warm seas.

● Genus *Leucozonia* Gray 1847

CHESTNUT LATIRUS *Leucozonia nassa* (Gmelin, 1791)   **Pl. 56**
    Range: Florida to the West Indies; Texas.
    Habitat: Shallow water.
    Description: About 2 in. high. Shell solid and fusiform, about 7 whorls, sutures quite distinct. Strong tubercles on body whorl form shoulders. Sculpture of revolving lines. Aperture oval, outer lip grooved within, operculum horny. Short open canal. Color varies from chestnut brown to almost black, usually with a paler band near base.
    Remarks: There is a smooth shouldered subspecies, *L. leucozonalis* (Lamarck, 1822) from the central part of the Caribbean.

WHITE-SPOTTED LATIRUS   **Pl. 56**
Leucozonia ocellata (Gmelin, 1791)
    Range: Southeast Florida to the West Indies and Brazil.
    Habitat: Shallow water.
    Description: About 1 in. high. A stoutly fusiform shell of some 5 whorls. Sculpture of revolving lines, with elongate knobs at shoulders. Canal short. Color dark brown, with a circle of whitish knobs at periphery and smaller white spots at base of shell. Nearly all mature shells have the apex white.

● Genus *Latirus* Montfort 1810

SHORT-TAILED LATIRUS   **Pl. 56**
Latirus angulatus (Röding, 1798)
    Range: Florida Keys to the West Indies and Brazil.
    Habitat: Shallow water.
    Description: About 1 to 2 in. high. With 8 knobby whorls, sutures well defined. Apex pointed; aperture moderate, notched above, short open canal below. Base of columella with weak plications. Sculpture of rounded vertical knobs. Color light brown, with numerous dark brown encircling lines.
    Remarks: *L. brevicaudatus* Reeve, 1847 is a synonym.

● Genus *Dolicholatirus* Bellardi, 1884

KEY WEST LATIRUS
Dolicholatirus cayohuesonicus (Sowerby, 1878)   **Pl. 46**
    Range: Florida Keys and the West Indies.

Habitat: Moderately shallow water.
Description: Height 1 in. An elongate, slender shell with 5 or 6 whorls, sutures indistinct. Sculptured with revolving ribs made somewhat wavy by a series of weak vertical folds. Color dull gray.

TROCHLEAR LATIRUS   Pl. 56
Latirus cariniferus Lamarck, 1822
    Range: Southeast Florida; Gulf of Mexico and West Indies.
    Habitat: Rocky reef areas in shallow water.
    Description: Up to 2 in., elongate, heavy, with 7 to 9 low, rounded ribs which are noduled by 2 spiral cords in the upper whorls and by 4 cords on the wide periphery of the last whorl. Numerous fine spiral threads present. Umbilicus variable, sometimes funnel-shaped. Color yellow, cream, or brownish. Lower part of columella with 2 weak folds. Aperture bright yellow.
    Remarks: *Latirus trochlear* Kobelt, 1876, is a synonym. Compare with McGinty's Latirus, which may be a Florida variant.

BROWN-LINED LATIRUS   Pl. 56
Latirus infundibulum (Gmelin, 1791)
    Range: Southeast Florida to the West Indies.
    Habitat: Moderately shallow water.
    Description: About 2 in. high. Shell solid and elongate, with about 7 whorls, a tall spire with blunt apex, sutures strongly marked. Each volution bears 6 vertical folds, and the surface is further decorated with prominent spiral ridges. The crests of the folds are commonly worn and shiny, obliterating the ridges at that point. Canal quite long and narrow, with 2 or 3 pleats on inner lip. Color grayish, the spiral ridges reddish.

McGINTY'S LATIRUS *Latirus mcgintyi* Pilsbry, 1939   Pl. 56
    Range: South Florida and the West Indies.
    Habitat: Moderately deep water.
    Description: About $2^{1}/_{2}$ in. high. Heavy and solid, with 8 or 9 whorls. Apex pointed, aperture narrow, funnel-shaped umbilicus. Sculpture of strongly rounded vertical ribs and coarse revolving ridges. Color yellowish, with dark brown stains between the ribs.
    Remarks: This is probably only a minor form of *L. cariniferus* Lamarck, 1822, a West Indian species.

● **Genus *Fasciolaria* Lamarck 1799**

BANDED TULIP SHELL   **Pl. 56**
Fasciolaria lillium G. Fischer, 1807
   Range: N. Carolina to Yucatan, Mexico.
   Habitat: Shallow water down to 100 ft.
   Description: Size 2 to 5 in. in length, whorls smooth, even at the sutures. The widely spaced, rarely broken, distinct, 7 to 11 spiral purple-brown lines and cloudy background are characteristic. Formerly known as *F. distans* Lamarck, 1822. There are five distinct subspecies, including the typical *lillium.*

• **Subspecies *lillium* G. Fischer, 1807**
   Range: Mississippi Delta west and southward to Yucatan, Mexico and the north side of Dry Tortugas.
   Description: Size 3 to 4 in. Second nuclear whorl with 7 axial riblets, followed by 13 riblets per whorl on the next two whorls. Last whorl with 9 or 10 spiral brown lines.

• **Subspecies *hunteria* (G. Perry, 1811)**   **Pl. 56**
   Range: Cape Hatteras, N.C. to Mobile Bay, Alabama, and all of Florida.
   Description: Size 2 to 3 in. No axial riblets on early whorls in shallow water colonies. Last whorl with 5 or 6 maroon spiral lines. Backgound ivory or bluish gray and with mauve axial flames. Upper whorls with two brown lines.

• **Subspecies *branhamae* Rehder and Abbott, 1951**
   Range: Gulf of Campeche, Mexico, and south Texas.
   Description: Size 4 to 5 in. Siphonal canal long and orange-brown. Last whorl with 8 to 12 spiral purple-brown lines.

• **Subspecies *tortugana* Hollister, 1957**   **Pl. 56**
   Range: Off the tip of the Lower Florida Keys; deep water.
   Description: About 2 to 3 in. Whorl after the smooth protoconch has about 7 riblets. Last whorl with 6 primary spiral black-brown lines. Background white with bright red axial flames.

• **Subspecies *bullisi* Lyons, 1972**
   Range: Deep water off northwest Florida. Uncommon.
   Description: Size 3 to 4 in. Very elongate, with 10 to 12 thin spiral lines, between which may be smaller ones. Background color pale yellow. No spiral ridge extending on to the parietal wall.

TULIP SHELL *Fasciolaria tulipa* (Linnaeus, 1758)   **Pl. 56**
  Range: N. Carolina to the West Indies and to Brazil.
  Habitat: Shallow water.
  Description: Height 4 to 6 in., rarely 10 in. Shell spindle-shaped and moderately high-spired, with 8 or 9 convex whorls and distinct sutures. Surface relatively smooth, with weak revolving lines and a few strong wrinkles just below each suture. Aperture long and oval, operculum horny, canal moderately short and open. Color pinkish gray to reddish orange, with interrupted spiral bands of dark brown and many streaks and blotches of reddish brown and amber.
  Remarks: This and the above species are voracious feeders upon other gastropods.

● **Genus** *Pleuroploca* **Fischer 1884**

FLORIDA HORSE CONCH   **Pl. 52**
Pleuroplaca gigantea (Kiener, 1840)
  Range: N. Carolina to Florida and to east Mexico
  Habitat: Shallow water.
  Description: Height reaches 2 ft. Shell ponderous in size and weight. About 10 whorls, the shoulders bearing large but low nodules. Spire high and somewhat turreted. Sculpture of revolving ridges. Aperture wide and oval, with lengthy canal. Columella bears 3 pleats, operculum leathery. Color brown, aperture orange-red; animal is brick red. Young shells are orange.
  Remarks: Easily the largest shelled snail to be found in American waters, it shares with one other species, *Syrinx aruanus* (Linnaeus, 1758) of Australia, the honor of being the largest univalve in the world. It used to be in the genus *Fasciolaria*. It was made the official shell of the state of Florida in 1969. A knobless or "bumpless wonder" variety is known as forma *reevei* (Philippi, 1851) (see Pl. 52).

◆ **SPINDLE SHELLS: Subfamily Fusininae**

Commonly large, rather spindle-shaped (fusiform) shells. Lip not thickened, umbilicus wanting. Operculum horny. The spire is tall, acuminate, and many-whorled. Canal long and straight. Found chiefly in warm seas.

● **Genus** *Fusinus* **Rafinesque 1815**

COUE'S SPINDLE *Fusinus couei* (Petit, 1853)   **Pl. 56**
   Range: Gulf of Mexico.
   Habitat: Deep water. Dredged up by shrimpers.
   Description: Height 4 in. A tall and graceful shell of 7 or 8 whorls, the sutures plainly marked. Sculpture of distinct spiral lines, no vertical folds. Aperture small, canal long and nearly closed. Inner lip reflected. Color white.

ORNAMENTED SPINDLE   **Pl. 56**
Fusinus eucosmius (Dall, 1889)
   Range: Gulf of Mexico.
   Habitat: Moderately deep water.
   Description: About 2¹/₂ in. high. With 9 whorls, a tall, sharply pointed spire, and a long thin canal. Volutions convex, sculptured with rounded vertical ridges crossed by wavy encircling lines. Sutures impressed. Aperture small, inner lip reflected, operculum horny. Color orange-white to pure white.

■ **OLIVE SHELLS: Family Olividae**

Members of this group tend to be cylindrical, with a greatly enlarged body whorl that conceals most of the earlier volutions. The shells are smooth and polished and often brightly colored. Widely distributed in warm and tropical seas. They feed on small shrimp and clams. The genus *Oliva* has no operculum; *Olivella* does.

● **Genus** *Oliva* **Bruguière 1789**

NETTED OLIVE *Oliva reticularis* Lamarck, 1810   **Pl. 60**
   Range: Southeast Florida to the West Indies.
   Habitat: Intertidal in sand.
   Description: Height 1¹/₂ in. About 4 whorls, short spire, sutures plain. Body whorl large, aperture narrow, inner lip with plications toward base. Surface highly polished. No operculum. Color white or grayish, with pattern of purplish brown reticulations.
   Remarks: A deep-water subspecies, *O. reticularis bollingi* Clench, 1934, has been obtained at 200 ft. off Miami,

Florida. *Oliva fulgurator* Röding, 1758, may be an earlier name for this species. A dark form, *pattersoni* Clench, 1945, is illustrated on Pl. 60.

LETTERED OLIVE *Oliva sayana* Ravenel, 1834   **Pls. 8, 60**
Range: S. Carolina to Florida.
Habitat: Intertidal in sand.
Description: Height $2^{1}/_{2}$ in. Shell strong and solid. Cylindrical, with short pointed spire. With 4 or 5 whorls, sutures deeply incised. Aperture long, notched at base, columella reflected at lower end. No operculum. Surface highly polished, bluish gray, variously marked with chestnut and pink.
Remarks: The pattern of dark markings suggest characters or hieroglyphics, hence the popular name of Lettered Olive. It used to be known as *O. litterata* Lamarck, 1810. The Coast Indians made necklaces of them long before white people set foot on American shores. There is a pale yellowish to nearly golden variety that is unspotted, a form eagerly sought by collectors. It has been named *O. sayana citrina* Johnson, 1911, the Golden Olive (see Pl. 60).

● **Genus** *Olivella* **Swainson 1831**

COMMON RICE OLIVE *Olivella floralia* (Duclos, 1853)   **Pl. 61**
Range: N. Carolina to Brazil; Bermuda
Habitat: Shallow water in sand.
Description: About $^{1}/_{2}$ in. high. Elongate, 4 or 5 whorls, no shoulders, well-defined sutures. Apex sharp. Aperture rather narrow, lower columella pleated. Small horny operculum. Surface highly polished. Color white or bluish white, a few darker mottlings at the sutures. Apex frequently orange.

MINUTE DWARF OLIVE *Olivella minuta* (Link, 1807)   **Pl. 61**
Range: South Texas; West Indies to Brazil.
Habitat: Shallow water in sand.
Description: Nearly $^{1}/_{2}$ in. high. A solid shell of 3 or 4 whorls, apex sharply pointed. Aperture elongate, base of columella grooved. Color bluish gray, whitish at base. Generally a white or brown band at sutures.

VARIABLE DWARF OLIVE *Olivella mutica* (Say, 1822)   **Pl. 61**
Range: N. Carolina to Florida and Bahamas.
Habitat: Shallow water in sand.

Description: About ¹/₂ in. high. Shell small but solid, about 5 whorls and short pointed spire. Outer lip thin and sharp, inner lip without plications. Small horny operculum. Surface highly polished, coloring variable. Specimens may be found that range from nearly white to dark chocolate, with or without bands, but the commonest color is yellowish white, with 2 or 3 revolving bands of purplish brown.

WEST INDIAN DWARF OLIVE   **Pl. 61**
Olivella nivea (Gmelin, 1791)
   Range: Bermuda; Florida to Brazil.
   Habitat: Shallow water.
   Description: About ³/₄ in. high. A slender shell of about 5 whorls, sutures plainly marked. Well-developed spire, sharp apex. Surface shiny. Color white, clouded with orange-brown, and commonly with suggestions of brownish dots encircling the shell near base and at shoulders.

● **Genus *Jaspidella* Olsson 1956**

JASPER DWARF OLIVE   **Pl. 61**
Jaspidella jaspidea (Gmelin, 1791)
   Range: N. Carolina to Brazil; Bermuda.
   Habitat: Shallow water in sand.
   Description: About ¹/₂ in. high. An oval shell of 4 or 5 whorls, short pointed spire, impressed sutures. Aperture narrow, inner lip weakly plicate toward base, operculum horny and small. Surface highly polished, color pale yellowish gray, with narrow band of chocolate just below sutures.
   Remarks: Formerly and sometimes still listed as an *Olivella*.

■ **MITER SHELLS: Family Mitridae**

The members of this family on our shores are mostly small shells. In the Pacific and Indian oceans they are much larger and often brilliantly colored. The shell is spindle-shaped (fusiform), rather thick and solid, with a sharply pointed spire. Aperture is small, notched in front, and there are several distinct pleats on the columella. Operculum elongate and horny. Chiefly inhabit warm seas.

● Genus *Mitra* Lamarck 1799

BARBADOS MITER *Mitra barbadensis* (Gmelin, 1791) **Pl. 62**
Range: Southeast Florida to Brazil; Bermuda.
Habitat: Shallow water under rocks.
Description: Height 1 to 1¹/₂ in. About 6 rather flat whorls, sutures not well impressed. Surface moderately smooth, but there are weak revolving lines. Aperture long and narrow, 4 or 5 slanting ridges on columella. Outer lip somewhat thickened. Color yellowish gray, often with whitish flecks.

BEADED MITER *Mitra nodulosa* (Gmelin, 1791) **Pl. 62**
Range: N. Carolina to Brazil; Bermuda.
Habitat: Shallow water.
Description: About 1 in. high. Shell elongate, with fairly sharp apex and 9 or 10 flattish whorls that are slightly shouldered. Sutures distinct. Surface sculptured with raised granules produced by vertical ribs crossed by revolving lines. Aperture quite short, notched at base. With pleats on columella. Color pale brown.
Remarks: Formerly listed as *M. granulosa* Lamarck, 1811.

ROYAL FLORIDA MITER *Mitra florida* Gould, 1856 **Pl. 60**
Range: South half of Florida and the West Indies.
Habitat: Among reef in moderately shallow water.
Description: About 1¹/₂ in., elongate, fusiform, smooth, with about 15 spiral rows of small, evenly spaced, roundish dots of orange-brown. With 9 columella folds.
Remarks: A handsome, uncommon species living near coral reefs. *Mitra fergusoni* Sowerby, 1874, is a synonym.

● Genus *Pusia* Swainson 1840

WHITE-LINED MITER **Pl. 62**
Pusia albocincta (C. B. Adams, 1845)
Range: Florida to the West Indies.
Habitat: Shallow water.
Description: Height ³/₄ in. A fusiform shell of about 6 whorls, sutures well indented. Aperture narrow, columella with 4 folds. Sculpture of numerous vertical ribs. Color dark brown, with encircling band of white on each volution.

LITTLE GEM MITER *Pusia gemmata* (Sowerby, 1871)
Range: Florida to West Indies.

Habitat: Shallow water.
Description: Height ¼ in. About 7 whorls, sutures distinct. Columella with 4 folds. Sculpture of rounded vertical ribs. Color black or dark brown, a whitish band showing on the crests of the ribs.

HANLEY'S MITER *Pusia hanleyi* (Dohrn, 1862)
Range: Florida to the West Indies.
Habitat: Shallow water in grass flats.
Description: Height ¼ in. A rather slender shell of about 5 whorls, sutures well impressed. Aperture narrow, columella with 4 folds. Sculpture of rounded vertical ribs. Color brown, with whitish encircling band.

MAIDEN MITER *Pusia puella* (Reeve, 1845)
Range: South Florida to the West Indies.
Habitat: Shallow water.
Description: Height ½ in. A stubby little shell of about 5 whorls. Apex rounded, sutures indistinct. Aperture small and very narrow, weak ridges on columella. Surface smooth, with just a suggestion of spiral threads. Color deep brown or black, commonly with a few encircling dots of white on body whorl.

■ CHANK SHELLS: Family Turbinella

Large, thick, heavy shells, often ponderous. There are several distinct pleats on the columella. The operculum is clawlike. These snails all are natives of tropical or subtropical seas. In India rare left-handed specimens are regarded as sacred and are mounted in gold and placed on altars. This family has also been called Xancidae.

● **Genus** *Turbinella* **Lamarck, 1799**

WEST INDIAN CHANK   **Pl. 52**
Turbinella angulata (Lightfoot, 1786)
Range: Bahamas and the West Indies.
Habitat: Shallow water.
Description: About 5 to 9 in. high. Heavy and ponderous, about 6 whorls with prominent knobs on shoulders. Sutures very distinct. Spire moderately high, apex bluntly rounded.

Sculpture of weak revolving lines. Aperture large, descending into a short open canal. Inner lip partly reflected, forming small umbilicus. Operculum horny, clawlike. Columella strongly pleated. Color yellowish white, with brownish periostracum. Interior delicate pink in fresh specimens.

Remarks: Formerly listed as *Turbinella scolymus* Gmelin, 1791.

■ VASE SHELLS: Family Vasidae

These are generally heavy shells, often ponderous. The outline is like an inverted vase. There are strong plications on the columella, the operculum is clawlike, and usually there is a heavy periostracum. Confined to tropical or subtropical waters.

● Genus *Vasum* Röding 1798

CARIBBEAN VASE *Vasum muricatum* (Born, 1778)   **Pl. 56**
Range: South Florida to the West Indies.
Habitat: Shallow water.
Description: About 3 to 4 in. high. Shell rough, heavy, and strong, with a fairly short spire and bluntly pointed apex. With 6 to 7 whorls, sculptured with many revolving ribs and ridges, and there is a series of rather sharp nodes on the shoulders, with a double row of spinelike nodes sometimes on lower part of body whorl. Aperture long, narrowing to canal, inner lip with transverse folds at center. Color yellowish brown, with tough brown periostracum.

■ HARP SHELLS: Family Harpidae

● Genus *Morum* Röding

WOOD LOUSE *Morum oniscus* (Linnaeus, 1767)   **Pl. 49**
Range: Southeast Florida to Brazil; Bermuda.
Habitat: Shallow water along edge of reefs.
Description: About $3/4$ in., with 3 rows of blunt tubercles; exterior brownish gray. Inner lip with raised white speckles. Operculum very small, corneous. Uncommon.

■ VOLUTES: Family Volutidae

The volutes are attractive, colorful shells and have always been great favorites with collectors, sharing honors with the cones and cowries. These shells exhibit a wide assortment of ornamentation and color. The aperture is notched in front and the columella bears several pleats. The group is noted for having a large, often bulbous initial whorl (protoconch) at the apex. Volutes are well distributed in tropical seas, living chiefly in rather deep water. For the collector who likes to add to his collection by purchasing specimens from dealers, the volutes can be the most costly of all marine shells.

● Genus *Scaphella* Swainson 1832

DUBIOUS VOLUTE *Scaphella dubia* (Broderip, 1827)
Range: South Florida; Gulf of Mexico.
Habitat: Deep water.
Description: Height 2½ in. A slender shell of about 5 whorls, a moderate spire capped by a rounded apex. Aperture long and narrow, weak plications on inner lip. Upper volutions ribbed vertically. Surface smooth, color yellowish brown with chocolate spots, but the spots are fewer — both in number of spots and number of rows — than in the better-known Dohrn's Volute.

KIENER'S VOLUTE   **Pl. 63**
Scaphella dubia kieneri Clench, 1946
Range: West Florida to Texas.
Habitat: Deep water.
Description: Height 6 in. A gracefully slender shell of 7 or 8 whorls. Apex sharp, sutures rather indistinct. Aperture long, lip thin and sharp. Columella without pleats. Surface smooth, color smoky brown with squarish spots of deep brown or black encircling the shell. Often these spots are in double rows.
Remarks: This was previously placed in the genus *Auriniopsis* Clench, 1953.

GOULD'S VOLUTE *Scaphella gouldiana* (Dall, 1887)   **Pl. 63**
Range: N. Carolina to the West Indies.
Habitat: Deep water.
Description: Height 2 to 3 in. About 5 whorls, spire well developed, sutures impressed. Surface sculptured with vertical

knobs at shoulders, and by very minute spiral lines. Aperture long and narrow, outer lip thin and sharp. Color yellowish gray, sometimes pinkish aperture; occasional specimens may be nearly white and others may show indistinct bands of brown.

Remarks: Unbanded forms are the variety or form *dohrni* (Sowerby, 1903) (see Pl. 63).

JUNONIA *Scaphella junonia* (Lamarck, 1804)   **Pls. 14, 63**
  Range: N. Carolina to Gulf of Mexico.
  Habitat: Moderately deep water.
  Description: Height 3 to 6 in. Shell spindle-shaped, strong and solid, 5 or 6 whorls, sutures distinct. Apex blunt, spire moderate. Outer lip relatively thin, inner lip with 4 oblique pleats on lower part. Canal short, no operculum. Color pinkish white, with slanting rows of squarish spots that may be chocolate brown or reddish orange.
  Remarks: This is one of the prizes in any shell collection. Good specimens have brought as much as $100 in the past, when the species was considered extremely rare. Every season a few examples are washed up on shore during storms, but the shrimp fishermen now bring them in quite regularly. There are only three known sinistral specimens. The subspecies *butleri* Clench, 1953, from the southwest part of the Gulf of Mexico has smaller spots and a whiter background. The subspecies or form *johnstoneae* Clench, 1953, from off Alabama has a darker, almost golden background.

■ NUTMEGS: Family Cancellariidae

Small but solid shells, with a striking cross-ribbed sculpture. The aperture is drawn out, with a short canal at base. The inner lip is strongly plicate, and the outer lip is ribbed within. There is no operculum. These snails are vegetarians and live in warm waters as a rule.

● **Genus** *Tritonoharpa* Dall, 1908

ARROW DWARF TRITON   **Pl. 62**
Tritonoharpa lanceolata (Menke, 1828)
  Range: N. Carolina to Brazil; Bermuda.
  Habitat: Offshore rocky bottoms.

Description: About 1 in. high. A slender, elongate shell of 5 or 6 whorls, each bearing many finely cut vertical lines and 2 distinct riblike varices. Aperture moderately small and narrow, canal short. Inner lip sometimes forms bladelike ridge. Color pale brown or yellowish buff, with scattered spots of orange-brown.

Remarks: Previously placed in the genus *Colubraria* in the family Buccinidae.

LEANING DWARF TRITON   **Pl. 62**
Tritonoharpa obscura (Reeve, 1844)
  Range: Florida Keys to the West Indies.
  Habitat: Moderately shallow water.
  Description: Height 1½ in. About 7 whorls, sutures faint. Aperture narrow, parietal wall reflected. Sculpture of weak revolving and vertical lines. Outer lip thickened; previous lips leave prominent varices at irregular intervals. Color pale brown, with marks of darker orange-brown, the varices decorated with vivid brown and white.

SWIFT'S DWARF TRITON
Tritonoharpa igniflua (Reeve, 1845)
  Range: Bermuda; West Indies.
  Habitat: Shallow water under rocks; uncommon.
  Description: Height ¾ in. A slender shell of 6 or 7 whorls, sutures faintly impressed. No varices on spire. Sculpture of distinct revolving lines and weak vertical ridges. Parietal wall reflected. Color yellowish gray, blotched with brown.
  Remarks: *Colubraria swifti* Tryon is a synonym.

● **Genus *Cancellaria* Lamarck 1799**

COMMON NUTMEG   **Pl. 60**
Cancellaria reticulata (Linnaeus, 1767)
  Range: N. Carolina to Brazil.
  Habitat: Shallow water.
  Description: About 1 to 1½ in. high. Shell strong and rugged, with 6 or 7 well-rounded whorls, sutures distinct. Surface sculptured with vertical ribs and revolving lines, producing a network of raised lines over the shell. Aperture moderately narrow, canal short. Inner lip with strong oblique pleats. Color bright or pale orange, with weak orange-brown bands.
  Remarks: *C. conradiana* Dall is a fossil relative. The Florida Keys' form *adelae* Pilsbry, 1940, is much smoother and has a pinkish aperture.

● Genus *Trigonostoma* Blainville 1827

PHILIPPI'S NUTMEG   Pl. 60
Trigonostoma tenerum (Philippi, 1848)
Range: South Florida
Habitat: Shallow water.
Description: Height ³/₄ in. high. A solid and sturdy little shell
of about 4 whorls that are sharply flattened at the shoulders
and form a winding terrace up the spire. Below this angle the
volutions show distinct slanting folds. Aperture fairly large,
with short canal at base, outer lip thickened. Color pale yellowish orange, sometimes with a row or two of chocolate
spots on body whorl.

● Genus *Admete* Kröyer 1842

COUTHOUY'S NUTMEG *Admete couthouyi* (Jay, 1839)
Range: Arctic Ocean to Massachusetts; California.
Habitat: Moderately deep water.
Description: About ¹/₂ in. high. A stout shell of 5 well-rounded
whorls, the body whorl relatively large, sutures well impressed. Spire sharply pointed, canal short and open. Sculpture of revolving lines, made nodular at shoulders by wavy
vertical ridges. Aperture rather large, outer lip thin and
sharp, inner lip deeply arched. Color yellowish brown.

■ **MARGINELLAS: Family Marginellidae**

These are small, porcelaneous, highly polished shells found
on sandy bottoms in warm seas. Spire short or nearly lacking
and the body whorl very large. Aperture narrow and long,
the outer lip usually somewhat thickened, the inner lip plicate.

● Genus *Marginella* Lamarck 1799

BANDED MARGINELLA
Marginella aureocincta Stearns, 1872
Range: N. Carolina to the West Indies.
Habitat: Shallow water in sand; common.
Description: About ¹/₈ in. high. Spindle-shaped, with moderate
spire. With 5 or 6 whorls, sutures indistinct. Elongate aperture toothed on both lips, with outer lip noticeably thickened. Surface very glossy, color yellowish gray, with 2 pale
brownish bands encircling the body whorl.

CARMINE MARGINELLA   Pl. 61
Marginella hematita Kiener, 1834
   Range: South Carolina to Brazil.
   Habitat: Offshore in sand from 50 to 500 ft.
   Description: About ¼ in., characterized by its glossy, bright
   rose color; with 4 strong columella teeth, a pointed spire
   and thickened outer lip bearing 12 to 15 small, rounded
   teeth. Uncommon.

DENTATE MARGINELLA   Pl. 61
Marginella eburneola Conrad, 1834
   Range: N. Carolina to the West Indies.
   Habitat: Shallow water.
   Description: Nearly ½ in. high. With 4 or 5 whorls, rather high
   spire for this group. Aperture narrow, about half the length
   of whole shell. With 4 strong pleats on columella, outer lip
   considerably thickened. Surface polished, color yellowish
   tan.
   Remarks: This shell looks very much like a small dove shell
   of the genus *Columbella*. *M. denticulata* Conrad, 1834, is a
   synonym.

● **Genus *Granulina* Jousseaume 1875**

TEARDROP MARGINELLA
Granulina ovuliformis (Orbigny, 1841)
   Range: South Florida to the West Indies.
   Habitat: Shallow water.
   Description: About ⅛ in. high. A glossy, small shell, rather
   globular, with a narrow aperture. Columella with 3 plica-
   tions, outer lip feebly toothed within. Color pure white.
   Remarks: The genus *Bullata* Jousseaume cannot be used for
   this group.

● **Genus *Prunum* Herrmannsen 1852**

COMMON MARGINELLA   Pl. 61
Prunum apicinum (Menke, 1828)
   Range: N. Carolina to Gulf of Mexico and West Indies.
   Habitat: Shallow water.

Description: Nearly ¹/₂ in. high. A solid shell of 3 or 4 whorls, with a low spire and a greatly enlarged body whorl. Aperture narrow, outer lip thickened, inner lip with 4 pleats. Surface highly polished, color varies from bright golden yellow to orange-brown. Outer lip usually white, sometimes with a pair of brownish spots.

Remarks: The most abundant marginellid on our shores. Very rarely it is sinistral. An example is illustrated on Plate 61. *Prunum* is sometimes used as a subgenus of *Marginella*.

ROOSEVELT'S MARGINELLA — Pl. 61
Prunum roosevelti Bartsch & Rehder, 1939

Range: South Florida and the Caribbean.
Habitat: Moderately deep water in sand.
Description: About 1 in. in length, extremely close to the Orange Marginella, differing only in being larger, in having a brown spot on the apex and 2 large chocolate spots on the outer lip.
Remarks: This rare species, named after President Franklin D. Roosevelt, may possibly be only a color form of *P. carneum*.

BELL MARGINELLA *Prunum bellum* (Conrad, 1868) — Pl. 61

Range: N. Carolina to Florida
Habitat: Shallow to deep water.
Description: Height ¹/₄ in. A flat-topped shell of 3 or 4 whorls. Aperture long and narrow, 4 pleats on inner lip. Outer lip thickened but without teeth. Whitish in color and glossy in appearance.

ORANGE MARGINELLA — Pl. 61
Prunum carneum (Storer, 1837)

Range: Southeast Florida and the West Indies.
Habitat: Shallow water.
Description: Height ³/₄ in. With 3 or 4 whorls, apex rounded, last volution constitutes most of shell. Aperture very narrow, outer lip rolled in and thickened. Inner lip with 4 pleats. Shiny orange, with whitish bands on body whorl.

SPOTTED MARGINELLA — Pl. 61
Prunum guttatum (Dillwyn, 1817)

Range: Southeast Florida to the West Indies

Habitat: Shallow water.
Description: About ³/₄ in. high. With 3 or 4 whorls, low spire, apex bluntly rounded. Aperture long and narrow, outer lip thickened, inner lip with 4 pleats. Color pinkish gray, with numerous whitish dots scattered over the highly polished surface. With 2 brown spots on apertural side of outer lip, and 3 or 4 at the edge on other side.
Remarks: This is one of the most colorful and attractive species of the group to be found on our shores.

ROYAL MARGINELLA *Prunum labiatum* (Kiener, 1841)
Range: Off south Texas and Mexico.
Habitat: Moderately deep water.
Description: Height 1 in. or more. A robust and solid shell of 3 or 4 whorls. Spire short, top of shell rounded, narrow aperture about as high as whole shell. With 4 very prominent pleats on inner lip, and the thickened outer lip has a number of small teeth along its inner margin. Glossy surface pale yellowish gray, with very weak bands of darker shade.

● **Genus** *Persicula* **Schumacher 1817**

PRINCESS MARGINELLA
Persicula catenata (Montagu, 1803)
Range: Southeast Florida to the West Indies.
Habitat: Moderately shallow water.
Description: About ¹/₄ in high. Apex very low, even concave, and usually covered by a callus. Narrow aperture runs full height of shell, outer lip only moderately thickened, with a series of iny teeth inside. Weak pleats on columella. Color grayish white, with encircling rows of triangular whitish and brownish spots and 2 separated rows of brownish spots.

● **Genus** *Hyalina* **Schumacker, 1817**

WHITE-LINED MARGINELLA
Hyalina albolineata (Orbigny, 1842)
Range: Bermuda; southeast Florida; West Indies.
Habitat: Shallow water.

Description: Height ¹/₄ in., sometimes slightly more. A slender, highly polished snail of 3 or 4 whorls; the last whorl makes up most of shell. Aperture long and narrow, lower columella with 4 folds. Banded with orange-yellow and white.

ORANGE-BANDED MARGINELLA   **Pl. 61**
Hyalina avena (Kiener, 1834)
   Range: N. Carolina to Brazil; Bermuda.
   Habitat: Shallow water.
   Description: About ¹/₂ in. high. Spire short but pointed, shell solid and highly polished. With 4 or 5 whorls. Long aperture narrow above and wider below. Outer lip thickened, inner lip with 4 distinct pleats. Color creamy white, generally with 2 or 3 pale orange bands.

OAT MARGINELLA *Hyalina avenacea* (Deshayes, 1834)
   Range: N. Carolina to Brazil.
   Habitat: Shallow water.
   Description: About ¹/₂ in. high. A slender shell of about 3 whorls, a short pointed spire, and an elongate aperture that widens noticeably at its base. Surface polished, color white or yellowish white.
   Remarks: Formerly listed as *Marginella succinea* Conrad.

VELIE'S MARGINELLA *Hyalina veliei* (Pilsbry, 1896)   **Pl. 61**
   Range: S. Carolina to west Florida.
   Habitat: Shallow water.
   Description: About ¹/₂ in. high. Shell elongate and thin, moderate spire. About 4 whorls, sutures distinct. Aperture wider at bottom, inner lip with 4 pleats. Highly polished, the color whitish or yellowish.

■ CONE SHELLS: Family Conidae

This is a large family of many-whorled, cone-shaped snails noted for their variety of colors and patterns. They live among the rocks and corals in tropical seas. This group is unusual among mollusks in that some of its members possess poison glands. The venom passes through a tiny duct to the teeth of the radula, some of which are modified to resemble small harpoons, and serves to benumb the gastropod's prey. None of the cones living in our waters are known to be dangerous, but all living examples should be handled with care. Certain South Pacific and Indian Ocean species are capable of inflicting serious and even fatal wounds. Many of the cones have a strong periostracum during life, which must be removed to display the shell's colors.

● **Genus *Conus* Linnaeus, 1758**

FLORIDA CONE *Conus floridanus* Gabb, 1868   **Pls. 15, 64**
  Range: N. Carolina to Florida.
  Habitat: Shallow water.
  Description: About $1\frac{1}{2}$ in. high. With 7 or 8 whorls, sutures distinct, spire elevated, apex sharp. Aperture long and narrow, notched at suture. Inner lip bears weak spiral ridges on lower margin. Color buffy yellow, marked with yellowish brown and white, generally in the form of broad bands.
  Remarks: There may be an earlier name for this cone, but the evidence is very weak. There are two minor color forms, one an extremely dark color form with spiral reddish brown dots and heavier mottlings, namely *Conus floridanus floridensis* Sowerby, 1870, and the other *Conus floridanus burryae* Clench, 1942, from off the Lower Florida Keys. It has spiral rows of brownish dots merging into solid lines, and with the lower part of the shell being blackish brown.

GLORY-OF-THE-ATLANTIC CONE   **Pls. 15, 64**
Conus granulatus Linnaeus, 1758
  Range: South Florida to the West Indies.
  Habitat: Moderately deep water.
  Description: Height 1 to $1\frac{3}{4}$ in. A handsome shell of 8 or 9 whorls, slender in build, the shoulders rounded so that the short spire lacks the sharpness of most cones. Surface shows distinct revolving lines. The color varies from orange to bright pink, with encircling rich brown markings. Generally

there is a darker area near the middle of the body whorl and another at the shoulder.

Remarks: An uncommon species, much desired by collectors. One must scuba-dive among reefs for this species.

JASPER CONE *Conus jaspideus* Gmelin, 1791   **Pl. 64**

Range: South Florida to West Indies and south to Brazil.

Habitat: Shallow water in sand.

Description: About 1 in. high. Shell trim and sturdy, with 10 whorls and a rather prominent spire that is frequently carinated. Apex sharp. Sculpture of evenly spaced spiral lines (especially on lower part of shell) and a few small tubercles. Color gray, with encircling rows of tiny spots of white and brown.

Remarks: Formerly listed as *C. pealii* Green. The more slender, darker subspecies, *stearnsi* Conrad, 1869, ranges from N. Carolina to west Florida (see Pl. 64).

WARTY CONE   **Pl. 64**
Conus jaspideus verrucosus Hwass, 1792

Range: South Florida to the West Indies.

Habitat: Shallow water.

Description: About ³/₄ in. high. A stocky shell of 10 or 11 whorls, the shoulders abruptly sloping, so that the spire appears angulated. Sculpture of rather stout revolving ribs, with regularly spaced beadlike pustules. Color pinkish gray, somewhat blotched with brown.

Remarks: This is only a beaded form of *jaspideus*.

JULIA'S CONE *Conus juliae* Clench, 1942

Range: Florida to the West Indies.

Habitat: Moderately deep water.

Description: About 1 to 2 in. high. Spire short, shoulders rounded, the whole shell having a substantial appearance. About 8 whorls. Color pinkish, with a fairly broad central band of white, and over all is a pattern of fine brownish lines and dots.

Remarks: Named in honor of Mrs. William J. Clench, wife of the distinguished malacologist of Harvard University.

MOUSE CONE *Conus mus* Hwass, 1792   **Pl. 64**
Range: South Florida to the West Indies; Bermuda.
Habitat: Shallow water.
Description: About 1 in. high. A rather stubby shell of 6 or 7 whorls, the spire short and rounded, apex blunt. Surface bears faint revolving lines. Color dull yellowish gray, spotted with reddish brown and generally with a light-colored central band. There may be a row of whitish spots at the shoulders.

CROWN CONE *Conus regius* Gmelin, 1791   **Pl. 64**
Range: Florida to West Indies and south to Brazil.
Habitat: Moderately shallow water.
Description: About 2 in. high, at times slightly more. Shell strong and solid, 7 or 8 whorls. Small spire, apex usually rounded. Surface sculptured with spiral threads or lines, more pronounced on the spire; some of these lines may be beaded. Mottled chocolate brown and purplish, sometimes more or less banded.
Remarks: Formerly listed as *C. nebulosus* Hwass. A yellow form is named *citrinus* Gmelin, 1791 (see Pl. 64).

SOZON'S CONE *Conus delessertii* Récluz, 1843   **Pl. 64**
Range: S. Carolina to Florida and Gulf of Mexico.
Habitat: Deep water.
Description: Height 2 to 4 in. A trim, shapely shell of 9 or 10 whorls. Well-developed spire, sharply pointed apex. Surface smooth. Color rich orange, with a pair of conspicuous white bands on body whorl, and over these is a series of distinct revolving lines of interrupted brownish dots.
Remarks: Many collectors would regard this as our handsomest cone. It is uncommon but not as rare as many others. *Conus sozoni* Bartsch, 1939 is a synonym.

ALPHABET CONE   **Pls. 15, 64**
Conus spurius atlanticus Clench, 1942
Range: Florida.
Habitat: Moderately shallow water.
Description: Height 2 to 3 in. With 9 or 10 whorls, the first few forming a short spire on the otherwise rather flat top. Aperture long and narrow, notched at suture. Operculum horny and very small. Color creamy white, with revolving rows of squarish orange and brown spots and blotches.
Remarks: The irregular markings often resemble letters of the alphabet. The shell was known for years as *C. proteus*

Hwass, but that name rightfully belongs to an Indian Ocean species our cone very closely resembles. The typical Alphabet Cone, *C. s. spurius* Gmelin, lives in the West Indies; its markings are usually arranged in revolving bands, whereas those of the subspecies *atlanticus*, found in Florida, are scattered so that ordinarily no banding is discernible. A yellow-banded color variation was named *aureofasciatus* Rehder & Abbott, 1951.

TURTLE CONE *Conus ermineus* Born, 1778   **Pl. 64**
Range: Gulf of Mexico and the Caribbean to Brazil.
Habitat: Offshore in sand in moderately shallow water.
Description: Length about 2 or 3 in. Shoulder well rounded and smooth, with slightly converse whorls. Spire with 4 or 5 fine spiral threads on the top of each whorl. Color grayish white to bluish with irregular mottlings of brown or blue-black; rarely all orange. Periostracum covers shell colors.
Remarks: Formerly called *ranunculus* Hwass, 1792. A young specimen found near Sanibel Island was called *Conus melvilli* by Louise Perry in 1939, and being a homonym, was renamed *perryae* by her friend, Dr. William J. Clench in 1942.

STIMPSON'S CONE *Conus stimpsoni* Dall, 1902   **Pl. 64**
Range: Southeast Florida and the Gulf of Mexico.
Habitat: Moderately deep water in sand.
Description: About 1 to 2 in. Sides of whorls flat; spire moderately high and pointed. Color yellowish white, with 2 or 3 wide, yellow-brown bands. Periostracum gray and rather thick. Uncommon.

CARROT CONE *Conus daucus* Hwass, 1792   **Pl. 64**
Range: Florida to Brazil.
Habitat: Moderately shallow water, in sand.
Description: About $1^1/_2$ in. Spire low; shoulder even and not knobbed. Color deep, solid orange-red or lemon yellow. Spiral rows of minute brown spots sometimes present. Interior of aperture rose. Uncommon.

■ AUGER SHELLS: Family Terebridae

These are slender, elongate, many-whorled shells, confined to warm and tropical seas. There are no pleats on the columella, but the base of the inner lip is twisted. Some members of this family are provided with a mild poison, but no American species is dangerous. Operculum corneous and thin.

● **Genus** *Terebra* **Bruguière, 1789**

GRAY ATLANTIC AUGER *Terebra cinerea* (Born, 1778) **Pl. 61**
Range: South Florida; West Indies south to Brazil.
Habitat: Shallow water.
Description: Height 1 to 2 in. About 10 rather flat whorls, the whole shell tapering gradually and regularly to a slender point at apex. Each volution sculptured with numerous fine vertical grooves. Aperture small. Surface shiny, color gray or brown, with a whitish band encircling each volution just below the suture.
Remarks: See Sallé's Auger (below) for a similar shell.

CONCAVE AUGER *Terebra concava* Say, 1827
Range: N. Carolina to Florida to Brazil.
Habitat: Shallow water.
Description: About 1 in. high. A slender shell of some 12 whorls, sutures fairly distinct. There is a line of beads just below the suture on each volution; middle of whorl is concave. Color gray, sometimes with a tinge of yellow.

COMMON AMERICAN AUGER **Pl. 61**
Terebra dislocata (Say, 1822)
Range: Virginia to Florida and Gulf of Mexico.
Habitat: Shallow water.
Description: About 1 to 1³/₄ in. high. Shell elongate, tapering gradually to a fine point. About 15 whorls, rather indistinct sutures. Surface decorated with wavy vertical folds and fine spiral grooves. A knobby spiral band encircles shell just below each suture. Aperture small, distinct twist at base of columella. Operculum horny. Ashy gray to pale brown, sometimes nearly white. See Florida and Sallé's augers (below) for comparison.
Remarks: The knobby spiral band just under the suture gives this shell the appearance of being composed of alternating large and small whorls. This gastropod is very common as a Pleistocene fossil in Florida and Bermuda.

FLORIDA AUGER *Terebra floridana* Dall, 1889 **Pl. 60**
Range: S. Carolina to Florida.
Habitat: Moderately deep water.
Description: To 3 in. high, with as many as 20 whorls. Tall and

spikelike shell, volutions marked with wavy vertical lines, and there is a distinct raised line running around middle of each whorl. Columella strongly twisted at base. Color yellowish white.

Remarks: This rather uncommon species may be mistaken for the Common Auger, but it can be distinguished by the lack of a "double suture" as well as by its larger size.

SHINY ATLANTIC AUGER *Terebra hastata* (Gmelin, 1791) **Pl. 61**
Range: South Florida to Brazil; Bermuda.
Habitat: Shallow water.
Description: About 1 to $1^{1}/_{2}$ in. high. With 10 to 12 whorls. The shell does not taper as rapidly or regularly as for most of this group but commonly remains nearly the same diameter until near the upper end, where it tapers rather abruptly. Sutures indistinct, each volution bearing fine vertical grooves. Surface shiny, color creamy white, with rather broad bands of pale orange.

FINE-RIBBED AUGER *Terebra protexta* Conrad, 1859
Range: N. Carolina to West Indies; Texas.
Habitat: Moderately shallow water.
Description: About 1 in. high. Shell narrow and tall, 12 to 14 whorls, sutures fairly distinct. Each volution bears several sharp-edged vertical folds. Aperture small, columella twisted at base, operculum horny. Color is a deep chocolate brown.

SALLÉ'S AUGER *Terebra salleana* Deshayes, 1859
Range: N. Carolina; West Indies south to Brazil.
Habitat: Shallow water.
Description: About 1 in. high. This shell looks much like the Gray Atlantic Auger (above), but it is smaller and slimmer, with fewer vertical ribs to a volution, and the apex is purple rather than white. Dark gray or brown, with a paler band at base of each whorl.

FLAME AUGER *Terebra taurinum* (Lightfoot, 1786) **Pl. 60**
Range: South Florida; Gulf of Mexico; and West Indies.
Habitat: Moderately shallow water.
Description: Height to 6 in. Our largest auger shell, tall and spikelike, with 25 or more whorls. Lower half of shell rather smooth, the upper volutions show vertical lines. Color yellowish white, streaked with spiral rows of reddish brown marks.
Remarks: Formerly listed as *T. flammea* Lamarck, 1822.

Once regarded as extremely rare, this shell has long been a collector's item; it is now known to be uncommon rather than rare.

■ TURRET OR TURRID SHELLS: Family Turridae

A very large family of gastropods, many of which are small and highly ornate. The general shape is fusiform (spindle-shaped), and the outer lip commonly has a slit, or notch. There are said to be more than 500 genera and subgenera in the family, and thousands of species. Many hundreds occur along our shores, mostly in deep water. Their classification is difficult and often causes argument among the specialists themselves. Only a few examples of the commonest forms can be discussed here.

● Genus *Crassispira* Swainson, 1840

CUBAN TURRID *Crassispira cubana* Melville, 1923
Range: South Florida.
Habitat: Shallow water.
Description: About ³/₄ in. high. Fusiform, with 7 or 8 whorls decorated with vertical ridges that form small knobs at the shoulders; these knobs commonly are white, the rest of the shell dark brown or black. Sutures indistinct, aperture elongate, canal open and short.
Remarks: *C. mesoleuca* Rehder, 1943, is a synonym.

SANIBEL TURRET   **Pl. 65**
Crassispira sanibelensis Bartsch & Rehder, 1939
Range: West Florida; Bahamas.
Habitat: Moderately shallow water.
Description: Nearly 1 in. high. About 8 whorls, an elongate spire, and sharp apex. Volutions ornamented with rounded vertical ridges and prominent spiral lines. Color pale brown or reddish brown.

TAMPA TURRID   **Pl. 65**
Crassispira tampaensis Bartsch & Rehder, 1939
Range: West Florida.
Habitat: Offshore in shallow water in sand and on rocks.
Description: About ³/₄ to 1 in., elongate, turreted, chestnut brown. About 18 slanting, rounded, axial riblets on the last

whorl, 17 on the previous ones. Faint spiral striations present. Aperture dark brown. Outer lip with a moderately deep "turrid" notch at the top.

Remarks: The form *bartschi* L. Perry, 1954, from off Sanibel Island has a few more ribs per whorl.

●Genus *Cochlespira* Conrad, 1865

STAR TURRID *Cochlespira radiata* (Dall, 1889)   **Pl. 65**
  Range: Off North Carolina to Gulf of Mexico; West Indies.
  Habitat: Fairly deep water down to 1,000 ft.
  Description: Length $1/2$ in. A delicate, glossy, translucent-white and highly ornamented species. Anterior canal very long. Shoulders keeled, with numerous, small, sharp, triangular spines.
  Remarks: This and the following rare species were formerly placed in the genus *Ancistrosyrinx* Dall, 1881.

ELEGANT STAR TURRID
Cochlespira elegans (Dall, 1881)
  Range: Both sides of Florida.
  Habitat: Deep water to 1,200 ft.
  Description: About $1^1/2$ in., similar to the Star Turrid, but with smaller, evenly sized, more numerous spines at the top of the whorls.

●Genus *Glyphostoma* Gabb, 1872

GABB'S MANGELIA *Glyphostoma gabbi* Dall, 1889   **Pl. 65**
  Range: Florida; Gulf of Mexico; West Indies.
  Habitat: Offshore; deep water.
  Description: About $1/2$ in. Shell white with two wide spiral bands of rose-brown. Fine spiral threads numerous. Notch deep, with thickened sides. Varix strong. Short ribs white in color.

● Genus *Monilispira* (Orbigny, 1842)

WHITE-BANDED DRILLIA   **Pl. 65**
Monilispira albomaculata (Orbigny, 1842)
  Range: Florida to West Indies.
  Habitat: Shallow water under rocks.
  Description: Height $1/2$ in. A rugged and stubby shell with about 5 whorls, sutures not deeply impressed. Aperture small, notched above, outer lip somewhat thickened, canal short. Surface decorated with revolving knobs, those on

shoulders larger and white, the areas between them dark brown or black.

Remarks: *M. albinodata* Reeve, 1843, is from the Eastern Pacific.

KNOBBY DRILLIA *Monilispira leucocyma* (Dall, 1883)   **Pl. 65**
Range: South Florida; Gulf of Mexico; and West Indies.
Habitat: Shallow water.
Description: About ¹/₂ in. high. A slender shell of 6 or 7 whorls, sutures indistinct. Sculpture consists of a row of knobs at the shoulders, about 12 to a volution. Aperture small and elongate, outer lip rather thick. Color grayish brown, the knobs whitish.

COLLARED DRILLIA
Monilispira monilis Bartsch & Rehder, 1939
Range: South Florida.
Habitat: Shallow water.
Description: Height ³/₄ in. A slender shell of about 8 whorls, sutures rather indistinct. Volutions bear rugged knobs at the shoulders and weak revolving lines. Aperture small and elongate, canal short. Brown, the encircling knobs paler.

● **Genus** *Neodrillia* **Bartsch, 1943**

GLORIOUS DRILLIA *Neodrillia cydia* Bartsch, 1943
Range: Florida to the West Indies.
Habitat: Moderately shallow water.
Description: Height ³/₄ in. A sturdy shell of about 8 whorls, sutures well defined. Aperture narrow, notched above. Parietal wall reflected. Sculpture of strongly rounded vertical ribs. Color white.

● **Genus** *Cerodrillia* **Bartsch & Rehder, 1939**

CLAPP'S DRILLIA
Cerodrillia clappi Bartsch & Rehder, 1939
Range: West Florida.
Habitat: Shallow water.
Description: About ¹/₂ in. high. A slender shell of some 6 whorls, made angular by a series of rather sharp oblique ridges. Outer lip thickened and notched above. Canal open and short. Color waxy white, sometimes with a weak band on body whorl.
Remarks: This may only be a form of *thea*.

Figure 63. Thea Drillia *Cerodrillia thea*

THEA DRILLIA *Cerodrillia thea* (Dall, 1883)   **Fig. 63**
  Range: West Florida.
  Habitat: Shallow water.
  Description: Height ¹/₂ in. High-spired, with 6 angled whorls, sutures only moderately distinct. Each volution has 12 or so slanting ribs. Aperture fairly large, inner lip reflected on body whorl. Color brown, the ribs yellowish, aperture dark brown.

● **Genus** *Fenimorea* **Bartsch, 1934**

JANET'S TURRET *Fenimorea janetae* Bartsch, 1934   **Pl. 65**
  Range: Florida to West Indies.
  Habitat: Moderately shallow water.
  Description: About 1 in. high. With 6 or 7 slightly shouldered whorls, sutures impressed. Sculpture of strongly rounded vertical ribs, about 12 on body whorl. Lip thickened. Color whitish, with pinkish brown blotches between the ribs, especially on lower portions of volutions.

MOSER'S TURRET *Fenimorea moseri* (Dall, 1889)
  Range: N. Carolina to Florida and Gulf of Mexico.
  Habitat: Shallow water.
  Description: Height ¹/₂ in. An elongate, sturdily built shell of about 10 whorls, sutures distinct. About 12 strongly curving ribs on each volution, plus an encircling ridge just below the

suture. Aperture somewhat lengthened, notched above. Color creamy white, with thin yellowish brown periostracum.

● **Genus** *Propebela* **Iredale, 1918**

CANCELLATE LORA
Propebela cancellata (Mighels & Adams, 1842)
    Range: Labrador to Massachusetts.
    Habitat: Moderately deep water.
    Description: Height ¹/₂ in. Shell rather slender, with 7 or 8 turreted whorls. Sculpture of numerous vertical ribs (about 20 on body whorl) that are crossed by raised revolving lines, giving the surface a cancellate appearance. Aperture narrow and small. Color pinkish white.
    Remarks: The generic status of this group is uncertain at the present time. They were once listed under *Bela* Gray 1847 and later under *Lora* Gistel 1848.

● **Genus** *Oenopota* **Mörch, 1852)**

HARP LORA *Oenopota harpularia* (Couthouy, 1838)
    Range: Labrador to Rhode Island.
    Habitat: Moderately shallow water.
    Description: About ³/₄ in. high. Stoutly elongate, with 6 to 8 whorls flattened somewhat above and forming slightly sloping shoulders. Sutures distinct. Each volution bears numerous oblique rounded ribs crossed by fine revolving lines. Aperture narrow and oval, canal a mere notch. Buffy flesh color.
    Remarks: See Remarks under Cancellate Lora.

● **Genus** *Pyrgocythara* **Woodring, 1928**

PLICATE MANGELIA
Pyrgocythara plicosa (C. B. Adams, 1850)
    Range: Maine to Gulf Coast of Florida.
    Habitat: Shallow water.
    Description: Height ¹/₄ in. A sturdy shell of 7 whorls, sutures quite distinct. Surface displays a network of vertical ribs and nodulous lines. Aperture narrow, outer lip thick, notched at top. Color dark brown.

● Genus *Glyphoturris* Woodring, 1928

FROSTED TURRET
Glyphoturris quadrata (Reeve, 1845)
  Range: Florida to the West Indies.
  Habitat: Moderately shallow water.
  Description: Height ¼ in. With 6 shouldered whorls. Sculpture of strong vertical ribs and sharp revolving lines. Aperture moderate, outer lip thickened. Color white.

● Genus *Daphnella* Hinds, 1844

VOLUTE TURRET   **Pl. 65**
Daphnella lymneiformis (Kiener, 1840)
  Range: South Florida to the West Indies.
  Habitat: Shallow water.
  Description: Height ¼ in. Thin in substance. With 7 or 8 whorls, the body whorl constituting about ⅔ of whole shell. Sutures well impressed. Aperture moderate, large below, notched above. Sculpture of distinct revolving lines. Color yellowish white, heavily blotched with orange-brown

■ **MELANELLA SHELLS: Family Melanellidae**

Small, high-spired shells, usually polished. The spire is often slightly bent to one side. This is a large family that lives chiefly in warm waters. Many of the species are parasitic on other forms of marine life. Formerly known as the Eulimidae, this group is now considered to be in the opisthobranchia Eulimidae.

● Genus *Melanella* Bowdich, 1822

GOLDEN-BANDED EULIMA
Melanella auricincta (Abbott, 1958)
  Range: N. Carolina to the West Indies.
  Habitat: Shallow water.
  Description: About ¼ in. high. A slender shell of about 12 flattened whorls, the sutures scarcely discernible. Aperture narrow and elongate, lip thin and sharp. Surface very glossy.

Color grayish white, with a thin brownish band encircling each volution.

Remarks: Formerly listed as *E. acuta* (Sowerby)

TWO-BANDED EULIMA *Melanella bifasciata* (Orbigny, 1842)
Range: South Florida to West Indies.
Habitat: Shallow water.
Description: Height ¹/₄ in. A slender spikelike shell of 10 or 11 flat whorls, sutures quite indistinct. Aperture narrow and elongate. Surface very glossy. Color yellowish white, with a pair of brown bands encircling each volution.

● **Genus *Balcis* Leach, 1847**

TWO-LINED BALCIS *Balcis bilineata* (Alder, 1848)
Range: N. Carolina to the West Indies.
Habitat: Shallow water.
Description: About ¹/₈ in. high. With 7 or 8 rather flat whorls, with very weak sutures, so that the taper from base to sharply pointed apex is very regular. Aperture rather small, outer lip somewhat thickened. Surface shiny, color milky white.

CONELIKE BALCIS
Balcis conoidea (Kurtz & Stimpson 1851)
Range: Cape Hatteras to the West Indies.
Habitat: Shallow water.
Description: Slightly more than ¹/₂ in. high. A slender shell of about 12 rather flat whorls, sutures quite indistinct. Shell tapers very regularly to a sharp apex. Aperture oval and small, lip thin. Surface highly polished, color pure white.

● **Genus *Niso* Risso, 1826**

HENDERSON'S NISO *Niso hendersoni* Bartsch, 1953
Range: N. Carolina to Florida.
Habitat: Moderately shallow water.
Description: About ¹/₂ in. high. A conical shell, rather wide at base, with 10 to 12 flattened whorls, the taper from base to apex very regular. Sutures indistinct, apex acute. Aperture relatively small. Surface polished, color pale brown, sometimes with patches of darker brown. Sutures marked with a reddish brown line.
Remarks: Formerly misidentified as the Eastern Pacific *Niso interrupta* (Sowerby, 1834).

■ PYRAMID SHELLS: Family Pyramidellidae

Small pyramidal or conical shells, usually white and often polished. Many-whorled. The columella is usually plicate (folded or pleated). They inhabit sandy bottoms, and the family contains a vast number of very small gastropods. Many of them are parasites.

● Genus *Pyramidella* Lamarck 1799

BRILLIANT PYRAM
Pyramidella candida (Mörch, 1875)
Range: N. Carolina to Florida, Gulf of Mexico, and West Indies.
Habitat: Moderately deep water in sand.
Description: Slightly more than ¼ in. high. A sturdy little shell of 9 or 10 moderately flattened whorls, sutures slightly channeled and indented. Aperture quite small, columella twisted to form 1 or 2 teeth. Color pure white, surface brightly polished.

CRENATE PYRAM *Pyramidella crenulata* (Holmes, 1859)
Range: S. Carolina to Florida.
Habitat: Shallow water.
Description: Height ¾ in. About 12 rather flat whorls, sutures plainly marked and slightly crenulate. Aperture moderate, lip thin. Operculum horny, and notched on one side to fit the plications on columella. Surface shiny, color whitish, with brownish mottlings.

GIANT ATLANTIC PYRAM
Pyramidella dolabrata (Linnaeus, 1758)
Range: Florida to the West Indies.
Habitat: Shallow water.
Description: About 1 in. high, our largest member of the genus. With 9 or 10 rounded whorls, sutures deeply impressed. The taper is rather abrupt, and the shell appears quite plump. Aperture semilunar, with 2 or 3 distinct ridges on columella. Small umbilicus and horny operculum. Surface polished, color milky white, with revolving lines of brown.

● Genus *Turbonilla*, Risso 1826

The genus *Turbonilla* is a large one, containing many species of very small, high-spired gastropods all much alike to the casual observer. The first (nuclear) whorl is coiled at a right angle to rest of the shell.

BUSH'S TURBONILLE *Turbonilla bushiana* Verrill, 1882
Range: Vineyard Sound to Long Island Sound.
Habitat: Moderately deep water.
Description: Height nearly ¹/₂ in. A slender shell of 10 or 11 rather flat whorls, sutures moderately impressed. Sculpture of weak vertical ribs, about 18 on body whorl. Surface between ribs smooth and polished. Aperture small and oval, columella slightly flattened. Color yellowish white.

DALL'S TURBONILLE *Turbonilla dalli* Bush, 1899
Range: N. Carolina to Florida and Gulf of Mexico.
Habitat: Moderately shallow water.
Description: About ¹/₄ in. high. With 12 well-rounded whorls, sutures sharply indented. About 18 strong and prominent vertical ribs to a volution. Surface also bears very fine revolving lines (striae). Aperture small, color bluish white.

HEMPHILL'S TURBONILLE
Turbonilla hemphilli Bush, 1899
Range: West Florida.
Habitat: Moderately shallow water.
Description: Nearly ¹/₂ in. high. A tall and slender shell of about 15 whorls, sutures distinct. Strong vertical ribs. Aperture small, operculum horny. Color white.

INCISED TURBONILLE *Turbonilla incisa* Bush, 1899
Range: West Florida.
Habitat: Moderately shallow water.
Description: About ¹/₄ in. high. Slender and high-spired, with 12 rather flat whorls, sutures distinct. Vertical ribs not as sharp as for most of this group. Color pale brown.

INTERRUPTED TURBONILLE   **Fig. 65**
Turbonilla interrupta (Totten, 1835)
Range: Maine to Florida and the West Indies.
Habitat: Moderately deep water.
Description: About ¹/₄ in. high. With 9 or 10 rather flat whorls, sutures only slightly impressed. Vertical ribs small and crowded, some 20 to a volution. Color pale yellow, the shell having a waxy luster.

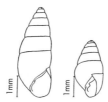

Figure 64. Ovoid Odostome *Odostomia laevigata*

CLARET TURBONILLE *Turbonilla punicea* Dall, 1884
Range: N. Carolina to Florida.
Habitat: Moderately shallow water.
Description: Height ¹/₄ in. A sturdy shell of about 12 whorls, sutures moderately impressed. Each volution bears about 16 rounded vertical ribs. Aperture quite small. Color yellowish white.

● **Genus *Odostomia* Fleming, 1817**

OVOID ODOSTOME   Fig. 64
Odostomia laevigata (Orbigny, 1842)
Range: N. Carolina to Brazil.
Habitat: Shallow water on shelly bottoms.
Description: Length ¹/₈ in., elongate-ovate, grayish white, with 4 to 6 slightly rounded, smooth whorls. Nucleus small and deeply and obliquely buried in the apex. Umbilicus chink-like or absent. Columella tooth weak.
Remarks: A very variable species with many synonyms: *ovuloides* (C. B. Adams, 1850), *schwengelae* and *cooperi* Bartsch, 1955.

THREE-BANDED ODOSTOME   Fig. 65
Odostomia trifida (Totten, 1834)
Range: Maine to New Jersey.
Habitat: Common in shallow water.
Description: Very small, 4 to 5 mm. (¹/₈ in.) Whorls with 3 or 4 spiral grooves which create spiral, raised bands. Grooves have microscopic axial threads. Most members of this genus live only for one or two years. They suck the juices of oysters and sea squirts.

● Genus *Boonea* Robertson, 1978

DOUBLE-SUTURED ODOSTOME   **Fig. 65**
Boonea bisuturalis (Say, 1821)
   Range: Gulf of St. Lawrence to Florida.
   Habitat: Shallow water.
   Description: About ⅛ in. high. With 7 or 8 whorls, somewhat
   flattened, sutures well defined. Apex sharp, aperture oval,
   columella with 2 oblique folds. A deeply impressed line on
   upperpart of each volution. Operculum horny. Color dull
   white, with thin brownish periostracum.
   Remarks: *Odostomia trifida* (Totten, 1834) is a synonym.
   This and the following two species were formerly listed under the genus *Odostomia.*

INCISED ODOSTOME *Boonea impressa* (Say, 1821)   **Fig. 65**
   Range: Massachusetts to Florida and Gulf of Mexico.
   Habitat: Shallow water.
   Description: Height ⅛ in. Shell elongate, consisting of 6 or 7
   rather flat whorls, with channeled sutures. Surface decorated
   with 3 equally spaced spiral grooves. Aperture oval, outer
   lip thin and sharp, occasionally flaring a little. Color milky
   white.

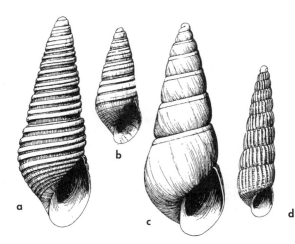

Figure 65. a) Incised Odostome *Boonea impressa* b) Three-
banded Odostome *Odostomia trifida* c) Double-sutured
Odostome *Boonea bisuturalis* d) Interrupted Turbonille *Turbonilla interrupta*

HALF-SMOOTH ODOSTOME
Boonea seminuda (C. B. Adams, 1837)
Range: Prince Edward Island to Florida and Gulf of Mexico.
Habitat: Shallow water.
Description: Height 1/8 in. Stoutly conical, with 6 or 7 whorls, sutures distinct. Sculptured with several revolving ridges cut by vertical striations, so surface appears beaded. Apex sharp, aperture oval, with oblique fold at base of columella. Color white.

■ SMALL BUBBLE SHELLS: Family Acteonidae

Small, cylindrical, solid shells with a short, sharp spire. The inner lip bears a single pleat. Surface is usually spirally grooved. Aperture long and narrow.

● Genus *Acteon* Montfort, 1810

ADAMS' BABY BUBBLE   Fig. 66
Acteon punctostriatus (C. B. Adams, 1840)
Range: Massachusetts to the West Indies.
Habitat: Shallow water to 360 ft.
Description: Nearly 1/4 in. high. With 3 or 4 whorls, sutures indented. Body whorl somewhat elongate, spire moderately extended. Surface smooth and glossy. Lower portion of last volution bears encircling rows of tiny punctate dots. Aperture large, broadest below; columella shows a twisted fold. Color white.
Remarks: Some workers place this species in the genus *Rictaxis* Dall, 1871.

Figure 66. Adams' Baby Bubble *Acteon punctostriatus*

■ PAPER BUBBLE SHELLS: Family Hydatinidae

Shells oval, inflated, and thin in substance. The surface is smooth, and there is no umbilicus. The spire is involute (rolled inward from each side). The animal is large, generally extending beyond the shell. Distributed widely in warm seas.

● Genus *Hydatina* Schumacher, 1817

BROWN-LINED PAPER BUBBLE
Hydatina vesicaria (Lightfoot, 1786)
   Range: South Florida to Brazil; Bermuda.
   Habitat: Shallow water.
   Description: About 1 1/2 in. high. A globose, well-inflated shell, thin and rather fragile. Spire not concealed as in *Bulla* (below), but top of shell is flattened and shows a small tight spiral. Surface smooth and polished. Color yellowish gray, with numerous thin wavy brown lines encircling the shell; every fourth or fifth line heavier than the others.
   Remarks: Formerly listed as *H. physis* (Linnaeus), which occurs in Japan, India, and Australia and used to be considered conspecific with our snail.

● Genus *Micromelo* Pilsbry, 1894

MINIATURE MELO *Micromelo undata* (Bruguière, 1792)
   Range: Florida to Brazil; Bermuda.
   Habitat: Shallow water.
   Description: Height 1/2 in. Semiglobular, thin and fragile in substance, nearly all body whorl. Aperture wide at bottom and narrower at top. Surface shiny, decorated with 4 or 5 encircling lines of reddish brown, these lines connected at intervals by curving vertical splashes of reddish hue.
   Remarks: If this shell were larger, it might well be one of the most sought after of our East Coast mollusks. Unfortunately it is not very common.

■ TRUE BUBBLE SHELLS: Family Bullidae

Oval in outline, the aperture flaring. Small to fairly large shells, usually rolled up like a scroll. The shell is thin and light. These are carnivorous snails, burrowing in the sands and muds for their prey, chiefly in warm seas.

● Genus *Bulla* Linnaeus, 1758

COMMON ATLANTIC BUBBLE   Pl. 65
Bulla striata Bruguière, 1792
   Range: N. Carolina to Brazil; Bermuda.
   Habitat: Shallow water.
   Description: About 1 in. high, sometimes more. Shell oval and inflated, spire depressed. Surface smooth and semipolished. Aperture longer than shell, rounded at both ends. A reflected white shield at base of columella. Color pale reddish gray, mottled with purplish brown; some individuals show traces of banding.
   Remarks: These gastropods inhabit grassy mudflats, slimy banks of river mouths, and brackish waters and conceal themselves in mud or under seaweeds while the tide is out, becoming most active at night. They feed upon small mollusks, which they swallow whole and crush with interior calcareous plates.

■ **GLASSY BUBBLE SHELLS: Family Atyidae**

Small and fragile shells inhabiting muddy and brackish waters, as a rule, chiefly in warm seas. The animal is too large for its shell, which is partially internal.

● Genus *Atys* Montfort, 1810

CARIBBEAN GLASSY BUBBLE   Fig. 67
Atys caribaea Orbigny, 1841
   Range: South Florida to the West Indies; Brazil.
   Habitat: Shallow to moderately deep water.
   Description: About $^1/_2$ in. high. A graceful species, rather elongate, the outer lip rising well above top of shell. Surface smooth and shiny, with a few obscure lines at both ends of shell. Color pure white.

Figure 67. Caribbean Glassy Bubble *Atys caribaea*

● **Genus *Haminoea* Turton & Kingston, 1830**

ANTILLEAN GLASSY BUBBLE   **Pl. 65**
Haminoea antillarum (Orbigny, 1841)
    Range: West Florida to the West Indies.
    Habitat: Shallow water.
    Description: About ¹/₂ in. high. Somewhat globular, aperture widely flaring. Outer lip thin, rising above top of shell. No depression at top. Color greenish yellow, the shell very thin and translucent.

ELEGANT GLASSY BUBBLE   **Pl. 65**
Haminoea elegans (Gray, 1825)
    Range: South Florida to Brazil; Bermuda.
    Habitat: Shallow water.
    Description: About ¹/₂ to ³/₄ in. high. Shell remarkably thin and fragile, and semitransparent. Shape somewhat short and squat, surface sculptured with very minute revolving lines, but the general appearance is smooth and glossy. Color greenish yellow.

SOLITARY GLASSY BUBBLE
Haminoea solitaria (Say, 1822)
    Range: Massachusetts to N. Carolina.
    Habitat: Shallow water.
    Description: About ¹/₂ in. high. Thin, delicate, well inflated. Aperture wide, small depression at top of shell. Surface shiny, with tiny but sharp spiral lines. Color bluish white.

AMBER GLASSY BUBBLE   **Pl. 65**
Haminoea succinea (Conrad, 1846)
    Range: Delaware to the West Indies; Texas; Bermuda.
    Habitat: Shallow water.

Description: About ¹/₂ in. high. More slender than most of the genus *Haminoea*, the aperture less flaring. Marked depression at top of shell. Surface with microscopic wrinkled lines. Shell substance very thin, translucent amber in color.

● **Genus *Cylindrobulla* Fischer, 1856**

BEAU'S GLASSY BUBBLE
Cylindrobulla beaui Fischer, 1856
   Range: Florida Keys to Brazil; Bermuda.
   Habitat: Moderately deep water.
   Description: Height ¹/₄ in. Broadly cylindrical, paper-thin in substance. Outer lip rolled over columella and practically closes the aperture, although it is open at bottom and top. Inner lip rather strongly reflected. Surface shiny, color soiled white.

■ **BARREL BUBBLE SHELLS: Family Retusidae**

Small cylindrical bubble shells, with or without a short spire. The sutures are deeply channeled and the inner lip usually bears a single fold. These tiny snails range from cold to tropical seas.

● **Genus *Acteocina* Gray, 1847**

CHANNELED BARREL BUBBLE   **Fig. 68**
Acteocina canaliculata (Say, 1822)
   Range: Canada to Mexico.
   Habitat: Shallow water.
   Description: Height ¹/₅ in. Shell cylindrical, with about 5 whorls, the summit of each with a shallow rounded groove. Spire slightly elevated, but body whorl makes up about ⁷/₈ of shell. Outer lip arches slightly forward, inner lip is overspread with a thin plate of enamel. Oblique fold near base. Color dull chalky white.
   Remarks: This diminutive snail commonly is found clinging to an old oyster or clam shell, and also on decaying, floating timbers. By gathering a few handfuls of broken fragments found in the coves of a shell beach and running the material through a sieve, one will usually find examples of this gastropod, as well as many other tiny varieties.

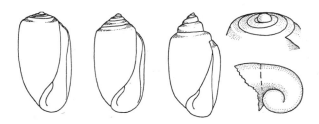

Figure 68. Channeled Barrel Bubble *Acteocina canaliculata*

CANDÉ'S BARREL BUBBLE   Fig. 69
Acteocina candei (Orbigny, 1842)
  Range: Cape Hatteras to the West Indies.
  Habitat: Shallow water.
  Description: About ¹/₁₆ in. high. Cylindrical, with short spire, the sutures slightly channeled. Aperture elongate, widest below, the inner lip with a distinct fold. Color milky white.

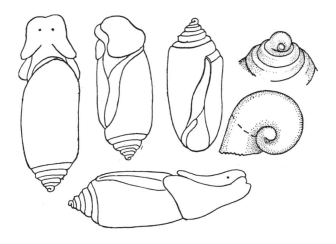

Figure 69. Cande's Barrel Bubble *Acteocina candei*

IVORY BARREL BUBBLE
Acteocina eburnea (Verrill, 1885)
Range: Cape Hatteras to Florida.
Habitat: Moderately deep water.
Description: About $1/4$ in. high. Oval in shape, the outer lip rising slightly above rounded apex of shell. Small chinklike umbilicus. Lip thin and sharp, describing a graceful curve from top to bottom. Surface smooth, color ivory-white.

■ CANOE SHELLS: Family Scaphandridae

Small to fairly large shells, usually rolled up like a scroll. The shell is thin and brittle. These are carnivorous snails, burrowing in the muds and sands for their prey, which are chiefly scaphopods.

● Genus *Scaphander* Montfort, 1810

COMMON CANOE SHELL   Pl. 65
Scaphander punctostriatus (Mighels & Adams, 1841)
Range: Gulf of St. Lawrence to the West Indies; Europe.
Habitat: Moderately deep water.
Description: Nearly 2 in. high. Oval in shape, narrower toward the top. Aperture large, flaring at base. Spire concealed. Surface bears numerous very fine revolving lines (striae), hardly to be seen with the naked eye. Color pale yellowish brown, with thin grayish periostracum.

■ BARREL BUBBLES: Family Cylichnidae

Small cylindrical shells, generally smooth and glossy. There is little or no evidence of a spire. Aperture long, widening at base. They prefer cold seas as a rule.

● Genus *Cylichna* Lovén, 1846

BROWN'S BARREL BUBBLE *Cylichna alba* (Brown, 1827)
Range: Greenland to N. Carolina; Europe.
Habitat: Shallow water to 6,000 ft.

Description: Height ¼ in. Spire sunken, so that there is a shallow pit at top of shell. General shape cylindrical, aperture narrow and elongate, widening at base. Surface bears very delicate lines of growth, but appearance is smooth and often shiny. Color white, with rusty brown periostracum.

ORBIGNY'S BUBBLE
Cylichna bidentata (Orbigny, 1841)
Range: N. Carolina to Florida to Brazil.
Habitat: Moderately shallow water.
Description: Height ⅛ in. Elongate-oval, rounded at top and bottom. Distinct fold at base of inner lip. Surface smooth, color yellowish white.

■ WIDE-MOUTHED PAPER BUBBLES: Family Philinidae

Small, loosely coiled shells with flaring apertures. The shell is partially internal, concealed by the mantle of the snail. They are chiefly mollusks of cold seas.

● Genus *Philine* Ascanius, 1772

FILE PAPER BUBBLE *Philine lima* (Brown, 1827)
Range: Arctic Ocean to Massachusetts.
Habitat: Moderately shallow water.
Description: Height ¼ in. Elongate-oval, top partially flattened. Flaring aperture begins below apex. Surface bears microscopic encircling lines but appears quite smooth. Color translucent yellowish white.
Remarks: Formerly listed as *P. lineolata* Couthouy.

QUADRATE PAPER BUBBLE
Philine quadrata (S. Wood, 1839)
Range: Greenland to N. Carolina.
Habitat: Deep water.
Description: About ¼ in. high. Thin-shelled, inflated, aperture flaring widely. Apex deeply excavated. Body whorl small. Color translucent grayish or whitish.

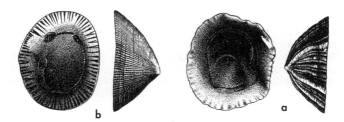

Figure 70. a) False Limpet *Siphonaria alternata* **b)** Striped False Limpet *Siphonaria pectinata*

ORDER BASOMMATOPHORA

■ FALSE LIMPETS: Family Siphonariidae

These snails look very much like the true limpets. The shell is roughly circular and conical, with a deep groove on one side that makes a distinct projection, or bulge, on the margin. The animals possess both gills and lungs and spend their time between the tide limits living a partially amphibious life, so they form a connecting link between the purely aquatic snails and the more highly developed air-breathing mollusks. Inside, the horseshoe-shaped muscle scar is open at the side instead of at the end as it is in the true limpets. They lay eggs in small, gelatinous blobs on protected rock surfaces.

● **Genus *Siphonaria* Sowerby, 1824**

SAY'S FALSE LIMPET   Fig. 70 & Pl. 65
Siphonaria alternata Say, 1826
   Range: Bermuda; south Florida; Bahamas.
   Habitat: Intertidal on shore rocks.
   Description: About ³/₄ in. long. Shell rather oval in outline, conical, open at base. A deep siphonal groove on right side makes a noticeable bulge on that margin, so the shell is not symmetrical. Surface decorated with numerous fine ribs that radiate from summit, the ribs varying somewhat in size. Apex commonly eroded. Color brownish, marked with white; interior glossy.

STRIPED FALSE LIMPET   **Fig. 74 & Pl. 65**
Siphonaria pectinata (Linnaeus, 1758)
   Range: Florida to Texas and West Indies.
   Habitat: Intertidal on shore rocks.
   Description: Length 1 in. Shape oval and conical, apex situated slightly behind center. Surface sculptured with fine radiating lines, all about same size. Strong bulge on right margin. Color pale gray, with brownish lines radiating from summit. Interior glossy.

■ SALT-MARSH SNAILS: Family Ellobiidae

These salt-marsh snails spend their time out of water to a considerable degree. These air-breathing snails usually occur in great numbers. The aperture is elongate, with a strong fold or two on the inner lip.

● Genus *Melampus* Montfort, 1810

SALT-MARSH SNAIL *Melampus bidentatus* Say, 1822
   Range: Nova Scotia to Texas; Bermuda.
   Habitat: Salt marshes.
   Description: Height $1/2$ in. Shell oval, thin, and shining when clean. About 5 whorls, the last one constituting most of shell and others flattened to form a short, blunt spire. Aperture long and narrow, broadest below; inner lip usually covered with white enamel and 2 folds cross the lower part. Deep within the outer lip are several elevated ridges. Color greenish olive. Young specimens are banded with brown, but old shells are often corroded and coated with a muddy deposit. Thin yellowish brown periostracum.
   Remarks: This is the commonest salt-marsh snail on the Atlantic Coast. It inhabits marshes occasionally flooded by the tide and is never very far from the high-tide mark. When the tide comes in these snails clamber to tops of the salt grass, as if to avoid getting wet for as long as possible. Formerly listed as *M. lineatus* Say.

COFFEE MELAMPUS   **Fig. 71 & Pl. 65**
Melampus coffeus (Linnaeus, 1758)
   Range: Florida to Brazil; Bermuda.
   Habitat: Intertidal near mangroves.
   Description: Slightly more than $1/2$ in. high. Shell thin but strong, with low spire. With 4 or 5 whorls. Outer lip thin and

sharp, crenulate within, inner lip with 2 white folds. Color pale chocolate, usually with 3 creamy white bands on body whorl. Thin but tough grayish periostracum.

Remarks: This species, as well as the Salt-marsh Snail, forms a very important food supply for wild ducks.

CARIBBEAN MELAMPUS   **Fig. 71**

Melampus monile (Bruguière, 1789)

    Range: Florida to the West Indies.

    Habitat: Salt marshes.

    Description: Height ½ in. An oval shell of 4 or 5 whorls. Short pointed spire. Outer lip thin and sharp, columella with deep fold at base. Surface polished, color yellowish brown, often with 3 encircling paler bands.

● **Genus *Pedipes* Ferussac, 1821**

MIRACULOUS PEDIPES

Pedipes mirabilis (Mühlfeld, 1816)

    Range: Florida to the West Indies.

    Habitat: Shallow water under rocks above tide line.

    Description: Nearly ½ in. high. With 4 rounded whorls, short spire. Sculpture of revolving lines. Aperture wide, with 3 prominent teeth on columella. Outer lip thickened, one tooth within. Color yellowish brown.

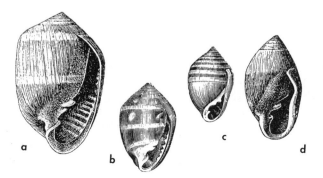

Figure 71. a) Coffee Melampus *Melampus coffeus* **b)** Caribbean Melampus *Melampus monile* **c)** Florida Melampus *Detracia floridana* **d)** Egg Melampus *Tralia ovula*

● **Genus *Tralia* Gray, 1840**

EGG MELAMPUS *Tralia ovula* (Bruguière, 1789) **Fig. 71**
   Range: Bermuda; Florida to the West Indies.
   Habitat: Salt marshes.
   Description: Height $^1/_2$ in. Oval, with short spire and about 4 whorls. Columella bears 3 teeth. Whitish glaze on parietal wall. Color yellowish brown.

● **Genus *Detracia* Gray, 1840**

FLORIDA MELAMPUS **Fig. 71**
Detracia floridana (Pfeiffer, 1856)
   Range: Delaware to Louisiana.
   Habitat: Abundant in salt marshes.
   Description: Length $^1/_3$ in., dark brown with a few bands of white. Columella with a large tooth. Above it on the parietal wall is a smaller, horizontal tooth. Behind the outer lip there are about 10 fine, spiral, white, raised lirae.
   Remarks: The late Dr. Joseph P. E. Morrison wrote an extensive account of the biology of this species in the Annual Report of the American Malacological Society, p. 15, in 1953.

BUBBLE MELAMPUS
Detracia bullaoides (Montagu, 1808)
   Range: Florida to the West Indies; Bermuda.
   Habitat: Salt marshes.
   Description: About $^1/_2$ in. high. Elongate-oval, 5 or 6 whorls, blunt apex. Aperture small, columella with a deep fold. Color brown, with encircling grayish lines.

ORDER THECOSOMATA

■ **SEA BUTTERFLIES: Family Cavolinidae**

The sea butterflies, or pteropods, are snails of the open sea, arriving on shore only by chance and generally after a violent storm with onshore winds. They exist in huge colonies, spending the day at considerable depths and rising to the surface at night to feed on plankton. Varied in shape, the shells may be globose, triangular, or thin and slender, according to the species of which there are many known and described. They are a main food of whales and young fish and seagoing squid.

● **Genus _Cavolinia_ Abilgaard, 1791**

GIBBOSE CAVOLINE _Cavolinia gibbosa_ (Orbigny, 1836) **Fig. 72**
   Range: Worldwide.
   Habitat: Pelagic; temperate and tropical seas.
   Description: Length about ¹/₄ in. Shell rather inflated. Ventral face with concentric ridges at periphery; dorsal face with several distinct radiating folds. Lateral spines short, middle spine stout. Color milky white.

INFLEXED CAVOLINE   **Fig. 72**
Cavolinia inflexa (Leseur, 1813)
   Range: Atlantic Ocean.
   Habitat: Pelagic; temperate and tropical seas.
   Description: About ¹/₈ in. long. Shell long and compressed. Ventral face relatively smooth; dorsal face with 3 radiating folds. Lateral spines small, middle spine long, stout, and curved upward. Color milky white.

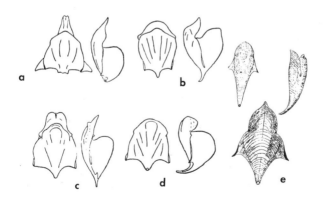

Figure 72. a) Long-snout Cavoline _Cavolina longirostris_ **b)** Gibbose Cavoline _Cavolina gibbosa_ **c)** Three-toothed Cavoline _Cavolina tridentata_ **d)** Uncinate Cavoline _Cavolina uncinata_ **e)** Inflexed Cavoline _Cavolina inflexa_

LONG-SNOUT CAVOLINE   Fig. 72
Cavolinia longirostris (Blainville, 1821)
Range: Martha's Vineyard to Gulf of Mexico and South Atlantic.
Habitat: Pelagic; temperate and tropical seas.
Description: About ⅛ in. long. Ventral face rounded and relatively smooth; dorsal face with 3 robust folds and extended in front by a long folded beak. Spines short and truncate. Color milky white.

THREE-TOOTHED CAVOLINE   Fig. 72 & Pl. 65
Cavolinia tridentata (Niebuhr, 1775)
Range: Worldwide.
Habitat: Pelagic; temperate and tropical seas.
Description: Nearly ¾ in. long, one of the largest forms in this group. Ventral face semiglobular and smooth; dorsal face with strong radiating folds. Spines sharp, lateral spines short, middle spine longer. Color translucent amber.
Remarks: Sometimes listed as *C. telemus* Linnaeus, 1758, but that name is questionable.

UNCINATE CAVOLINE   Fig. 72
Cavolinia uncinata (Rang, 1829)
Range: Atlantic Ocean. Worldwide.
Habitat: Pelagic; temperate and tropical seas.
Description: About ¼ in. long. Ventral face swollen and smooth; dorsal face with 3 strong radiating folds. Spines along sides compressed and curved slightly backward, middle spine short, stout, and turned upward. Color pale amber.

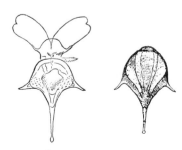

Figure 73. Three-spined Cavoline *Diacria trispinosa*

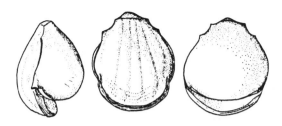

Figure 74. Four-toothed Cavoline *Diacria quadridentata*

● **Genus *Diacria* Gray, 1847**

THREE-SPINED CAVOLINE   **Fig. 73**
Diacria trispinosa (Blainville, 1821)
   Range: Worldwide; pelagic.
   Habitat: Pelagic; temperate and tropical seas.
   Description: Length about ¼ in. Shell compressed, with 3
straight spines, the middle one long and stout. Ventral face
shows faint ridge on each side; dorsal face with sharp radiat-
ing folds. Color translucent smoky white.

FOUR-TOOTHED CAVOLINE   **Fig. 74**
Diacria quadridentata (Blainville, 1821)
   Range: Worldwide oceans; pelagic.
   Habitat: Pelagic; temperate and tropical seas.
   Description: Slightly less than ¼ in. Dorsal lip thickened into
a pad. Without lateral spines. Ventral side greatly inflated.
Upper lip longer than the bottom one.

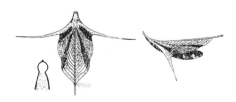

Figure 75. Cuspidate Clio *Clio cuspidata*

● Genus *Clio* Linnaeus, 1767

CUSPIDATE CLIO *Clio cuspidata* (Bosc, 1802)   **Fig. 75**
  Range: Worldwide.
  Habitat: Pelagic; temperate and tropical seas.
  Description: Length about $1/2$ in. An extremely fragile opaque white shell. Surface wrinkled, 3 dorsal folds. Thin and delicate spines along sides.

PYRAMID CLIO *Clio pyramidata* Linnaeus, 1767   **Fig. 76**
  Range: Worldwide.
  Habitat: Pelagic; arctic and temperate seas.
  Description: About $1/2$ in. long. Somewhat variable in shape. General form is kitelike, with no spines along sides. Color translucent white.

WAVY CLIO   *Clio recurva* (Children, 1823)   **Pl. 65**
  Range: Worldwide; warm and temperate seas.
  Habitat: Pelagic within 100 ft. of the surface.
  Description: About $3/4$ in., with lateral keels along its entire length. With 3 dorsal ribs. Fragile translucent shell. Abundant.

ORDER GYMNOSOMATA: NAKED SEA BUTTERFLIES

Cold-water northern and southern seas swarm with schools of minute, shell-less snails known as the Naked Pteropods or Naked Sea Butterflies. Usually less than a half inch in size, they occur as free-swimming, pelagic mollusks in such numbers that they serve as a regular food for baleen whales. These snails are carnivorous, feeding mainly on shelled pteropods. They ascend to the ocean's surface at night and sink to lower depths in the daylight hours.

■ Family Clionidae

● Genus *Clione* Pallas, 1774

COMMON CLIONE   *Clione limacina* (Phipps, 1774)   **Pl. 68**
  Range: Arctic seas to North Carolina; Alaska to n. Europe.
  Habitat: Seasonally abundant on the high seas.
  Description: About 1 in. Body cylindrical, tapering at the posterior end. Front end with 2 short tentacles and 2 or 3 pairs
  of conical mouth appendages. Fin lobes translucent, small
  and oval. Translucent-white with reddish internal organs
  visible. No shell, jaws, or gills.
  Remarks: Serves as a food of whales. Sometimes cast ashore
  after strong northeast winds in New England. Photo courtesy of Norman Katz of Beverly, Mass.

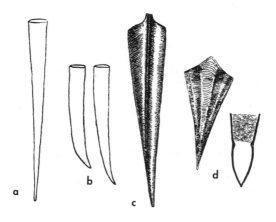

Figure 76. a) Straight Needle Pteropod *Creseis acicula*
b) Curved Needle Pteropod *Creseis virgula* **c)** Keeled Clio
Styliola subula **d)** Pyramid Clio *Clio pyramidata*

● Genus *Styliola* Lesueur, 1825

KEELED CLIO *Styliola subula* (Quoy & Gaimard, 1827)   **Fig. 76**
  Range: Worldwide.
  Habitat: Pelagic; temperate and tropical seas.
  Description: Length nearly $1/2$ in. A straight, elongate, conical shell. There is a marked dorsal groove. Surface smooth, color whitish. This is the only species in the genus.

● Genus *Creseis* Rang, 1828

STRAIGHT NEEDLE PTEROPOD   **Fig. 76**
Creseis acicula (Rang, 1828)
  Range: Worldwide.
  Habitat: Pelagic; temperate and tropical seas.
  Description: Nearly $1/2$ in. long. This is merely a long slender cone that tapers to a sharp point, the larger end open. Surface smooth and shiny, the color white or yellowish white.

CURVED NEEDLE PTEROPOD   **Fig. 76**
Creseis virgula (Rang, 1828)
  Range: Pelagic; Atlantic and Pacific oceans.
  Habitat: Near the ocean surface; abundant.
  Description: About $1/3$ in. in length. A long slender, tubelike shell with its narrow end hooked to one side. The amount of bend of the hook is variable.

● Genus *Cuvierina* Boas, 1886

CIGAR PTEROPOD *Cuvierina columnella* (Rang, 1827)
  Range: Worldwide.
  Habitat: Pelagic; temperate and tropical seas.
  Description: About $1/2$ in. long. Shell cylindrical and bottle-shaped, rounded at one end, open at other. Cross section almost circular. Surface smooth, color white. The only species in the genus.
  Remarks: Formerly in the genus *Herse* Gistel, 1848.

ORDER: SACOGLOSSA

■ SEA-HARES: Family Aplysidae

Sea-hares, or sea pigeons, bear little resemblance to any snail. The shell is completely internal, buried away in the soft parts of the back, and is really no more than a thin, triangular, shelly plate. The animal of Atlantic species may be as long as 10 in. and is soft-bodied; the mantle forms broad swimming lobes and the narrowed front end bears a pair of earlike tentacles that make it look a bit like the head of a rabbit. Colors frequently brilliant, with greens, purples, and bright reds in irregular patches of blotches or spots. This mollusk secretes an entirely harmless deep purple fluid. The largest known living snail is the Giant Black Sea-hare of southern California which may reach a length of 30 inches and a weight of 35 lbs. All *Aplysia* daily feed on large amounts of seaweeds. They lay spaghettilike, gelatinous strands of eggs.

● Genus *Aplysia* Linnaeus, 1767

WILLCOX'S SEA-HARE *Aplysia brasiliana* Rang, 1828   **Pl. 66**
Range: Massachusetts to both coasts of Florida.
Habitat: Shallow water among marine grasses.
Description: Length of animal about 8 in. Color mottled brown, with round yellowish markings on inner margin of lobes. Shell about 2 in. long and internal; thin and rather flat; color glossy white on the attached side, with a thin yellow periostracum.
Remarks: *A. floridensis* (Pilsbry, 1895) and *A. willcoxi* Heilprin, 1886 are synonyms.

SPOTTED SEA-HARE *Aplysia dactylomela* Rang, 1828
Range: S. half of Florida; Bermuda; West Indies to Brazil.
Habitat: Shallow water among marine grasses.
Description: Length of animal 4 to 5 in. Color pale yellowish to greenish with a few large, irregular circles of violet-black. Shell internal, thin and chitinous. Gives off a harmless purple ink when disturbed. Feeds on seaweeds.

● Genus *Stylocheilus* Gould, 1852

BLUE-SPOTTED SEA-HARE   Pl. 68
Stylocheilus longicauda (Quoy & Gaimard, 1824)
   Range: South Florida; West Indies; Bermuda.
   Habitat: Shallow water among rocks and seaweeds.
   Description: About ¹/₂ to 1 in. in length, with sparse filaments;
   greenish with many gray pencil lines and occasional very
   small blue "eye" spots surrounded by orange circles.

● Genus *Bursatella* Blainville, 1817

RAGGED SEA-HARE *Bursatella leachii pleii* Rang, 1828   Pl. 66
   Range: N. Carolina to Forida; West Indies to Brazil.
   Habitat: Grassy, mud-bottom shallow areas.
   Description: About 4 inches long, elongate-oval, plump, soft
   and flabby. Greenish gray to olive in color, sometimes with
   white flecks. Surface covered with numerous, ragged filaments. Shell absent in adults.

■ Family Umbraculidae

● Genus *Umbraculum* Schumacher, 1817

ATLANTIC UMBRELLA SHELL   Pl. 67
Umbraculum umbraculum (Lightfoot, 1786)
   Range: S. Florida to off Texas and Caribbean; Bermuda.
   Habitat: Shallow water on rock bottoms and sponges.
   Description: Soft, orange body 4 or 5 in. long; oval in shape.
   The oval white, flat shell sits on top of the animal. Its top
   surface is covered with a thin, tan periostracum.
   Remarks: An uncommon species that was first discovered in
   Bermuda in the late 1700s.

■ Family Elysiidae

● Genus *Elysia* Risso, 1818

PAPILLOSE ELYSIA *Elysia papillosa* Verrill, 1901   Pl. 69
   Range: Southeast Florida; Caribbean; Bermuda.
   Habitat: Shallow water, on the alga *Halimeda*.
   Description: About ¹/₃ in.; color gray with one or two trans-

verse brown bands on the rhinophores and with numerous conical, white papillae sprinkled over the surface. Rhinophores large.

Remarks: Photos of *Elysia* courtesy of Dr. Kerry Clark of Melbourne, Florida.

TUCA ELYSIA *Elysia tuca* Marcus & Marcus, 1967   **Pl. 69**
Range: Southeast Florida; Caribbean.
Habitat: Shallow water among algae.
Description: About 1/3 in., elongate, with a long flap on each side. Color dark green, clouded with yellowish. White on neck; parapodial side flaps have a straight edge.

PAINTED ELYSIA *Elysia picta* Verrill, 1901
Range: Southeast Florida; Bermuda and the West Indies.
Habitat: Intertidal on green algae.
Description: About 1/2 to 3/4 in., elongate, with slightly rolled edges on the parapodial flaps. Color blackish brown with iridescent bands of red, blue, green, and yellow. Rhinophores with red and blue bands. Eggs are in orange ribbons attached to the bottom.
Remarks: *Elysia duis* Marcus and Marcus, 1967, is a synonym.

ORNATE ELYSIA
Elysia ornata (Swainson, 1840)
Range: Florida; Bermuda and the West Indies.
Habitat: Shallow water among algae.
Description: About 3/4 in. Body translucent green, with white spots. Rhinophores orange with a black border. Moderately common.

● **Genus *Stiliger* Ehrenberg, 1831**

DUSKY STILIGER   *Stiliger fuscata* (Gould, 1870)   **Pl. 70**
Range: New Hampshire to Virginia.
Habitat: In shallow water near salt marshes; uncommon.
Description: About 1/4 in., sluglike, with 2 simple rhinophores. Dark slate gray above. Foot pale yellowish. Cerata long, club-shaped, black and white at the ends.
Remarks: Belongs to the subgenus *Ercolania* Trinchese, 1872. Photo courtesy of Kerry B. Clark of Melbourne, Florida.

● Genus *Tridachia* Deshayes, 1857

COMMON LETTUCE SLUG   Pl. 68
Tridachia crispata (Mörch, 1863)
   Range: South Florida; Bermuda and the Caribbean.
   Habitat: Shallow water near the open ocean; common.
   Description: About 1 or 2 in. long; green or bluish with white
   spots on the back and the edges of the undulating, folded
   parapodial flaps.
   Remarks: A rather common, active tectibranch. Photo cour-
   tesy of Kerry B. Clark of Melbourne, Florida.

■ **BIVALVED SNAILS: Family Juliidae**

● Genus *Berthelinia* Crosse, 1875

CARIBBEAN BIVALVED SNAIL   Fig. 77 & Pl. 67
Berthelinia caribbea Edmunds, 1963
   Range: South Florida to Brazil.
   Habitat: Shallow water in the green alga *Caulerpa verticil-
   lata*, near mangroves.
   Description: Only ⅛ in. long, this sluglike animal carries two
   bivalvelike shells on its sides. Color greenish gray with
   faint radial rays of yellow.
   Remarks: A remarkable sluglike snail having two shelly
   valves. Photo by Ronald J. Larsen in Puerto Rico.

Figure 77. Caribbean Bivalved Snail *Berthelinia caribbea*

ORDER NUDIBRANCHS

These are small, sluglike, and often very beautiful, marine univalves that have no shells. There are several hundred species in our Atlantic waters, most of them feeding on hydroids or sponges. Their identification sometimes depends upon internal anatomical and radular characters. Only a few examples are presented here, since their identification requires specialists who have extensive literature at hand. Most lose their shape and natural colors when preserved in alcohol or formaline.

■ Family Chromodorididae

● Genus *Hypselodoris* Stimpson, 1855

FLORIDA ZEBRA DORIS   **Pl. 69**
Hypselodoris edenticulata (White, 1952)
  Range: South Florida and the Caribbean.
  Habitat: Shallow, coral waters down to 180 ft.
  Description: About $1/2$ to 1 in., elongate, deep blue-black with stripes and small circles of bright yellow. About 10 branchial plumes at the posterior end. Rhinophores blue-black.
  Remarks: A brightly colored nudibranch photographed by the late Alice Barlow. Photo courtesy of the Bailey-Matthews Shell Museum on Sanibel Island.

■ Family Cadlinidae

● Genus *Cadlina* Bergh, 1878

WHITE ATLANTIC DORIS   **Pl. 70**
Cadlina laevis (Linnaeus, 1767)
  Range: Arctic seas to Cape Cod; Europe.
  Habitat: Shallow water among sponges.
  Description: About 1 in., translucent white with numerous very small yellowish dots. Rhinophores opaque white or yellowish and with 12 or 13 leaflets. Back with numerous, very small tubercles. Branchial plumes of 5 imperfectly tripinnate, whitish plumes.
  Remarks: Photo by Seven F. Barry of Florida.

■ Family Polyceratidae

● **Genus** *Polycera* **Cuvier, 1817**

DUBIOUS POLYCERA *Polycera dubia* (Sars, 1829)   **Pl. 70**
Range: Labrador to Connecticut; Greenland.
Habitat: Below low tide from 18 to 120 ft.
Description: Length about ¹/₂ to 1 in. Frontal margin with fingerlike processes. Rhinophores nonretractile and without sheaths. Appendices on the top of the back are small and numerous. Color yellowish with fine longitudinal lines.
Remarks: Photo by Dr. Kerry B. Clark of Melbourne, Florida.

HUMM'S POLYCERA
Polycera hummi Abbott, 1952
Range: North Carolina to northwest Florida.
Habitat: Shallow water among hydroids.
Description: On either side are 3 or 4 extrabranchial processes that are cylindrical with pointed tips. Gills with 7 to 9 plumes. Rhinophores with 14 or 15 leaflets and without sheaths. Colors blue and orange.

■ Family Phyllidiidae

● **Genus** *Phyllidiopsis* **Bergh, 1876**

PAPILLOSE DORIS *Phyllidiopsis papilligera* Bergh, 1890   **Pl. 71**
Range: South Florida; West Indies.
Habitat: Offshore in moderately deep water.
Description: Length about 1 in., flattish, oval, with large black warts on a white surface. Small white-tipped tubercles are in the center of the black warts. No dorsal branchial gills but with lanellae under the sides of the mantle. Rhinophores on the dorsal side of the mantle. Anterior border of the foot slightly notched.
Remarks: Photo taken on coral at 90 ft. by Ronald J. Larson in Puerto Rico.

■ Family Tritoniidae

● **Genus** *Tritonia* **Cuvier, 1798**

BAYER'S TRITONIA *Tritonia bayeri* Marcus, 1967   **Pl. 71**
Range: Georgia to Southeast Florida.

Habitat: Shallow water among hydroids and gorgonian sea-whips.

Description: About $1/2$ in.; translucent in color with an opaque white diffused network on the smooth back. Branchial gills white.

Remarks: Photograph taken in Puerto Rico by Ronald J. Larson.

■ Family Dotoidae

● Genus *Doto* Oken, 1815

CORONATE DOTO *Doto coronata* (Gmelin, 1791)   Pl. 72

Range: Newfoundland; eastern U.S.; Europe.

Habitat: Shallow water on hydroids.

Description: Length $1/3$ in. Small body widest at the front and tapering behind to a point. With a series of 5 to 8 papillae on each side, each bearing minute tubercles. Rhinophoral sheaths long and trumpet-shaped. Color pale yellowish white with reddish dots on the tubercles and the back.

Remarks: Fairly common. It lays eggs on the hydroid *Obelia*. Photo taken by Dr. Kerry B. Clark of Melbourne, Florida.

■ Family Facelinidae

● Genus *Facelina* Alder and Handcock, 1855

BOSTON FACELINA   Pl. 72
Facelina bostoniensis (Couthouy, 1838)

Range: Nova Scotia to Connecticut.

Habitat: Among the hydroid *Obelia*, on the kelp weed *Laminaria*; 6 to 120 ft.

Description: Length 1 in.; rhinophores light brown with 20 to 24 lanellae. Body rosy tan with a rosy head. Tentacles with a bluish to white dorsal streak. Cerata thin, clumped into 5 or 6 oblique rows, each with 8 to 12 cerata with a white ring at the tip.

Remarks: Photo by the late George Moore of the University of New Hampshire. Courtesy of the Museum of Comparative Zoology, Harvard University.

■ Family Favorinidae

● Genus *Favorinus* Gray, 1850

AIRY FAVORINUS *Favorinus auritulus* Marcus, 1955   **Pl. 72**
   Range: South Florida to Brazil.
   Habitat: Shallow water among hydroid growths.
   Description: About ¹/₃ in. With two pairs of oral tentacles. Slender head tentacles are knobbed. Body and cerata translucent with opaque white splotches.
   Remarks: Photo taken in Bermuda by Kerry B. Clark.

● Genus *Dondice* Marcus, 1958

WESTERN ATLANTIC DONDICE   **Pl. 73**
Dondice occidentalis (Engel, 1925)
   Range: North Carolina to Florida and to Brazil.
   Habitat: On hydriods in shallow water.
   Description: Length up to 1¹/₄ in. Color white with a central red stripe along the head. Slender cerata in clumps, elongate, gray with a clear, pointed end, below which is an orange ring with a central red ring.
   Remarks: Photo taken by Dr. Kerry B. Clark of Melbourne, Florida.

■ Family Aeolidiidae

● Genus *Spurilla* Bergh, 1864

NEAPOLITAN SPURILLA   **Pl. 73**
Spurilla neapolitana (Delle Chiaje, 1823)
   Range: Florida to Texas; Caribbean to Brazil.
   Habitat: Common in weeds in shallow water.
   Description: Length 1 to 1¹/₂ in., long, ivory-colored with rose tints. Cerata numerous, crowded, curved and translucent gray. Back with chalky white spots.
   Remarks: Feeds on sea anemones and retains the stinging cells in its cerata, which it uses later to ward off intruders. Photo courtesy of Dr. Kerry B. Clark of Melbourne, Florida.

PAPILLOSE EOLIS *Aeolidia papillosa* (Linnaeus, 1761)   **Pl. 73**
   Range: Arctic seas to Maryland; Europe; North Pacific.

Habitat: Shallow to deep water; intertidal pools.

Description: About 1 to 3 in. in length. Branchiae set in numerous, close, transverse rows; with 4 simple tentacles; foot broad, anterior angles sharp. Color brown, gray, or yellow and spotted and freckled with lilac, brown, and opaquewhite.

Remarks: Although usually found in fairly deep water, this common species can occur in shallow estuaries. They ingest the stinging cells of sea anemonies and store them in their cerata without discharging them. Later, they are used to defend themselves from predators. Photo courtesy of Norman Katz of Beverly, Mass.

■ Family Dendronotidae

● Genus *Dendronotus* Alder & Hancock, 1845

FROND EOLIS *Dendronotus frondosus* (Ascanius, 1774)   **Pl. 71**

Range: Arctic seas to New Jersey; Europe; Alaska to s. Calif.; Japan.

Habitat: Shallow rocky bottoms among hydroids.

Description: Up to 2 in. Grayish white, overlaid with browns, yellows, and whites. Conical papillae on back are yellow or white-tipped. Rhinophores with 8 to 12 large leaves, interspaced by about 15 smaller ones. Rhinophores as long as the first pair of cerata. Able swimmers; common.

3

CLASS POLYPLACOPHORA (Amphineurans): CHITONS

These are the chitons, or coat-of-mail shells — mollusks that usually live in rocky situations close to shore. They are nocturnal in habit, feeding chiefly upon decaying vegetation at night and spending the daytime clinging to the undersides of stones and dead shells, safely out of sight. They are not exclusively herbivorous, however, and many will feed upon animal matter to some extent. All members of this class are marine.

The chiton shell is composed of 8 separate but overlapping plates (valves). This forms a sort of shield, which when empty and turned over suggests a small boat. The girdle is the leathery skin in which the plates are embedded, and it generally extends beyond them — all the way around — to form a thin border. This girdle may be smooth or granular, or it may be covered with scales or tufts of hair. Frequently it has the appearance of snakeskin.

They cling to rocks with surprising tenacity, and it is not easy to remove a specimen without injury. Slipping a thin knifeblade under one is the best way to dislodge it. In death they commonly curl up like a pillbug, but they can be relaxed by being soaked in water, then spread out on a thin board, such as a lath, and secured by wrapping with strong thread. Place the tied-down chitons, board and all, in a container of some kind (2-quart fruit jars do nicely) and cover them with a 70 percent solution of alcohol. If a specimen is large you can dig out most of the fleshy part before fastening it to the board. After soaking for about 2 weeks, the chitons can be taken out and allowed to dry slowly in a shady place. Then they may be removed from the boards and are ready for the collection, although there will be some shrinkage of the girdle. There also will be some loss of color, so the chitons rarely make as attractive cabinet specimens as do the snails and clams.

Some collectors remove the 8 plates of the shell and clean

292

and reassemble them. The resulting specimens are things of beauty, exhibiting an unexpected range of colors from pure white to rich blue-green, with splashes of yellow, rose, or orange. The attractiveness of the collection is enhanced by displaying a few cleaned plates in the tray along with the complete specimens. To prepare them, simply boil the chiton for about 5 minutes, then remove the plates and place them in pure Clorox for $1/2$ hour. This softens any adhering tissue so that its removal with a stiff brush is easy. After drying the plates on a paper towel, glue them together in the proper sequence. When completely dry and set, they can be wiped lightly with mineral oil to which a small amount of neat's-foot oil has been added; then they are ready for your cabinet.

■ CHITONS: Family Lepidochitonidae

● Genus *Tonicella* Carpenter, 1873

MOTTLED RED CHITON   **Pl. 74**
Tonicella marmorea (Fabricius, 1780)
   Range: Circumpolar; Arctic Ocean to Massachusetts.
   Habitat: Moderately shallow water.
   Description: About 1 to $1^{1}/_{2}$ in. long. A solid and robust species, oval in shape. Plates keeled; each bears a slight projection at the rear. Color reddish brown, marked with angular whitish lines. Girdle is without scales, is leathery in texture, tan, and sometimes speckled with red.

RED CHITON *Tonicella rubra* (Linnaeus, 1767)
   Range: Arctic Ocean to Connecticut; Alaska south to California.
   Habitat: Shallow water to 480 ft.
   Description: About $3/_{4}$ in. long. Oval shape, plates strongly keeled, bearing elevated lines of growth. Color pale brick red, with a few lines of deeper red. Girdle reddish brown and set with elongate scales. Animal itself bright red.

■ CHITONS: Family Acanthochitonidae

● Genus *Acanthochitona*, Gray 1821

DWARF GLASS-HAIRED CHITON
Acanthochitona pygmaea (Pilsbry, 1893)
   Range: Florida to the West Indies.
   Habitat: Shallow water.

Description: About ¹/₂ in. long. Rather elongate, with a high, somewhat arched back. Plates microscopically dotted. Girdle leathery, covering major portion of plates, margins decorated with minute tufts of hair. Color may be yellowish, brownish, or mottled, sometimes with greenish.

■ CHITONS: Family Ischnochitonidae

● Genus *Calloplax* Thiele, 1909

RIO JANEIRO CHITON
Calloplax janeirensis (Gray, 1828)
  Range: Florida Keys to Brazil.
  Habitat: Shallow water.
  Description: About ³/₄ in. long. Strongly sculptured, each plate bearing a pair of heavy ribs along its front margin that radiate from the center to the sides; rest of plate deeply scored by vertical grooves. A fanlike display of ribs at each end of shell. Girdle shows some fine silky hairs. Color greenish brown, dotted in places with red; interior of plates white.

● Genus *Chaetopleura* Shuttleworth, 1853

COMMON EASTERN CHITON   Pl. 74
Chaetopleura apiculata (Say, 1830)
  Range: Massachusetts to Florida.
  Habitat: Shallow water.
  Description: About ³/₄ in. long. Oval, the plates heavily scored with longitudinal grooves. Edges marked with rows of tiny elevated dots. Color grayish or pale chestnut.

● Genus *Ischnochiton* Gray, 1847

WHITE CHITON *Ischnochiton albus* (Linnaeus, 1767)
  Range: Circumpolar; Greenland to Massachusetts; Aleutian Islands in n. Pacific.
  Habitat: Shallow water.
  Description: About ¹/₂ in. long. Somewhat elongate, plates weakly marked with growth lines. Narrow girdle sandpapery. In life the color is bluish black, but this rubs off easily, and cabinet specimens vary from pale cream to nearly white.

● Genus *Stenoplax* Carpenter & Dall, 1879

SLUG-SHAPED CHITON   **Pl. 74**
Stenoplax limaciformis (Sowerby, 1832)
   Range: South Florida.
   Habitat: Shallow water.
   Description: About 1¹/₂ in. long. Slender, plates broad and
   rough, with heavy but not keeled longitudinal lines. Girdle
   rather wide, smooth, and delicately marked with black and
   gray. Color of back whitish or pale green, mottled with gray.
   Formerly listed as *Ischnochiton floridanus* Pilsbry, 1892.

■ CHITONS: Family Chitonidae

● Genus *Chiton* Linnaeus, 1758

MARBLED CHITON *Chiton marmoratus* Gmelin, 1791   **Pl. 74**
   Range: Southeast Florida to the West Indies.
   Habitat: Shallow water on coral shore rocks.
   Description: Length 2 to 3 in. Broadly oval. Surface quite
   smooth, almost polished. Plates without ridges or pustules,
   presenting a silky appearance. Color variable, ranging from
   olive-gray to greenish black, often with longitudinal streaks
   of paler shade. Girdle broad, resembles snakeskin, alter-
   nately banded with greenish white and dark brown. Interior
   of plates blue-green.

SQUAMOSE CHITON   **Pl. 74**
Chiton squamosus Linnaeus, 1764
   Range: Southeast Florida to the West Indies.
   Habitat: Shallow water.
   Description: Length 2 to 3 in. Oval, strong and solid. Plates
   with sharp longitudinal lines at center, sides with transverse wavy lines. Color greenish gray, with brownish
   streaks. Girdle broad, strongly scaled, gray-green, with irregular patches of darker green.

COMMON WEST INDIAN CHITON   **Pl. 74**
Chiton tuberculatus Linnaeus, 1758
   Range: Florida to the West Indies.
   Habitat: Shallow water on wave-washed rocky shores.
   Description: Length 2 to 3¹/₂ in. Broadly oval, plates strongly
   keeled. Each plate divided into a broad triangle toward

front, and 2 wedge-shaped triangles at sides. Main triangle marked with longitudinal grooves, side triangles bear transverse wavy ridges. Front and back plates pimpled with small tubercles. Color olive green, clouded and speckled with greenish. Conspicuous girdle heavily scaled; pale green, with squarish patches of black or dark green, suggesting a border of snakeskin.

● Genus *Acanthopleura* Guilding, 1829

FUZZY CHITON   **Pl. 17**
Acanthopleura granulata (Gmelin, 1791)
  Range: South half of Florida; West Indies.
  Habitat: Upper intertidal rocks.
  Description: About 2 or 3 in. in length, usually quite eroded. Girdle matted with coarse, hairlike spines and colored gray with occasional black bands. Underside of valves green, with the middle valves having a black splotch.

● Genus *Tonicia* Gray, 1847

SCRAMM'S CHITON   **Pl. 74**
Tonicia schrammi (Shuttleworth, 1856)
  Range: Southeast Florida; West Indies; Bermuda.
  Habitat: Intertidal waters on rocks.
  Description: About an inch in length, colored a brownish red with darker speckles. Interior of valves white with a red stain. Lateral areas of the upper side of the valves peppered with about 75 microscopic black "eyes." Girdle light brown and smooth.

4

CLASS SCAPHOPODA: SCAPHOPODS

An external, tubular shell, open at both ends and somewhat curved, covers the animal in this class. Shape of the shell is responsible for the popular names of tusk shell and tooth shell which are generally applied to members of this group. Found only in marine waters, where they range from just below the low-tide mark to depths of several hundred fathoms, they show a preference for clean sand but are sometimes found living on muddy bottoms. The typical shell is long and tapering, cylindrical, gently curved, and usually pure white, although some tropical species may be pale green or pink. The surface may be smooth and glossy, dull and chalklike, or ribbed longitudinally. They live in the sand with the small end uppermost; from the larger end protrudes the foot, a tough elastic organ admirably suited for burrowing. In fact, the name scaphopod means "plow-footed."

In primitive times the shells were used for money and adornment by various Indian tribes, particularly from our Northwest, where the tubular shells were cut into short sections for beads.

■ TUSK SHELLS: Family Dentaliidae

● Genus *Graptacme* Pilsbry and Sharp, 1897

IVORY TUSK SHELL *Graptacme eboreum* (Conrad, 1846)   **Pl. 17**
Range: N. Carolina to Texas and the West Indies.
Habitat: Shallow water in sand.
Description: About 2 in. long. Thin and delicate, gently curved. Surface smooth and polished, with a few raised lines at the small end. Color white or ivory-white, sometimes flushed with pinkish or yellowish. Apical slit narrow and on the convex side.

● **Genus** *Antalis* **H. & Adams, 1854**

RIBBED TUSK SHELL
Antalis occidentale (Stimpson, 1851)
   Range: Newfoundland to Cape Hatteras.
   Habitat: Moderately deep water.
   Description: About 1 in. long. A rather solid shell decorated with about 16 well-defined longitudinal ribs. Surface not polished, color a soiled white, sometimes with tinges of ivory.

● **Genus** *Fissidentalium* **Fischer, 1885**

FLORIDA TUSK SHELL   **Pl. 60**
Fissidentalium floridense Henderson, 1920
   Range: Southeast Florida and the West Indies.
   Habitat: Fairly deep water, buried in soft sand.
   Description: About 2 to 3 in., with numerous fine longitudinal riblets. Apex with a long, simple slit. Roundish in cross-section. Color yellowish. Apex hexagonal. Ribs increase to 24 anteriorly.

● **Genus** *Dentalium* **Linneaus, 1758**

TEXAS TUSK SHELL
Dentalium americanum Chenu, 1843
   Range: N. Carolina to Texas.
   Habitat: Shallow water in sand, offshore.
   Description: About 1 in. long. Surface bears weak longitudinal ribs, the spaces between them rather flat. In cross section the shell is hexagonal. Color dull grayish white.
   Remarks: Formerly known as *D. texasianum* Philippi, 1848.

PANELED TUSK SHELL
Dentalium laqueatum Verrill, 1885
   Range: North Carolina to Florida; West Indies.
   Habitat: In mud and sand from 20 to 1,200 ft.
   Description: From 1 to 1$^1/_2$ in., thick-shelled and dull white in color. Apex sharply curved. With 9 to 12 strong, elevated primary ribs. Fine reticulation over the entire shell.

■ SWOLLEN TUSK SHELLS: Family Siphonodentaliidae

● Genus *Polyschides* Pilsbry and Sharp, 1898

These tusk shells differ from the genus Dentalium by being short and generally swollen in the middle.

CAROLINA CADULUS
Polyschides carolinensis (Bush, 1885)
Range: N. Carolina to Florida and Texas.
Habitat: Moderately deep water, from 18 to 600 ft.
Description: About $1/4$ in. long. Shell rather solid but slightly swollen at middle. In cross section it is round. Small end bears 4 tiny slits. Surface highly polished, color milky white.
Remarks: Formerly placed in the genus *Cadulus* Philippi, 1884.

5

CLASS CEPHALOPODA: SQUIDS AND OCTOPUS

The cephalopods are highly specialized mollusks, keen of vision and swift in action. The head is armed with a parrot-like beak and surrounded by long flexible tentacles studded with sucking disks. Besides the octopuses, this class includes the beautiful Pearly or Chambered Nautilus of the w. Pacific and the Indian Ocean. The class is abundantly represented in the past by a bewildering variety of nautiloids, belemnites, and ammonites known only as fossils, some of the latter from the Cretaceous with a diameter of more than 3 ft. Four members of the shell-bearing cephalopods may be found on our shores, in addition to several kinds of squid lacking external shells.

SUBCLASS COLEOIDAE

■ RAMS' HORNS: Family Spirulidae

● Genus *Spirula* Lamarck, 1801

COMMON SPIRULA *Spirula spirula* (Linnaeus, 1758)   **Pl. 16**
   Range: Worldwide.
   Habitat: Pelagic; shells washed ashore.
   Description: Diameter about 1 in. Shell thin and rather fragile, flatly but loosely coiled, the coils not in contact. Shell divided into many chambers by concave partitions (septa). Last partition shows a small hole (opening of the siphuncle — a structure connecting the chambers). Color pure white.
   Remarks: This is an internal shell, located at the rear of a

small squidlike mollusk, and it may serve as a balancing device or may enable the creature to rise or sink at will. The small snow-white shells are washed ashore from Cape Cod to Florida (rather rarely in north but not uncommonly in south) and can be picked up on beaches all around the world in warm and temperate seas; the complete mollusk is almost never seen, and then only when taken by dredging or trawling in water 180 to 3,000 ft.

ORDER SQUIDS

There are over 100 kinds of squids found in our American waters, most of them living in deep water well beyond the reach of the average mollusk collector. However, three abundant species belonging to the "dibranchiate," or two-gilled, subclass Coleoidea, are familiar to those who use them for fish bait. The other subclass, the Nautiloidea, or the "tetrabranchiate," or four-gilled, cephalopods are represented in the southwest Pacific by the well-known Chambered Nautilus.

The Sepia squids from Europe, sometimes called cuttlefish, have a white, chalky, internal cuttlefish bone which is rarely cast ashore in Florida and Texas. Our East Coast squids have a thin, transparent, internal pen. Harvey's Giant Squid, *Architeuthis harveyi* Kent, 1874, found off Newfoundland, reaches a length of 40 to 55 feet, and so far has only been found dead.

■ HOOK-ARMED SQUIDS: Family Gonatidae

● Genus *Gonatus* Gray, 1849

FABRICUS SQUID *Gonatus fabricii* (Lichtenstein, 1818) **Fig. 78**
Range: Arctic seas; Nova Scotia to Rhode Island.
Habitat: Pelagic in cold waters.
Description: Length, including the arms, about 1 ft. The tentacular arms are long and have numerous small discs at the ends, as well as several small distinct, horny hooks. The fins are spread out at the posterior end.

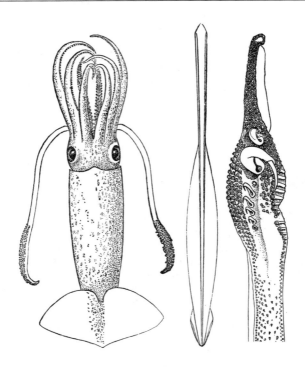

Figure 78. Fabricius Squid *Gonatus fabricii*

■ LOLIGO SQUIDS: Family Loliginidae

● Genus *Loligo* Schneider, 1784

ATLANTIC LONG-FINNED SQUID   **Fig. 79 & Pl. 16**
Loligo pealeii Lesueur, 1821
   Range: Nova Scotia to the Gulf of Mexico; Bermuda.
   Habitat: Pelagic, in large schools.
   Description: Length, including the 10 arms, from 1 to 2 ft.
Body with 2 long, triangular fins. Arms with 2 rows of suck-
ers provided with horny, toothed rings. Eyes large. Living

specimens brightly colored with specks of red, purple, and pink. The female receives the sperm sac of the male upon a specially developed pad below the mouth. A very abundant species caught commercially for fish bait in New England.

● Genus *Lolliguncula* Steenstrup, 1881

BRIEF THUMBSTALL SQUID   **Fig. 79**
Lolliguncula brevis (Blainville, 1823)
   Range: Maryland to Texas and to Brazil; Bermuda.
   Habitat: Pelagic in warm waters.
   Description: Total length, including the 2 long tentacular arms, 5 to 10 in. Eyes large. Characterized by its short, rounded fins and very short upper arms. Body and top of fins heavily spotted. Underside of fins white. The internal pen is illustrated at the top of Fig. 79.

■ SHORT-FINNED SQUIDS: Family Ommastrephidae

● Genus *Illex* Steenstrup, 1880

COMMON SHORT-FINNED SQUID   **Fig. 79**
Illex illecebrosus (Lesueur, 1821)
   Range: Newfoundland to northeast Florida.
   Habitat: Pelagic, in cool waters.
   Description: Total length, including the 2 short tentacles and 8 arms, is 12 to 18 in. Eyes very small, with a small, narrow notch in front. Two short triangular fins at the narrow back end. A common squid used for fish bait, sometimes seen in large schools near shore in New England in the summer.

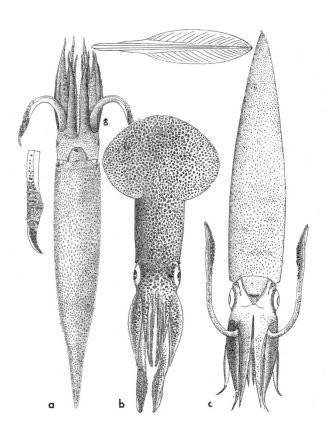

Figure 79. a) Common Short-finned Squid *Illex illecebrosus* **b)** Brief Thumbstall Squid *Lolliguncula brevis* **c)** Atlantic Long-finned Squid *Loligo pealeii*

ORDER OCTOPODA

■ OCTOPUSES: Family Octopodidae

● Genus *Octopus* Lamarck, 1798

There are only six valid species of littoral octopuses so far recorded along our Atlantic coast. Technical characters concerning the length of the arms and the relative length of the ligula (the tiny padlike extension on the third right arm of the males) make identification impossible for the average observer. The largest, rarely reaching a radial span of 7 feet, is *Octopus vulgaris* Cuvier, 1797, which ranges from Connecticut to Florida and the West indies as well as Europe.

JOUBIN'S OCTOPUS *Octopus joubini* Robson, 1929   **Pl. 16**
Range: South half of Florida; West Indies.
Habitat: Shallow water near shore.
Description: A small species, rarely over 10 in. in diameter. Skin is smooth, except for fine pimples. Eggs amber-colored, $1/2$ in. in size.
Remarks: Prefers to hide in dead pairs of bivalves.

■ PAPER ARGONAUTS: Family Argonautidae

● Genus *Argonauta* Linnaeus, 1758

COMMON PAPER ARGONAUT   **Pl. 74**
Argonauta argo Linnaeus, 1758
Range: Worldwide in warm seas.
Habitat: Pelagic.
Description: Diameter to 8 in. Shell somewhat flattened, forming a roundish spiral; thin and brittle, not chambered. Exterior bears a double keel and is decorated with knobs and swollen lines. Color milky white, tinged with brown at the keels.
Remarks: There are no muscular attachments to the shell, and the animal may discard it at any time. This puzzled the early naturalists, for it was contrary to all known varieties of shellfish; the general belief was that the cephalopod lived in the shell of some mysterious "sea snail" after the manner of

a hermit crab. Another puzzling fact was that all specimens found were females. About 1840 it was discovered that the female has 2 "arms" broadly expanded to form a pair of web-like appendages and that these organs secrete the shell, not the mantle as in the usual mollusk. The shell is begun when the female is only a few weeks old; eventually it will serve as a case for her eggs. The male argonaut is much smaller than the female and has no shell at all, so it is understandable that for many years the life history of this mollusk was so imperfectly known.

Empty shells are occasionally washed up on the beaches of Florida, and rarely as far north as New Jersey. This species has been named *A. americana* Dall, but today most scientists regard it as conspecific with the European and Pacific forms, and they are all listed as *A. argo* Linnaeus, 1758.

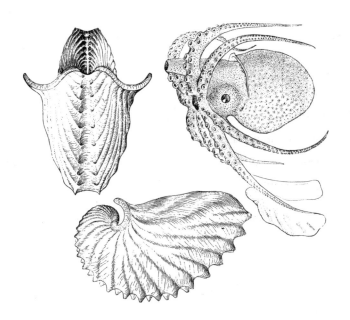

Figure 80. Common Paper Argonaut *Argonauta argo*

BROWN PAPER ARGONAUT   Pl. 74
Argonauta hians Lightfoot, 1786

Range: Worldwide in warm seas.
Habitat: Pelagic.
Description: Length 1$\frac{1}{2}$ to 3 in., soft brown in color and with fairly strong nodules on the keel of the "shell."

APPENDIXES
INDEX

APPENDIX A
GLOSSARY OF CONCHOLOGICAL TERMS

Acuminate — tapering to a point.
Acute — sharply pointed.
Animal — the fleshy part of the mollusk.
Annulated — marked with rings.
Anterior end — end toward which the beaks point in a bivalve shell; posterior end is opposite. Front end of shell.
Aperture — the entrance or opening of the shell.
Apex — the tip of the spire in snail shells.
Apophysis (pl. **apophyses**) — a shelly brace or peglike structure located inside under each beak to support muscles; also called myophore.
Axis — the central structure (column) of a spiral shell.

Base — *snails*, the extremity opposite the apex; *clams*, the margin opposite the beaks.
Beaks — the initial, or earliest, part of a bivalve shell; umbones.
Bivalve — a shell with 2 valves (or shell parts).
Body whorl — the last whorl of a snail shell.
Byssus — a series of threadlike filaments that serve to anchor the bivalve to some support.

Calcareous — composed of hard lime.
Callum — thin calcareous covering of the gape in some clams.
Callus — a calcareous deposit, such as enamel.
Canal — usually a somewhat narrow prolongation of the lip of the aperture containing the siphons in many snails.
Cancellate — having longitudinal and horizontal lines or ribs that cross each other.
Carinate — with a keel-like, elevated ridge.
Cartilage — an internal, elastic substance found in bivalves that controls the opening of the valves.
Chondrophore — an internal spoonlike projection on the hinge of some bivalves.

Columella — the pillar around which the whorls form their spiral circuit.

Compressed — having the valves close together.

Concentric — applied to curved ridges or lines on a bivalve shell which form arcs with the beaks at the center.

Conic — shaped like a cone.

Coronate — crowned, usually with knobs.

Costate — ribbed.

Crenulate — notched or scalloped.

Cuspidate — prickly pointed.

Deck — a shelly plate under the beaks; also called a platform.

Decussated — having lines cross at right angles.

Denticulate — toothed.

Dextral — turning from left to right; right-handed.

Discoidal — having the whorls coiled in one plane.

Dorsal — belonging to the back.

Ear — *see* Wing.

Epidermis — *see* Periostracum.

Equivalve — when both valves are the same size and shape.

Escutcheon — an elongated depression behind the beaks in a bivalve shell.

Foot — muscular extension of the body used in locomotion.

Fusiform — spindle-shaped.

Gaping — having the valves only partially closed.

Gastropod — a snail (or slug).

Genus — a separate group of species, distinguished from all others by certain permanent marks called generic characters.

Globose — rounded like a globe or ball.

Granulated — covered with minute grains or beads.

Growth lines — lines on the surface of a shell indicating rest periods during growth; also called growth laminae.

Hinge — where the valves of a bivalve are joined.

Inequivalve — having valves that differ in size or shape.

Inner lip — portion of aperture adjacent to the axis, or pillar.

Involute — rolled inward from each side, as in *Cypraea.*

Keel — a flattened ridge, usually at the shoulder or periphery.

Lamellibranchia — an older name for pelecypods (bivalves).

Lanceolate — shaped like a lance.

Ligament — a cartilage that connects the valves.

Linear — relating to a line or lines; very narrow.

Lineated — marked with lines.

Lips — the margins of the aperture.

Lirate — resembling fine incised lines.

Littoral — the tidal zone.

Lunule — a depressed area, usually heart-shaped, in front of the beaks in many bivalve shells.

Lyrate — shaped like a lyre.

Maculate — splashed or spotted.

Mantle — a membranous flap or outer covering of the soft parts of a mollusk; it secretes the material that forms the shell.

Margin — the edges of the shell.

Mesoplax — an accessory plate.

Mouth — the aperture of a snail shell.

Myophore — *see* Apophysis.

Nacre — the pearly layer of certain shells.

Nodose — having tubercles, or knobs.

Nodule — a knoblike projection.

Nucleus — the initial nuclear whorls.

Operculum — a plate or door that closes the aperture in many snail shells.

Orbicular — round or circular.

Outer lip — the outer edge of the aperture.

Ovate — egg-shaped or oval.

Pallets — a pair of simple or compound chitinous or calcareous structures to close the tube when the siphons are withdrawn.

Pallial line — a groove or channel near the inner base of a bivalve shell, where the mantle is made fast to the lower part of the shell.

Pallial sinus — a notch or embayment at the posterior end of the pallial line where the retracted siphons are held.

Parietal wall — the inner lip area.

Pelagic — inhabiting the open sea.

Periostracum — the noncalcareous covering on many shells; sometimes wrongly called the epidermis.

Peristome — edge of the aperture.

Platform — *see* Deck.

Pleat — applied to folds on the columella.

Plicate — folded or pleated.

Posterior end — the back end; opposite anterior; *see* Anterior end.

Produced — elongated.

Protoconch — the initial whorls of a snail shell; the nucleus.

Quadrate — rectangular-shaped.

Radial — pertaining to a ray or rays from a common center.

Radiating — applied to ribs or lines that start at the beak and extend fanwise to the margins.

Radula — the "tongue," or dental apparatus, of gastropods.

Resilium — internal cartilage in bivalve hinge; causes shell to spring open when muscles relax.

Reticulate — crossed, like network.

Rostrate — beaked.

Rostrum — a beak, or handlike extension of shell.

Rugose — rough or wrinkled.

Scabrous — rough.

Sculpture — the ornamentation of a shell.

Semilunar — half-moon-shaped.

Septum (pl. **septa**) — the platform or deck; in plural usage it can mean partitions.

Sinistral — turning from right to left; left-handed.

Sinuate — excavated.

Sinus — a deep cut.

Siphon — the organ through which water enters or leaves the mantle cavity.

Siphuncle — a membranous tubular extension of the mantle that runs through chambers of *Nautilus.*

Species — the subdivision of a genus, distinguished from all others of the genus by certain permanent marks called specific characters.

Spire — the upper whorls, from the apex to the body whorl.

Striae — very fine lines.

Subglobular — not quite globose.

Sulcus (pl. **sulci**) — groove or furrow.

Suture — the spiral line of the spire, where one whorl touches another.

Teeth — the pointed protuberances at the hinge of a bivalve shell; in snails, the toothlike structures in the aperture.

Trochiform — top-shaped.

Truncate — having the end cut off squarely.
Tubercle — a small knob.
Turbinate — top-shaped.
Turreted — having tops of the whorls flattened.

Umbilicus — a small hollow at the base of the shell in snails; visible from below.
Umbo (pl. **umbones**) — beak, or prominent part, of bivalve shells above the hinge.
Univalve — a shell composed of a single piece, as a snail.

Valve — one part of a bivalve shell; one of the 8 plates that make up the dorsal shield of a chiton.
Varicose — bearing 1 or more varices.
Varix (pl. **varices**) — an earlier margin (a kind of rib) of the aperture; a prominent raised longitudinal rib on surface of a snail shell caused by a periodic thickening of the outer lip during rest periods in shell growth.
Ventral — pertaining to the underside.
Ventricose — swollen or rounded out.

Whorls — the turns of the spire.
Wing — a somewhat triangular projection or expansion of the shell of a bivalve, either in the plane of the hinge or extending above it; also known as an "ear."

APPENDIX B
BIBLIOGRAPHY

Abbott, R. Tucker. *American Seashells.* Second Edition. New York: Van Nostrand Reinhold, 1974.

—. *Collectible Florida Seashells.* Melbourne, Fla. American Malacologist, 1984.

—. *Kingdom of the Seashell.* Melbourne, Fla. American Malacologist, 1993.

—. *Seashells of North America.* Revised Edition. New York: Golden Press, 1986.

Amos, William H. *The Life of the Seashore.* New York: McGraw-Hill in cooperation with World Book Encyclopedia, 1966.

Arnold, Augusta. *The Sea-beach at Ebb-tide.* New York: Century, 1903. Reprint by Dover Publ., N.Y.

Carson, Rachel. *The Edge of the Sea.* Boston: Houghton Mifflin. 1955.

Dance, S. Peter. *Shell Collecting: An Illustrated History.* Berkeley: Univ. Calif. Press, 1966.

Gould, Augustus A. *Report on the Invertebrata of Massachusetts.* 2nd ed., edited by W. G. Binney. Boston: Wright and Potter, 1870.

Hausman, Leon A. *Beginner's Guide to Seashore Life.* New York: Putnam, 1949.

Jacobson, M. K., and W. K. Emerson. *Shells of the New York City Area.* Larchmont, N.Y.: Argonaut, 1961.

—. *Shells from Cape Cod to Cape May, with Special Reference to the New York City Area.* New York: Dover, 1972.

Johnson, Charles W. *Fauna of New England: List of the Mollusca.* Occas. Papers Boston Society of Natural History, Vol. 7. No. 13 (1915).

—. *List of the Marine Mollusca of the Atlantic Coast from Labrador to Texas.* Proc. Boston Society of Natural History, Vol. 40, No. 1(1934).

Johnstone, Kathleen Yerger. *Sea Treasure: A Guide to Shell Collecting.* Boston: Houghton Mifflin, 1957.

La Rocque, Aurele. *Catalogue of the Recent Molluscs of Canada.* Natl. Museum of Canada Bull. No. 129. Ottawa, 1953.

Lipe, Robert E., and R. Tucker Abbott. *Living Shells of the Caribbean and Florida Keys.* Melbourne, Fla. American Malacologists, Fla. 1991.

Miner, Roy Waldo. *Field Book of Seashore Life.* New York: Putnam, 1950.

Morris, Percy A. *Nature Study at the Seashore.* New York: Ronald Press, 1962.

Morton, J. E. *Molluscs.* 4th ed. London: Hutchinson, 1967.

Perry, Louise M., and Jeanne S. Schwengel. *Marine Shells of the Western Coast of Florida.* Ithaca, N.Y.: Paleontological Research Institution, 1955.

Pratt, Henry Sherring. *A Manual of the Common Invertebrate Animals.* Rev. ed. Philadelphia: Blakiston, 1935.

Rios, Eliezes C. *Coastal Brazilian Seashells.* Rio Grande do Sol, Brazil: Museu Oceanografico de Rio Grande, 1970.

Rogers, Julia E. *The Shell Book.* New York: Doubleday, Page, 1908. Reprinted 1951 by C. T. Branford, Boston, with names brought up to date in the appendix by Harald A. Rehder.

Turner, Ruth D. *A Survey and Illustrated Catalogue of the Teredinidae.* Cambridge: Museum of Comparative Zoology, Harvard University, 1966.

Vaught, Kay C. *A Classification of the Living Mollusca.* Melbourne, Fla. American Malacologists, 1989.

Verrill, Addison E., and S. T. Smith. *Report upon the Invertebrate Animals of Vineyard Sound and Adjacent Waters.* Washington: Government Printing Office, 1874.

Warmke, Germaine L., and R. Tucker Abbott. *Caribbean Seashells.* New York. Dover Publications.

Zim, Herbert S., and Lester Ingle. *Seashores.* New York: Simon and Schuster, 1955.

JOURNALS

American Conchologist: Quarterly bulletin of the Conchologists of America, 1222 Holsworth Lane, Louisville, KY 40222-6616.

How to Study and Collect Shells: A publication written by dozens of experts in their fields. Subjects covered include shore collecting, reef collecting, dredging, collecting mollusks from fish, land collecting, freshwater collecting, and many others. Obtainable from the American Malacological Union (3706 Rice Blvd., Houston, TX 77005).

The Nautilus: A quarterly journal written for and by malacologists. Technical and semipopular articles. c/o Division of Mollusks, Smithsonian Institution, Washington, D.C. 20560.

Johnsonia: Monographs of the marine mollusca of the western Atlantic. Vols. 1-4, William J. Clench, Editor. Museum of Comparative Zoology, Harvard University, Cambridge, Mass. 02138.

APPENDIX C
SOME EASTERN SHELL CLUBS

COMPLETE ADDRESSES are given below for only those clubs with permanent addresses. Additional information may be obtained from the Conchologists of America, Inc. (see below) or from *Sources of Information on Mollusks*, Smithsonian Institution, 1000 Jefferson Drive S.W., Washington, D.C. 20560.

American Malacological Union, 1 Herman Circle, Houston, TX 77030
Astronaut Trail Shell Club, Brevard, Florida
Bailey-Matthews Shell Museum, P.O. Box 1580, Sanibel, FL 33957
Boston Malacological Society, Museum of Comparative Zoology, Cambridge, MA 02138
Broward Shell Club, Pompano Beach, Florida
Central Florida Shell Club, Orlando, Florida
Chicago Shell Club, c/o Field Museum of Natural History, Chicago, IL 60605-2496
Conchological Club of Southern California, Los Angeles County Museum of Natural History, Los Angeles, CA 90007
Conchologists of America, Inc., c/o 2644 Kings Highway, Louisville, KY 40205-2649
Georgia Shell Club, Marietta, Georgia
Greater Miami Shell Club, North Miami, Florida
Greater St. Louis Shell Club, St. Louis, Missouri
Hawaiian Malacological Society, P.O. Box 22130, Honolulu, HI 96823-2130
Indianapolis Shell Club, Indianapolis, Indiana
Jacksonville Shell Club, Jacksonville, Florida
Long Island Shell Club, Long Island, New York
Louisville Conchological Society, Louisville, Kentucky
Naples Shell Club, P.O. Box 1991, Naples, Florida

National Capital Shell Club, c/o National Museum of Natural History, Washington, D.C. 20560

New York Shell Club, Mollusks, American Museum of Natural History, New York, NY 10024

North California Malacozoological Club, Novato, California

Oregon Society of Conchologists, Portland, Oregon

Paleontological Research Institute, 1259 Trumansburg Rd., Ithaca, NY 14850

Philadelphia Shell Club, Academy of Natural Sciences, Philadelphia, PA 19103-1195

St. Petersburg Shell Club, St. Petersburg, Florida

Sanibel-Captiva Shell Club, P.O. Box 355, Sanibel, FL 33957

Sarasota Shell Club, Sarasota, Florida

Suncoast Conchologists, Palm Harbor, Florida

Western Society of Malacologists, Santa Barbara Museum of Natural History, Santa Barbara, CA 93105

Wilmington Shell Club, Delaware Museum of Natural History, Wilmington, DE 19807-0937

INDEX

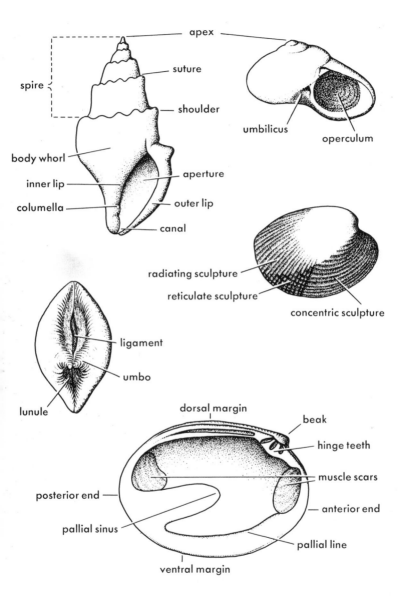

TERMINOLOGY OF UNIVALVE AND BIVALVE SHELLS

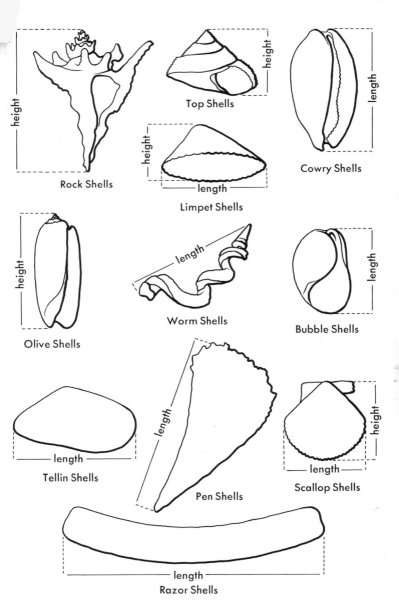

Rock Shells

Top Shells

Cowry Shells

Limpet Shells

Olive Shells

Worm Shells

Bubble Shells

Tellin Shells

Pen Shells

Scallop Shells

Razor Shells

SHELL MEASUREMENTS